O9-ABF-861

to Mark Baker's *Nam* and Al Santoli's *Everything We Had....* From the start, CHARLIE COMPANY'S great material (supplied at some emotional cost by the veterans interviewed), set forth in punchy prose and sharp dialogue, gives a feel of the grunts' experiences...compelling."

Philadelphia Inquirer

"TO DATE THE MOST POIGNANT EYEWITNESS ACCOUNT OF THE WAR AND ITS STARTLING AFTERMATH."

Penthouse

"CHARLIE COMPANY IS BETTER THAN THE NEWSWEEK ARTICLE EVER COULD HAVE BEEN....It tells more of the story and it tells it better....It shows what happens when a government takes advantage of its citizens' patriotism to involve them in what turned out to be a futile exercise. And as we move to put the nightmare of Vietnam behind us and focus our attention on Central America, this book and others like it should serve as a grim reminder of what can happen."

Dallas Times Herald

"A VERY FINE BOOK, BALANCED AND WISE IN ITS ATTITUDES, admirable above all in its avoidance of hype and hyperbole....Since it refrains, in large measure, from moralizing, it compels the best sort of moral reflection. ...It is very hard, sad reading, because there is so much suffering in it, so much pain and death and anger, because so many of these men were so heartbreakingly young when they fought, and because they are ours, our brothers and sons, our people, ourselves."

Esquire

"INFORMATIVE, REFLECTIVE, SOBERING...SHOWS THE DEPTH OF FEELING—RESENTMENT, BITTERNESS, AND HATRED—OF MEN WHO WENT THROUGH VIETNAM."

The Associated Press

"THE MANY NARRATIVES ARE GRAPHIC AND OFTEN TOUCHING... They tend to offset the Hollywood and television view of each Vietnam veteran as a walking timebomb, and of the war as an olive-drab acid trip. The reader is more inclined to sob over the many quiet tragedies that dogged Charlie Company throughout the war and back home...the book's cumulative effect is powerful."

Newsday

CHARLIE COMPANY:
WHAT VIETNAM DID TO US

PETER GOLDMAN
and TONY FULLER

with

Richard Manning
Stryker McGuire
Wally McNamee
Vern E. Smith

A Newsweek Book
BALLANTINE BOOKS • NEW YORK

Grateful acknowledgment is made for permission to reprint the following:

On page 10, lines from the song "Ruby, Don't Take Your Love to Town," by Mel Tillis, copyright © 1966 & 1967, Cedarwood Publishing Co., Inc., 39 Music Square, East, Nashville, Tennessee 37203.

On page 176, a line from the song "Gonna Give Her All the Love I've Got," words and music by Norman Whitfield & Barrett Strong, copyright © 1966, Jobete Music Co., Inc. International copyright secured. Used by permission. All rights reserved.

On page 188, a line from the song "Colour My World," words and music by James Pankow, copyright © 1970, Moose Music and Aurelius Music. All rights reserved. Used by permission.

On page 331, lines from the song "Changes in Latitudes, Changes in Attitudes," words and music by Jimmy Buffett, copyright © 1977, Coral Reefer Music & Outer Banks Music. BMI. Used by permission.

On pages 327–341, excerpts from the CBS News documentary *CBS Reports* "Bittersweet Memories: A Vietnam Reunion," copyright © 1982, CBS, Inc. All rights reserved.

Library of Congress Catalog Card Number: 82-14375

ISBN 0-345-31496-4

This edition published by arrangement with William Morrow and Company, Inc.

Printed in Canada

First Ballantine Books Edition: May 1984

To the men of Charlie Company

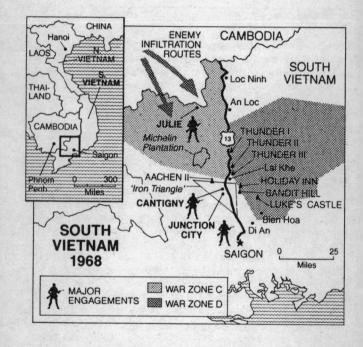

CHINA

Hanoi

N.
VIETNAM

LAOS

S.
VIETNAM

THAI-
LAND

CAMBODIA

Phnom
Penh

Saigon

0   300

Miles

**SOUTH
VIETNAM
1968**

ENEMY
INFILTRATION
ROUTES

CAMBODIA

Loc Ninh

**SOUTH
VIETNAM**

An Loc

13

JULIE

*Michelin
Plantation*

THUNDER I
THUNDER II
THUNDER III

Lai Khe

AACHEN II
'*Iron Triangle*'

CANTIGNY

HOLIDAY INN

BANDIT HILL
LUKE'S CASTLE

Bien Hoa

**JUNCTION
CITY**

Di An

SAIGON

0   25

Miles

MAJOR
ENGAGEMENTS

WAR ZONE C

WAR ZONE D

FOREWORD

There were no homecoming parades for the million men and women who served in combat in the longest war America has ever fought and the only war it has ever lost. There were no brass bands or crowds cheering at the dock or celebratory speeches floating across village greens. The veterans of the failed United States mission in Vietnam returned instead to a kind of embarrassed silence, *as if*, one of them thought, *everybody was ashamed of us*. They were obliged to bear an inordinate share of the blame for having fought at all and for not having won. Some paid a terrible further cost in stunted careers, shattered marriages and disfigured lives. Most have endured with that same stubborn will to survive they had brought to the least popular war in our history—a war that has never really ended for them or for their countrymen. They have tried to forget Vietnam as we have, casting it out of mind as they have buried its medals and memorabilia out of sight in cardboard cartons and dresser drawers. But the effort has not succeeded, for them or for us. "There are too many of us," said Tom Swenticky, who was an infantryman in 'Nam, "for them ever to forget."

This is a book about sixty-five of those nearly forgotten men who, like Swenticky, soldiered in the late 1960s in a gook-hunting, dirt-eating, dog-soldiering combat infantry unit called Charlie Company. They were boys then, nineteen or twenty years old on the average. The Army had snatched them up out of towns named Ottumwa and Puxico and Sun Prairie, suited them up as soldiers with the Big Red One of the First Infantry Division on their shoulders and the Black Lion of the Second Battalion, 28th Infantry Regiment on their blouse pockets, and sent them off to a place they could not locate on a globe to fight a war they could not understand. They served a year apiece there, those who survived, and then came back to fight a second war, this one waged at home and in the mind. They waged it alone for the most part, their stories and their scar tissue unknown even to their wives and parents. It was, one of them thought, as if they were the bearers of some unspeakable disease. Until a team of *Newsweek* correspondents sought them out between the late summer of 1981 and the spring of 1982, some of them had never been asked what they had experienced in the war, or back home in what the grunts in the bunkers of 'Nam thought of wistfully as The World.

Their story is not military history in any formal sense; it is not, that is, the record of general staffs and grand strategies, or of territory seized and held, or of great battles won or lost. Vietnam was not that sort of war, and Charlie Company's piece of it was fought over bloodied patches of ground that could not be found on maps and that nobody really wanted anyway. Neither is this book a moral commentary on the war, or an analysis of its geopolitical origins and consequences, or an account of the travail of the Vietnamese people, or an attempt to assess the relative virtue and valor of those Americans who served as against those who chose not to. It is instead the chess game viewed, or, more accurately, remembered, by the pawns. It is a collective memoir of the war and the homecoming, filtered through layers of time and pain, anger and guilt, bitterness and forgetfulness. It is history at ground level, witnessed through gunports and coils of concertina wire, with Presidents and generals only dimly, intermittently and warily glimpsed in the distance.

The view of the Presidents and the generals in 1968 and 1969, when most of the men in these pages were soldiering in Vietnam, was that the war was going rather well on the ground and paradoxically badly back home. Charlie Company's time in the field was roughly bracketed by two decisive events in the psychohistory of the failing American effort in Indochina: the Communist Tet offensive of January 1968 and the scandal late in 1969 over the massacre of 347 Vietnamese noncombatants in a hamlet called My Lai. The My Lai atrocity was an aberration in the war, so far as is known, a paroxysm of murderous violence by a grunt company drunk on blood and war-weariness. The Tet offensive, viewed in purely military terms, could be counted a defeat for the Viet Cong and their North Vietnamese allies; their synchronized attacks on practically every city, town and American military base in South Vietnam were carried out at devastating cost in lives and matériel and did not succeed as intended at igniting a general uprising in the countryside. But the media imagery of Viet Cong guerrillas penetrating the American Embassy grounds in Saigon at Tet and of the bodies of old men, women and children rotting in a ditch in My Lai had a shattering effect on America's image of itself as invincible on the one hand and humane on the other.

The two events accordingly reinforced the two separate and contradictory peace movements then at loose in the American countryside: the up-scale, campus-centered opposition that believed the war to be criminal, and the larger, more inchoate silent majority who saw that it could not or would not be won. It was the organized antiwar movement that seized the attention of the media with its teach-ins, its flag burnings, its clinics in draft resistance, its siege of the Democratic convention in Chicago in 1968 and its mass marches on Washington for the Moratoriums of October and November 1969. The movement was in flood during Charlie Company's time in the war, filling the newspapers from home; it was spreading from college campuses to Army camps in the States and was transfiguring American presidential politics.

But it was Middle America's slow, painful turning against the war that made its prosecution impossible under the military and political constraints imposed upon it. During its long ride up the escalator toward a peak commitment of 542,000 men and women in January 1969, the Johnson administration had made a conscious decision not to drum up a fever of jingoism at home, partly to keep the war from getting out of hand, partly to leave some money available to finance Lyndon Johnson's Great Society domestic programs. "We tried to do in cold blood perhaps what can only be done in hot blood, when sacrifices of this order are involved," Johnson's Secretary of State, Dean Rusk, said in retrospect. It was workaday America that was stocking the Charlie Companies in Vietnam with its sons and was receiving a widening stream of them home in burn dressings, wheelchairs and reusable metal body containers, all to no discernible purpose.

The song that heralded the end of America's tolerance for the war was not the anthem of the antiwar movement, "Give Peace a Chance," but rather Mel Tillis's painful "Ruby, Don't Take Your Love to Town," the country-and-western lament of a paraplegic soldier to his wandering wife:

It wasn't me that started that old crazy Asia war,
But I was proud to go and do my patriotic chores.
Oh, I know, Ruby, that I'm not the man I used to be—
But Ruby, I still need your company.

When "Ruby," published in 1966, became a gold-record best seller in 1969, the message was unmistakable. Support for the war was collapsing among the men and women providing its cannon fodder. As a Gallup Poll confirmed, the boys of Charlie Company were fighting a war regarded by a majority of their countrymen and, increasingly, their own parents, as a mistake.

With the ground turning to sand under their feet, first Johnson and then Richard Nixon resolved in nearly identical words not to become the first American President to have lost a war. Winning wars had always seemed as much an American birthright as life, liberty and the pursuit of happiness, but by 1968–69, there was no longer much talk of winning, given the nearly limitless commitments of time, manpower and money that victory would take. The irony, pressed on Washington by General William Westmoreland as commander in the field, was that the decimation of the enemy after Tet had left the United States and its South Vietnamese allies with a military advantage fairly begging to be pressed. The Viet Cong were licking their wounds and having trouble recruiting replacements; the North Vietnamese Army was skinning back to platoon- and squad-size hit-and-run operations, retiring its main-force units to sanctuaries in Laos and Cambodia to await the final implosion of America's will to carry on. When Westmoreland asked Johnson for 206,000 more men so he could mop up, the request was arguable militarily and insupportable politically. Johnson was then at the point of abdicating his hope for a second full term, his presidency a casualty of his war and the candidacies of Eugene McCarthy and Robert F. Kennedy against it.

Nixon followed Johnson to the White House, committed to "end the war and win the peace," but he failed at the latter objective and could not achieve the former during Charlie Company's tour in Vietnam. The secret and still germinating plan he brought to office was, in Henry Kissinger's phrase, "to get out of it quietly" by liquidating the American effort on the ground, thus reducing the weekly casualty counts to less demoralizing levels, and by massively expanding the bombing across all Indochina as a prop to the militarily suspect South Vietnamese armed forces. The troop withdrawals began in mid-1969 and continued through the year. Charlie Company missed those first planes home and was left behind in Vietnam, fighting a diminuendo gypsy war whose objectives were to tempt the enemy out into the open, stack up and count the bodies of his dead, and move on to the next encounter. It was a strategy of attrition, not conquest, baffling to the men and senseless even to some of their commanders. A postwar West

Point textbook by a lieutenant colonel called it "bankrupt," a strategy that "uses blood in lieu of brains." Its larger purpose had got lost for the boys of Charlie Company and sometimes, it seemed, for their leaders. Composing his speech of November 1969 summoning "the great silent majority of my fellow Americans" to rally behind what remained of the war, Nixon had to write a note on his yellow legal pad reminding himself to "include a paragraph on *why* we are there."

That the war still had to be explained in the fifth year of America's massive commitment to it was a measure of how different it was from our past wars, and how much more scarring to so many of the men who fought it. The experience of being in combat—the total immersion in fear and noise, in chaos and sudden death—was not objectively worse for the grunts in Vietnam than for the men we sent to other, less divisive wars. The doughboys of World War I and the dog soldiers of World War II commonly served longer tours under more sustained fire; where a combat hitch in Vietnam lasted for precisely 365 days, a Big Red One infantryman at Cantigny in 1918 or on Omaha Beach in 1944 knew that he was in the war to stay until it was won or he was carried from the field, wounded or dead. But those who fought in our wars before Vietnam were at least fighting with popular support for territory that could be measured and causes that could be easily understood. They were received as liberators abroad and, if they survived, as conquering heroes back home.

There was no such solace for the grunts of Charlie Company or a million others like them, no bands or parades or blizzards of ticker tape. It was a dozen years before Congress, in embarrassment over the national orgy of celebration over the return of fifty-three American hostages from Iran in January 1981, voted the veterans of Vietnam an official and fleetingly observed day of recognition. A monument to the 57,692 of them who had died in the war was in planning for Washington, two low slabs of black granite among the soaring white cenotaphs honoring the earlier heroes of the republic. Until its sponsors thought better of it, the monument was to bear no mention of Vietnam at all, only the roll of the dead, as if, *The New Republic* wrote, they were "the victims of some monstrous traffic accident."

Those who did come home returned to a nation that was itself a victim of the war, its politics embittered, its economy ravaged by inflation, its educated young in revolt, its faith in its own military might and moral rectitude badly wounded. "America had, like us, changed forever," David Brown of Charlie Company reflected years later, and it received its returning sons as if they were to blame for the bad news they bore. It was painful enough for Tom Swenticky being called a baby-killer when he deplaned in San Francisco; it was worse when he got off the bus in South River, New Jersey, where he had lived all his life, and nobody seemed to know who he was. George Hesser's father wept, seeing his boy off for Charlie Company's war, and offered to help him escape to Canada. Hesser said no, he wanted to go, and he did, serving with valor as a machine gunner. But on the flight home to Oklahoma City, no one wanted to sit next to him. "What's the matter with me?" he asked his father at the airport. "Do I smell bad? Is something wrong with me?"

The common denominator for the boys of Charlie Company was pain, in some measure, in the war and in the return to The World. Most of them survived the reentry as they had survived the war, by putting what hurt too much out of mind and moving forward. But hardly a man among the sixty-five located by *Newsweek*'s team of correspondents was untouched by Vietnam. Four of them had come home in government-issue coffins. One had committed suicide. Two others had died young, one of heart failure, one in an auto accident, both in states of anguish over the war. Some had experienced the symptoms of why psychiatry, since Vietnam, has formally recognized as "post-traumatic stress disorder"—nightmares, flashbacks, rages, binges, panics, melancholic silences, numbed feelings, guilt at having survived at all and at what survival sometimes required of them. Marriages had stretched thin and died, often of noncommunication. Careers were delayed or derailed; some of the men were still adrift from job to job twelve and thirteen years later. Several had disquieting physical symptoms they associated with Agent Orange, a defoliant widely used in their area of operations. Two had been in mental hospitals, one in jail. One had deserted the Army, preferring life in flight to a war and a military regimen he feared might be driving him insane. One was blind.

They had grown accustomed to silence, most of them, by the time *Newsweek* came knocking at their doors starting in August and September 1981. Our calculation, in seeking them out, was that they would be easy to find and hard to interview—that silence would have become *too* settled a habit over the decade since the last of them came out of Vietnam. We were wrong on both counts. Locating them turned into an exercise in detective work that stretched out over three months before we had enough leads on enough addresses even to begin reporting. But when our correspondents found the men, they were almost painfully eager to speak—to spill out their stories of the war and the homecoming in poignant personal detail because somebody had finally asked.

We had chosen Charlie Company almost out of a hat. It was only as our reporting progressed that we found the close family resemblances between our small, unscientific sample and a 1,380-interview profile of Vietnam veterans by the Center for Policy Research in the most authoritative study now extant. We had set out looking for a grunt company, because Vietnam was preeminently a grunt's war; our only further criteria were that the unit be one that had tasted heavy combat and had served in the crucible years of 1968–69. With the generous help of the Society of the First Division and its secretary, Arthur L. Chaitt, we winnowed eight such companies out of the annals of the Big Red One and, of the eight, chose Charlie Company. What attracted our notice to it was an ambush on May 3, 1969, in which the company had been pinned down for fourteen bloody hours and had finally fought its way free. We discovered in the course of our interviewing that that action had run together in memory with too many others too much like it. Charlie Company, it turned out, had experienced far more harrowing days and weeks in the war.

We had first to track down enough of the men to stand as a fair slice of the life of the company, at war and in The World. The Army was as helpful and even as enthusiastic as the law permitted; it started us out with the computerized roster of the 162 enlisted men who made up Charlie Company on April 30, 1969, three days before the ambush that had caught our attention, and was equally obliging in helping us identify officers. But the laws pertaining to privacy forbade the Army's furnishing us last-known addresses or any other clues to the whereabouts of any of the men except the three—one officer and two sergeants—who were still on active duty. It took part of a spring and summer to attach addresses to half the names we had, and not all of those were accurate; one turned out to be a vacant lot under a bridge in Oregon. Art Chaitt and his Society once again helped us mightily, though only a single alumnus of Charlie Company had joined; the veterans of Vietnam are notoriously leery of organizations. Individual members of the company, as we found them, steered us to others. A few more leads turned up in newspaper clippings from those rare occasions when the press got out to Charlie Company's godforsaken patches of brush and jungle.

Most of the addresses on our working list were dated; some

were twelve years old. Some led us to parents wary of telling us where their sons had gone. Some consisted of a hometown, nothing more. To track those men, our correspondents worked sources ranging from city directories and small-town newspaper files to water-commission records and police traffic-ticket rolls. Richard Manning found himself searching for a Smith in Chicago and Stryker McGuire for an equally commonplace Gonzalez in the San Joaquin Valley, each without success. Manning, the chief of *Newsweek*'s Detroit bureau, traced one veteran on his list to a mountain cabin in Montana and made contact by nailing a note to the doorjamb with the flat of an axe. Their ensuing interview began in a saloon at ten one evening and continued past dawn the next morning in a pickup truck with a vodka bottle lying empty between them. McGuire, our Houston bureau chief, discovered that another company alumnus was a habitué of a gay bar in the Northwest and left messages for him there. The messages were received but not answered; the man was the only one we found who would not speak with us. Vern E. Smith, chief of the *Newsweek* bureau in Atlanta, discovered how profound the silence enveloping the men had been in the course of an interview with one of them, Roy Rosson, in Ranger, Texas. Rosson's wife was eavesdropping on their conversation, hearing her husband's stories of the war, Smith realized, for the first time.

Our four principal correspondents and a fifth member of the team, Wally McNamee, a staff photographer assigned to *Newsweek*'s Washington bureau, traveled an aggregate 65,000 miles in our original sweep; they interviewed forty-seven veterans of Charlie Company and the surviving families of six others, scattered from Maine to California and from Puerto Rico to Alaska. Ron Moreau, a *Newsweek* Paris correspondent who had covered the war, traced a fifty-fourth man—still an Army sergeant—to a basement supply room in West Germany. Their reporting ran to more than 100,000 words, supplemented by reams of transcriptions of tape-recorded interviews. The resulting special report, at 25,000 words, filled half the December 14, 1981, issue of *Newsweek* and was the longest single article in the magazine's half-century history. The response of our readers was voluminous and emotional—"You gave us our parade," a Vietnam veteran wrote us—and the judgment of our peers was kind.

Yet those of us most closely engaged with the project felt that we had only begun to tap the riches of our raw material. What had made it an extraordinary reporting experience was the affecting eagerness of the men to speak and be heard, to lay bare what they had experienced in the war and in the dozen years since. "I think what much of it comes to," Rick Manning cabled in a progress report at mid-passage, "is having Vietnam bottled up inside them, like a trapped prisoner trying to get out—*screaming* to get out—and unable to do so. One of the most common complaints I've heard is not that they were called baby-killers but that they were unable to talk about the war, unable to find a friendly ear. I think that's why many of us, on leaving these interviews and thanking the men for their time and their wasted evenings, have had them turn to us and thank *us* for coming. A large part of heroism is in the telling of the tale. The men who fought at Guadalcanal and Pusan were heroes in part because their tales fell on receptive ears. But who wanted to hear, in 1969, about how Charlie Company held its ground at Fire Base Julie or Cantigny or Junction City? Nobody. That's why they thank us. We're doing what nobody would do twelve years ago. We're listening."

The decision to lengthen and deepen the story of Charlie Company into a book was accordingly easy. A store of material was in hand and more was added as more alumni of Charlie Company found their way to us. One was a delayed casualty of the war, a suicide; a newspaper clipping of his death mentioned his service in our company, a year or two earlier than most of the other men, and led us to his survivors. Another was a postman who was out on his route in Kentucky delivering subscription copies of *Newsweek* and saw the faces of a couple of wartime buddies staring back at him from the cover. A third noticed the same photo accompanying a *Reader's Digest* condensation of the article one insomniac night and recognized himself in it. A fourth wrote us from Australia, where he was living as an expatriate and working as a railroad brakeman. A fifth, a schoolteacher in Boston, sat for an interview himself and helped us find a pair of brothers who had survived Charlie Company's war together, one whole, one terribly maimed in body but not in spirit. We added the stories of eleven more men in all to our growing store. Our sample increased in the process from fifty-four to the sixty-five men whose lives are threaded through this group portrait.

Two of us have signed the book, but the story of Charlie Company was born as a work of newsweekly journalism and as such was the collaborative effort of many talented hands. Our colleagues Rick Manning, Stryker McGuire and Vern Smith in particular brought to it their extraordinary gifts at reporting not just the surface of the story but the emotions at play under its skin. Single interviews of comparable quality were conducted by Ron Moreau in Germany, Richard Sandza in Alaska, Carl Robinson in Sydney and Stuart A. Seidel in Minneapolis, the latter on a sort of busman's holiday after having managed the complicated logistics of reporting the magazine version. Wally McNamee, a photographer who deserves that sometimes inflated title "photojournalist," contributed most of the pictures of the men as they are today and his own sharp-eyed reportorial insights as well. Photo editor Guy Cooper directed a search for the best of hundreds of war pictures taken by the members of Charlie Company themselves, the jacket photo by Greg Etzel among them. Deborah Witherspoon, Katherine Koberg and Peter Salber provided valuable background research. Lynn Povich, a senior editor at *Newsweek*, was a source of ideas and encouragement from the start and was the magazine's liaison with CBS News at the finish for a follow-up television documentary on a reunion of Charlie Company. Our colleagues Sheldon Czapnik and Peter Fitzpatrick led us through the mysteries of money and the law as they pertain to writing books, and inflicted this manuscript on themselves along the way.

Our special thanks belong to two of our editors at *Newsweek*. In a book about a company of grunts, it is perhaps appropriate to mention one's superior officers last. But Lester Bernstein, who had the vision and daring to gamble half an issue of his magazine on this project, and Maynard Parker, who believed in it and walked point for it every suspenseful step of the way, belong first in our professional and personal regard. Neither *Newsweek*'s special report nor this book would have been possible without them.

Other hands helped the story become a book. Bruce Lee, our editor at William Morrow & Company, read the *Newsweek* version and was first to see a book inside it trying to get out. His enthusiasm has not flagged; he has been the source of constant encouragement and wise advice. Betsy Cenedella volunteered her skills as a copy editor, a gift above and beyond the obligations of a twenty-year friendship with one of the authors. Rollene Saal got us together with Morrow in her new role as editorial consultant to *Newsweek* for this and future books. Erna Helwig typed most of this one, with great speed and precision. Helen Dudar, the writer and critic, read the manuscript in installments with patience, insight, a sharp pencil and requited love. In her other incarnation as Helen Goldman, she along with Kathy Fuller, Diane Manning, Marie Smith,

Nikki McNamee, Lela Cooper, Stephen Shepard and others near and dear to the members of our team endured our nearly total immersion in the world of Charlie Company for periods as long as a year.

Last and most, we are grateful to the men of Charlie Company. This is their book and, we hope, their parade, a thank-you for their service to their country and their openness in talking about it twelve and thirteen years later. In token of our gratitude to them, *Newsweek* is creating a scholarship fund for the sons and daughters of the men whose stories appear in these pages.

New York City
July 1982

CONTENTS

PART I MEMORIES OF VIETNAM   I

HELLO, WAR 3 • A SMALL CORNER OF HELL 20 • A TRIP OUTSIDE TIME 36 • BEER, SMOKE AND BRAGGADOCIO 39 • "OUR OWN MEN HAVE SHOT US" 44 • A VIETNAM DEATH TRIP 53 • "I WANT GOD TO STOP THE LIGHT SHOW" 55 • "WAR IS A PAIN IN THE ASS" 67 • A BODY COUNT FOR CHRISTMAS 68 • FRIENDLY FIRE 79 • IN THE ASHES OF FIRE BASE JULIE 85 • THE COLOR OF WAR 90 • "ALL HEROES DO IS DIE GOOD" 95 • "MY DEAR WIFE . . . I'VE KILLED" 118 • "PEOPLE DIE IN TECHNICOLOR" 123 • THE DYING OF THE LIGHT 127 • GOODBYE, WAR 134

PART 2 THE WAR COMES HOME   141

GREG SKEELS: "ONE DAY, YOU HAVE A LICENSE TO KILL . . ." 143 • OMEGA HARRIS: "I AM NOT BREAKABLE" 145 • JERRY DICKMANN: ORDINARY PEOPLE 151 • RICHARD ROGERS: "I ASKED GOD NOT TO LET ME BE A COWARD" 153 • LLOYD COLLINS: THE DEATH OF THE HEART 157 • DAN COLFACK: A KILLING GROUND IN HEAVEN 159 • ROY ROSSON: LOOKING FOR SOMETHING ELSE 161 • ANTONIO RIVERA PARILLA: A PETITION FOR HELP 165 • FRITZ SUCHOMEL: "BRING THEM SAFELY AND QUICKLY HOME" 167 • KIT BOWEN AND DON STAGNARO: THE BEST OF FRIENDS 169 • JOE BOXX: "IT WAS THE YOUNG BOY YOU KILLED" 178 • DENNY PIERCE: ALL THE WAY HOME 181 • SKIP SOMMER: ON THE RUN 183 • BILLY

JOHNSON: THE WAY LIFE IS 190 • ALBERTO MARTINEZ: "THEY BURNED MY MIND UP" 192 • EDMUND LEE VI: AT HOME ABROAD 200 • KEVIN ABBOTT: "THEY WANTED US TO GO AWAY" 203 • DAVID AND MICHEL RIOUX: ON HIS BLINDNESS 206 • TARAS POPEL: "I HAVE NO RE-GRETS" 214 • FRANK GOINS: IF YOU'RE BLACK, GET BACK 216 • DAVID BROWN: WHAT THE ARMY TAUGHT ME 219 • CLYDE GARTH: HE WANTED TO DO THE THINGS MEN DO 225 • BERT KENNISH: A QUESTION OF SELF-ESTEEM 227 • BOB BOWERS: "SNEAKING IN THE BACK DOOR" 231 • JIM SOIKE: BREAKING AWAY 235 • MIKE FETTER-OLF: KING OF THE MOUNTAIN 237 • CHARLES RUPERT: A $10 MILLION MISUNDERSTANDING 243 • J.C. WILSON: "WE WERE FOOLS" 244 • STEVEN MCVEIGH: VIETNAM AND THE ART OF GARAGE DOOR INSTALLATION 248 • BOB SELIG: STAYLING ALIVE 249 • CHESTER WARD: "THERE WAS SO MUCH DEATH" 252 • HARRY FOXWELL: THE PAST IS AN-OTHER COUNTRY 254 • DAVID BEAN: "WHAT'S WRONG WITH ME?" 259 • ROBERT MASTROGIOVANNI: FIVE DAYS OUT OF THE WAR 266 • BOBBY EUGENE JONES: A DEATH IN THE FAMILY 268 • CURTIS GILLILAND, JR.: "WE JUST KILLED 'EM" 271 • DAVID SPAIN: HARD TIMES 277 • ED SCHWEIGER: ONE DAY AT A TIME 280 • MIKE MACDON-ALD: BREAKING THE SILENCE 281 • RICHARD GARCIA: A HERO COMES HOME 289

PART 3 THE BOYS OF CHARLIE COMPANY   291

THE MEN OF CHARLIE COMPANY 309
ABBREVIATIONS AND ACRONYMS 313
A BIBLIOGRAPHICAL NOTE 315
INDEX 317

I am an Infantryman,
A killer, a hunter,
The VC is my game.
I am an Infantryman,
A grunt,
To so many is the name . . .

But when the war is over,
And all the guns of battle cease to ring,
And all the facts are brought to light,
I, the Infantryman,
Shall be crowned King.

—From "The Infantryman's Plead,"
an anonymous GI folk poem circulated
among members of Charlie Company,
Second Battalion, 28th Infantry Regiment,
First Infantry Division, during the
war in Vietnam

PART I

MEMORIES OF VIETNAM

*We are the unwilling working for the
unqualified to do the unnecessary for the ungrateful.
This is about as truthful as you can get.*

—KIT BOWEN of Charlie Company,
in a letter to his father, 1968

HELLO, WAR

The war began for Greg Skeels the moment his plane touched down at Bien Hoa, north of Saigon, in June of '68 and disgorged its cargo of raw new troopers onto the runway apron. Skeels was a curly, breezy kid of nineteen out of Flint, Michigan, and he had joined in the nervous schoolboy banter aboard the chartered jet, pointing at the jungle rising beneath them and kidding about whether there were really any gooks down there. But his grin vanished when they opened the door and he started down the ramp with the rest of the new meat into the war in Vietnam. He could feel his Class A khakis soaking through in the enveloping heat and could smell the sharp scent of gunpowder in the air—a smell that would stay with him through his tour in 'Nam and long after he got home. And then he was marching with the rest of the recruits past a file of combat veterans who had done their time in the war and were headed back to what they thought of, with wistful irony, as The World. The vets looked old at twenty or twenty-one. They watched the FNGs—the fuckin' new guys—in leaden silence. Some shook their heads. None said a word. *Shit*, Skeels thought under their sad gaze. *What have I gotten myself into?*

What he had got himself into was a distant and ugly war fought by post-adolescent boys who could not or would not evade it—teenagers who, like Skeels, saw *American Graffiti* years later and recognized themselves in its filmscape of drive-ins, drag races and puppy love. *I can't believe it— that's me,* he thought, seeing the picture on TV, and so it was. He had grown up car-crazy, a child of the automotive culture of Detroit and its satellite factory towns the way they were in the fat times. The center of his life starting halfway through Ainsworth High was his pet Goat, the '66 Pontiac GTO he bought practically the moment he came of driving age; it was him, the source of his cachet with the girls at the Dairy Queen and his authority among the guys burning rubber and nineteen-cent-a-gallon gasoline on the long, flat straightaways outside of town. That was what you did in Flint in those days, that and drink beer and listen to the radio and graduate straight out of school into a low-skill, high-wage job on the line at Buick or Chevrolet or Fisher Body. Except Skeels couldn't wait; he signed on at Chevy final assembly two months before the class of '66 graduated from Ainsworth, and spent the next year and a half attaching fender brackets, tossing hubcaps into half-finished cars and watching the mailbox for his draft notice.

It came in January 1968, and Skeels accepted it as a condition of life, as common to his crowd as marrying young and as inescapable as the weather. More privileged boys in those days were skipping to Canada, or cooling out on college deferments, or wangling direct commissions, or tracking through the snow in New Hampshire soliciting votes for Eugene McCarthy's peace candidacy for President. But those options never crossed Greg Skeels's mind. In his world, it was simply accepted that when the country called, men went, as generations had since the Revolution and as Skeels's own stepfather had in World War II. *This is just something that happens to everybody*, he thought in his turn when his papers came. He shrugged, said goodbye to his girl, slogged through basic and advanced infantry training and finally shipped out to 'Nam.

Skeels had only the haziest notion then of where he was and no idea whatever of what the war was about. It didn't even occur to him to be frightened until the moment he pitched up at C Company barracks at the sprawling U.S. Army base at Lai Khe. His welcome there was a sign emblazoned with the Big Red One of the First Infantry Division and the rampant Black Lion of Cantigny, the emblem of the Second Battalion of the 28th Infantry Regiment. CHARLIE COMPANY, the sign announced to the world. DUTY FIRST. NO MISSION TOO DIFFICULT, NO SACRIFICE TOO GREAT. Skeels dropped his duffel bag into the red dust and stood staring at the words for maybe five minutes. He felt suddenly alone, 12,000 miles from home and—for the first time—scared. *This is serious*, he thought. Hello, war.

He had at that moment fallen reluctantly heir to the tradition of a division heavy with honors dating to World War I. It was said in Charlie Company that the Big Red One shoulder patch was born the day a doughboy in the Great War caught a piece of shrapnel in the ass, ripped off a fragment of what was left of his underpants, daubed a numeral "1" on it with his own blood and fixed it to his sleeve. The division brought back five Medals of Honor from that war, winning what some historians consider the turn-of-the-tide battle at a wayside town in France called Cantigny. It rang up sixteen more cutting a swath of fire across North Africa, Sicily, France, Belgium and Germany in World War II. It also made a reputation as a particularly fierce and sometimes unmanageably rowdy outfit—"increasingly temperamental," General Omar Bradley once lamented, and "disdainful of both regulations and senior commands. It thought itself exempted from the need for discipline by virtue of its months on the line."

Both traditions followed the Big Red One into Vietnam in October 1965, at the beginning of Lyndon B. Johnson's massive escalation of the war, and were layered over with fresh tales of bravery and bravado by the time Skeels arrived with the class of '68–'69. The division's mission was dirty work even by the standards of what had by then become a singularly dirty and doom-haunted war. Its A-O (for Area of Operations) embraced war zones C and D, stretching north from Saigon to the Cambodian border and the North Vietnamese sanctuaries just beyond, and was counted one of the toughest in the country. It was, for the grunts, an alien landscape of scrub brush and bamboo jungle, of working rubber plantations and abandoned rice paddies. It was dangerous terrain as well; through it ran the main enemy infiltration routes into the heart of South Vietnam—that lacework of roads, trails, footpaths and subterranean tunnels known collectively as the Ho Chi Minh Trail. It was the Big Red One's duty to rove the middle and northern reaches of that territory on in-and-out, hunt-and-kill operations, its successes measured not in acreage but in those new and notoriously unreliable statistics of war called kill ratios and body counts. "Our mission was bigger than any little piece of real estate," Orwin C. Talbott, then the Big Red One's commanding general, said years later. "The objective was the enemy, not territory—to stop the infiltration and stabilize the area so that the local people could go about their business. The goals were achieved. The enemy was stopped. It was considered a success."

If so, it was a success bought at great cost to the flesh and spirit of the grunts who soldiered in the line when the war was going sour. Their predecessors had come over gung ho in 1965 and 1966, when, with the encouragement of the government, people still believed the war could be won. The first C Company of Black Lions made the passage by ship, not plane, anchoring aboard the troop carrier U.S.S. *General Sutton* in the South China Sea and putting ashore in landing craft as men had hit the beaches in World War II. They slogged inland with blank cartridges in their M-14 rifles, in token of the ambiguity with which the United States then still approached an inexorably widening war. The great base at Lai Khe was hardly a base at all until they got there and carved it out of the red earth. Laboring in the rain, a charter Charlie Company grunt named James Bryan Bowling dug a foxhole for himself and crawled in. It was the only home he had, and when the sun came up after an all-night downpour, he was sleepless and shivering in water up to his chin.

Bowling saw a lot for a nineteen-year-old boy out of the Indiana Soldiers & Sailors Children's Home during that first year of America's ride up the escalator. The men-children of the first Charlie Company in Vietnam had to pacify the village of Lai Khe before they could go anywhere else; so hostile were their neighbors that even the aged mama-san who came on the base to sell them French bread and Cokes lingered behind to map the positions of their bunkers. They did battle with fear and mud and leeches, with powdered eggs and wilting heat and an enemy apprenticed at guerrilla war for more than twenty years. They learned to pack their own dead in body bags and to count the enemy's without gagging—four hundred of them, some charred black by napalm, in one particularly fierce engagement. They were fired on once by their own helicopters, until Bowling and some others despaired of straightening out the mistake in identity and started firing back. They endured everything their successors in Charlie Company would endure after them. But it was made somehow more bearable for them by their innocent sense that they were fighting for a discernible national purpose and were winning. "All this time we stuck together

and our morale was high because we defeated the enemy,"
Bowling wrote years later in a longhand chronicle of his war.
"I was really proud to be the owner of a Combat Infantry
Badge and a member of 'C' Co."

Tales of those days still circulated in the semipermanent
tin-roofed hooches that succeeded the tents and foxholes as
Charlie Company's habitation in Lai Khe. It was said that
when a Black Lion spotted a Viet Cong in the early times,
he would stand straight up like Audie Murphy in VistaVision,
blow him into the next life and leave his body rotting in the
sun with an ace of spades and a Black Lion patch nailed to
his forehead; it was said that the VC in return had circulated
leaflets offering a reward to any of its men who came back
with a patch, or a pair of ears, removed from a Black Lion.
Charlie Company in particular made, and for a time basked
in, a barracks notoriety as a rough, tough, take-no-prisoners
fighting force that seemed to trail trouble in its magnetic
field. When another company would get in a jam and have
to be lifted out by chopper, it was Charlie Company that
went back for the bodies. When Colonel George S. Patton
III, the son and namesake of the World War II legend, led
his 11th Armored Cavalry through a long fallow spell without
a kill, it was Charlie Company they sent for to change his
luck—and Charlie Company that led his tankers into a bounteous nest of enemy troopers the first day out.

But the guts-and-glory esprit of the early days was dying
long before Greg Skeels set foot on the tarmac at Bien Hoa
in 1968; in the carnival-mirror war that Vietnam had become,
even measures designed to sustain that esprit conspired instead to suffocate it. The Army had adopted a policy it had
test-marketed in the similarly limited and similarly nasty war
in Korea: rotating men individually "in-country" and out
again a year later, if they survived, instead of shipping them
in together in units and committing them to battle together
for the duration. "The one-year tour gave a man a goal,"
General William Westmoreland wrote in his Vietnam memoir; its intent was thereby to brace up morale in the line and
to diffuse pressure in the States to bring the boys back home.
The gains were negligible on both counts and were bought
at some cost to that cohesion of purpose that had helped
American soldiers to endure and prevail in past wars. The
160 men of Charlie Company were not really men but boys,

nineteen and a half years old on the average as against twenty-six in World War II, and were not a company at all until they were flung together in the field by the vagaries of chance and alphabetical order. Their war as a consequence atomized into 160 private wars in which winning was not nearly so important an object as staying alive for 365 days.

For the men in the bunkers, winning seemed to be a receding possibility in any case, in a war confined by the boundaries of South Vietnam and the strained tolerances of American politics. Most of them accordingly lowered their sights from victory to survival; you humped the boonies, hunted for gooks, lived in varying degrees of physical and emotional pain, and counted down the days to your personal DEROS—date eligible for return from overseas. Most were making it through. Some were coming home in reusable metal containers. Some were surviving in body but dying in spirit; by 1966 and 1967, the war had begun producing the kind of casualty whose wounds were invisible to the eye and unacknowledged by the keep-'em-fighting canons of military psychiatry in fashion at the time.

One of them, in Charlie Company, was Ernesto Alberto Martinez—Al, to his friends—and it wasn't even his war. He was a Cuban, not an American citizen, the son of a jockey who had migrated to the States when little Al was four, to work the *yanqui* tracks in Ohio, Maryland and West Virginia. But Martinez accepted it as his obligation to serve the country he had grown up in and thought of as his home. He tried the Air Force and the Navy; both turned him down because his arm had been badly broken in a traffic accident and, three years later, was still incompletely healed. But the Army swept him up in the draft, put him and his lame wing through the rigors of infantry training and sent him his orders for Vietnam.

"Go to Canada," his father begged when the papers came. "I'll give you the money."

Martinez said no.

"We'll *all* go to Canada," his father said. "There's racing up there, I can always get a job, and we'll just live there."

"No," Martinez said again. "This is my country. It's my duty to fight for the country I believe in."

So he went over a happy-go-lucky kid in 1966 and came back a psychic cripple in 1967, autodestructing on sadness and death. He told his brother and sister the stories he hadn't been able to bring himself to put in his letters home. He told them about the officer they nicknamed Zippo 6 for the day he burned down a Vietnamese village and only then, when it lay in ashes, radioed battalion headquarters for leave to put it to the torch. He told about the day the company was set down by chopper in some lonely barren somewhere and was bombed by American warplanes, leaving six of them dead and seventy-four more wounded. He told about all the times he tried to go on sick call with what he later discovered was osteomyelitis eating into the bone of his game arm; the doctor would smile, tell him it was all in his mind, tranquilize him with Librium and send him back out to the field.

And finally he told about how he and his best buddy were ordered out on an operation the day they were due to go home, because the Army had mislaid their papers. He found out only afterward that the papers had come through ten minutes after they left; by then, his buddy had stopped an enemy bullet, and Martinez had spent his last day in 'Nam hunkered down in a foxhole with the corpse. "They burned my mind up and it's gone," he told his family when he finally got home. "Blood they want, blood they'll get," he said, except the blood they finally spilled fifteen years later, on a highway out of Miami, was his own.

Stories like Martinez's weren't the tales of 'Nam that found their way home to the boys who followed him into Charlie Company in the summer and fall of 1968. The lifers who had taught them the arts of war at infantry school had taken a certain extracurricular pleasure in teasing them about what lay ahead: *Hey, buddy, you know what's going to happen to you, buddy, you're just meat, buddy, you're going to bite it over there*. But most of the lifers had never seen 'Nam and most of the twinks—the new recruits—had little idea of where they were going and none whatever about what would become of them when they got there. One of them, Taras Popel, a streetsmart college dropout from a Ukrainian enclave on Chicago's West Side, looked up Vietnam in the *Britannica* out of morbid curiosity when he got his orders and read how France had lost *its* war there at Dien Bien Phu fourteen years before. *My God*, he thought, *we're flogging a dead horse*.

Yet Popel went, like most of the others, without question

or complaint. Some were scared and some eager; some went because it was an adventure and some because it was simple patriotic duty. "Keep your head down. Don't volunteer," Bob Bowers's father, a combat veteran of World War II, told him on the ride from their home outside Elwood City, Pennsylvania, to the Pittsburgh airport. Bowers nodded and smiled and wasn't even anxious until they got to the gate and his father suddenly burst into tears. *I've never seen him cry before*, Bowers thought, feeling his own buried fears steal over him. *I must be in trouble*.

George Hesser's dad wept, too, a great, strapping man's man standing in the middle of Will Rogers Airport in Tulsa with his eyes flooding over.

"You don't have to go," he stammered. "I'll send you to Canada."

"It's all right," Hesser answered awkwardly. "I want to go ahead and do it."

And so, one by one, they made their goodbyes, headed for San Francisco and boarded the chartered jetliners for the journey to a war half a world away from home. Some of them tried to talk down their apprehensions with jokes and chatter and little gusts of machismo. But mostly they kept to themselves, alone with their anxieties in a silence that deepened as they began the descent into 'Nam. In the daylight they could see the craters pockmarking the landscape and the helicopter gunships skittering over the treetops; at night, the red streaks of tracer fire and the brilliant white glare of illumination rounds. The last wisps of conversation died. The stewardesses looked sad.

Like a wake, Omega Harris thought; a planeload of guys wishing they had a drink to get their heads right, wondering which faces would be missing from the flight back and covering their bets by taking out life insurance on one another, and there he was among them, not quite twenty and married thirteen days, and he didn't even know enough to be scared. Not yet. All he knew was that his brother, Byrum, was down there somewhere with Charlie Company, Second of the 28th, and where Byrum was, he was going; what Byrum could do, he could do too. Just like the old days, the Harris boys, Byrum and Omega, a couple of bloods messing around at the edges of the street-gang life in Buffalo's black ghetto.

War? *War ain't no big deal*, Harris told himself going in. *Me and Byrum. Be like gang-bangin' on the block.*

Byrum was why Harris was in the Army in the first place. They had always been competitive at everything, even for their mother's love; it was Omega who bought her a card and made her a present every Mother's Day and Omega who brought home the better report cards, but it was Byrum who got the $265 silk suit for graduation. So when Byrum and a buddy came swaggering around to Omega's girl's place one day, woofing about how they were joining up and flashing their enlistment papers in his face, he took the bait. The word on the street even then, in 1966, was that if you were black and the Army got you, it was the same as a ticket to Vietnam, and the idea made Omega a little nervous. But Byrum and his buddy were teasing him that he was scared, and before he knew it he was headed downtown to sign up too.

He had been getting restless anyway, living at home with his mother and marking time in his junior year in high school. He had been raised part-time by his grandparents in Camden, South Carolina, after his parents split up, but his granddaddy had died and left a big empty place in his life. The Army was at least a way out of the house. It took some selling to the recruiting sergeant, who counseled him to finish school first, and to his mother, who had to sign his papers, but he was determined and he prevailed. *Byrum can't do nothing I can't do.*

A wild child, his mother had always called him, and he had to be tamed first. He found himself billeted at Fort Dix for basic with five home boys, buddies from his old neighborhood in Buffalo, and they picked up where they had left off, beering and brawling their way through training as if they were still back on the block. They were six street bloods with quick hands and quicker attitudes; one of them decked a white joker with a single punch for calling him nigger. The Army tried to break them without success, loading them down with scut work. The effort collapsed one Saturday when their platoon guide routed them from their bunks to clean latrines and Harris's partner Baby Huey, six feet six and 250 pounds of pure muscle, picked the dude up like a rag doll and tossed him down the barracks steps.

Next day their sergeant haled them in with a little surprise.

"Well, since you guys can't do nothing and nobody else can do anything with you," he said, glowering straight at Harris, "I'm going to make you squad leader. I'm gonna give all your friends to you, and it'll be up to you to get your details done." Harris gulped an okay and the sergeant dismissed them. Outside, everybody fell out laughing, until Harris said something about him being leader now and they saw he was serious.

"Aww, man," somebody groaned.

"Hey," Harris said, cutting them short, "we gonna outdo all of these other jokers. We gonna show 'em we better soldiers than them."

To their astonishment, they did precisely that. The six bloods from Buffalo graduated basic all spit-shined and strack, the Army honorific for a Class A soldier; a colonel who inspected their barracks was so pleased at the way Harris folded his gear that he ordered him promoted to Pfc. on the spot and sent for a draftsman to diagram his footlocker for the benefit of the rest of the battalion. Harris was finding a calling, and when he went on to leadership school to get his sergeant's stripes for real, he embraced it. He was Byrum Harris's baby brother and he wanted his mother to be proud of *him* this time; he was a black man in a white man's world, and he wanted someone to look up to him for a change. The Army was his point of entry to respect. *Hey*, he told himself, *this is what I want to do*.

Harris spent nineteen months thereafter in Mannheim, Germany, at eighteen the youngest and sharpest sergeant in his battalion. "I'm gonna send your little smart ass to Vietnam, see how smart you is," his first sergeant, a tough old lifer from Watts, used to tease him. Harris figured he was kidding, or hoped he was, but then the plane put him down in Bien Hoa and it was all coming true. He looked around at the mocking sign that said WELCOME TO VACATIONLAND and the guys waiting to board the freedom bird home, some of them missing arms or legs. *Shit*, Harris thought, and then somebody was yelling "Incoming!" and mortar rounds were thudding down and he was running like everyone else for cover.

It took some talking to get himself assigned to Charlie Company, and when he finally got there, he discovered it wasn't going to be what he had thought, him and Byrum rumbling with the VC, because Vietnam wasn't gang-banging and Byrum wanted out. Omega was waiting at the base camp in Lai Khe when Byrum and the guys came in from an operation, and they had barely popped the tops off a couple of Miller High Lifes when a siren went off, rockets started exploding and everybody was running again. *Must be us firing at them*, Omega thought, sipping at his beer and wondering why he was all alone at the snack bar. Byrum came scrambling back for him, and even then Omega took his sweet time sauntering behind his brother to a bunker. "Get your dunce head down here, man. They incoming!" Byrum yelled at him. Omega—*dumb little cluck me*—sauntered on; he didn't even know what incoming meant until Byrum told him that they were under enemy rocket attack and that he had better get used to it, because it happened so often they called Lai Khe "Rocket City."

Byrum told Omega that and a lot more, brother initiating brother in what the war was really about. The war had been getting to Byrum. He had been badly burned by a rocket round while Omega was still in Germany, and Omega, in a spasm of worry and rage, had dumped his dog tags, his ID and his uniform U.S. pin on his own first sergeant's desk and stormed, "My brother die, you might as well send me home or lock me up because I will not stay in this Army one day."

The sergeant had followed him back to his barracks and found him sitting miserably on his bed with a letter from the Red Cross about Byrum. "Harris, you can't do that," the sergeant said, and Harris knew it. They fixed Byrum up anyway and sent him back to the company, but he wanted out of the war and Omega was his ticket; the Army rules said you couldn't force two brothers to fight in the same war zone.

"One day you'll understand," he told Omega, leaving him and 'Nam behind just two weeks after their reunion. Goodbye, Byrum. Hello, war.

And still the planes kept coming in at Bien Hoa and Tan Son Nhut and Cam Ranh Bay, delivering their freight of men-children to Vietnam. In July it was David Bean's turn, stepping out into the heat and the dank, sticky smell of the jungle and wondering why the stewardesses avoided looking you in the eye. Bean was a short, wiry towhead straight out of a bored and restless adolescence in country Minnesota, first in Comfrey and later Mountain Lake. He had never been on a plane before the day he flew out to Fort Lewis, Washington, for basic, and by then he was ready to go. He had felt himself a round peg in a very square hole, a truck driver's son coming of age in a small and mostly Mennonite town of fewer than two thousand souls and smothering in its conservative folkways. There were no movies, no dances, not even a senior prom—*nothing to do*, Bean often thought, *except drive out to the lake, make a U-turn and drive back.* He took up with what passed for the looser crowd, a half-dozen or so kids like him, sliding through high school on easy C's, going out drinking on Saturday nights, slipping away to the dances in Sanborn when Mitch Ryder and the Detroit Wheels were passing through. Once there was a car accident and they found Bean sodden behind the wheel; he said somebody put him there, but they kicked him off the high-school basketball team anyway. Life in the fast lane. Which way out?

The Army was one way, and Bean didn't even wait till his number came up to take it. He had partied through a single quarter in junior college sixty miles down the road in Worthington, then dropped out and volunteered for the draft so he could go off to basic at Fort Lewis with some buddies. He knew from watching Walter Cronkite every night that maybe five hundred guys a week were coming back in tin boxes, but it never sank in that one of them might be him. The Beans had lived in America for three hundred years and had gone off without question to all of America's wars; a great-grandfather had been a POW at Andersonville in the Civil War, and Bean's own father had served in World War II. Going to war was part of the rhythm of life, the cycle of generations, and you didn't run away from it; you served.

You didn't even think of running. On their way to 'Nam, Bean and a pal treated themselves to a boozy few days in San Francisco, with a sympathetic topless dancer named Bonnie as their tour guide. The last day, at her place in Berkeley, Bean saw a guy his age across the room lacing up a pair of hiking boots. Bean said hello. The guy didn't answer. "He's going to Canada," Bonnie said. It didn't register; Bean didn't know what people were going to Canada for—not until he got to 'Nam himself and went out on patrol and saw Sergeant Williams lying waxy in the bush with a bullet hole through his helmet and his forehead. Goodbye, World. Hello, war.

In September it was J.C. Wilson, and all he could think about was how the Army had lied to him. It wasn't going to Vietnam that bothered him, since he didn't understand what was happening there anyway. Didn't *nobody* understand it down home in Waverly, Tennessee, because nobody from Waverly had been to the war before Wilson. Not even his first glimpse of the jungle from the plane coming in disturbed him. He had grown up in the woods, running barefoot over the rocks and branches till his soles were as tough as shoe leather and his skinny body as hard as a tenpenny nail; he could come up downwind of a deer without so much as popping a twig or even drawing a breath for two or three minutes on end. *Hell, this'll be a piece of cake,* he thought, staring out at the thick cover of foliage below him. *Playin' a game.* No, it wasn't the war that was bothering him; it was the lies. It was all that recruiting sweet talk about him having a future in construction engineering, learning to handle heavy equipment, until they had his signature on the enlistment papers; then they shipped him off to infantry school, and when he asked whatever happened to construction engineering, they told him he didn't have the training for it—infantry was what he was trained for, so infantry was what he would do.

Learning to run a bulldozer had been a meager dream, but Wilson always figured he had grown up too fast for dreaming anyway. His boyhood began dying while he was still in grade school, the day his daddy fell off the Nazarene church roof. He was one of ten children, with five older sisters and four younger brothers, sharing a hardscrabble patch of ground two miles out of Waverly with a couple of hogs and eight or ten chickens. Their father worked for the WPA and did odd jobs to keep them all on the near side of hunger, and saw to their spiritual nourishment every Wednesday night and Sunday morning at their holiness church. But their life was always pinched at the edges. The boys couldn't go out for sports, because sports meant staying for practice after the school bus left and the Wilsons didn't have a car to fetch them home in. When J.C. came along, it was almost as if they couldn't afford a whole name for him and had to christen him with initials instead.

Still, the Wilsons were scraping along all right until that day a two-by-four broke under J.C.'s daddy while he was helping put up the roof of their new church and spilled him from the rafters to the ground. "It broke him all to pieces," they told the family. They put him back together with a metal pin and a length of his own leg bone to prop up his spine, but he was paralyzed from the waist down and the doctor warned the Wilsons that it wouldn't be long before his mind went too.

It wasn't long. The elder Wilson's life fell into a depressive round from bed to wheelchair and from melancholy to rage. His pain was constant. He said his legs felt like they were on fire. J.C.'s mother remembered what the doctor had told her—*his mind could go like that*—and, just in case, she hid his single-shot .22 out of his reach under some clothes in a box. But with a guile born of descending madness, J.C.'s father talked one of the girls into bringing it to him in his bed.

"You know I got it, don't you?" he told J.C.'s mother after that. It was the day before Thanksgiving. J.C., nine years old, was in school.

"Don't worry about the gun," his mother told his father. "I got the gun put up."

"You don't think I've got it," his father answered, "just look around here and I'll show it to you."

His mother looked. The barrel of the .22 was peeking out of the bedclothes. She stared at it, and him, and went running terrified to his sister's place to call the sheriff to come take the gun away. She was on the way back when she heard the shot. With his two littlest boys watching wide-eyed from the foot of the bed, J.C.'s daddy had put the rifle to his head and pulled the trigger.

A big sister found J.C. at lunch at school and fetched him home to his inheritance: a childhood too short and too poor for dreaming. The family bumped along for a while on Social Security survivors' benefits, and J.C. lasted in school till the tenth grade. That was the furthest a Wilson had ever made it at the time; his parents came from big, hard-pressed families—bigger and harder pressed than his own—and had never gone to school at all. J.C. liked school and wished he could stay, but there wasn't any money, and he was the man of the house at sixteen. So he said goodbye to boyhood and went to work for a feed company, grinding cow and hog feed six days a week for $4 a day.

He held off the draft board as long as he could, till he was going on twenty-one, but the eldest of his kid brothers was coming on working age, and he went to see the recruiter about volunteering.

"If I go in now," he asked, "will you let me pick what I want?"

"Yeah, sure you can. Any field you want."

"Construction engineering?"

"Fine, we've got openings," the man said, pushing the papers toward Wilson.

So Wilson signed and was still waiting for his first bulldozer lesson the day they lined everybody up in formation in a big field at Bien Hoa for assignment to their units. The 101st Airborne had taken some fearful losses—"Dyin' like wild flowers," guys were saying—and the roll call for replacements got all the way down to the W's, one name before Wilson's, before they made their quota. Wilson watched the FNGs piling into a convoy of trucks, nobody armed yet except the drivers and the guys riding shotgun, and rumbling off toward Highway 1 to hook up with the 101st. He was just getting his own assignment to the Big Red One and, ultimately, Charlie Company when they heard the blast and the chatter of gunfire and saw the smoke mushrooming up a mile or two in the distance. They heard later that the replacements for the 101st had run into an ambush—or, more nearly, a massacre—and that seventy-five or eighty of them had been blown away. *This damn game is real*, Wilson thought, and it had come within an ace of killing him on his first day out. Hello, war.

In October it was Doc and Stag, the medic and the radioman, strangers leading separate lives a world apart until lot cast them up in Vietnam and war bonded them together like brothers. Doc was Kit Bowen, Thomas Kitrick Bowen on his birth certificate, the hellion eldest child of a prominent and prosperous insurance man in Portland, Oregon. Stag was Donald Stagnaro, the grandson of an Italian immigrant and son of a fisherman working the boats out of San Pedro, California. They made an oddly matched set, the two of them: Bowen had been raised in comfort where Stagnaro had gone to bed hungry when the day's catch was poor; Stagnaro had a core of seriousness even when he was playing hard, where Bowen was a barely grownup Katzenjammer kid. But differences tended to melt when you were new to 'Nam and headed for the field and you had to wait for the body bags to come off the chopper so you could get on. There was something leveling about 'Nam with its democracy of death. 'Nam made friendship hard because there were too many painful goodbyes. But 'Nam made friendship necessary because you needed friends to survive.

The friendships Stagnaro had left behind were mostly with his car-club buddies—the sons of fishermen and longshoremen, like himself, grabbing a little playtime and dreaming of a world beyond the boats and docks where their fathers worked. In a California generation that sorted into surfers and low-riders Stagnaro was a low-rider, the possessor of a no-longer-recognizable ten-year-old Pontiac with a souped-up motor and a chassis dropped so rakishly low it nearly scraped the ground. It was the vehicle for his fantasies, the metaphor of his escape from the boats. He drank beer, chased girls, played football, hacked at a piano in a rock band and hung out with the other low-riders at their clubhouse, a rented storefront on Skid Row. But he wanted something more than a precarious livelihood fishing like his father and his grandfather, and he never lost sight of where he was going. He kept up a better-than-B average through high school and enrolled in the fire science program at Harbor Junior College to learn to be a fireman.

It didn't take, and he dropped out after a semester to work in a warehouse and wait for the draft. "Hey, you're crazy. You should stay in school," guys in the car club told him; half his buddies were doing just that, clinging to their student deferments. But going to war didn't bother Stagnaro. It was more than just having grown up in a close, conservative town like San Pedro where you answered the call when your country needed you; he felt a positive tug—*kind of a John Wayne thing*—to test and prove himself, as nearly every generation of Americans had before him, in combat. He left behind a houseful of weeping women when he got his papers, but the edge of apprehension he felt taking off yielded to the pumped-up rush of adrenaline as the Vietnamese coastline

came into view. *This is right and proper*, he told himself.
He thought he knew where he was going.

Bowen didn't and didn't much care. He was the roustabout of the Portland Bowens, a born kidder pinballing
through young manhood on mother wit and a gift of gab still
twinkling at four generations' remove from Ireland. School
was too easy for him; while Stagnaro was earning B's and
playing football in the trenches as a center and a linebacker,
Bowen was sliding by on gentleman's C's and gentlemanly
sports—track and swimming. He stuck a toe in the waters
of higher education, at Portland Community College, and
almost as quickly withdrew it. *This is way too soon*, he
thought; he lasted roughly three weeks, then dropped out
and went to work as a carpenter. It was too soon, and he
was too young, to be serious. His father, a man of similarly
Celtic humors, feigned despair. "If the phone ever rings after
midnight," he told Kit, "I'd ask what hospital is he in and
how much is the bail."

Even his passage into the Army and off to Vietnam had
the quality of accident about it, like bumping into a door.
His best friend Richard was going into the service; Bowen
and a buddy got smashed on beer sending him off, and the
next thing he knew he was volunteering to be drafted early
to make Richard feel good. *Logic*, he thought later. *Oh, God.*
The day he presented himself, he informed the Army
straightaway that he couldn't cook and couldn't possibly be
a medic either—"Blood and I are out." They told him not
to worry, it couldn't happen. But the day his name came up
was the day the Army needed medics, and being B-for-Bowen
didn't help in an institution in which alphabetical order had
the force of physical law. He spent ten weeks at Fort Sam
Houston learning a lot about how to make hospital beds and
not enough about what you do with a severed leg or a sucking
chest wound: *Stop the bleeding, treat 'em for shock and get
'em on a helicopter.*

He didn't think about where he was going, not really,
until he got there. The closest he came was the day before
he left for 'Nam, rummaging through a drawer at his grandmother's place and coming upon a trove of medals and clippings about his father's heroics as a bombardier in World
War II. He hadn't seen them before, and he was still going
through the reliquary when his father found him. They looked

at each other, the father solemnly consecrating the son to war. "Let me tell you," his father said, "the bravery comes all the way down this family, and I don't want you to let us down."

Oh, God, Kit thought, stealing another glance at the medals, *here it comes. I'm not going to try to match him.*

"If you want to be really proud of your heritage," his father was saying, "let me tell you about your great-grandfather. When the Irish rebellion started to break out, he and his best friend said, 'No, we don't think so,' and they dressed up as women and came over to America on a freighter."

They laughed, father and son, and Kit understood the message. *He's telling me just keep your jets cool*, Kit thought, and he did. He wasn't nervous flying over, or descending into 'Nam, or stepping out into the stifling heat, or waiting out his processing through Bien Hoa and Di An. It didn't get to him till he was on the bus to Lai Khe and Charlie Company, gazing out at the passing landscape through a shield of heavy mesh screen.

"What's this for?" he asked aloud. "Shrapnel? Bombs?"

"There's one of the reasons," a sergeant who had been in-country for a while told him. They were lumbering through a ville, past a knot of South Vietnamese, and suddenly fruits and vegetables were splattering against the mesh and people were yelling, "Fuck you, GI!"

These are the people I'm protecting, Bowen thought. Hello, war.

A SMALL CORNER OF HELL

It was the eve of his first big operation commanding Charlie Company, and Captain Richard Lee Rogers didn't know if his men were up to it. He wasn't certain yet that he was, either. He was in a sense an accidental officer in the first place; he had grown up skinny and poor in East Texas and had enrolled in advanced ROTC at Northwestern State College in Louisiana partly because he needed the $27 monthly stipend to help pay his way through school. At twenty-eight, he had already done one tour of Vietnam, behind the lines, in 1965 and had been tempted thereafter to leave the Army; he had been offered a PR job in California at flatteringly high pay and had never quite let go of his alternate dream of a career in football, playing pro or coaching. But at the last he could not bring himself to quit, not with the struggle over Vietnam coming to a rolling boil. *I have to find out about myself*, he thought. He was a soldier, his country was at war, and he had to go see for himself in combat whether he was a coward or not.

So Rogers, nearly alone among the boys of Charlie Company, had gone to Vietnam because he wanted to. He had in fact had to outscramble other ambitious career officers to get there. He was one of them, slender and trig, his patient eyes and softly accented voice masking the asceticism and the aspirations of a committed professional soldier. Having chosen the Army, he understood that upward mobility in wartime meant getting a piece of the action. There were never enough combat commands to go around in a theater as small and a war as limited as Vietnam; the Army cut back the standard command tour from a year to six months, in part precisely to satisfy the intensely competitive demand. But going to 'Nam was more than simple ticket-punching for Rogers. He saw it as a proof of his patriotism and a test of his nerve; it was his daily prayer to God not to let him be afraid.

The command he drew proved a trial of his by-the-book professional standards as well. He had found Charlie Company in what he considered rusty shape when he took over in August 1968—*stale*, he thought, from having gone too long a time with too little contact with the enemy. They had taken a terrible pounding in a major battle some months before and then had gone for weeks on end humping the boonies in vain search of action. There had been a passage in the summer when the most memorable contact they encountered had been with the mama-sans who followed them up a stretch of Highway 13 called Thunder Road on bicycles and serviced them in the bushes at $3 a ten-minute trick. Discipline had gone slack, and one of Rogers's first acts as CO was to institute a heavy schedule of training in such rudiments as ambush techniques and rifle marksmanship. The older hands didn't much like taking lessons in war from a pink-cheeked ROTC captain, and Rogers could feel their resentment.

He sensed that they were measuring him, too; wondering, perhaps, if he would crack up under fire like a past Charlie Company officer who had called in artillery on his own position and had finally been relieved of command in the field. Rogers was not impervious to doubt in himself. Early in his tour he had lost his first man, a sergeant named Raymond Williams. They had stopped for a break on a routine patrol in the bush and he had sent Williams off a hundred meters or so to set up an observation post. They heard a *pop-pop-pop* in the trees and a sudden, urgent voice on the radio, and David Bean was running with a couple of other guys toward the sound. Williams was dead when they found him, and Bean, the towhead from the Minnesota lake country, was staring at where the bullet had passed clean through the sergeant's helmet into his skull. *Oh, Christ*, Bean thought; he had never seen a man killed before, and he guessed later that Rogers hadn't either.

Rogers hadn't, not on his own watch; he felt torn apart by it, and when he had to face the men at a memorial service in the chow hall back at Lai Khe, he couldn't hack it. There hadn't been long enough for him to get to know Williams, or even to match the name to the face, and Rogers meant only to say a few words of farewell at the service. But when he rose to speak, he was too choked with sorrow to say anything at all. The words stuck in his throat, and then, in full view of the company, he was crying. It took him a few moments to get hold of himself and do a soldier's homily about how you had to bury the dead and carry on and how armies at war go flat when they don't see enough action. He didn't know then that some of the men liked him rather better for his show of caring whether they lived or died. In his own eyes, he had surrendered to emotion, and he was afraid the men might see his surrender as he had—as a sign of weakness in himself.

And now, in October, he had to find out whether they would follow him into a small corner of hell: a jungle outpost barely two klicks—kilometers—from the Cambodian border and smack astride one of the main NVA (for North Vietnamese Army) infiltration routes into the heart of South Vietnam. Lyndon Johnson was then already tapering down the bombing of North Vietnam toward a full stop on November 1, a few days before the American presidential election. His emissaries were in secret contact with the North Vietnamese in Paris, and he thought he had a wink-and-a-nod understanding that Hanoi would reciprocate by easing off its own pressure on the south and entering serious peace negotiations.

There had indeed been a lull of several weeks in the ground war by mid-October. But Army intelligence had picked up signs that the entire First NVA Division was massed perhaps three thousand strong in a Cambodian sanctuary called Base Area 353, north of Tay Ninh, and was operating on both sides of the border. In response, the American command was sending up three battalions, the Black Lions among them, to set up fire bases in the area and try to tempt the enemy into the open. "We're going to use you for bait," Rogers told his lieutenants and noncoms in a hooch at Lai Khe. There were two thousand to three thousand regular NVA troops at the border, on their way to Saigon if nobody stopped them. So the battalion was going up to get in their way. "We're going to be bait for those guys," Rogers told his people. "We want them to hit us."

His further instruction was not to tell the men the nature of the mission. But the word spread quickly that where they were going was hot, and given their affinity for trouble, most of them simply assumed that wherever Charlie Company wound up would be the hottest. On the morning of the 18th they stood inspection at their Lai Khe base camp, then marched to the airfield, the tension palpable among them. The field was covered with choppers, more than they had ever seen before for a single operation. They filed aboard, clattered north over the jungle into far Tay Ninh province and set down in a brush and bamboo wilderness within spitting distance, as it turned out, of a main-force NVA base camp. Their purpose by then was no longer a well-kept secret. *We're here to draw fire*, Edmund J. Lee VI was thinking. Robert E. Lee lurked somewhere in the branches of his family tree, but the impulse to command and to heroism had thinned in the Lee bloodline by the time it reached him, and all he could think was, *We're going to catch it*.

That day and the next, they carved Fire Support Base Julie out of the jungle, the farthest north and most exposed of the three in the Army's battle plan. A circle of ground was stripped of foliage down to the bare red dirt; bunkers were dug and sandbagged in clock formation near the edge, Charlie Company drawing the sector from six o'clock to ten o'clock; coils of sharp-edged concertina wire were strung around the perimeter; trees were blown away and humps of earth knocked flat with explosives to clear fields of fire against the moment when the enemy chose to come at them. They worked largely unmolested at first. But they could feel the NVA watching them in the daytime and could hear the rumble of supply trucks in the night, just across the Cambodian border from their outpost.

The quiet lasted less than thirty-six hours. On the night of October 19, Julie's NVA neighbors lobbed in some mortar rounds, just enough to spoil their sleep, Edmund Lee thought, and to keep them nervous. The 20th was quiet. On the 21st a Huey helicopter took a burst of ground fire trying to airlift a stranded long-range reconnaissance patrol out of a jam, and went down in flames. They sent Charlie Company out to find the wreckage and bring back anyone or anything in shape to save. The men headed off into the jungle, double-timing so they could get back to base by nightfall, and almost tripped over a three-man North Vietnamese rocket team that had stolen within five hundred meters of Julie's outer ring of wire.

The NVAs were dozing near a stream bed in the afternoon sun, and Charlie Company wasted them before they could scramble to their rifles. But the gunfire brought a furious answering volley from a larger enemy force on the far side of the stream, and suddenly they were the bait challenging the shark, a company rapping at the front door of an enemy division. Rogers pulled them back and radioed for artillery and air strikes. The mission to the fallen chopper was abandoned till the next morning; when they finally reached it, it was a charred skeleton, the bodies of the dead hanging from its blackened remains.

The cycle continued, quiet one night, rockets and mortars the next, and Rogers was worried for his men. He could feel the pounding build toward a crescendo and was afraid they might buckle under it. The round of patrols by day and bombardment by night had left them haggard, sleepless and rumbling with discontent at what he and they considered a disproportionate share of the danger. A lot of them were coming down with dengue fever, a nasty second cousin to malaria, but Rogers sensed that the worst was coming and felt that he could not spare them; he ordered that no one be evacuated with a temperature under 103.5 degrees, and he stayed in action when his own hit 104.5. Each new night assault, each new day run seemed to stretch them closer to the end of their string. "Sir, I don't know if they can go out again today," Rogers told Lieutenant Colonel Vernon Coffey, the towering black swashbuckler who commanded the battalion, when yet another hazardous detail fell to them. And later: "Sir, I don't know if they *will* go out again."

Rogers's anxiety grew with his belief—half premonition, half empirical judgment—that the decisive battle for Fire Base Julie was at hand. "I think the twenty-fifth will be the day," he told Colonel Coffey. The day came, and he was trying to steel his men and himself for it when somebody brought him an urgent letter from his wife. Rogers ripped it open and started reading. She was begging him to get to a phone and call home; their son, Richard, seven months old, was in the hospital with what looked like meningitis, and she was afraid he might die. It was no help to Rogers in that moment that the diagnosis would prove to be a false alarm. His wife was asking him to choose between his family and his duty, and he did what he felt he had to do. He folded the letter, stuffed it in a pocket, said a prayer for Richard's recovery, and went back to the war.

Omega Harris was worried about his men too. It was why they called him Sergeant Rock, not just because he was good with an 81 mm mortar but because he was concerned about getting them home alive. He was just back from five days' R&R with his wife, Jean, in Honolulu, and it had been half spoiled for him by his guilty feeling that he had deserted his guys. "Look at this, just look at this!" he had raged, his head still in 'Nam. Jean had asked what it was she was supposed to be looking at, and he said, "Look at all these bastards walkin' around free and easy, and people over there in Vietnam dyin' for them!" He stayed out the five days, his pleasure at being with Jean in constant tension with his misery at thinking he wasn't where he belonged. And then he went home to the war and to Fire Base Julie on his third day back, and found his man Clyde Garth fallen under a spell of impending doom.

It wasn't like Garth. Garth was a sunny black kid out of Aberdeen, Mississippi, the kind of guy people naturally liked and wanted to look out for. Harris had taken Garth under his wing almost like a baby brother; he was actually a year younger than Garth at nineteen, but he was a sergeant and Garth a private straight out of infantry school, and Garth looked up to him. In the weeks before Julie, Garth had sought out Harris and unburdened himself of a dilemma of the heart. He had a lady named Leome at home; he loved her, he had stood by her and paid all the bills for the two baby girls she had borne him, and his heart melted every time he heard O.C. Smith sing "Little Green Apples" on Armed Forces Radio because it reminded him of her. But there was another woman he was a little soft on and, he told Harris, he didn't know which of them he wanted to marry. Harris didn't want to push, but he made sure he called Garth over to his hooch every time "Little Green Apples" came on, and he talked about how hard it had been for his own mom to raise her five kids when she and his father had split up. Garth thought about his baby girls and made up his mind. He was going to marry Leome, as he had promised when he left, and he sent away for two mail-order diamond rings.

But the premonition of death that sometimes infected men in the bush had stolen over Garth and crept into his letters home. He complained that he was tired. He sent home a snapshot of a buddy, a white dude in Harris's weapons platoon; the guy had been hit, the letter said, and had died with his head in Garth's arms. He wrote finally about how he had been lying in his bunker one night when a mortar round hit nearby; it might have killed him if he hadn't rolled out of the way just in time. "I won't always be so lucky," he wrote Leome. "I'll be coming back home but it won't be alive." He was at Fire Base Julie when the rings he had bought her arrived at mail call. Something made him take them to Harris and ask him to hold them, just in case. It was October 24.

Just past midnight on the 25th the mortars opened up yet again, softening up Julie for what was to be the NVA's do-or-die last assault. The first rounds fell fifty feet short of the wire while Harris's team was at work shoring up its own emplacement with sandbags. *Not even close*—Harris shrugged, but his guys were running toward him yelling that Garth was dead.

"How's Garth dead?" Harris demanded, not wanting to believe it.

"I'm not kidding, he's really dead," somebody said.

Guys were crying and Harris was double-timing after them to where Garth lay sprawled on his back in the mud. Harris looked at him. There was no blood, no gaping wound, and Harris was still resisting it. "Man, get up and stop playing around," he ordered. Garth lay still. They discovered only later that a fragment of shrapnel no bigger than the end of a ballpoint pen had pierced his chest and found his heart.

His death was a portent for the others, an omen of what was to come. In the distance beyond their encampment, they could hear the trucks lumbering closer, moving men and supplies into position for the attack. Mortar rounds showered in, then rockets, then mortar rounds again. On an ambush run maybe half a kilometer beyond Julie's perimeter, Sea-Tac Olson and Larry Samples and Jerry Dickmann and some others heard the sound of Vietnamese soldiers moving and whispering in the foliage. The men looked at one another. They had come out in bush hats instead of helmets—*real slinky*, Olson had thought at the time, but now they were regretting it and looking for a place to hide.

Olson, the squad leader, motioned them into a stand of bamboo that had been ripped up by mortars the day before. They found a crater big enough for all eight of them, scrambled in and watched what looked like the whole NVA marching past them in the darkness. *Hundreds of guys*, Dickmann thought, wide-eyed. Thousands, maybe, with AK-47 rifles and RPG grenade launchers and an ox dragging a heavy machine gun, all filing by them in the night and pointed straight at Fire Base Julie.

The eight of them lay in place, terrified, belly down and trying to will themselves into the earth. Olson's heart was pounding so hard he thought he must be bouncing off the ground. Artillery was flying over their heads out of Fire Base Rita to the south. Mortars were popping on both sides and banging down all around them. One round hit close to their hole. Olson felt a bit of shrapnel skip off his head, leaving a painful knot, and another man was gasping and groaning, clawing at a sucking wound in his side. They were still trying to quiet him when their own men back at the base lit the sky over their heads with illumination rounds. "Stop the fuckin' flares, will ya?" somebody whispered into the radio. "Come get us—we're trapped!"

But the NVA was between them and Julie; their buddies couldn't get near them, and their SOS brought only a single enemy soldier who overheard their voices, mistook them for comrades and wandered into the bamboo chattering at them in Vietnamese. Samples leveled a .45 automatic at him and blew him away, but as he fell dying, he yanked the pin out of a fragmentation grenade and tossed it into their hideaway.

The grenade clumped onto the dirt and rolled to their feet. For one freeze-framed moment they stood paralyzed, and then Samples had it, turning to shield the others with his body. He was trying to throw it away when it went off in his hand. The spray of shrapnel hit practically everyone who wasn't wounded already, all but Dickmann and Chico the Indian. But it was Samples who paid the dues, his chest and stomach blown mostly away.

Samples was black and Dickmann didn't like black people; he hadn't known many, coming of age in Saukville, Wisconsin, and didn't particularly care for what few he had met. But Samples was different, Dickmann thought. Samples was okay; he didn't spend his time bitching like some of the others about what the government owed him. And now he was dying, and Dickmann was watching him, thinking, *He's a fuckin' hero.*

He didn't die easily. He was groaning and weeping for what seemed an endless time, and the others were begging him not to cry—he would give them all away. "I know, I know, I know," Samples moaned, "but, God, it hurts. I'm dying." He wouldn't quit and he wouldn't die, and finally Chico and Dickmann took hold of his head, clamping his jaw closed to smother his cries. After a while he shuddered all over once, and again, and died. The survivors lay in the night with his body, aching for dawn. *Where is the sun?* Dickmann was thinking. *Where the hell is the sun?* A second NVA blundered into their position and they opened up on him, blowing his head to bits. The night dragged on. *One dead and one maybe dying,* Olson was thinking, and both of them his buddies; they were the first he had lost in the war, and he was feeling awful about that and worse about what was going through his mind. *Better them than me*, he was thinking, *even if they are my friends*. Where the hell was the sun?

The sun wouldn't come, and the NVA troops kept moving through the dark in clusters of fifty toward Julie. The three-man listening posts stationed a hundred meters or so outside the wire heard them first, saw their silhouettes passing in the night and started clicking the on-off switches on their radios, the signal that trouble was coming so close by that it was too dangerous even to whisper. The barrage had let up, and in the stillness J.C. Wilson, sitting up on his bunker inside the perimeter, could hear the clicks from the listening posts run together into an ominous sputter—*clicking and popping and snapping*, he was thinking, *like popcorn in a pan*.

And then the mortar and rocket rounds were cascading down again, everybody was scrambling for cover, and waves of NVA regulars were hurling themselves at the wire on Charlie Company's section of the line. Battalion radioed for Danger Charlie 6, Captain Rogers's call name, wanting to know how heavy the assault looked. "Heavy," Rogers answered. "We can't take it much heavier."

They were coming at Julie like breakers on a beach by then. Rogers clicked off and was scurrying from pressure point to pressure point, trying to brace up the line, when the NVA finally blasted a way through the wire with bangalore torpedoes and came spilling inside. Tracers streaked red across the clearing, "Sort of like the Fourth of July back home," Jim the Fox Erwin wrote in his notebook later, "except these weren't for display, these were for Death." Flares turned the night into day. Shadowy forms were moving toward the bunker line, backlit by the glare, walking straight up and stiff like B-movie zombies through Charlie Company's fields of fire.

Greg Skeels and some buddies lay in a bunker watching them coming and couldn't believe it was the NVA at first—not walking in that way. "You GI? You GI?" some of Skeels's pals yelled at the shadows. But they kept coming, and Skeels and his buddies opened up, the sticky scent of blood already rising around them, shooting gooks, Skeels thought, as if they were popping balloons with BBs on a carnival midway.

Only they wouldn't quit coming; they seemed to be everywhere, flittering through the night and the firestorm like water through a wide-mesh strainer. Five of them made it to cover in a tank trailer ten feet inside the wire, until Omega Harris's No. 1 mortar team dropped a round right on target and blew it, and them, to pieces. One got to the lip of a bunker and stopped; they found him squatting there, a barely teenaged boy, too frightened either to go on or turn back. Men were shooting and shouting and yelling for medics, and in the middle of a Niagara of noise, Bob Mastrogiovanni was crouched in a bunker with George Hesser thinking he had only been in the field for two days and wasn't going to live to see the third. In the next bunker he could hear a sergeant in hand-to-hand combat with an NVA, slashing him to death methodically with a knife. In the middle distance he could hear a scream rise above the din of battle. "Mommy!" somebody was crying in the dark. "Mom—where are you?"

Billy Johnson—Doc Johnson inevitably, because he was a medic—was in his own bunker with his M-16 near at hand. He carried a Bible inside his helmet liner with a letter from his girl folded inside, but Johnson, unlike some medics, had no conscientious objection whatever to defending his own life. He had grown up poor, the son of a Missouri share-cropper come north to Rockford, Illinois—for the food, Johnson liked to say, and the indoor plumbing. He had been working his way through Drake University as a part-time pre-med student when the Army swept him up and set him down in 'Nam practicing more traumatic medicine in a month than a lot of doctors see in a lifetime. And now he was hunched down behind his sandbags, watching Sergeant Racie Reid scramble off into the blackness toward a machine-gun emplacement. A minute dragged by, then another; then Reid was yelling for him and Johnson was low-crawling through the night toward the voice.

At the edge of a forward bunker he saw a form in the dark and thought it was one of his own guys until he heard a metallic click-click-click—a firing pin in an empty AK-47 chamber. *A gook*, Johnson thought, too astonished to be angry or even scared. *He's trying to kill me*. The gook— they were all gooks in the language of the bunkers—swung the AK-47 at Johnson's head and connected, knocking his helmet, his Bible and the letter from his girl into the dirt.

There wasn't time to shoot or even think of shooting; instead, Johnson stood parrying blows with his own M-16 and then swung back, as hard as he could. His rifle stock splintered over the gook's head, but he kept swinging the bared steel, again and again, and all he could hear in the eye of a hurricane of noise was the rasp of his own breathing, the sound of his own grunts each time the remnants of his rifle struck home.

He quit only when his enemy lay bloody at his feet and the whine of tracers and the pop-pop of flares welled up again in his ears. Then he jumped down in the bunker to see to Reid.

"Is he dead?" Reid asked.

"I don't know," Johnson answered. "He's not moving."

Reid handed Johnson his own rifle. "Shoot the gook," he said.

Johnson shot him, once in the heart, and went back to Reid. Reid was fucked up bad; the gook had dropped a grenade into the bunker, practically on top of him, and the blast had laid open a shoulder, an arm and a leg. The arm was spouting blood from a main artery. Johnson stuck his fingers in the holes to slow the hemorrhaging long enough for him to get a pressure bandage in place. *Stop the bleeding, treat 'em for shock, get 'em to a chopper*. It wasn't pretty, and it wasn't textbook medicine, but Reid was going to make it.

Captain Rogers saw Johnson after that, still carrying his splintered M-16, and recognized him as the embodiment of the odds they were up against, viewed from the short end. The men had brought an NVA prisoner to Rogers's command bunker. Rogers, who had learned Vietnamese for his first tour in-country, had questioned him and confirmed how badly outnumbered they were—a single battalion trying to hold off elements of four or five of the enemy's. The assault waves were still breaking over the concertina wire, and for a desperate passage Rogers was afraid they might be overrun.

But overwhelming American firepower finally achieved what Julie's overmatched defenders could not do for themselves. David Spain saw a guy fire a machine gun till the barrel glowed red, yipping like a chihuahua and popping skulls like watermelons under a sledgehammer. A plane they called Puff the Magic Dragon circled low overhead, a refitted

Air Force transport spewing six thousand rounds a minute from its Gatling guns. A single NVA sniper was shooting back at the plane out of a crater until J.C. Wilson popped a couple of grenades at him with an M-79 launcher; the second hit the sniper's ammo supply and incinerated him in a ball of orange flame. Howitzer rounds thundered in from Fire Base Rita to Julie's south. Omega Harris's mortar teams were pounding away at the gaps in the wire, chanting to their own rhythm of firing, loading and firing again: "Here's one for you, sucker! Here's one for yo' mama!" They kept on firing, and when they came near the end of their ammo, Jim Erwin had to scuttle off to Bravo Company and back through the dark, half-running, half-crawling to Harris's mortars with armloads of fresh rounds.

The ordnance of death saturated the night and turned Julie into a killing ground. Bodies piled on bodies, so deep at points that Rogers had to order his men out of their bunkers to clear them so they could see to kill more. Some didn't want to move; he was shouting commands at them but they weren't budging, and Rogers, fighting his own demons, was seeing just how paralytic fear could be if men surrendered to it. It struck him in that instant that if he couldn't get them above ground, maybe one of their own could. He turned to a black kid private named Poindexter and told him, "Get these men moving!" Poindexter popped to. "Charlie Six says let's move," he shouted, "*so let's move!*" The men moved, and Rogers made a note to himself to put Poindexter in for sergeant as soon as the smoke cleared.

The siege finally let up by five-thirty, and with first light, a platoon set out from Julie to try to bring Olson's trapped ambush party back from its hideaway in the bamboo. The rising sun revealed a nightmare landscape strewn with the bodies of the dead and dying. They came upon the remnants of a machine-gun emplacement that had been overrun; the gunner had been hit sixteen or seventeen times and was half paralyzed, but he had kept firing, the corpses piling up around his position. The platoon was bringing the survivors in when the enemy opened up again, wounding a grunt named Cisco. Frank Goins, a muscular black kid from South Georgia, had to crawl to base with Cisco slung across his brawny back.

They moved out again and were barely fifty meters beyond the wire when they walked into the main element of an NVA force regrouping for a second suicide attack on Julie. They could see the flash of mortars in the reeds, and they were scrambling for cover with the rounds screaming in around them. Goins saw a guy go down clutching his belly, trying to hold his guts inside; he scrambled to help and was dragging the guy toward a trash pit for cover when a rocket exploded behind him, nearly tearing away his own left leg.

A fresh barrage from Omega Harris's mortar section snuffed out the attack before it got seriously started, and the attackers fell back at last, leaving most of their dead behind. The bodies were everywhere when the men crept topside for a look around, some still hanging from the wire, some mounded like cordwood on either side. Some were already beginning to decompose in the settling morning heat. Shards of arms and legs were scattered on the ground and dangling from blackened tree limbs. Overhead, a helicopter bearing a cargo of replacements and network news teams to Julie swooped low for several passes so the cameramen could film the slaughter, and Harry Foxwell, one of the FNGs, felt a stab of fear. He had been drafted out of community college in Long Island, put through the Army's shake-'n'-bake in-stant-noncom school, shipped to 'Nam with the stitching on his sergeant stripes still fresh, and shuttled by air-conditioned bus to Di An and Lai Khe for assignment. He had drawn Charlie Company, suddenly in need of new meat; his first contribution to the war had been unloading the body bags containing the American dead from Julie, and now he was looking down at the harvest of enemy corpses, thinking, *This is what the war really is. It's not the air-conditioned buses—it's people lying on the ground that are dead.*

All that remained that morning was to count them. "You want to run & vomit & cry but you can't," Jim the Fox Erwin confessed to his steno notebook a few days later. You couldn't, because in a war without battle lines or territorial objectives, the only measure of success was to number the dead, subtract ours from theirs and declare victory. So the men set out poking among the bodies and rifling their uniform shorts, some pocketing whatever money or souvenirs they found, some misting up at the discovery that the other side carried around wallet photos of their wives and kids just like Americans did.

It was painful work, and sometimes deadly dangerous.

J.C. Wilson was rounding up a patrol for the sweep when a kid radioman, just seventeen years old and three days in-country, came to him too paralyzed by fright to leave the base. He told Wilson a piteous hard-luck story: a dead daddy, a bedridden mama, ten brothers and sisters dependent on his monthly allotment check. A chopper had dumped him at Julie with the food and water only the day before, and he had cowered through the NVA assault in his bunker, never once firing a shot. His eyes were filling when Wilson saw him after daybreak. "Sarge," he begged, "can I stay here this morning? I'm scared to death."

There were echoes of Wilson's own stunted boyhood in the kid's story and he sympathized. His lieutenant did not. "No, ain't *nobody* staying here," he told Wilson. "I want every swinging man we got in line."

The kid was weeping.

"What can I do?" Wilson told him. "When the lieutenant says go, you got to go."

So they went out and started counting bodies, the kid humping his radio and fighting his terror. Just outside the perimeter they found several NVA troopers clumped together in attitudes of death. The kid flipped one of them over for a look and saw only then, in the last moment of his own life, that the gook wasn't dead yet; then a bullet was tearing through his chest, and he was falling forward onto the gook, dying, and a medic was running toward him, and the gook got him, too—hit him in the eye and blew away the side of his face with a dying last shot.

The count went on and reached 128 enemy dead, to 8 Americans. The Army was pleased; there was talk that General Westmoreland himself was coming out for a look at the night's kill, and the bodies were left temporarily in place for his inspection. Westy didn't make it. But on his personal order, or so Charlie Company heard, four or five choppers set down at Julie loaded with cold Cokes and ice cream, and they feasted within eyeshot of the festering dead. Only afterward did they bulldoze the bodies into a common grave and layer them over with the red earth. *Just like they're building a road*, Bob Mastrogiovanni thought. He wanted to retch but was too scared even for that.

The celebratory mood at Saigon headquarters did not travel well to Julie in any event; most of the men of Charlie Company were too spent, and many too full of grief and fury to share the pleasure of the generals in their victory. A sergeant from New York went mad with sorrow for the dead medic; he crashed off into the trees with his M-16 on rock-and-roll, firing clip after clip at nothing till they pulled him out, shot him up with sedatives and sent him back to Lai Khe. J.C. Wilson was lamenting the medic, too, regretting that they had let themselves get close to each other. *It messes up your mind when they die*, he thought; he promised himself he wouldn't make that mistake again. Omega Harris was in mourning for Garth, and when a lieutenant tried to console him by offering to write Garth up for a Bronze Star, Harris exploded. "Sir," he told the lieutenant, "if I could take your life and give him his back, I'd give *you* a Bronze Star. How do you think his family is gonna feel, lookin' at him in a coffin? They don't want no goddam medal—the man's layin' there dead!"

Doc Johnson was sore, too—raging at the blood of buddies crusting on his fatigues and at Captain Rogers for having led them into harm's way in the first place. Some of the men liked the way Rogers had handled himself in his first real test and saw the exhaustion and the sadness shadowing his eyes as a reflection of their own. "It showed how he hated to loose his men," Jim Erwin wrote in his notebook. "There isn't any thing he wouldn't do to save a mans life or limb. He's been here about 3 months and he really loves these guys. But he too must follow orders like us, so we follow him."

But Doc Johnson wasn't buying it, not then and not for years afterward. He stormed into Rogers's tent and started haranguing him for having taken them to Julie at all against impossible odds, a battalion as bait for a division. Rogers had soldiered bravely after all, and so had Johnson; Rogers was putting him in for a Silver Star. But he did not try to answer Johnson's fury. Instead, he sat letting it spill over him, head down under the tumble of accusation, nodding in what Johnson understood to be silent agreement.

A TRIP OUTSIDE TIME

David Bean was back in Lai Khe on an unexpected little holiday from the war when they came to him and told him they needed him to identify Larry Samples's body. Till then, Bean had been congratulating himself on his luck. He had gone up to Fire Base Julie with the company knowing it was bad-ass territory and was so overwound by the time he got there that he jumped off his chopper while it was still hanging eight feet off the ground. And then a guy in his squad who had been scheduled for a three-day break in Lai Khe was caught sleeping on an LP, a night listening post outside the wire. His transgression was reported up the line to Captain Rogers and the verdict came back down: The liberty time would go to Bean instead. So Bean said goodbye to Julie, flew back to Lai Khe, took a shower, smoked a joint and was just getting mellow when they told him his man Samples was in the morgue in Bien Hoa waiting to be identified so they could send the body home. *Fuck, man*, Bean thought, his heart sinking. *Samples*.

Samples had been Bean's partner, his buddy, his tour guide to a world as alien to him as the dark side of the moon. Bean, three months into his tour, was still the unseasoned Minnesota lake-country kid revealed in his favorite Vietnam photo, posed against Black Virgin Mountain, his thin chest bare, his expression solemn, a cigarette dangling from his lips; a straw-blond boy trying to look like a soldier. He had never really known anybody black before, and Samples even at that was his nearly perfect opposite, a streetwise ghetto brother out of Alabama via the tenements and the asphalt basketball courts of New York City. But they had formed another of those mismated friendships the war kept producing, and Samples had seen to his continuing adult education.

Samples had been there to ease him down the day David

Spain turned him on to marijuana. Spain had been success-
fully resisting going out with the company into combat, on
the ground that he had a brother fighting in the 25th Infantry,
and had spent considerable time at Lai Khe acquainting himself with the plentiful local cannabis; they called him L.
David Stone for his devotion to it. But Bean had never tried
it until Spain extended his pack of joints, rolled tight and
sealed in cellophane just like Luckies at $20 a carton for the
GI market.

"Here, smoke some," Spain said.

Bean lit up, smoked one joint down without feeling anything much and started another. Spain was grinning at him.
He finished the second and was into a third before it hit him,
hard. He was conscious of Spain laughing at him and walking
away. Bean wafted into his hooch, flopping backward onto
his bunk, and Samples was there.

"Hah," Samples said. "First time you got high."

"Yeah," Bean said.

"Okay," Samples said. "Take it easy."

"Can I walk around?" Bean asked. The motor signals from
his legs were not promising.

"Yeah, you can do anything you want," Samples said,
and Bean knew he would be all right.

Only that was summer and this was fall, and when it was
Samples who needed Bean, Bean hadn't been there. He
hadn't even known what had happened until a guy came to
him and said, "Dave, you know Samples." He had said yeah,
and the guy told him, "Well, you're going to fly down to
Bien Hoa and identify his body."

He was thinking, *Fuck, man*, and saying, "Yeah, I'll go,"
and a little later he was in the morgue looking at Samples's
corpse. He hadn't known a black guy could look pale, but
Samples did, ashy pale, as if he had literally been drained
of life. "Yeah, that's him," Bean said. He signed a form and
walked away, thinking, *I was supposed to be with those guys
and I wasn't*.

That was when David Bean fell out of time. Time had
been playing tricks on him for a while anyway. He had noticed it one night on Thunder Road in the summer when a
patrol he was on walked into an enemy ambush; they were
running for cover and the tanks coming to bail them out were
rumbling straight at them, dark hulks three abreast in the

moonlight, and Bean was yelling into the radio, "Hey, don't fire, we're coming in!" and the tanks were pumping round after round practically in their faces. He could see the muzzles flashing and hear the rounds shrieking overhead, and when it was over he didn't know whether it had lasted for one second or eight minutes. He didn't know whether what was left of that night had lasted a night or a week, either— only that he was lying sleepless in the dark, thinking, *Oh Jesus, let's go home*. Time took a holiday for him on Thunder Road, and when Samples died, it was as if time's loosening hold on him had died too.

Bean left Samples's ashy body behind in the morgue and started walking. He walked maybe a mile along a road, carrying his M-16, feet pounding in the red dirt, half-conscious of the peasants glancing incuriously at him from the paddies. *I was supposed to be with those guys*, he was thinking. A GI came by in a three-quarter-ton truck, and Bean thumbed a ride, looking for a bar that somebody had told him about somewhere fifteen miles away. *I was supposed to be right with them*, he was thinking; but he hadn't been, and Samples was lying ashen in an Army morgue, the first guy close to him who had ever died. *I don't understand anything anymore*, he was thinking. All he knew was that he had to get drunk.

He found the bar, had some drinks, bought a $10 bag of marijuana from a Vietnamese kid and lurched aboard a bus back to Bien Hoa, totally wrecked. He really belonged in Lai Khe waiting for Charlie Company; Bien Hoa was where they billeted the twinks waiting to be assigned to their units. But Bean was past caring. He wandered into a barracks, picked out an empty bunk and crashed. He slept and got drunk and slept and got drunk again, stashing his rifle and gear under the bed whenever he went outside and losing himself in the anonymous swirl of new men. *Out of the way*, he thought; *fuckin' AWOL*, he thought, from the Army and from time. *Fuck, man. Samples*.

They were coming after Bean when Bean went back to them—when he reentered time and reconnected with Charlie Company four days later. Nobody even asked where he had been—no officers, anyway. The guys were just back from Julie, those who were still alive and still walking, and Bean posed them for some pictures with the weapons they had captured and brought back for souvenirs. But it wasn't like before. People were missing—Frank Goins with a piece of his leg blown away; Tom Swenticky, the big Polish kid from Jersey, so badly riddled with shrapnel that they had mistaken him for dead; Edmund Lee VI, distant cousin to Robert E., with an ingloriously nasty-looking wound in the groin an inch or so from his genitals. Guys who had made it were muttering, about Rogers and the Army and the war.

Everybody's changed, Bean thought; he was and they were. *The death thing*, he thought. They had seen too much death at Fire Base Julie that night when Larry Samples got killed, and, after Julie, people really seemed to get serious about staying alive.

BEER, SMOKE AND BRAGGADOCIO

Joe Pentz and Ronald Warehime got their first taste of life in Charlie Company that night at Lai Khe, when the guys came down from Julie, showered away most of the red dust and some of the weariness, and went pinwheeling off on their several roads to oblivion. Warehime, a plain-folks Marylander, did the sensible thing and hid under his bunk with another new guy, wishing he were back stocking shelves at the Safeway store in New Windsor. A firefight had broken out between hooches, the tracers whining from tin roof to tin roof, and some guys were being held hostage in the mess hall, and Warehime was lying under a bed composing his own obituary for the Carroll County *Times* on his very first night in the war. *Oh dear*, he was thinking. *I can see this:* GI DIES AND NEVER MAKES IT TO FIELD.

Joe Pentz was bolder, and he went out for a look. Pentz was a college dropout from Seattle, drafted out of a holding-pattern job as a janitor in a public school. He had gone off willingly, as his father had to World War II and his grandfather to World War I, and had been a strack soldier until he realized with only three weeks left to go at instant-noncom school that they were training him to lead a platoon into battle in Vietnam. The realization lit his future like an illumination round, and he didn't like what he saw. He went AWOL for a weekend holed up at his parents' house, and when his top sergeant threatened to send the MPs for him, he went back to his shake-'n'-bake sergeants' class at Fort Benning no longer caring whether he graduated or not. His schoolmasters thereafter found reasons not to like the way he shined his shoes or made his bed and finally drummed him out.

His days as the dewy-eyed model soldier thus were light-years behind him, but he was still unprepared for what he saw on his get-acquainted tour of his new home ground. *His* first glimpse of Charlie Company was of a man ambling along the road toward him, stripped down to sunglasses, Jockey briefs and thong sandals, waving a whiskey bottle and bellowing, "Club's open! Club's open!"

Pentz watched the figure disappear through a crimson door into a windowless prefab ornamented with a Big Red One, a Black Lion and the words BIG CHARLIE'S PLACE pretzeled into the shape of a *Playboy* bunny.

"Who's that?" Pentz asked a GI idling nearby.

"Oh," the GI answered, "that's one of your officers."

Oh, great, Pentz sighed inwardly. What they hadn't taught him at Benning, or Ronald Warehime at radio school, was the unbuttoned animal-house ferocity that fighting men could bring to their play—a release of emotion as explosive and occasionally as dangerous as a claymore mine popping out in the bush. Both men learned that day at Lai Khe. Warehime lay cowering under his cot, listening to his marauding comrades come thundering through with a loaded M-79 grenade launcher. *Oh, dear*, he thought, *I have to get out of here*, but there was no way out until a black grunt known as Lady Bird Johnson broke up the war party and took the M-79 away.

Pentz continued his own inspection tour, as goggle-eyed as Alice on the far side of the looking glass. He saw one GI careening through the company area with a live grenade in each hand, pins pulled, primed to explode if he had dropped them. He passed a hooch where another grunt, wrecked on drugs and paranoia, had set out claymores at both doors and wired them to go off if anybody came in. He walked over to the clubhouse with the red door and stepped into the gloom just in time to see the officer in underpants flatten a sergeant with his whiskey bottle, by now drained dry. Pentz ducked back out, smack into the middle of a knife fight between a Puerto Rican and a black.

Oh, great, Pentz thought, but what he was seeing was only Charlie Company come in from the heat as they always did, raucous as frat boys and mean as snakes, nearly as fearsome to the cadre on their own home base as they were to the VC out in the boonies. A convoy of deuce-and-a-half trucks would deliver them sweat-stained and filthy from the helicopter pad into Black Lion Country, a fiercely held corner of Lai Khe where the sign said THIS LION RULES THIS DAMN JUNGLE and anybody else proceeded at his own risk. The last truck would clear, and the MPs, in tribute to the company's feral reputation, would draw the concertina wire across the road behind them—*as if to say, okay,* Kit Bowen thought the first time he saw it, *we don't want you people going anywhere, and if anybody escapes,* we're gonna kill you.

The procession would stop in the company street, and guys who hadn't had so much as a bath in a month except when they were fording a stream in their fatigues would have to wait in attendance on their CO. Sometimes the captain of the moment would stand up in his jeep—*a scene right out of* M*A*S*H, Bowen thought later—and would instruct the men solemnly through a bullhorn that the beer and the showers and the fresh uniforms would have to wait until they had cleaned their rifles. He would still be standing there talking when the grunts had stampeded past him, stripping naked on the run toward Lethe and the showers, the juicers popping open cans of Carling Black Label, the smokers ripping up the barracks floorboards to get at their stashes of el-primo no-seed, no-stem marijuana laid in at $50 the six-pound sandbag full. "Oh, fuck it," the captain would say only then and sit down.

Lai Khe was where the men of Charlie Company were permitted to be boys again—to be as rowdy as hell week at the Deke house and as macho as a street gang defending its turf. Sometimes their play would turn deadly serious, in boozy imitation of the war they had left behind in the bush.

Guy gets a Dear John letter, Omega Harris thought, *he's in a situation where he can retaliate. You got guns, you got grenades—you can start your own war.* But mostly the sport at Lai Khe was of a post-adolescent sort, half beer bust and half pot party, drinking or smoking in part to forget where you were and in part so you could brag the morning after about how wrecked you had got the night before. It was all for laughs, and sometimes the quality of the wit could be unmercifully strained; there was, for example, the day they hotwired the toilet seats to a crank telephone and levitated an unsuspecting sergeant three feet in the air.

The management of America's first teenaged war understood that boys would be boys and for the most part despaired of taming them. Once, after a particularly drunk-and-disorderly firefight among the hooches, Charlie Company was exiled from Lai Khe for a month. The night they came back, the juicers soaked up all the beer at the enlisted men's bar and adjourned to the NCO club for more. The NCOs closed the door. The deputation from Charlie Company broke it down and demanded service. Somebody sent for the MPs—*a mistake*, Bob Bowers reminisced years later, the memory by then transfigured in the retelling into legend; *a challenge to our honor, y'know, the MPs trying to take care of the Black Lions.* It was instead the Black Lions who took care of the MPs, at least in Bowers's recollection, leaving behind a litter of splintered chairs, tables, window glass and banged-up military policemen.

From there, the boys of Charlie Company marched on the old plantation house where the Big Red One's commanding general lived and found a lawn party in tinkly progress, the brass and the USO girls mixing under a big open-sided tent. They watched from the edges for a while, grousing among themselves about how the USO girls never wanted to have anything to do with them. The noise level rose. There were complaints. The boys of Charlie Company took the complaints badly. Some of them slithered up close through a drainage ditch and, soaking wet, lobbed six tube flares onto the tent top. It caught fire; the general's party dissolved in a swirl of burning canvas, scrambling brass and screaming women, and Charlie Company immediately thereafter was exiled back to the war. "They're a bunch of animals," one of their betters said of them. "They belong in the jungle."

Their antic humors followed them into the field, at least in those slow times when nobody was shooting at them. There was one idle patch working Thunder Road with the Armored Cav, the men walking the highway behind Colonel Patton's tanks looking for mines. "Put your foot out and close your eyes and you're a mine detector," Kit Bowen used to kid, but they hardly ever detected any, and their days fell into a low-gear round of writing letters, skinny-dipping in a muddy swimming hole and wandering down to the nearest ville for a taste of a popskull native rice whiskey called 45.

And then one sweet day they were sitting around nursing their hangovers at their NDP—their night defense position of the moment—when a flatbed truck came barreling up from Saigon with a load of beer and flipped over practically in their laps. "Oh, my God, gotta go help that boy," a tanker near Bowen was saying reverently, and suddenly two or three tanks were clanking out toward the cases of Carling Black Label strewn all over the roadway.

Bowen followed them out, did a couple of deals on behalf of his platoon and came back with a piece of the booty—enough cases of Carling's to line the walls of their bunker and raise a parapet around it six feet high. *Best-looking bunker in the whole NDP*, Bowen thought, surveying his handiwork; *all squared-off and beautiful with sandbags on the outside*. The CO was surprised and pleased at how strack it looked, unaware at first of the secret of its architecture. But Charlie Company's stay dragged on for a week or so, and as Bowen's platoon started drawing down its reserves, their bunker started imperceptibly shrinking.

Its deterioration escaped notice for a while, and the men of the Second Platoon continued their nightly beer-klatches, sitting up till three in the morning dealing cards, drinking Carling's and feasting on stolen officer-grade steaks pan-broiled in a steel plate ripped off the back of a claymore mine. But one night three of the guys took a case out on listening post and killed it; they were found zonked out in the morning, their radio microphone half-buried in the dirt and their position surrounded by empties. In the disciplinary inquisition that followed, a lieutenant poked his head into the Second Platoon bunker and glanced around. "Oh, my God," he gasped. The prettiest bunker in the NDP had shrunk by then from six to three feet high; its corners were no longer square, and its innards were piled deep with drained bottles, crumpled cans and glassy-eyed GI's.

They were boys at play in those interludes when the war did not require them to be men; their sport and their memory of it were all beer, smoke and braggadocio. But there was a strain of desperation to their comedy as well, a primal scream of laughter in the valley of the shadow of death. You would party all night, Bowen remembered, but in the morning you had to shake off your hangover, go over to headquarters and take care of business. "You'd have all your buddies that you lost to say goodbye to," he remembered. "They weren't there, but their rifles and everything was— their boots and their rifles with the helmets on top. And that was kinda hard. That was tear-jerking, 'cause you had to say goodbye."

"OUR OWN MEN HAVE SHOT US"

You had to say goodbye and go back out and keep on fighting a will-o'-the-wisp war—*like somebody in the Pentagon had a map*, J.C. Wilson thought, *and they were throwing darts at it, and wherever that thang stuck, that's where you went.* In November they went to Fire Base Rita, Julie's twin sister to the south, for a week or ten days to relieve the battered garrison there and to patch the holes in their own decimated ranks. New men had begun coming aboard the morning after the siege on Julie lifted and were still showing up daily on the supply choppers: Kit and Stag and Foxwell and Tiny Scott, a six-foot-two hulk out of the Ohio coal country, and Deacon Johnson, a barber from Indianapolis who had promised the Lord he would repent and believe if the Lord would only let him have his estranged wife back. *God, we don't have very many guys*, Stagnaro thought, looking uneasily around. They taught you at infantry school that there were supposed to be 160 men in a combat company, but the fortunes of war and the ravages of dengue fever had reduced Charlie Company to 25 or 30 at low ebb—less than the rated strength of a single platoon.

They were whole again but heavy with new meat when, just before Thanksgiving, an eagle flight of choppers airlifted the battalion out over the embattled Iron Triangle north of Saigon to set up a new fire base called Cantigny. The name had been chosen for heroic effect out of the annals of the Big Red One and the Black Lions in World War I; they had assaulted the fortified French town of Cantigny in broad daylight in May 1918, wrested it from the Germans in half an hour, held it at terrible cost against a series of furious counterattacks and so won America's first unambiguous victory of the war. But Cantigny's successor in the bush in Vietnam was a rather less promising theater of battle from the moment the choppers set the men down.

It was, most of them reckoned afterward, the wrong place at the wrong time. They were to have encamped on a rise commanding a wide sweep of land below, but the signals were changed in mid-flight and the choppers deposited them instead on the low ground, thicketed with elephant grass six and eight feet high. It was what they called a hot LZ, a landing zone swarming with enemy troops and alive with sniper fire from the moment they set down—*as if*, Captain Rogers thought, *they had our plans*. The snipers kept potshotting at them on the hike to their campsite, and when they got there they could glimpse enemy bunkers through the tree line, no more than five hundred meters off. They had walked into the middle of a main-force concentration of North Vietnamese regulars, and they were arriving too tired and too late in the day to get their defenses properly set up.

They fell to work clearing the site first, and trampling the elephant grass flat for thirty or forty meters around to open fields of fire; it was pushing five before they began wearily stringing their concertina wire and digging their bunkers. "We're in some pretty shit here," the older hands were saying, still jumpy from Julie. One of them, a guy named Ty, took an avuncular liking to Stagnaro and told him to be sure to volunteer for daylight duty on an observation post outside the perimeter—you didn't want to be out there at night when the shit hit the fan. Stagnaro got the assignment. Ty didn't;

instead, he was sent out after dark with two virgin FNGs, neither of them more than ten days in-country, to hunker down in the high grass and watch for what everybody knew was coming.

So sure were the older hands of their premonitions that they saw little purpose in putting anybody outside the wire at all. A platoon from each Black Lion company was supposed to go out to night ambush positions, but Charlie Company's said no—they were hungry, the area was hot and they weren't going anywhere in the dark. Rogers was furious, but while he was dressing down the platoon's lieutenant, the battalion command decided to call the platoons back anyway. That left the listening posts, and some of the men were after Rogers to bring them in too. The radios were beginning to click, signaling the first enemy movement; the LPs were scared and wanted to come back, but by the time Rogers gave the order, a dozen NVA troopers had swept by them and were running under a rain of covering mortar fire toward the wire.

Danger Dan Colfack was on one of Charlie Company's LPs, new to the war and terrified, but he was with two seasoned men who knew how to handle themselves and they made it back. Ty's team did not. Rogers was on the horn saying come in, but there were enemy troops between them and the wire, one of the twinks had been hit in the leg, and they didn't think they could make it. They hesitated, as it turned out, a beat too long; then Ty sent the two new guys crawling toward the wire and hung behind them to cover their backs. The rookies came through the brush line, shadowy forms in the night with NVAs running and howling all around them, and the men inside the wire couldn't see if they were GIs or gooks or what. One of the shadows stood upright, frozen for a moment in panic between the NVA's guns and America's, and then disappeared in the crossfire. Somebody popped a claymore mine on the other, practically in his face. David Bean, hunkered down with six other guys in a hole too small to hold them, saw the red and yellow flash and, against it, the silhouette of a man flung two or three feet off the ground. Then it was dark again, and somewhere within twenty feet of the wire, a kid trooper with no legs left moaned, "I'm dying! I'm dying!"

Guys were yelling from the rear to quit shooting till the

LPs came in, and in the moment's lull that followed, Ty came scrambling inside the perimeter to what passed at Cantigny for safety. But he had barely made it when enemy fire blew holes in both his calves, and it was too late for the kids beyond the wire. Kit Bowen was pinned down in a bunker and could not get to them; whenever he poked his head up into view, a burst of NVA fire would force him down again. So he lay in the night listening to the guy with no legs moaning, "Oh, my God, oh, my God, our own men have shot us!"

Bowen sank down at last in helpless rage, cursing the war and the Army and himself for not being able to do anything. Doc Johnson found him there and told him that he suspected a trick anyway—that there were gooks who had picked up enough battlefield English to yell for a medic and tempt somebody out into the open. "Just let it lay, man," Johnson told Bowen softly. "You can't get to 'em."

You couldn't do anything at Cantigny except find whatever meager cover there was and pop grenades at ghosts in the pitch blackness. They were paying dues for their late start; they had been laboring from dusk until midnight, but half the men didn't even have bunkers to hole up in, and only a single strand of concertina wire stood between them and the enemy troopers coming at them out of the brush. The gooks were on their front porch, and they weren't even supposed to fire their M-16s because the muzzle flash would give their positions away. That was SOP, a trick of the trade you were supposed to learn in infantry school, except Jeff Hicks forgot it when the NVAs were inside the area, and then it was Doc Johnson's turn to feel the pain of his powerlessness against death.

Johnson was normally the fatalistic sort, the kind who humped along through the war and got through the bad days telling himself, *This is the way life is right now.* But Jeff Hicks was the best friend he had in 'Nam. Hicks was everyone's buddy, really; he and Johnson were home boys from Missouri and had a special bond, but Hicks was an outgoing kid with a sunny line of chatter and enough contagious optimism to go around. He had sat up only the night before sharing it with some of them. Deacon Johnson was there, new and nervous, and Joe Boxx, a twink who had barely set foot outside Ottumwa, Iowa, before he got drafted; Tom Swenticky was there, too, just back from a MASH hospital with fifty-six stitches suturing up the nine shrapnel wounds he had suffered at Julie and a headful of angst that he was about to get it again. Some of them thought later that Hicks must have seen the apprehension in their eyes. He rattled brightly on about his girl and his wedding plans and all the things he was going to do when he got back home, and the others found themselves drawn along in his train, caught up in his infectious presumption that there would in fact be life for them after Vietnam.

There would be for the rest of them, but not for Hicks. He was lying out in the open with Sea-Tac Olson, caught without cover. Off to the right, they could see some NVAs stealing up on one side of a mound of dirt and some of their own buddies flattened out unsuspecting on the other side. Olson lobbed a grenade their way but it was a dud, and Hicks opened up on them with his M-16 on automatic. It was a twink's mistake; the muzzle flash and the intermittent tracer rounds were like a homing beacon for the NVA machine gunner in a crater just beyond their position. There was an answering rattle and Hicks fell silent, a bullet between his eyes. David Bean crawled out with a grenade launcher and silenced the machine gun. But Hicks was beyond help. Olson grabbed his wrist, looking for a pulse, and couldn't feel anything. *Move*, Olson's nerves were screaming at him; as he broke for cover, a grenade hit precisely where he had been, and Hicks was finished. There was no more than the faintest vestige of a heartbeat when his pal Doc Johnson got to him. Johnson picked him up. The back of his head was gone, and there was nothing Johnson could do except wait while Hicks died in his arms.

There wasn't time yet for grieving; when Johnson looked up, gooks were running past him in the dark, and guys were firing at them point-blank with M-16s now, or anything else that came to hand. Tiny Scott was trying to hide his 220 pounds behind a rucksack, shooting at sounds and shadows. Danger Dan Colfack was flattened out behind a little hummock of earth with his rifle spewing rounds as quickly as he could empty one clip and rip the paper batting off another.

Harry Foxwell looked up and saw an NVA trooper standing at the lip of his bunker. Foxwell was still new to the war and had never fired at anybody he could see face to face; he wasn't even thinking of the man as his enemy when he shot him—only as another hapless person like himself. But circumstances had made them adversaries, armed them with rifles and placed them face to face in the bush in Vietnam, and it was Foxwell, the skinny math major from Long Island, who survived. *I killed someone*, he thought afterward, turning the new fact over in his mind; he found regret there but no guilt—only the mathematical certainty that he had done what he had to do.

Kevin Abbott had to kill, too, and it was tough, but he had hesitated for a split second when a gook was coming at them with a grenade; suddenly Abbott's best friend was dying, and Abbott got mad. Abbott was no George Patton. He was a streetwise Irish kid from Flatbush who hadn't thought much about the war until his draft board sent him his induction notice and a single subway token so he could report. He was clerking at Morgan Guaranty Trust at the time; he hadn't had the grades to go to a city college or the money to pay the tuition anywhere else. He looked unhappily at the token. *A one-way trip*, he thought. *It's game time. The last mile.* But it was something you had to do, so he said goodbye to his parents, his big brother and his three sisters at home—he didn't want any teary scenes at the induction center—and presented himself to the Army.

His training at Fort Jackson, South Carolina, reaffirmed for him that he was not Patton. His sergeant hazed him because his electric razor wasn't shaving close enough, and an assembly-line dentist solved small problems with three teeth in the Army way, by pulling them; there was blood on the pillow and snow on the ground when Abbott woke up the next morning, and he was thoroughly miserable. His spirits did not improve when he got his orders for Vietnam. His father delivered him to John F. Kennedy Airport with some GI pals and their parents, and this time there was a scene. A friend's father started bawling, and Abbott's father told him, "You'd better leave now, because if you don't, I'm going to be the same way." They left and, when they got to San Francisco, stretched two days of liberty time to three with a raucous AWOL tour of the joints in Berkeley and Haight-Ashbury. *Saying goodbye to The World*, he thought, because they knew where they were going.

He discovered only when he got there that he hadn't really known after all. He had been scared descending into 'Nam, a kid of twenty staring silently out at the flares and the helicopter lights in the darkness, and he had humped through his early months in-country, fighting his deepening suspicion that the war didn't make any sense. But he soldiered well; they gave him his stripes and a squad to lead, and when the NVA got him mad at Cantigny, the kid who was not Patton and did not want to kill was an army all by himself.

What got to him was the gook with the grenade blowing away his best friend. Abbott had seen the guy coming toward their bunker, running straight at them. *It could be the LPs*, he thought; he didn't know whether they had made it in or not and didn't want to give away his position by calling out to them. So he held his fire for one uncertain moment, and the NVA got close enough to drop a grenade on the field kitchen a few yards to their right. Beside Abbott, Stagnaro yelled, "Oh, my God!" and closed his eyes tight, but could still see the flash and feel the concussion flipping him over onto his back.

Men were bleeding and yelling for medics, and Bowen was scuttling around bandaging, soothing and raging inwardly at not being able to get choppers in to get the wounded out. His pal Stag had caught it in the back and side, and Bowen patched him together with pressure bandages. But he couldn't help Abbott's best friend. Abbott's friend had been getting short, just a month left to go in the war, and had begged to be reassigned as a cook off the line. He had sensed that his time was up, and now it was. The grenade had laid open his head; he was going to die, and Abbott was mad.

Somebody yelled that the gook who had tossed the grenade was right on top of their bunker. In a fury of motion, Abbott snatched up his M-16, jabbed it out through a gunport and blew him away with a burst. But he could see more enemy troops erupting from the tree line, and too many guys in the bunker were already bleeding. "We can't stay in this hole," Abbott said, and then he was scrambling topside to an M-60 machine gun and firing till it overheated and finally burned out. Bowen, looking up from his work, saw a skinny arm lobbing grenades their way out of a crater in front of their bunker. He gave Abbott a poke. Abbott dropped the machine gun and snatched an M-79 grenade launcher away from Stagnaro. Stag had been fumbling with it, trying desperately to remember his M-79 training, but Abbott really knew how to handle it. Abbott poked back up out of the bunker, popping grenades into the crater as fast as he could load and shoot, and when his supply ran out, he scrambled alone under fire to the ammo dump for more.

There were four or five bodies in the crater when the attackers fell back at last under punishing air and artillery attack; seven more hung on the wire or lay on either side of it, and there were blood trails leading off into the brush where the NVA had carried away others of their fallen. Eight or nine Americans had died, but guys were saying how much worse it could have been if it hadn't been for Abbott. Abbott ought to get the Medal of Honor, they were saying, but Abbott was thinking about his best friend dying and the kid from his squad lying dead outside the wire with both legs gone and the fraction of a moment when he might have shot the NVA with the grenade but didn't.

Abbott was crying.

Doc Johnson was angry. He was trying to compose a letter to Jeff Hicks's parents. He didn't put in how fucked up he thought the mission had been—how they had arrived late and set up camp within sight of the NVA's bunkers. He didn't say anything about the kid LPs caught out in no-man's-land, dying in the crossfire. He didn't mention the lieutenant who had collapsed in terror, pretending to be wounded, when the shit started flying. "Jeff was just laying on the ground fighting," he wrote the Hickses. "He didn't suffer any pain." That was all; he folded up the letter and sent it, and resolved, as men did in the anguish of a heavy hail and farewell, that he would never let himself get too close to anybody again.

David Bean was scared. He was out on a death detail, assigned to truss a rope around the NVA corpses festering in the hot morning sun and flip them over one by one from a distance in case they had been booby-trapped with grenades. He tossed one body, then came close and started going through the pockets. The head came off and cracked open. The brain spilled out onto the ground. *It doesn't bother me*, Bean told himself. *I don't care. I'm alive and they're dead. They're like animals and I'm a hunter*. It didn't help, not really. Bean drifted back to the base, found an empty bunker and fished his last joint out of hiding in a pack of Winstons. He never smoked dope in the field—you had to be alert all the time—but he was suddenly nervous and he lit up. It was cool in the bunker. He was fighting down the image of the severed head and dreaming of his R&R in Bangkok. He was due to leave the next morning and he didn't want to die now—not before he made it to the plane.

Kit Bowen was exhausted. He was flaked out in his own bunker, trying to grab some rack time, when a sergeant dipped down to see him, wanting to talk about how well they had done. "Hey, leave him alone. He's asleep," somebody said, but Bowen opened his eyes and the sergeant sat down beside him.

"What a good job—" the sergeant started saying.

"Hey, I don't even want to hear your shit," Bowen cut in. The last of the wounded had just been dusted off by a chopper to field hospitals, his new pal Stagnaro among them. His own hands were still red from the fingertips to the elbows with the blood of his wounded and dying buddies. He was tired. He didn't feel like talking.

"It was a real rough evening," the sergeant persisted, "but we're on our way. We're makin' some progress. Look here."

He shoved a copy of *Stars and Stripes* at Bowen and pointed at a story. Bowen scanned it. It reported urgently that, after five weeks of dickering, the peace conferees in Paris had finally agreed on the shape and seating configuration of the negotiating table.

"We're on our way out," the sergeant was saying. Bowen looked at him, saw he was serious and turned away. *You ignorant fucker*, he was thinking, *get out of my face. All this time haggling over what shape the table should be and this idiot thinks we can hear those freedom birds startin' their engines now. Oh, boy, this is a joke*, Bowen thought. *This is a real sad joke.*

A VIETNAM DEATH TRIP

Something was happening to Lloyd Collins. Collins was a good-time guy, a born clown, all gags and grins and post-adolescent cynicism, but he was turning moody; he was moving in widening swings between the laughter that had been his natural habitat and the ice that seemed to be forming around his soul. Some of the men guessed that it had started at Julie, when Collins, then a corporal, had taken a squad out for the body count and had had to apply the *coup de grâce* himself to a crimson blur of dying Vietnamese. One NVA was still crawling with five or six bullets in him, and Collins wasted him at point-blank range. Another wouldn't die even after a grunt named Washington put three rounds in him. "Shoot him," Collins ordered.

"I already shot him three times," Washington answered. Collins, exasperated, did it himself with an M-79 grenade launcher. The gook exploded, and after that it was as if Collins were engorged with blood and vengeance.

After that, it was if he weren't Collins any more. He was a big, brawny kid out of Peoria, blond as cornsilk and strong as a Caterpillar tractor. Growing up, he had liked school but loved sports better, to a point where they had become mutually exclusive. He won a baseball scholarship to junior college, then lost it when he flunked a couple of courses and had to drop out. His coach promised nevertheless to try to help get him on the team at Illinois State University at Normal when he got back from 'Nam, and most of the men in Charlie Company who thought they knew him figured that was what he would do. "Christ, I have to go back to Peoria," he would bitch, but Collins was always either kidding or complaining about something, and even his pals lost track of when to take him seriously.

Collins resented being in 'Nam and let everybody know

it. But for all the complaint and the comedy, he was a good
and sometimes a recklessly daring soldier—the kind who
would stand straight up and exposed in the thick of a firefight,
grinning at death and hosing down the enemy line with bullets. It struck his pal Mike MacDonald that, behind the mask
of casualness, Collins was driving himself perhaps too hard
and holding himself in perhaps too tightly. Even in combat
the mask stayed in place. Once, when they were cowering
together in a bunker under heavy fire, Collins took his helmet
off his head and dropped it over his crotch.

"Collins," MacDonald asked, "what the hell are you
doing?"

Collins grinned and tapped his skull. "They can get this
head, but," he said, gesturing toward his penis, "there's no
way they're getting this one."

A moment later, tired of cringing, he crawled out in the
open toward the enemy, and MacDonald once again demanded to know what he was up to. "I'm out of bullets,"
he said back. "I'm going to go pick 'em up and use 'em
again."

That was the Collins they knew in Charlie Company—
medium crazy, Sea-Tac Olson thought, making a gag of his
own heroics and laughing or pissing by turns at everything
else. The routines of an army at war seemed to grate on
Collins almost as much as combat. The men would spend
two hours packing their gear for a five-day operation, all
except Collins; he would dawdle, and guys would be saying,
"Come on, Collins, hurry up," and at the last moment he
would stick a box of C-rations inside his shirt and announce
himself ready to go. He was notoriously slack on daytime
observation-post duty outside the perimeter wire. He would
sally two hundred yards into the bush, rig up his poncho for
shade and sit reading a book with only a .45, a machete and
an acute sixth sense for protection. Sometimes he would
break out his ample stash of grass, smoke a joint or two and
fall asleep so soundly that the man relieving him couldn't
wake him up. Once he radioed in that he had seen movement,
and everyone in camp went belly down in a panic wanting
to know what it was.

"I'm making them out now," Collins radioed, his voice
tense. "I'm just barely making them out."

"Collins," MacDonald whispered urgently into the horn, "what have you got?"

"God, he's screwing her," Collins's voice answered reverently; he was, he explained, watching two dinks fucking in the grass.

There had been a time before the ice started forming when Collins could laugh in the face of death itself. He was out on an operation one day when two men were killed and a third wounded by enemy fire, and headquarters once again wanted to know what was happening. "Well," Collins answered, laconic as Gary Cooper, "we got three popsicles, two melted." But after Julie, he seemed less frequently able to cauterize his wounds and suppress his angers with a laugh. He was still the joker, but there were days when rage came over him like a summer storm, and he would pick a meaninglessly violent fight with one of his own comrades in arms. At Julie, Collins had fired at men who, however tenuously, were still alive and dangerous. In the body sweep after Cantigny, it didn't matter anymore whether they were moving or not; some of the men saw him standing over an enemy corpse with his M-16 on rock-and-roll, emptying clip after clip at it until the skull had turned to pulp and his own breathing had come back again.

"I WANT GOD TO STOP THE LIGHT SHOW"

Taras Popel was two days shy of nineteen and brand-new to Charlie Company's war when they got hit again, this time on a hot, dusty rise called Junction City, north of Lai Khe. Most of his new comrades in arms were out at a night ambush position along Highway 14, well outside the wire, but Popel had been assigned to Omega Harris's mortar section, and they had stayed behind at the base with two other Black

Lion companies to tend their guns. They had worked past midnight digging in and sandbagging their emplacement and, afterward, had crashed behind their bunker under the night sky trying to sleep. It was, for Popel, a losing battle with the outsize native mosquitoes. The score was already BUGS 1, POPEL 0, when the mortars and the rocket-propelled grenades started coming down around him, and he became suddenly reacquainted with prayer.

Popel till then had fancied himself a tough guy from a tough neighborhood, a brick and cement microcosm of the Ukraine on the West Side of Chicago. He grew up in the close, warm bosom of its Catholic ethnicity, *about 30 cents removed*, he used to think, *from orthodox Jewish*. But Popel was a born rebel, a bright, verbal kid with an unrealized and unacknowledged streak of intellect and an instinctive disdain for authority. He ran with the boys from the gangs that ruled the neighborhood streets—the C Notes, the Gay Lords, the War Lords—and partook of their lesser vices, smoking dope and sniffing glue and lighter fluid. When his worried mother wanted to send him to military school, he bridled and chose Lane Technical High School instead. He breezed home in the top 10 percent of his class and went on to college, in part to make it up to his mom. College didn't take; Popel dropped out just before his freshman-year finals and enlisted in the Army.

He was just eighteen, and as he would reflect later, *eighteen-year-olds know everything*. He knew, for example, that he was fluent in Ukrainian and German; that he had fallen arches, a slight hernia, a positive TB skin test and scars on both lungs; that he had scored a barely passing 84 on his infantry test as against a solid 130 or 140 for radio, clerical and mechanical aptitude. *They'll never put me in the infantry*, he thought, but they did. *They'll never send me to Vietnam*, he told himself, but they did that, too—suited him up, trained him to kill and deposited him on a hilltop called Junction City in the middle of a war. Popel shrugged. Not even his cram course in the *Brittanica* on how the Viet Minh had routed the French at Dien Bien Phu weighed heavily on him. He was a hard guy, and war was the ultimate romantic experience.

Charlie Company was in strung-out shape when he got there. Captain Rogers had had to drive them hard, shaping them up for combat and flogging them through it at Julie and Cantigny; they had had Thanksgiving dinner out in the field, the stink of the Vietnamese dead spoiling their appetites and mocking the purpose of their feast. Tempers were fraying and growling rebellious. Rogers kept telling them to take care of one another, and then kept leading them into situations where they would have to. Guys who knew how to take care of one another kept disappearing anyway, and green recruits kept arriving to take their places—Cowboy Rosson, an aspiring rodeo rider out of Muskogee, Oklahoma; Head Hedspeth, a teacher grown restless in the Missouri bootheel initiating eighth graders into the mysteries of science; Tore Pearson, a Swede who had emigrated to America at fifteen and had barely got his citizenship when the Army swept him up and off to 'Nam.

And Taras Popel, the tough guy from Chicago, cowering in a bunker at Junction City under a hail of grenades and mortar rounds and realizing that he wasn't that tough after all; *a kid with a bad mouth*, he realized suddenly, *but I lost all the fights*. He and Ed Schweiger and three other guys had plunged into the bunker when the shooting started, forgetting their rifles and their steel-pot helmets in the rush. They were huddling together with no shelter at all except sandbags, mud and prayer against a blizzard of flying shrapnel. The world was exploding around them, and inside his skull, Popel could see his parents and his sister and his pals back on the West Side of the other side of the world. *My nineteenth birthday is only two days from now*, he was thinking, *and they'll never know if I reached it*. He tried the Lord's Prayer and made it a third of the way through; then he got more elemental. *I want God to stop the noise*, he prayed. *I want God to stop the light show. I want God to stop the yelling and screaming.*

It occurred to him finally that God was not going to stop the assault—that the men would have to do it for themselves. The realization was still settling over him when a rocket-propelled grenade found the ammo dump and blew it away in a ball of flame. For a moment afterward there was a hush, and Popel heard something land with a *clump* on the bunker floor. He looked. It was a grenade. *I'm gone*, he thought. *This is the last moment of my life. This is my last breath. It's over*. Nothing happened. Popel looked at the grenade again. It was American. The blast in the ammo dump had blown it their way. The pin was safely in place. The grenade was harmless.

The firing died down. Popel was ordered topside to hump ammo for the mortars, hauling forty pounds per trip in a scrambling low crawl. Afterward, he finally slept.

The enemy was falling back then, straggling off in twos and threes along Highway 14 into the arms of Charlie Company's ambush position. The men there had been counting their blessings, thinking how lucky they were, for a change, to have been posted somewhere away from the bull's-eye; Swenticky heard later that two guys in his bunker had been messed up when the ammo dump went off. And then the stragglers were limping toward them in the darkness, and it was easy; it was like popping tin cans off a fencepost with a .22.

It was almost too easy for Roy Rosson II, the Cowboy, lying in the blackness on his first night in the field and watching a dim form coming up the road toward him. He lay there feeling sorry for the shadow; Rosson was raw meat, twenty years old, and he had never even thought about hurting another human being in his life. All he had ever wanted was to be a rodeo cowboy, and the dream had seemed within his reach when the Army got him. He had been working four hundred acres outside Muskogee with his father, raising and training horses, running fifty head of his own cattle and riding bulls in rodeos every chance he got. He was a gangly farmboy of nineteen when, in 1967, he placed fifth in the all-around in the Oklahoma Junior Rodeo. But the draft had caught up with him the next year, and the dream had to be deferred.

"Maybe I ought to go to Canada like the rest of these guys," he told his father at the time, meaning it as a joke. It didn't go over. Both his parents had been in the service in World War II, and Roy Sr. was not amused.

"You'll go over there," he flared, "and do your job."

He went, and now it was dues time on Highway 14, the Cowboy watching the spectral shape passing along the road and wishing it would go away.

"I think I see a gook," he told his platoon sergeant.

"Drop a grenade right out behind him," the sergeant ordered.

The gook was moving by, and Rosson was thinking about

what the grenade was going to do to him. *Why doesn't he just take off?* he was thinking. *Man, you better run*, he was thinking, but the guy wouldn't run. *I never tried to kill anybody before*, he was thinking, but he tossed the grenade and, reflexively, poked his head up to watch it hit. The grenade exploded, the shadow fragmented, and the concussion blew away Rosson's innocence of war along with his two lower front teeth.

The company killed five men in all, before the NVA caught on to their position and switched to an alternate line of retreat, and forty-four more bodies were heaped up at the wire when the men got back to Junction City. *Like store-bought mannequins*, Rosson thought. He had been in the war less than twenty-four hours, and death was already becoming an abstraction for him as against the single central reality in the life of a grunt in Vietnam: the will to survive.

Survival was what it was about, in a war with no higher objective evident to the men fighting it. Junction City taught Rosson that—Rosson and Taras Popel and Ed Schweiger. Popel wakened with the first light and looked around. Two unexploded RPGs—rocket-propelled grenades—were lying within five feet of the weapons pit. A lieutenant instructed Popel to take them out to the perimeter. Popel was learning fast and he refused. The lieutenant found three less resistant men from another company to do the detail. The RPGs blew up in their hands; the census of the American dead at Junction City rose from one to four, and Taras Popel resolved that whatever else happened in the war, he was going to make it home alive.

Schweiger was up early too. He clambered out of the bunker where he and Popel and the others had huddled through the night and sat staring at some pebbles aglow in the wakening morning. He had always thought of his life as a novel in progress, a picaresque adventure hop-skipping along without visible design from one experience to the next. The previous chapter had found him idling through the University of Wisconsin, stretching two years of academic work over three years and wondering why he was doing it at all. He had enlisted two days after his last exam in May 1968 on what struck him later as a slightly suicidal whim; it was that or sell his '67 MGB-GT and go to Europe, and he chose the Army. He regretted his decision almost immediately, laid

plans to split to Canada and stayed in the end only because
he knew it would destroy his parents if he deserted. He
wound up in 'Nam, *Candide Amongst the Gooks*, and in the
midnight siege at Junction City his nerves had screamed that
the novel of his life was over, finis, THE END; he was going
to die. The siege lifted, the sun came up, and Schweiger was
staring like a newborn child at the pebbles in the morning
light. *Like a drug reaction*, he thought later; he was staring
at pebbles, sermons in stones, and seeing how beautiful life
was. Life was all that mattered. He didn't want to let any
of it go.

None of them did; Rogers was having to push harder
against the undercurrents of resistance and fear running
among them, and while some of them understood that he
was following orders, too, some resented him for placing
their lives at hazard. They operated out of Junction City
through much of December and into the new year, conducting what had been called search-and-destroy missions
until the name fell into bad political odor back in The World.
The preferred new term of art was reconnaissance in force,
RIF for short, but the objective was essentially unchanged—
hunting down and killing the enemy—and so was the level
of danger. One day, still weary from the siege, they slogged
back to Cantigny to see if the NVA had moved in when the
Black Lions moved out, and discovered under fire that they
had. A few days later, they were headed back to Lai Khe
for a breather and had to battle through a nest of Viet Cong
riflemen just to get to their choppers.

The Army saw substantial profit in what they were doing;
they came upon and neutralized several good-sized NVA
supply bases and, between Junction City and Cantigny, a
major underground field hospital as well. But the enemy was
pecking away at them—*nickel-and-diming us to death*, one
of them thought—and occasionally the normal daily knot-in-
the-stomach anxiety of war would give way to paralytic terror. Once, a shake-'n'-bake sergeant showed up fresh out of
Fort Benning, and Rogers, strapped for noncoms, had to put
him in charge of a squad before he was ready. The concern
Rogers felt doing so was confirmed for him the first time the
squad came into contact with the NVA. The sergeant fell on
the ground, frozen in fear, and would not go on. There was
enemy artillery out front of the squad's position, and Rogers

was afraid they would be wiped out if they didn't move. But the sergeant lay there, immobilized. He was sick, he pleaded. He was exhausted. He begged to be left where he was.

"Move the squad," Rogers radioed an E-4 who had taken charge. "Drag him if you have to."

"Sir," the E-4 answered, "we've already tried that and we can't get him to move."

Rogers thought for a moment, then radioed the squad again. Leave him, he said. "He'll go with you when you start moving out. Believe me—he'll go with you."

No, the E-4 replied, the men wouldn't do it. They wouldn't leave the sergeant lying there alone.

They're fixin' to get hit, Rogers thought. He had to get them out and there was no one left to do it for him, so he went forward to the squad's position and moved the sergeant himself by main force—seized him by the hair, dragged him to his feet and yanked and shoved and hauled until he was in motion on his own. The squad moved with him, but the sergeant was finished in Rogers's book and, Rogers felt, in the eyes of the men. He had buckled under pressure and put them all in danger, and Rogers doubted he could ever win back their confidence. He could not tolerate surrender to the fear all of them felt, so he broke the man as an example— busted him to Pfc., and shipped him off to another unit.

But Rogers could not banish fear as he did the sergeant. It was his obligation as CO to require men to risk their lives in a war whose tactics and larger purposes they did not understand, and the harder he had to run them, the more his imperative to win came into conflict with theirs to survive. One of them fell prey to the conviction, endemic in war, that his number was up, that the next patrol was going to be his last, and he refused to go out. *If you allow that*, Rogers thought, *pretty soon you don't have anybody*. He told the man he had to go. The man answered that he'd sooner rot in jail, and Rogers threw him into the stockade.

Three days later the word came that the GI wanted to rejoin the company. "Come on back, but I'm still going to courtmartial you," Rogers replied. He said he would testify that the man had come back of his own accord, but he could not relent on the basic principle that a soldier cannot be allowed to choose when he will or will not fight.

The man returned, and on a patrol his first day back, he

was killed, just as he had foreseen he would be. "He chose to come back and be a man," Rogers wrote the GI's parents, but it did not appease their sorrow or his own pain. The boy's mother answered his letter, and Rogers, years later, could still quote her reply from memory. "Johnny told me that as long as you were there, he'd be safe, nothing would happen to him," she wrote. "Captain Rogers—where were you?"

Rough, he thought, but it never got easier; the orders kept coming down from battalion, and Rogers was whipping the men from RIF to RON (a remain-overnight operation) to ambush at a steady, debilitating price in blood and spirit. *He's really good*, Bob Bowers thought, and Bowers didn't normally care much for his officers. Bowers was tough and insubordinate, a rebel with a choirboy face, but he thought Rogers had more guts than most, and more concern for his men. Some other, older hands were less enthusiastic. A combat command consists quite literally of life-and-death decisions taken under agonizing pressure, and when the outcome was death, there were men who blamed Captain Rogers without asking whether or not the decision had in fact been his.

It was that way the day near the turn of the year when the Top bought it along with a couple of other guys, right in the middle of an NVA base camp. The Top was Charlie Company's top sergeant, an eighteen-year lifer named Jones on his second tour in-country but still so new to Charlie Company that the men hadn't even had time to learn his first name by heart. Early in his run, they went out on a three-day RIF and were working their way back through the jungle and the rolling terrain toward Junction City when they came upon the camp. They smelled it before they saw it, by the stink of fresh human excrement hanging fetid on the air. They sighted and killed a few enemy soldiers going in, but Rogers kept them moving, and they caught most of an NVA war party asleep in its bunkers.

Rogers sensed they had struck pay dirt, a potentially rich harvest of prisoners and intelligence information. His hopes vaulted higher when two NVA officers were coaxed out of hiding by the company's Vietnamese scouts, enemy troopers who had surrendered and switched sides under a program called *chieu hoi*, for open arms. They were moving toward the next bunker and three more officers trapped inside when battalion headquarters told Rogers to pull back. Rogers was upset; he had the initiative, he felt, and a good feel for the ground, and he wanted to keep going. But a new commander had taken over the battalion, and he cut off Rogers's arguments with what Rogers considered an error on the side of caution: Pull out and wait until artillery and air strikes could snuff out any further resistance.

They pulled out and waited. Cobra helicopters raked the encampment with bullets. Artillery whistled in overhead, the rounds time-delayed to explode underground, cave in bunkers and tunnels and entomb anybody in them alive. A pair of jets screamed down from three thousand feet to treetop level, unloaded their freight of bombs and wheeled upward again in a bravura victory roll. The pounding went on for most of an hour before the brigade and battalion commanders dipped down in a loach—a light observation chopper—to look at the rubble. The bunkers, viewed from the air, were like open wounds. The brass pronounced themselves satisfied.

Rogers was not. He knew the bunkers were well reinforced, strong enough to take a good shellacking; he knew as well that he had lost the edge of surprise and would not catch the NVA sleeping a second time. But his superiors reckoned that any enemy remnants would surely have fled the camp, and they ordered Rogers to go back in. Rogers swallowed his own doubts and did not share them with his men. A lieutenant was protesting at one elbow and Bowen, the medic, at the other, but he transmitted the order as his own. He told the men to be careful, and they started back.

They took a different line of approach the second time and moved in behind two point squads, Bob the Roadrunner Selig's on the left and Harry Foxwell's on the right. They stopped at a line of twigs stuck into the ground; it looked to the Americans as if some little kids had been building a play fence a couple of inches high, but the *chieu hois* read it as a sign. "No go in here," one of them warned Selig in fractured Franglais. "Beaucoup NVA! Beaucoup NVA!"

Selig didn't like the look of it. He was a college dropout who had been drafted from behind a clothing counter at Shriver's Department Store in Sioux Falls, South Dakota, and assembly-lined through the Army's instant NCO factory into Vietnam. He had arrived gung ho but he became a passionate survivalist in a mop-up operation after the assault on Julie. An NVA had dropped a grenade on his squad and wounded three of his men. Selig, furious, had scrambled behind a hummock of dirt and lobbed a grenade at the NVA. The NVA tossed one back at him, and then they were trading grenades, volleying back and forth like Laver and Ashe at Wimbledon, until the NVA landed one close enough to blow Selig's helmet off.

This guy's trying to kill me, Selig thought. *Not just anybody—me*. The war turned suddenly, vividly, personal for him at that moment; he came up to his knees in a rage, his M-16 rat-tatting on automatic until the grenades weren't coming at him anymore. His private war aims changed after that. "I don't care if you kill anybody," he began telling new guys joining his squad. "I just want to go back home and I want to take you with me. If you want to be heroes, you can transfer to another squad."

He hadn't lost a man yet, but now he had led them to the edge of danger and his CO was ordering him to walk them straight on into it. A fire team went in first in a cloverleaf pattern and found nothing. The *chieu hois* were saying that it didn't mean anything; the NVA hadn't abandoned the camp. They had only fallen back out of sight in the jungle and were waiting for the round-eyes to walk right into their gunsights. Selig and Foxwell pressed Rogers for more artillery to soften up the area. "We're gonna walk into a whole bunch of crap," they were saying, and Kit Bowen was spluttering, "Hey, bullshit," but Rogers had his own orders, and he told them to keep going.

They were within shouting distance of the lead bunker again when they spotted an NVA popping out, then disappearing underground again when he saw them coming. They closed around the bunker and heard voices inside. The *chieu hois* chattered back at them in Vietnamese, trying to talk them into surrender. *The glory part of the war*, Selig was thinking, except he didn't like the way the men were clumping up together in front of the bunker, an irresistibly fat and easy target. "You guys spread out," he ordered. He and Foxwell led the way and had barely moved their men out of the bull's-eye when the AK-47s and the machine guns opened up on them from point-blank range.

Guys were ducking and falling and scattering and shouting

and flattening out. Kit Bowen was trying to hide his whole body under his helmet. Skip Sommer was doing everything except ripping off his buttons to get closer to the ground. Cowboy Rosson found himself looking down the barrel of a sniper rifle not ten feet away, staring into the muzzle flash; then he was sinking to the jungle floor with wounds in his arm and chest. They were caught between two enemy machine guns, and one was raking Selig's area. A grunt came stumbling away clutching his belly, the blood seeping out between his fingers. A sergeant spun down with a bullet in his back. Selig was yelling at him not to move, they would come get him, but the sergeant rolled from his side to his stomach trying to get lower. The NVAs saw the movement and hit him again. By the time Selig and the others could get to him, he was gone.

The Top never even made it to the ground for cover. He had moved up with Rogers and his core group, with Bowen still bitching that it was a bullshit operation. "We're gonna go in and we're gonna pull right back out," the Top had reassured him. "Let me work on the captain." So Bowen had moved off with a couple of other guys for a look inside the bunker, thinking, *Hmmm, what can I get as long as we're here?* They had barely left the Top's side when the shooting started. Rogers and his radioman scuttled forward for a look, but the Top lingered behind and had barely knelt behind a bush for a wisp of shelter when a dozen rounds ripped him open from his right knee up to his left shoulder.

Skip Sommer was new, but he already felt close to the Top, and he and a buddy crawled over to see what they could do for him. There wasn't much. The last and deadliest of the machinegun rounds had torn away the side of the Top's neck and angled up through the crown of his head; his blood was puddling in a big pool on the jungle floor beneath him, and Sommer found himself quaking with fear. "Doc," Bowen heard someone scream, "over here!" Bowen slithered over and went to work, knowing from the moment he saw the wound and the spouting arterial blood that it was hopeless. He went into the Top's neck with his hands and pinched off the carotid artery. Then he jammed open his jaws to administer mouth-to-mouth resuscitation. The Top's brains were in his mouth. Bowen closed it and sank back in fury again, at Rogers and what he perceived to be Rogers's war. *Oh God*, he was thinking, *I'm pissed. I'm pissed, man.*

It took Charlie Company three or four hours to retrieve its dead and wounded and fight its way back out far enough to permit them to call in the jets and the arty and the Cobras again. The barrage went on this time until the ground was trembling under them, and it didn't quit until the enemy guns fell still. The men heard later that the pilot of a spotter plane that had gone in to mark the target area with white phosphorus had called it the biggest NVA base camp he had ever seen. But when the men went back in at last, it was deserted, a cratered moonscape without a soul or a body in sight. They never knew whether the NVA had melted into the jungle and escaped or had died and been incinerated by napalm in the bombardment.

They had to hump a mile and a half through the jungle to get to a clearing big enough for medevac choppers, the point men hacking at the brush and trees with machetes, the dead bouncing along on litters, the wounded walking if they could. It was sweaty going, the sun and the terrain hilly. You might be grieving for a lost buddy, Joe Pentz thought afterward, and hate him at the same time—hate him for dying and weighing you down and slowing your own passage out of danger. Guys got that cold, living with death. Bowen could feel it creeping over him, too; he was helping lug one of the dead sergeants, a man he had been drinking and kidding with for a couple of months, except now the sergeant's arm kept flopping off the litter and tripping them up, and Bowen was having to fight down the impulse to ask permission to cut it off.

They limped at last into Junction City with their freight of death and sorrow and grievance. Rogers was nearing the end of his run as CO; he had presided over some of Charlie Company's worst moments in the war, and the strains they had imposed on him and the men were palpable. Some of them understood that it was in fact battalion, not Rogers, that had ordered them into what they perceived as a death trap. But for some—for Bean and Bowen and Selig and some others—Rogers was the visible embodiment of the Army and its arbitrary power over whether they would live one day longer or die. Some had never forgiven him for Julie or the death of the kid LPs at Cantigny and would not now absolve him of blame for losing the Top. Some of the men were nursing resentments deep and bitter enough to outlive the war and last for a dozen years.

"WAR IS A PAIN IN THE ASS"

"Dear Aunt Sis," Harry Foxwell wrote during their brief December stand-down in Lai Khe. "I've got so much to say I don't know where to begin."

What Foxwell wanted to talk about was the war and his changing attitude toward it. He didn't like to write his mother about that; she was having a bad emotional time of it, agitated over his safety, so he kept his letters to her determinedly cheery and chatty, all about whom he had met and how much he had liked the last batch of brownies she had sent and very little about what he was enduring. He had held himself back from close friendships with men or emotional entanglements with women before he left, to minimize the pain of being away. So he sent his war news mostly to his aunt Sis and even then imposed a kind of censorship on it, leaching out most of the blood and gore and signaling by his implacable calm that he was all right. His account of the siege at Junction City was accordingly spare, and when he talked about a firefight between his squad and three VCs a few days afterward, he assured his aunt that they had been less scared than p.o.'d at being delayed in their return to Lai Khe.

"Got your letters of the 24th and 29th," he wrote then. "You keep saying how bad it must be over here and what 'hell' I go through. As long as we have our wits about us, it isn't what you'd think. The guy who said 'war is hell' should have said 'war is a pain in the ass.' (Pardon me.)"

But the war was changing Foxwell, not in fits, starts and spasms of angry illumination, but slowly, as by a series of proofs in mathematics. Math had been his major when the draft plucked him out of Suffolk County Community College, a field suited to his cool temper and his linear habits of mind. He hadn't been a politically aware sort then, and while he was irritated at the interruption in his life, it did not occur to his accepting spirit to resist. His father, a machinist, had fought on a destroyer in World War II; it was his turn now to serve his country, he had thought, and that was that. And then he had come to 'Nam. He had seen death and tasted fear and killed a man face to face in combat, and it was changing him.

"Don't kid yourself about what we do over here being 'justifiable,'" he wrote his aunt Sis. "None of it is, but it has to be done. I'm not bursting with pride about what we do over here, when you realize that most of the people we're fighting (and killing) are younger than us and know less about the war than we do. All I'm doing is acting the best way I know how to bring me and my men home in a year without harm."

Foxwell read through the passage. He hadn't meant to sound preachy, so he wrote "end of speech" at the bottom of it, tweaking himself, and filled two more pages with chat. The leaves were PX stationery with a blue-tinted photo of three columns of grunts out on a highway sweep, faces impassive and rifles at port arms. It could have been a picture of Charlie Company, doing what had to be done. Foxwell wrote "Love, Har" on the last sheet, folded the letter into an envelope and sent it home to The World.

A BODY COUNT FOR CHRISTMAS

When they came down from junction City in Lai Khe after Christmas, Skip Sommer had been in the war for only a month or so. But he was already choking on it. He had come to it a spare blond boy, drafted at eighteen out of the sheltered Westchester County suburbs above New York City in a brief hiatus between junior college and college. His father was an oil company executive of conservative bent, a church-every-Sunday Lutheran who raised his two boys to fear God, honor the flag, stay out of trouble and serve without question when their country called. In his own young life, Sommer had never experienced anything more violent than the gladiatorial combat that goes on in the line in a high-school football game. But he had already seen more dying in a month than he could stomach, and now he was in Lai Khe staring at a big blackboard listing the latest body counts, company by company. *This is crazy*, he thought. He had been there along the Saigon River on Christmas Eve; he knew what lay behind Charlie Company's handsome score. *A game*, he thought, looking at the tote board. *A friggin' game, only they're using human beings*.

The war had been a death trip for Sommer almost from the moment he arrived. He had had his first mild anxiety attack coming in, smoking up half a pack of cigarettes during the descent, and had stepped out into a day so hot he could hardly breathe. He was processed through Di An and Lai Khe and loaded aboard a chopper with the day's resupply of twinks to join Charlie Company at Junction City just after the siege there. He felt like a kid on the first day of summer camp, embarrassed by how pasty white he looked and how hopelessly green he felt. But his noncoms lost little time seeing to his catch-up education.

His initiation into warfare was the interment of the Three Wise Men—the corpses of three fallen NVA attackers who had been left to rot between the wire and the bunker line as an example and a deterrent to their comrades. They had lain there for several days, a gesture of bravado by men at once afraid of dying and hardened to death. THIS LION RULES THIS DAMN JUNGLE, they announced to the world. But the stench of decomposing flesh was beginning to get to the men when the wind was wrong, and a general who came bearing congratulations to the Black Lions for another fine body count was offended by its residue when he saw the Wise Men from his chopper. "Get them buried!" he ordered. The men played dumb at first, pretending they hadn't realized the bodies were there. But the general's wish passed down the line to Mike MacDonald, a sawed-off kid from Minneapolis who had been in-country for barely a month, and MacDonald, like a pledge master during hell week, rounded up a detail of men even newer than he—Curtis Gilliland, a farm boy from Kentucky; Jim Soike, a city boy from the Polish South Side of Milwaukee, and John G. Sommer, a suburban boy out of the leafy affluence of Ardsley, New York.

It wasn't easy, not even when they put on gas masks against the stink of death. MacDonald went out first to cinch the bodies up into a single, manageable heap. They were pretty far gone after two or three days in the ninety-plus heat. Maggots had invaded the flesh. An arm came off when MacDonald moved it. The smell was overwhelming his mask and nauseating him. He went back to his party of twinks to work out a strategy. Gilliland was numb. Soike was scared. Sommer was trying not to be sick.

Somehow, they buried the dead—or, more accurately, covered them. They started by maneuvering thirty or forty feet upwind of the bodies and filling a sandbag apiece with dirt. Then, tightening their gas masks and holding their breath, they ran past the Wise Men one by one and dumped the earth out of the bags onto the bodies in full flight. It took several relays before the cadavers were thinly layered over, all except a single toe poking up out of the dirt as if to mark the grave site. By then, Sommer was a casualty. It had all come up in his throat—the corpses, the stench, the maggots, the blanketing heat, the amusement of the noncoms grinning from a safe distance at their discomfort. He couldn't go on. He turned away, retching uncontrollably.

The burial party was only Sommer's first glimpse into the kingdom of death that Vietnam would become for him. He was caught in a war of attrition in which the objective was not to conquer territory but to bloody the enemy, systematically and unrelentingly, until he submitted. Counting the dead thus became an indispensable part of the bookkeeping of war—a proof of merit for ambitious career officers, a measure of success for the tacticians in Saigon, an instrument of persuasion for the leaders in Washington attempting to justify Vietnam to the nation and to themselves. But body counts seemed to the men of Charlie Company to obsess some officers past caring what Vietnamese bodies got counted or how many American bodies were worth forfeiting for a fat score. *This is their only opportunity to have a war*, Bert Kennish thought, surveying the lifers among his brother officers. Kennish was a lieutenant and so nominally one of them, but his aim was to do his time and go home, while theirs, he thought, was too often to accumulate capital for advancement in the principal available currency: the corpses of the enemy dead.

The men in Washington set great store by these numbers. The boys of Charlie Company did not. They were keenly aware that some of the counts were approximations—a patch of blood on the ground, for example, counted as a body on some scorecards if it was six inches or more in diameter— and some were pure fabrications. Once, two squads inadvertently crossed paths on an ambush, and before they could identify themselves to one another, somebody fired a single, wild shot. The muzzle flash had barely died away when the battalion commander radioed for a body count. *"One,"* the men radioed back; they had rooted around in desperation to appease him and had found a decaying two-week-old cadaver. Another time they came upon a cache of rifles, rusting and broken, in a bunker that looked like a reliquary of the Viet Minh war with the French a decade and a half before. A rifle counted as a kill in Vietnam; one dead man carrying three rifles counted as three bodies. The rifles moldering in the bunker were tallied accordingly. *Oh, jeez, this is crazy; we didn't get one guy*, Stagnaro thought, but they put in a body count of roughly fifty.

What hurt worse was their sense that, for some of their officers, their own lives were expendable in the interests of a good count so long as the kill ratio of Vietnamese to Americans stayed in favorable balance. Some men in Charlie Company's second platoon posted a $2,500 price on the head of one such man, a lieutenant colonel. No one collected or seriously tried; it was the expression of their feeling that mattered. Another senior officer was known as The Parasite or, later, The Leech for his particularly fierce fixation with the bottom line. The Leech was the kind who would monitor their radio traffic and, at the mere suggestion of contact with the enemy, would be on their ass for a body count without even asking how many of their own guys got maimed or killed bringing it in. *You see your buddy laying here dead,* Omega Harris thought, *and some sucker asks you what's the body count. Now who in the hell is going out there and count bodies?*

The priorities implicit in the demand sat badly with the men, and The Leech became the object of their special and nearly mutinous loathing. Once, on an operation, they found some enemy bunkers. The Leech ordered the men to check them for bodies. They made the search but skipped one bunker, crumbling with age and crawling with red ants.

"You didn't check this one over here," The Leech said.

They told him it was too old; there wouldn't be any bodies.

"Check it," he said. He was turning red.

They stood their ground.

"Well, then, *I'll* check it," The Leech said, hot and blustery. He went in. The men exchanged trail-wise glances and waited. It didn't take long. In a matter of moments the Leech came back out in a flurry of motion, slapping himself wildly, peeling off clothes and picking the last of an occupying army of ants off his buck-naked body.

The men had no tears for him, and some in fact dreamed of a rather more terminal comeuppance. It almost came to pass one day when Lieutenant Kennish's platoon flushed a covey of NVA regulars in a clearing in the jungle. There was a firefight; then the NVAs were sprinting for cover in the bamboo and Kennish was standing behind in the clearing, calling for a medevac helicopter for a badly wounded GI.

"Get me a chopper!" he was yelling into his radio. "Get me a chopper!"

"To hell with the wounded, *get those gooks!*" The Leech cut in from his own loach—a light observation chopper—whirring overhead.

It was too late anyway; Kennish watched the NVAs melt into the tree line, flitting easily through woods too densely thicketed for American grunts with their bulkier bodies and their cumbersome packs. "Let's shoot the son of a bitch down," a voice said at Kennish's elbow. Kennish turned. It was his machine gunner, and he wasn't talking about the gooks; he had tilted his M-60 skyward and was blasting away at The Leech's loach in a blind rage until Kennish managed to calm him down.

Skip Sommer's furies had not yet boiled that high when he was introduced to the surreal outer limits of body counting on Christmas Eve; he was still raw, a new boy only just learning to smell death without gagging, and his response was less rage than a steep, vertiginous free-fall into despair. Sommer shared the upset of the men that they had to go out at all that night. The parties to the war had agreed to a thirty-six-hour Christmas cease-fire starting at six o'clock, and under its terms, neither side was supposed to move men or matériel anywhere before sunup on the 26th.

But the provisions for the stand-down did not include a moratorium on the suspicions that each side held for the other. A large force of North Vietnamese had just taken a bad battering at the hands of the 25th Infantry Division to the south of Junction City and was moving through Black Lion country, apparently headed for sanctuary in Cambodia to regroup. Curtis Gilliland, hunkering down scared on an observation post in a B52 crater, saw a couple of them walk by in broad daylight within a klick or two of Junction City. An observation chopper went up for a look and spotted more enemy troops, moving along a trail toward a sampan moored on the Saigon River. Nothing in the cease-fire terms forbade their moving by day, if they could get away with it. But they would be at least in technical violation of the truce if they were still in motion after dark, retreat or not. The order accordingly came down to monitor the roadways and trails, and Captain Rogers led three platoons from Charlie Company out to ambush positions, taking care that they were themselves in place before the ban on movement went into effect at six o'clock.

The operation went down badly with the men. The battalion was having a Christmas do at Junction City; the choppers were descending onto the pad there all day, disgorging turkey dinners, Red Cross girls, the Big Red One band and a network camera crew to record that the Prince of Peace was alive and well in the boonies of Vietnam. But Charlie Company, girding for battle, wasn't in a Christmas mood. First, a guy came around telling them to put their shirts on for the cameras and the girls—*Put our shirts on*, David Bean thought, *when it's hotter than hell and we're in a goddam war*. Then they were lining everybody up in choir formation—everybody, that is, who hadn't drawn ambush duty—to be filmed singing carols for a network special. Bean, packing his gear and glowering in his bunker fifty feet away, felt a sudden urge to swat one of the cameras with his M-16. He had been seized with a premonition of his own death and had begged Captain Rogers to reassign him off the line, serving beers at the bunny club in Lai Khe. Rogers had held him off, and now the choir was singing "Silent Night" and he was going out on an ambush he thought might be his last. *What the hell are we going out for*, he was thinking, *if it's a truce? We're supposed to see if they're breaking it, and we go out in the field and try to knock somebody off. So who's breaking what?*

None of them liked it, not Bean or Foxwell or Gilliland or Skip Sommer. But they had their orders and they slogged four or five klicks from Junction City to where a heavily used trail ran into a road nearly at a right angle, one branch running along the river bank, the other back through the jungle. They arrived late in the afternoon and had to hurry to get their claymore mines in place, each packed with *plastique* and rigged to spray seven hundred balls of steel in a sixty-degree arc of death at the tug of a tripwire. Then they took cover in three separate positions spaced two kilometers apart. They were in a free-fire zone in which the often constricting rules of limited war didn't apply; they could shoot without permission at anything Vietnamese that moved on the presumption that it must be the enemy.

They waited, but not for long. The clock had barely ticked past six when they heard and then saw the first party of NVA moving toward them in infiltration formation, three cells of three men each. Rogers watched them coming. He was under orders to hold his fire, movement or no, unless he felt his own men were endangered. The decision was his— *the leader's call*, he thought—and when the enemy troops were ten meters away from overrunning them, he called it. The men, at his order, popped the ambush. The enemy soldiers never had time to return fire; they were caught in a sudden squall of bullets, pellets and *plastique*, and when it lifted, all nine of them lay dead in the trail.

Rogers caught a bit of heat for what he had done; the new colonel at battalion was on the radio reminding him that the truce was on and asking him rhetorically if he was aware of it. Rogers said yes, but the other side was moving men through their position in violation of the truce, and they weren't just innocent villagers out for a Sunday stroll, either; they were armed soldiers, a danger to his men, and he wasn't about to ask them if their intentions were peaceable or not.

There were more spasms of violence and more anxious calls from battalion before quiet settled in. Christmas Eve had melted into Christmas morning and some of the men were dozing when, ten minutes past midnight, they heard the chatter of voices in Vietnamese once again coming toward them far down the trail. *Noisy as hell*, Skip Sommer thought; the men couldn't imagine why they would be so careless except that it was dark, the sampans were close and a cease-fire was on so that the round-eyes could celebrate Christmas. They waited. The voices got closer and turned into vague shapes in the darkness. Claymores started popping; the flashes lit the night like strobe lights, pellets of steel the size of ballbearings were flying everywhere and a machine gun was burning up the trail.

Skip Sommer was a distance from ground zero, lying with some other guys in the dark with bullets flying by and tree branches crashing down around them. An AK-47 round came their way with Curtis Gilliland's name on it, except it went through Bean's foot first and veered off its collision course with Gilliland's head. Both men were praising God, Gilliland for the gift of his life, Bean for the million-dollar wound he knew would get him off the line. Sommer was thanking God, too, and not just for his own deliverance; he was thanking God that he hadn't been in the party doing the shooting. He could hear a high, keening moan through the cacophony of battle, and he sensed then that not all the people who had passed into their free-fire zone were soldiers—that some were women and children and were dying.

It was all over in a matter of minutes. Then the surviving NVAs pulled out, the din died away, and Sommer lay in anguish in the night, listening to the sounds of Bean groaning in pain beside him and the women and children keening in the trail. No one could have seen them in the dark, but that didn't help. Neither was it much comfort to Sommer that women and children routinely served the enemy as ammunition bearers and sometimes, to deadly effect, as combatants. All he could hear through his pain was their crying, and he lay wondering bitterly what women and children know about cease-fires or wars.

The moaning was getting to all of them. "I can't take this," Sommer could hear guys muttering to themselves; some were hefting grenades and some were urging them to lob a couple into the trail—"Do something," they were muttering, "to shut those bastards up." But there was nothing they could do. They couldn't throw grenades without giving away their position, and they couldn't leave without violating the cease-fire themselves and walking smack into the next American ambush in the process. So they lay where they were until Christmas morning dawned, in thrall to the sounds of dying on the trail.

Ten or twelve bodies lay strewn in the roadway when some of the men walked up in the daylight for a look. Their memories of what they saw or heard assumed different shapes over the dozen years thereafter, filtered as they were by time and their varying degrees of pain. Some, Captain Rogers among them, didn't believe there were any women or children at all. Some believed that there were, but that the women had been ammo bearers and the children were not children by enemy standards; they were teenagers quite old enough to fight, and to kill. But Sommer and some others were seeing something else in the road, and in the memories and nightmares of it that followed them home from the war. Sommer was seeing two or three women and two or three children, none more than nine years old. Only one, a boy, was even twitching. A couple of guys put him out of his misery with an M-16 round. Sommer felt sick.

They still couldn't move, so they passed their Christmas in their patch of jungle, each sorting the events of the night. Curtis Gilliland was nursing a wound in one hand and looking in wonderment at the bullet pocks in the ground where he had lain through the night; he reckoned that it had only been by the will of God that he had survived. Tiny Scott was turning down $100 bids on a 9 mm pistol he had liberated; he had wasted its previous owner, a Chinese payroll officer, and one of the kids on the trail besides, and suddenly guys were calling him Killer instead of Tiny.

David Bean was playing his exit from the field like Errol Flynn. He posed for a picture displaying his bloody foot, a Camel dangling insouciantly from his lips. A medic asked if he wanted morphine. "Naw," Bean answered, waving him away. There was a half-inch hole through his foot, and it hurt like hell, but he was savoring it; it was his ticket out of the war, and coming as it had just after midnight on Christmas morning, how else could he interpret it except as God's present to His blue-eyed boy David Bean?

But Skip Sommer was sinking in his despair. A colonel had come out at first light to satisfy himself finally that Rogers had been within the rules and, having done so, to commend the men for their work. Sommer watched him, despising him for his spit-shined shoes, his razor-creased pants, his Patton-style .45 and what seemed to Sommer and some of the others his absorption with the statistics of death. "Good job, boys," he told them, and was gone.

There were extra sodas waiting for them at Junction City, and a half-dozen unscheduled in-country R&Rs as well, and when they got back to Lai Khe for a break they found the scoreboard further celebrating their night's kill. Sommer stared at it. Charlie Company was out front in the company standings, with two or three dead mama-sans and two or three dead kids, by his own calculation, fattening its score. Sommer felt lost and empty. *Like a contest*, he thought. *A friggin' game. All we have are dead bodies to prove we are right.* He felt he had descended into madness, or maybe hell. He knew then that he had to get out.

Sommer soldiered on after that, bravely; he walked the exposed point position at the head of the column on patrols; he was promoted to sergeant and decorated for his valor in combat. He fought like most of the others to survive—*survive*, he thought, *so you don't die so you can go home*. He imagined that he killed men in the process; he sheltered himself from the probability, as many of the men did, by telling himself that he did not certainly know. But he could feel himself turn as brittle as glass. Walking point was making him jumpy, suffusing him with a nascent paranoia. The treadmill futility of the war was clawing at his nerves. In the night, he could still hear the moaning of women and children dying on a lost jungle trail on Christmas morning.

He felt finally that he was succumbing to the insanity he saw around him—that he was in fact half-mad himself. He dragged himself through ten and a half months in the line, then went to Tokyo with his buddy Larry Cottrell for a week's R&R and realized that he could not take it anymore. Cottrell had a fat-rat job awaiting him on their return, standing guard on the bunkers in Lai Khe. Sommer did not; he felt himself a man under sentence, imprisoned in bedlam with no way out. *I'm breaking up*, he thought when his leave time was up. *I can't go back out there. I can't pull that trigger anymore.*

He was caged in his nightmare, rattling at doors in search of an exit and finding none. There was no medical ground for his deliverance under the Catch-23 canons of military psychiatry then in vogue, which no longer recognized battle fatigue as a disorder; the term of art instead, beginning in Korea, was "acute situation reaction" and the standard course of treatment was a short rest, a hit of Thorazine in the worst cases and a speedy return to one's unit. There were no off-the-line openings left at Lai Khe either; Cottrell pulled what strings he could for Sommer without success.

So Sommer walked through the last door left to him and presented himself to the recruiting sergeant waiting behind it with a reenlistment blank and a cat-and-canary grin. It was the Army's practice then to keep its numbers up by doing deals with combat soldiers who, like Sommer, had reached a certain pitch of desperation: re-up for three years and get reassigned off the line. The sergeant was pushing the papers toward him. "Can't take it anymore, huh, boy?" Sommer heard him saying. "Well, this is what you want, this is what you're gonna have to do, boy, if you want out of it. If this is it, boy, sign right here."

Sommer sat there hating it all—the war, the Army, the sergeant's face mocking him across the desk as if to say he had lost his nerve when what he most feared losing was his mind. But he was out of options. *I can't swim 13,000 miles home*, he thought miserably. *I'm going to get my ass out of here, and as soon as I get back into the States, I'm gone.* The sergeant was waiting expectantly. Sommer accepted the pen and signed.

FRIENDLY FIRE

The first time he ever laid eyes on the rookie lieutenant, Omega Harris marked him for a loser. The company had gypsied east and south from Junction City through an indistinguishable blur of NDPs and fire bases, from Thunder Two to Thunder One and then to a grandly named circle in the dirt north of Di An called Luke's Castle. Along the way they had picked up a number of freshly minted brown-bar second lieutenants; and Captain David Arthur, who had succeeded Rogers as CO, directed Harris to conduct a briefing for them on what it is a mortar section can do for you in a tight spot. Harris was just in the process of explaining how to call in supporting fire when he noticed one of the brown bars—*this one little sucker*—engrossed in a book about something else. The first thing Harris himself had learned in 'Nam was that the lowest-ranking dog soldier around, if he had been incountry for a while, could teach you something that might save your life. *But this guy's not interested in what I got to tell him*, he thought, going on with his lesson. It struck him later that if only the lieutenant had been listening, he might not have called down a mortar barrage on his own men.

It was at once accepted and resented among the boys of Charlie Company that they were as much in peril from America's own instruments of war as from the other side's. The possibility of death or injury by what the statisticians of war chose to call "friendly fire" was the surreal flip side of the vast technological edge America brought to Vietnam. The Viet Cong might send a guy at you with an AK-47 and six bullets, where the American arsenal ranged from jeeps to tanks, from jets to helicopter gunships, from .45 automatics to six-thousand-round-per-minute miniguns. It was almost as if there were too much killing power around, and in in-

79

experienced or inexpert hands, it could be undiscriminatingly dangerous to friend and foe alike.

There was, for example, the night a major from the Rangers—the Army's trained-for-trouble combat elite—marched a platoon from Charlie Company from one ambush position to another within earshot of a party of men talking and moving in the bush. "These are some smart gooks," the major said. "They sound just like Americans." But before he asked the logical next question, the two sides were firing wildly at each other in the dark. The major radioed the NDP for supporting mortar fire. Harris did some quick calculations, then radioed back: "Sir, that movement you got is the second platoon." The shooting stopped without serious casualties. The major moved on afterward to another command. The word drifted back to Charlie Company later that he had been killed in action; the official version was that he had been the victim of an enemy ambush, but the barracks chatter was that he had been fragged by his own men.

There was, for another example, the time they went out in a patch of jungle thought to be alive with enemy troops and set up a classic hammer-and-anvil trap. Some of the men hid in the trees at one edge of a clearing and waited for the others, in company with a line of tanks, to drive the enemy into their arms. The trouble was that there weren't any NVAs between the hammer and the anvil; the men in the trees saw the tanks rumble into view shooting straight at them. "Fall back, fall back," they were begging their own lieutenant, but he was saucer-eyed with fear and wouldn't move. The tanks were still coming, blowing away their cover, when they finally made radio contact across no-man's-land. "If you don't stop shootin'," somebody told the tankers in unmistakable English, "we're gonna start shootin' back." The advance halted. The guns went silent. Curtis Gilliland had been hiding behind a tree. When the shooting stopped, the tree was gone.

And there was the day when it wasn't only tanks but Cobra attack helicopters—when their paranoia was made flesh and they felt as if they had blundered into a proving ground for the whole arsenal of democracy. They had surprised some enemy soldiers in a clearing and had radioed for help. A couple of tanks lumbered in first. The men got up to wave at them. The tanks started shooting, and guys were nose down in the dirt thanking God that it was only high explosive shells they were catching and not fleshette rounds, the kind that burst in flight and saturate the air with steel darts sharp and fast enough to tear through trees. They were waving and cursing and popping smoke grenades and yelling at the tankers that everybody was on the same side. The tankers finally got the message and quit shooting.

Some of the men scrambled up when the dust settled and were dog-trotting along a trail looking for the vanished enemy troopers when two Cobras showed up. The Cobras were in radio contact with the tanks, not the men, and the tankers told them that there was enemy movement a hundred yards ahead. The grunts from Charlie Company had progressed about that far when they looked up and saw the Cobras coiling into a tight circular attack pattern. The men were scuttling into a ditch for shelter when the first chopper swooped low, its painted dragon teeth leering at them and its minigun chewing a trench through the patch of trail they had just abandoned. The second Cobra followed, spitting rockets into the trail. The first was circling for another pass when the word got through that the men were friendlies. The choppers paused in flight, lifted straight up and, without so much as a sorry-about-that, disappeared.

Most of Charlie Company's friendly-fire tales were like that: hairbreadth escapes in which the men lived to tell the tale and even, in time, to laugh about it with a kind of seditious merriment. But there was no happy ending the day the rookie lieutenant called the mortars in on them, and nothing to smile at in the memory. Some of the men wanted to kill the lieutenant for it. A couple might have if they hadn't needed his help to carry away the wounded.

The lieutenant was in part the victim of bad beginner's luck when he took a platoon out of Luke's Castle on a night ambush operation. There were seasoned men who might have put him straight if they had been there—Roadrunner Selig for one, the squad leader whose single war aim was to get himself and his men home alive; Bowser Bowers for another, an experienced woodsman who always carried a map and compass, knew how to read them and never hesitated to back-sass an officer he thought was wrong. But Selig was temporarily off the line and Bowers was laid up with a head injury; somebody had dropped an M-79 grenade launcher by accident the day before and a grenade had bounced off the back of his skull at 250 feet a second. A lot of other, older hands had fallen out in battle at Junction City or rotated out when their one-year tours were over. Half the men in the lieutenant's platoon were as new and raw as he; it was the greening of Charlie Company, and some of the surviving combat veterans didn't like the look of it.

They set out nevertheless that late afternoon, Cowboy Rosson walking point and breaking a path through the trees. The terrain was rough and hilly; they weren't precisely sure where they were or how far they had come, but they reckoned later that they were a kilometer or so from Luke's Castle when Vitt Vittorini thought he picked up some movement off their left flank. They fired a machine-gun burst toward the sound. There was no answering fire, not even a rustle in the trees in response, and the men got ready to move on. The lieutenant held them up. He took out his map, made some calculations and radioed Harris's mortar team back at the base for a marking round.

Harris made his own calculations. "Hang it in the hole," he ordered. Somebody dropped a round into the tube. "Fire in the hole!" Harris sang out. They fired and dropped a marking round roughly where the lieutenant had asked for it, one hundred meters off his left flank.

"We got two tubes loaded, dropping six rounds," Harris radioed the lieutenant. "Call it."

The lieutenant looked at his map again. The older hands among the grunts thought he was shooting at phantoms, but he seemed set, so Bowen and Stagnaro stood at his elbows trying frantically to catch him up on the rudiments he appeared to have missed at the mortar briefing—how to walk in rounds in giant steps one hundred meters apart until the entire flank was covered. But the lieutenant said, "No, we're just going to bring 'em in a hundred meters to the right."

"You're crazy," Bowen told him. "That's right on top of us."

"No," the lieutenant said, "on this map it says—"

Bowen broke in. "Don't call—"

"Now, Doc, listen," the lieutenant said, cutting him short. "I've gone to school."

"Don't," Bowen pleaded and Stagnaro was arguing, and Harry Foxwell was telling the lieutenant he had it wrong.

"Right a hundred," the lieutenant radioed Harris. "Fire for effect!"

"That's right on top of us," Rosson told his buddy Whitey White. They could hear the first *thoooomp!* of Harris's mortars in the distance and the shrill *eeeeeeee* of the round whistling toward them.

"Well—goodbye, sir," somebody told the lieutenant, and then Rosson was yelling at everybody to hit the ground and Bowen was saying *'bye* to Stagnaro, and Stagnaro was saying *'bye* back to Bowen, and Kevin Abbott was belly down cursing into the dirt, and Danger Dan Colfack was shivering and praying fast, and Omega Harris's radio back at Luke's Castle was picking up the voices still screaming at the lieutenant, "You called that shit right on us!"

It was too late by then to stop; Harris's mortars had lobbed in a half-dozen textbook-perfect tree bursts right on target, the rounds exploding in the branches and spraying shrapnel downward like a deadly rain. Vittorini lay in the brush hearing them coming—*thooomp, eeeeeeee, bam!*—and with every hit, somebody else would be screaming. Abbott, the hero of Cantigny, was sprawled on the jungle floor with two chunks of made-in-U.S.A. metal in his back. Whitey White got hit, and Little Brother Pierce, and one guy was missing a piece out of the top of his head, and another, a *chieu hoi*, had a gaping hole in his leg. One of the twinks was spilling tears for a lost friend, wailing, "He's dead! My buddy's dead!" Another, a black kid, was staring at the bloody stumps of three fingers, asking over and over, "What's going on?"

They lay praying and counting rounds to themselves till the barrage lifted and the branches quit crashing down around them. Then they got up and began picking up the pieces. The precise casualty count faded over time like a repressed memory; the consensus among the survivors a dozen years later was that one, two or three men had died and that only half the grunts who had followed the lieutenant into the jungle that day walked out whole. There were more casualties, in any event, than Bowen could tend to alone; Foxwell helped out, patching guys back together with pressure bandages, and even then it took them nearly an hour. They called for a dust-off helicopter to evacuate those who were too badly fucked up to walk. But they were in double-canopy

jungle and the chopper couldn't land; it had to hover overhead instead, lifting the wounded out in a rope rigging, and
one man fractured an arm when the rigging broke with him
in it, dumping him back into the trees.

Guys were yelling at the lieutenant, calling him an ignorant son of a bitch, and they could hear the CO's voice on
the radio from Luke's Castle chewing him out: "You don't
even know what the fuck you're doing there. You're in the
wrong fucking place!" That the lieutenant survived owed
largely to his own luck during the barrage and the charity of
his men thereafter; they couldn't spare anyone in shape to
walk out, so they let him off with a warning—the cautionary
tale, possibly apocryphal, of an earlier brown-bar who had
been blown away with a grenade one night for sins a good
deal less deadly than his. But they made it plain to the lieutenant that, as far as Charlie Company was concerned, he
was finished. On orders from battalion headquarters, he told
them to gather up the guns and the ammo—they were going
ahead with the original mission. Bowen and Stagnaro looked
at each other, then at him. "We're beyond ya," Bowen told
him. "We're going back in. Fuck you."

They did go back in, Vittorini carrying six rifles and still
jawing at the lieutenant. When they reached Luke's Castle,
somebody hung the caved-in helmet of one of the dead out
on a pole where everyone could see it. It stayed there long
after the lieutenant had gone. *They disappeared him*, Vittorini thought. The men never saw him after that night; they
heard later with bitter amusement that he had been reassigned off the line, training South Vietnamese troops in the
arts of war.

IN THE ASHES OF FIRE BASE JULIE

The day David Brown came eyeball to eyeball with his first gook and blew half his face away with a submachine gun, he thought there must be some reason for what he was doing. The day he met his last and killed him with his bare hands, he had no purpose left except his own survival. Brown had put in eight or nine months by then trying to make sense of Charlie Company's apparently aimless wandering from one disposable fire base to another. He had been shot at by both sides, nearly incinerated by American napalm, nibbled at by fire ants and junior officers, and obliged by circumstance to put at least five or six of his fellow human beings to death. He had been transfigured as a man as well, introduced to his fears and to the lengths of violence to which fear could drive him. But he never figured out what it was for. *I was just fighting there*, he thought when he was finally out. *It was for nothing.*

It hadn't always been that way; Brown had submitted to the draft and the inevitability of Vietnam on the unquestioning premise that he lived in America and America was supposed to be right. He was himself a child of the American middle, a machinist's son from Trenton, New Jersey, with a better-than-average high-school record and a two-and-a-half-year start toward a degree in education at Trenton State College before the money ran out. His notions of war were formed in darkened movie theaters watching John Wayne decimate whole tribes of Indians and regiments of Japs in causes that were presumptively just. He was less than happy about being called when his time came, and he felt undernourished by the Army's course in WHY VIETNAM? at noncom school—*a bunch of facts*, he thought, on rice and rubber production without much attention to the practical or moral purposes of the war. But Brown, a chunky young man with

85

a broad, square face set on a wrestler's body, did not feel it was his to reason why. It was enough, he supposed then, that he was paying his dues to his country.

Charlie Company was still at Luke's Castle when Brown arrived in March 1969, a freshly milled sergeant so green, by his own reckoning, that he didn't even know which direction was down when all he had to do was fall that way. The ground war was in an adagio passage when he got there, but the daily cat-and-mouse pursuit of the enemy continued, and Brown learned fast. He was dozing beside Tom Swenticky on his first night ambush when he heard the *thooomp-thooomp* of NVA mortars in the near distance.

"Tom," he said, shaking Swenticky awake, "they're shooting at us!"

"What are they shooting at us with?" Swenticky asked, still fogged with sleep.

"Mortars—don't you hear them?"

"Oh, that's nothing," Swenticky answered. "They're just trying to find us. It'll stop at five or six rounds. Go back to sleep."

Brown counted the rounds to himself—*four-five-six*. They stopped. He was breathing again. He went back to sleep.

He was still gung ho and still green when they made a point man of him, in part for precisely those reasons; he didn't understand how dangerous it was until they gave him a badge merely for having done it for three months and lived. He had in fact almost bought it one day when he was up front whacking a path for the men through a tangle of six-foot elephant grass and found himself face to face with an NVA soldier.

Brown froze.

He could see the gook leveling an AK-47 at him and squeezing the trigger. Time crawled to a stop. Brown couldn't move.

He heard a dull click.

The round was dead, and Brown was suddenly alive, unlimbering his submachine gun while the gook was still fumbling with the AK-47, and emptying a thirty-round magazine point-blank at the gook's head. Brown was outside time; it was as if the bullets took two or three minutes in flight, and he was watching them. He was seeing the gook's skull explode and half his face disappear, and the image of it was exploding in Brown's own head, filling it so completely that he couldn't even remember afterward whether he had seen the gook's body hit the ground or not.

The picture burned itself permanently into Brown's memory and his dreams, but he had been losing his heart for the war anyway. It seemed to him not a war at all but a mindless, purposeless exercise in which men were required to kill or be killed but were not permitted to win. The company kept going out on its endless round of daylight patrols and night ambushes, humping sixty pounds of bullets, grenades and claymores per man and shucking everything in their C-ration kits except the peanut butter, jelly and crackers to accommodate more ammo. They were literally loaded down with their killing power, so heavily, Brown thought, that the sheer noise they made humping through the trees and brush was almost calculated to scare the enemy into hiding. They had everything, where the other side, so guys kept telling themselves in the bunkers, consisted of this little gook running around the jungle with a rifle and six cartridges. And yet with all of it, they were not winning.

They were not winning in part, Brown supposed, because they were muscle-bound by the very technological imbalance they brought to the war. Tanks used to knock down trees in those John Wayne movies he had seen back in Trenton, but in Vietnam they threw their treads if they tried; they couldn't even leave the roads for the nine rainy months of the year anyway without miring down in the mud. B-52s, denied access to military and industrial targets in the North, were flattening suspect rural areas in the South—*making a beautiful golf course out there*, Brown thought, without visible effect on the other side. Not even the great American edge in those small arms more suited to a close-in jungle war seemed to impose insupportable pain on an enemy toughened by twenty years of fighting on his home ground in a cause for which he was prepared to die. Once two Viet Cong blundered into a squad-sized ambush on a jungle trail, and the men opened up with devastating force—first with an "animal," twenty claymores jury-rigged to go off all at once and loose a hailstorm of 14,000 flying steel balls; then a saturation spray of rifle and machine-gun fire at the sitting-duck distance of ten feet. When they broke cover afterward to count the dead, they found none—not even a blood spot in the trail. They had squandered it all, Brown thought, where that gook with six rounds had six targets to expend them on and had walked maybe a thousand miles to get at them.

They might have won anyway, Brown thought, if they hadn't been bound down like Gulliver in Lilliput by the rules and the tactical restraints of a limited war. *A nine-to-five war*, Brown thought; they could have used all that power to blow the whole country to hell, but instead they kept bumping around on little nickel-and-dime, hit-and-run operations trying to secure America's control of the daytime and challenge the enemy's possession of the night. He didn't even know where he was most of the time; they didn't issue him a map until he got his own platoon, and then it was a small area map—*as if*, he thought, *they don't want us to go someplace on our own*. The symbol of Charlie Company's war for him was the Michelin rubber plantation, a vast and thickly wooded sprawl favored by the Communists as an ammunition cache and a training base. The company would ride in on armored personnel carriers, smoke out the enemy, run them off in a firefight, then sign chits to Michelin for the damage to the rubber trees and pull out until the next time. There always seemed to be a next time, and for Brown, the Michelin came to stand for the apparent purposelessness of the entire war. *The French had forts in Vietnam and they couldn't do it*, he thought. *So what are we going to do walking around the country?*

The last of his gung-ho spirit oozed away when he heard somewhere that it cost the Vietnamese an average of 27 cents to kill one American as against $10,000 for America to kill one Vietnamese. He didn't like what the numbers said about the quality of the U.S. war effort or about the bargain-basement price on his own head. His commitment to winning the war accordingly shrank in inverse proportion to his interest in living through it.

He was already a seasoned survivalist when his CO of the moment ordered the men to walk from point A to point B along an exposed road instead of through the brush, where they would have some cover. Brown sat down and said no, he wouldn't go. His friend and lieutenant Bert Kennish told him they had to do it—they had only thirty minutes to move two thousand yards and if they lost time hacking through the brush, they would miss their choppers out. Brown ended his mutiny, satisfied for once that there was a purpose in something they were doing. They set out down the road, and on the way to the choppers, as Brown's sixth sense had warned him, a big blond twink from Alaska walked into a sniper's rifle sight and died before the convention of American society had recognized him as a man.

The irony of Brown's passage through Vietnam was that, when he won the Silver Star for gallantry, it was for killing a man face to face to save himself; even the Army, or at least its more sensitive line officers, understood by then that the impulse toward survival in a failing war represents not a failure of courage but an access of common sense. The encounter shouldn't have happened at all except that Brown had been in-country for eight or nine months and was showing off his experience a bit for the new boys. They had come to an empty bunker leading into a subterranean network of tunnels, and Brown, with a touch of swagger, had pulled the pin out of a grenade and gone in. The grenade was safe as long as he kept it in his balled fist, holding its firing lever to its side. But when the gook jumped down into the bunker practically in his face, he was in trouble.

The gook was in front of him. The grenade was in his hand, primed to blow in four and a half seconds if he dropped it or even loosened his grip. He was cursing himself for having pulled the pin and cursing the gook for being there. *You stupid shit, you've either got to kill me or we're both going to get killed when this thing goes off,* he was thinking, except there wasn't time to think, only to move. He swung once, then again, the grenade adding a pound of steel to his punch, and with the second blow he felt his fist stave in the gook's skull as if it were heavy-duty cardboard.

It was necessary, Brown reflected afterward, but in that instant he had discovered a violence in himself that he had not known was there. He left the war not long after that, white-knuckling out of the bush aboard a loach doing 150 knots six feet off the ground to avoid enemy fire, and he still didn't understand any of it. *What did we do?* he was thinking. *Cut their population down a little. Wreck the rice fields for a year. But were we defending the country?*

In the latter part of his tour, Charlie Company's peregrinations led it on a walk through what once had been Fire Base Julie. Brown hadn't been there, but he had heard the older grunts talk about it—about the sweat they had expended carving it out of the bush and the blood they had spilled defending it from the enemy. When Brown saw it, it was a wasteland, denuded by the defoliant Agent Orange, scorched by napalm and blackened by ashes and decay. *So why*, he puzzled to himself, trudging through the detritus, *did they have such a great big fantastic battle at this place if nobody wanted it?* He wasn't the gung-ho boy noncom anymore; he was walking in the ashes of his war and America's, thinking, *This was for nothing*.

THE COLOR OF WAR

On a day off from the war, Charles Rupert, a son of the streets on the black East Side of Detroit, walked into his mama-san's hooch in the village of Lai Khe and surprised her with another boyfriend—a VC guerrilla sitting cross-legged on the floor in his black fighting pajamas. Rupert grabbed at his M-16 and the VC scrambled for his AK-47, but the mama-san got between her two men, yelling, "Don't shoot! Okay! He Number One GI!"

So they laid aside their rifles, lit up a joint and called their own cease-fire for as long as it took to smoke it down to a glowing roach. The VC did most of the talking, trying to make common cause of their color—you and me, GI, brown and black against white. "We no want to fight soul brother," he said. "You go home. This white man's war. You soul brother, you go home."

Wild, Rupert thought, walking out of the hooch and back to the war; wild, but white folks weren't his problem in Vietnam—the war was. He hadn't wanted to go to 'Nam in the first place. He had been a basketball star at Southeastern High and was dreaming of a college athletic scholarship when his draft notice came. *It ain't too bad, three meals a day and all*, the brothers on the block told him. But his mother had to talk him out of fleeing the four miles from her place to Canada when he got his orders for Vietnam, and once he was there, he got so strung out on the heat, the rain, the red ants, the jungle and the sheer vagrant aimlessness of the war that he actively contemplated shooting himself in the foot to get out of it. The charge that it was a white man's war, as the VC in his mama-san's hooch had argued, was not part of his own bill of grievances then or afterward. He was carrying around his own black man's burden of prejudices toward whites, the mirror image of the white man's prejudices toward him, but his own body-counting told him that whites were dying, too, in Vietnam.

The war was by no means color-blind; the heavy freight of color and caste antagonisms followed the flag in-country and was never very far from the surface of consciousness—not, in any case, in those times between operations when men were free to indulge them. There were whites who put it about that blacks were slow-witted at everything except staying out of action, when in fact the black ninth of the American population was furnishing a disproportionate sixth of the combat troops in Charlie Company and the war. And there were blacks who looked on whites indiscriminately as their enemies. It was said around Lai Khe that a dozen or more white troopers had been mysteriously shot on guard duty after Martin Luther King, Jr., was assassinated in April 1968. The air cooled thereafter, but when Larry Samples bought it at Fire Base Julie in October, one black eating a grenade to save seven whites, a shudder of paranoia coursed through the ranks of his black comrades in Charlie Company; a couple of them refused to go out in the field after that and were court-martialed.

At Lai Khe in particular, life between engagements tended to reproduce the tracery of color lines the men had grown up with back in The World. Grunts of every hue might stand side by side defending Black Lion Country against trespassers from the Armored Cav or the Artillery, but once the dust had settled they would mostly go their separate ways. *Los morenos, los hispanos y los americanos*, thought Antonio Rivera Parilla, a Puerto Rican from San Juan; blacks, hispanics and whites repairing to their respective watering holes off-duty and keeping to themselves. An official inquiry into racial problems on the base concluded that there were none worth the Army's serious concern. Unofficially, at Lai Khe as in Harlem or in Birmingham, Alabama, there were places where a man of the wrong color simply did not go.

Kit Bowen lurched across the divide into a black NCO club one night, already in extra innings in his off-duty encounter with demon rum, and wondered afterward how he ever got out alive. At the time, the question didn't even occur to him; he was too used to the easy banter between blacks and whites in the field and too well oiled to notice the distinctly unamused stares he was attracting. He marched up to one dude with a sprained hand freshly swathed in tape. "Who wrapped that?" Bowen demanded with transcendent professional scorn. It was in fact perfectly taped, but Bowen undid it and started over.

It took some time, given the state of his hand-eye coordination, and the finished dressing was a boozily loose and asymmetrical mess. Bowen looked up from his work, grinning. His hat was on sideways. Nobody was smiling back. Somebody had pulled the plug on the jukebox. The room was silent. A couple of guys were unlimbering their short-sticks, the chunky batons that grunts would carry and notch day by day when their time in-country was running out. *I'm a nice guy*, Bowen thought in sudden desperation, but it wasn't niceness that bailed him out in the end; it was his medic's badge.

"Now, bro," somebody was whispering to somebody else, "if you get hurt, it don't matter what race you are—ol' Doc here is gonna be patchin' you up."

A chuckle broke the silence, then a pealing laugh. "Doc, you must be the most wackiest idiot in the world to even come in here," a guy was saying, but the tension was gone; they bought Bowen a couple of beers and sent him on his wobbly way home.

Charlie Company's own racial ethos was formed in the heat of combat; the stress lines between races were accordingly looser off the line and practically nonexistent when the bullets and the shrapnel started flying. Some guys were naturally at ease anyway on either side of the gulf. J.C. Wilson, for one, was brought up southern, poor and white, but he figured prejudice was the direct consequence of slavery and the Wilsons never did have no such thing as slaves. Blacks in the company took to calling him "the white soul brother" for his unaffected camaraderie with them. Others were less comfortable at first but were made comrades and even friends by their common will to survive and their mutual dependence on one another if they were to do so. Death was democratic in Vietnam, and was a democratizing force. When they carried you off the battlefield dead, Omega Harris thought, it didn't matter what color you were—*The boots hang over the side of that poncho the same way.*

Color no longer mattered to Smitty the day in April when Fritz Suchomel died, his lungs screaming for air at the bottom of an abandoned well. Smitty hadn't much liked white folks when he came to Vietnam. Until he hooked up with Suchomel, he didn't like them at all. Smitty was a pavement-tough ghetto brother from Cleveland or Philly or the Deep South or somewhere, with a vivid police pedigree, by his own account, and a black chip on his shoulder. He told those buddies he would talk to that he had killed a man once in a fight over a woman; they were supposed to go at it bare-handed in a Mississippi Death Circle formed by members of their two families, but somebody tossed the other dude a knife and Smitty took it away and stuck him. The authorities had given him his choice between the Army and the slammer after that, he said, and he had chosen the Army, packing his baggage of racial resentment with him. And then he had run into Suchomel, a little blond kid off a farm outside Sun Prairie, Wisconsin. Suchomel liked Smitty, and Smitty, against his impulses, found himself liking Suchomel back.

Smitty had never known anyone like Suchomel before; to a brother off a ghetto street corner, the gently rolling hills of south central Wisconsin might have been the far side of the moon. Suchomel was barely five feet four, but he was tough and wiry, with a shelfful of high-school baseball and wrestling trophies back home; he had pitched Sun Prairie High to the finals of the state baseball tournament in his senior year and had lost a 1–0 heart-stopper to a guy who later made it in the big leagues for five years. He had hoped for an athletic scholarship, but it didn't work out, and he wound up soldiering side by side with Smitty in Charlie Company. The men liked him for his no-sweat manner, and for his guts. At Cantigny, an NVA made it to the brow of Suchomel's bunker and trained an AK-47 on his back. The rifle misfired. Suchomel heard it, wheeled toward the gook and, cool as autumn in Wisconsin, blew him away.

In April, Suchomel got a Dear John letter from a girl back in Wisconsin. He was miserable, and some of his buddies sat up most of one night with him in a bunker at Bandit Hill, their fire base of the moment, sharing some joints and trying to cheer him up. The next morning he went out with a squad on recon, and at the outskirts of a village they came upon an abandoned well. The enemy routinely used wells as ammo caches. Somebody tossed in a couple of concussion grenades just in case. Somebody else had to go down for a look, and Suchomel, given his size and agility, was the ideal tunnel rat.

So he started down on a rope, and nobody figured until he was deep inside that a concussion grenade will blow the oxygen out of an enclosed space along with everything else. They heard him call out after ten minutes or so that he was feeling dizzy and faint, and they hauled him up for a breath of air. Then he dropped back down again. Another ten minutes oozed by, and they heard him again. "Hey, guys," he was saying, "pull me out. I think I'm gonna faint."

They started pulling. Suchomel went limp at the end of the rope. They tugged. He was lodged at a bad angle and they couldn't budge him. A medic started in and came right out, and then Smitty was bulling forward, headed for the well, the man who hated whites bent on saving his white buddy's life.

They lowered Smitty in. He made it to Suchomel's lifeless body, heaved him onto his own shoulder and started up the rope, trying to hold his breath in the airless passage. He was eight feet from the top when he couldn't hold it any longer. He was gasping for oxygen but there wasn't any, and he and Suchomel fell back down.

An armored personnel carrier finally backed up to the well. Another rope was lowered, the medic went down for the bodies and the APC hauled them out. It was Fritz Suchomel they carried away on a poncho, his boots hanging over the side. Suchomel was dead and his friend Smitty was the next thing to it, his brain starved of oxygen and, the men heard later, permanently damaged.

"ALL HEROES DO IS DIE GOOD"

One day in the war, a flight of choppers lifted off into the blood-red dusk over the Iron Triangle, an embattled wild in the vee between two rivers north of Saigon, bearing the grunts of Charlie Company back to Lai Khe for a breather. Their trail-weary legs dangled from open doors. They hugged their M-16s to their bare and mostly scrawny chests. Their teenage faces were masks of impassivity, gazing without expression at the deserted outpost receding swiftly beneath them. They had hacked it out of a gordian tangle of trees and vines, held it at a steady daily price in sinew and spirit, and then abandoned it as they had Julie and Cantigny and the rest. All that remained to show that they had even been there were their buried refuse, their empty dugouts—and, spray-painted across one deserted bunker, the single, exasperated word CRAZY.

The graffito was their primal scream to the world that the war was mad and they were not. It made sense enough to the brass back in Saigon with their battle maps and body counts and to their new civilian masters in Washington. Richard Nixon had come to power in January 1969 committed to liquidating America's involvement in the war without being seen to have lost it. The tightrope device he chose was called Vietnamization; reduced to simplest terms, it meant drawing down the U.S. commitment, ceding the ground war gradually to the South Vietnamese and propping them up at least for a time with the renewal and massive escalation of the bombing.

But the name Vietnamization itself was an index of how completely Americanized the war had become over the five years just past and how ill-prepared America's Vietnamese clients were to defend themselves. It did not suit Nixon's domestic or geopolitical purposes to let them go under before

95

a decent interval had passed, and so, even as the freedom birds began flying the first 25,000 boys home in June, Charlie Company and scores of line outfits like it were obliged to linger behind and fight what was becoming a rearguard action against the Communist forces infiltrating from the North. The American command imagined that that effort was succeeding, for which there was some supporting evidence for a time, and that the men were happy in their work, for which there was almost none. In his memoirs, General Westmoreland proclaimed their morale "the highest... I have seen among United States soldiers in three wars" and blamed the withdrawal, not the war, for its deterioration.

A few of the men in Charlie Company might have seconded his assessment. Curtis Gilliland for one thought of himself as just an old Kentucky boy displaced and scared in Vietnam, but he felt himself falling in love with the Vietnamese and angry that his own country was preparing to cut and run from its commitment to them. Antonio Rivera Parilla, for another, had grown up surrounded by the poverty of Puerto Rico and saw in the poverty of Vietnam a plea for succor. Greg Etzel, for yet another, didn't even know where Vietnam was when the draft took him away from his wife, his Corvette and his job at the post office in the Rockland County exurbs of New York. But he was a go-with-the-program guy who considered the war a duty, not a burden, and thought the Americans should have stayed as long as it took to guarantee the survival of an independent South Vietnam. Charlie Company's mission, as he understood it, was to help stop the Communists and not ask questions. Etzel felt particularly moved the day the men had been assembled to watch the division command pass to a new general, who had told them: "You have to realize, gentlemen, that right now you are making history. You don't understand, but what you are doing is making world history."

What most of Etzel's buddies were doing was in fact something rather more elemental than that: trying to live through a war whose means and ends they did not understand. They had come to defend freedom in a country where the population seemed to them indifferent to the result and where even the land seemed hostile. The war for them was humping the boonies for weeks on end under their sixty- and seventy-pound packs, officially hunting Communists, privately hoping that the racket they made crashing through the foliage would frighten the enemy away. Their Vietnam was a platoon of fire ants devouring your arms and thirty or forty leeches sucking blood from your legs. It was heat so oppressively constant that you stopped feeling it until you started to move, and rain so heavy that you could set out your helmet and collect enough within an hour to make yourself a whole pot of hot chocolate. Its indelible smells, for Jerry Dickmann, were sulfur, diesel, death and burning excrement. Its lingering echo, for Don Stagnaro, was the jeering sound of an indigenous lizard whose cry in the night sounded uncannily like *fuck you! fuck you!*

The boys of Charlie Company fought their war with six- and eight-foot elephant grass tearing at their arms and legs and double- and triple-canopy jungle bouncing their own grenades back in their faces. They operated in thickets of bamboo and rubber trees so dense they could not see the sun and could not move more than one hundred feet in an hour; once, a VC sniper hidden in the bush put an AK-47 practically at their point man's ear, shot him dead and ran off without anyone having seen him. Their fatigues stiffened with mud and sweat, unwashed unless they happened to wade a stream wearing them. Red dust wore into their skin; Bert Kennish was complimenting himself on the progress of his suntan until he got under a shower at Lai Khe and it washed off. Scorpions stung them and jungle rot turned the bottoms of their feet so soft and sore you could scratch them and draw blood. Mike MacDonald came down once with a bad case of jungle rot compounded by ringworm, and exhausted the usual Army-issue salves, powders and unguents trying to keep it from spreading all over his body. His skin was an archipelago of red blotches when Doc Johnson finally whipped him up a home-brew remedy. Mosquito repellent was the only active ingredient MacDonald recognized, and the potion made him scream in pain when he daubed it on, but it worked well enough to serve the purpose of military medicine. It got him back to the war.

The very terrain seemed to the men to be their enemy and was treated as armies treat enemies, with the application of deadly force. For a time in 1969, Charlie Company worked in tandem with an armada of Rome plows, huge armored earthmovers that stripped great swaths of jungle down to the naked ground and sometimes buried enemy troopers alive in their spider holes and tunnels. The intended consequence was to deprive the Communists of cover from their American pursuers; the demoralizing side effect was to turn the company's own base of the moment into a wallow of mud so deep that men went hungry rather than wade through the ooze to the mess tent.

The war against the land was conducted from the air as well, with planeload after planeload of the defoliant Agent Orange laying waste to 3.5 million acres of rice paddies and mangrove forests. The Big Red One's area of operations was fairly soaked with it in an effort to denude Hanoi's southbound infiltration routes. The men in Charlie Company saw its leavings, the trees that turned orange before they died and then were burned to black ash with napalm, and one day they were working along the Saigon River when an Air Force C-123 lumbered low over their heads and sprayed the land all around them. They did not know what the spray was and did not ask. But the image haunted their memories years later when the papers began reporting the damage Agent Orange could do to the human body.

The alien landscape only sharpened the sense of isolation stealing over them, caught as they were between the failing support for the war back home and the thanklessness they felt among the people they had come to save. A few like Gilliland tried to reach out and touch the Vietnamese; a few more formed close comradeships with the *chieu hois* who soldiered with them and shared their common danger. But most held the Vietnamese at a wide and undifferentiatingly wary distance. The Vietnamese they knew cut their hair, washed out their fatigues, sold them Cokes and marijuana, saw to their sexual needs and burned their excrement with diesel fuel in big oil drums, all the while smiling at them. But sometimes the smiles masked a deadly intent, an unwon heart or mind. Charlie Company was still in Vietnam when the scandal over the massacre of civilians at My Lai broke in the autumn of 1969; reading about it, a few of the men thought about those smiles and the hatred they sometimes concealed and felt a pang of empathy for William Calley, the lieutenant accused of having presided over the bloodletting. *Well*, Leroy Pringle thought, *what did they send him over here for?*

There were no My Lais in Charlie Company's war, but there was no presumption of the innocence of civilians either—not, in any case, after the night they popped an ambush on a party of Viet Cong and found the bodies of their barber and two manicure girls among the dead. *They laugh in your face today*, Pringle thought, *and tonight they shoot at you*. The war from the perspective of Charlie Company was limited only on their side; it was total for their enemy, and women and children were not infrequently combatants. An aged mama-san stood at a roadside hawking Cokes one day as they were setting out on an ambush run, and Cowboy Rosson saw her head bobbing in time with their passage. *She's counting us*, Rosson thought. It flashed through his mind that he ought to kill her, but he trudged on. In a total war, even the little kid running at you yelling, "Candy, GI!" might be carrying a live hand grenade, and if you saw it in time, J.C. Wilson remembered, *you shot him*.

Even among friendly Vietnamese, the men felt as alien as Martians among Earthlings, contemptuous of them as a fighting force and baffled by their apparent apathy as to whether they were delivered from Communism or not. In token of America's commitment to Vietnamization, they changed the name of one of their fire bases from Mahone to Kien in honor of a fallen Vietnamese officer and shared it for a time with a force from the Army of the Republic of Vietnam. But the experiment in brotherhood fizzled in the eyes of the grunts, if not the generals, when an epidemic of pilferage broke out on the base and when the ARVNs flung down their rifles and ran the first time an enemy mortar round landed near them. *Only thing they beat us to is the chow line*, Omega Harris thought; otherwise, it seemed to him that the ARVNs were somewhere behind the lines polishing their made-in-U.S.A. weapons. Even when they did go out on ambush, Harris was suspicious of the way they kept coming back clean. He looked at them and thought, *They been sleeping*.

Neither were the men welcomed in the villes as liberators, as Americans had been in earlier wars. It was a commonplace in Vietnam that the Americans owned the daytime but the VC ruled the night, and the population whose hearts and minds they were contesting seemed kindly disposed to whichever side was around. It struck the men that they had no secrets that were not accessible to the other side; it was the whores at Lai Khe who had told them that they were going up to Fire Base Julie before they had it from their officers, and the men presumed that the same intelligence had been passed in a spirit of equity to the enemy. The indifference they felt all around them as to the outcome only deepened their puzzlement as to why they were in Vietnam at all. *We're as much of a threat to the villagers as the Viet Cong are*, Don Stagnaro, the fisherman's son from San Pedro, thought by the end of his tour. *Their whole lives have been surrounded by war. They don't really care one way or the other—they just want to be left alone.*

In the absence of evidence that the Vietnamese cared, some of the men became uncaring toward them; they were abstractions at the edge of the war, an enigmatic presence viewed across the vast chasm between America and Asia, between a technological and a peasant society. George Goldstein, the single Jew in Charlie Company for most of his tour in 'Nam, was struck by the nearly painful beauty of the country. It was, he thought, like living in a landscape by Modigliani if Modigliani had painted landscapes. Once he bathed in a jungle stream as pure and lambent as sunlit crystal; once he read the Psalms in a tiny Buddhist sanctuary on a hilltop; both times he felt powerfully moved. But, under Western eyes, a discontinuity seemed to him to open between the land and the people who inhabited it. The memories of the sanctuary and the stream were mixed in his mind with the images of a Viet Cong corpse trussed up to a tree as an example to his comrades; of some of his buddies throwing C rations and candy bars *at* the villagers begging along the roadside, instead of *to* them; of a GI garbage truck discharging its load, and a half-dozen Vietnamese peasants standing under it in a rain of nearly liquefied refuse, trying to catch America's leftovers in buckets to feed their own families. Goldstein felt ashamed; it was as if the people they had come to serve were somehow less than human to them.

The men had rather more respect for the other side; some came to envy the enemy his skills at war and his sense of calling to it—a commitment, wanting in themselves, to a cause worth dying for. They thought of him as a gook with six rounds, but they knew at first hand what six rounds could do in motivated hands. Charlie Rupert, the schoolyard ballplayer from Detroit, saw one VC knock a helicopter gunship out of the sky with a rifle. He saw another empty his rifle at a search party of GIs, then hole up in a bunker refusing to surrender until they blew him apart with a grenade and his ear wound up stuck to Rupert's knee. To the men, the enemy seemed unafraid of anything, perhaps excepting B-52's and Cobra attack helicopters—anything, that is, that Charlie Company could bring to bear against him in the normal course of business. *We're playing games and they're fighting for keeps*, Kit Bowen thought. *They've got a destination—they have to take over Saigon. We've got nothing.*

In the absence of a destination, some of the men were afflicted with a sickened sense of the meaninglessness of the bloodletting on both sides. Its epiphany, for them, was the day they were choppered out of a base called Thunder Three to bail out a mechanized convoy that had been ambushed on Highway 13 north of Saigon. Trucks and half-tracks were burning in the roadway when they got there, a fallen helicopter was smoldering down to a charred ruin, and a long line of civilian and military traffic was stalled while a patrol went out ahead to sweep for mines. Some of the men clambered aboard an armored personnel carrier and were waiting for something to move when a Volkswagen bus loaded with civilians pulled out of line, trying to beat the jam and slip to the head of the column.

The bus was almost abreast of the APC when it hit a mine and lifted eerily into mid-air. *"Uh-oh,"* Gilliland was saying, and then glass was spewing outward, and a tire caromed off the APC next to Ronald Warehime, and arms, legs and heads were flying through the roof and windows. A two- or three-year-old boy landed near Rivera Parilla, all his clothes and both his legs blown away. Johnny McClure heard someone screaming and followed the sound to a twelve-year-old girl, dying, with nothing left from the waist down except a puddle of blood. Harry Foxwell jumped from the APC and found an old woman with one hand gone, trying to crawl back into the bus in search of a child. The child was a mangled corpse on the far side of the wreckage. Foxwell didn't tell the woman that; he steered her gently away to a medic instead, wondering what purpose could be served for either side by blowing children to bits on a highway.

Still, the men felt almost nothing in common with the

moral certitudes of the peace movement boiling among their contemporaries back in The World—only a sense of estrangement from their own generation and abandonment by their own country. That sense owed partly to the simple fact that they were there, *getting shot at and landing on our face in the mud in a half-assed operation*, Bob Mastrogiovanni thought, *while everybody else our age is going to college and getting laid and having a good time.* But it flowed as well from the nearly polar distance between the bunkers and the campuses as vantage points from which to view the war in Vietnam. The men would read about students back home burning flags, shredding draft cards and calling them baby killers, Danger Dan Colfack remembered, and guys would be muttering, "After we finish this, let's go get some hippies." The peace movement decried Richard Nixon's secret decision to loose the B-52's on the North Vietnamese sanctuaries in Cambodia; the boys of Charlie Company lay on the ground watching with the earth literally bouncing under their bellies and celebrated it for pulverizing people who might otherwise be shooting at them. The movement preached at the gates of the Pentagon that the war was immoral; the men fighting it protested instead that it was futile—that it ought to have been fought to win or not at all.

Few of them doubted that they could have won it if they had been allowed to. *It could have been over within six months*, Frank Goins thought. *Easy. We could have took the 57,000 troops that got killed and put them all in a line behind tanks and APCs instead and just started them at one end and walked on across the country.*

The nuances of saving face and showing steel, of limited war and superpower politics, were beyond their ken and their patience; they were boys of nineteen and twenty, dying and killing piecemeal in a war they supposed could have been ended by vaporizing Hanoi in a single big bang. They chafed at the rules of engagement dividing their world into free-fire zones, where they could shoot at anything walking, and no-fire zones, where they had to let the other side shoot first. They raged at the petit-point quibbling among the peace conferees feeling one another out in Paris. *We're in the jungle with two canteens and two C-rations*, Vitt Vittorini thought, *and they're arguing about what kind of fuckin' table they're going to talk around. If those guys were walking around the fuckin' jungle, they'd forget the shape of the table and sit down right now and make peace.*

But the talks were stagnating in the spring and summer of 1969, and Charlie Company kept fighting its wandering war of attrition with no front line and no territorial objective—only the unending round of going out, seeking "contact," spilling blood, counting the dead and moving on. Fire bases came and went, Mosby and Mahone, Aachen Two and Mons Six, Bandit Hill and Holiday Inn, the lot of them running together in memory like the eight countries on a seven-day package tour of Europe. They were way stations in a war whose objective was not conquest but killing, each an obstruction in the path of the enemy and a jump-off point for hit-and-run, hide-and-seek operations against him. They seemed to the men as disposable as Dixie cups, to be seized and held only as long as the Communists seemed actively interested in capturing them. When the shooting stopped, the Americans would pull out and the enemy would walk in, dig up the refuse pit and scavenge whatever remnants of food, ammunition and radio batteries the men had left behind. Once, when the battalion abandoned a base, Charlie Company was posted in the bush to watch what happened. They had waited less than three hours before a party of NVA arrived and started digging; the poachers were fish in a barrel when the gunships came at Charlie Company's call and blew them away.

To have turned the American engagement in Vietnam into a war for real estate would have required a vastly larger army of occupation than public opinion back home would support—by some estimates a million men or more. But to the grunts on the ground, obliged to take and retake the same forlorn patches of bush two and three times over, the Army's uninterest in holding what they had won came to stand for what seemed to them the aimlessness and the endlessness of the war. Mastrogiovanni for one doubted that it made sense even to their officers, and he was right; an after-the-fall survey of the 173 surviving Army generals who had managed the war disclosed that 70 percent of them had been uncertain of what they were fighting for.

As a consequence, there was no one to explain it satisfactorily to the boys in the bunkers, and cynical theories flourished in the vacuum. They were there, they speculated, for the enrichment of the munitions makers, or the rubber companies, or the heroin traffickers, or Lyndon Johnson, or all of the above; or alternatively they were there, as Bert Kennish guessed, so that the Americans and the Russians could field-test a few new weapons without having to shoot them at each other. No other explanation seemed to them to wash, and none was offered to them. *Why are we here?* Frank Goins would wonder, homesick for piney South Georgia. *They ain't got nothin' but rice and rubber trees, so what's the battle for?*

In the absence of answers, the men had to come variously to terms with a war whose strategy reduced their mission to hunting and killing the enemy on the installment plan. *What difference does it make*, Stagnaro puzzled, *whether you kill three or four guys in an ambush? There'll be three or four more tomorrow night, and the next night, and the next.* The Army's response to them was to keep stacking up the bodies against the far-off and constantly receding day when the Communists would be bled white and would submit.

Some of them made peace with what they were doing, and some could not. Some found refuge from their anxieties and their guilts in the fact that, in most of their operations, everybody was shooting at once in the dark and nobody could surely say that it was his bullet that killed anybody. Some saw the bodies pile high and could not find shelter at all. Peter DeCarlo was only in Vietnam for two months and two days before his family got him sent home to Cambridge, Massachusetts, with a hardship discharge, but his psychic baggage was heavy with the memory of the day Charlie Company had cleaned up a bounteous harvest of bodies after a B-52 raid. They were NVA troopers, sharp and tough-looking, DeCarlo thought, and there were pictures of babies in their wallets. *They're no different than us*, DeCarlo found himself thinking. *We're in their country, and they were doing what they thought was right. What are we doing here?* he was thinking. *What am I doing here?*

The answer most men came to, with no larger purpose discernible to them, was that they were trying to survive; it was at once an accurate description of their daily lives and an armor against guilt for what survival sometimes required of them. Staying alive has been the foot soldier's first imperative on every battleground since Peloponnesus and

Agincourt, but in Vietnam, by 1968 and 1969, there were no serious competing imperatives—no follow-the-flag sense of mission or of victory, no cheers of gratitude from the delivered for their deliverance, no evidence in the news from home that their own country was behind them; nothing, that is, that seemed to them worth the forfeit of their own lives. Everything focused on the single business of counting away 365 days and making it to the freedom bird in one piece. You killed to keep from being killed; you watched your buddies' backs so they would watch yours. Heroism, in the circumstances, became a synonym for madness. *All heroes do*, George Stover thought, *is die good*.

The handmaiden of trying to survive was the fear that they would not. Even when the war slowed to second gear in the spring and summer of 1969, the Communists hunkering down under the renewed bombing and waiting for the Yankees to go home, fear was a constant, gnawing presence among them. It varied in degree from man to man and situation to situation. Some learned to sit eating their C's at the rear of the column while the men up front were in a blistering firefight; some refused to leave a movie during a rocket attack on Lai Khe because they hadn't been to a flick in months and wanted to see how it came out. But few of them were immune to fear moving through the jungle at night, in the unseen presence of an enemy who could find his way in the dark because he was home. Some never quit feeling it in the pits of their stomachs. Some got ulcers at nineteen. Some were plagued with constipation, the hangover of too many tight-assed nights out on ambush when you didn't want to foul your own position and didn't want to be even ten yards away from your buddies if the enemy attacked.

Some feared being maimed, paralyzed or blinded even more than death. Mike MacDonald and some buddies made a compact that if one of them got fucked up, the others would put him swiftly and surely out of his misery—blow his brains out, maybe, or drop a grenade beside him and run. MacDonald knew he couldn't really go through with it and sensed that the others wouldn't either, but it was important for them to preserve the assurance that they would never go home vegetables—that they had friends close and strong enough to see to that.

Mostly, they appeased their nerves by promising themselves they would survive and by developing the repertoire of tricks and dodges that made survival possible. Taras Popel and three buddies were dispatched one day with orders to secure a supply drop for a tank column—four men assigned to defend 20,000 gallons of diesel fuel, 20,000 pounds of ammunition and 5,000 pounds of miscellaneous supplies. *Christ*, Popel thought, *a twelve-year-old with a popgun could blow that whole mess sky high.* He took a carton of chocolate milk from the stockpile, wandered two hundred yards away, hid in the bush, drank the milk and went to sleep until the tank column showed up five hours later. There were equally effective and equally seditious techniques of self-preservation on night listening-post duty outside the wire. Sometimes, Tore Pearson remembered, three LP teams would head dutifully off to their scattered separate positions and then bunch up together as soon as they were out of sight, nine or twelve men in one place seeking comfort in body heat and security in numbers. "Team one?" the CO's command bunker would call.

"Okay," a voice would radio back.

"Team two?"

"We're okay."

"Team three?"

"Okay," the answer would come back, and nobody would notice that it had been the same voice each time.

The pitch of anxiety would rise, and the resort to the arts of survival would multiply, when a man was getting short and dreaming of the freedom bird home. It struck Stagnaro that a grunt's tour in 'Nam fell into a recurring three-phase cycle—a time of apprenticeship when you were constantly afraid; a middle passage when you became confident and even crazy brash as you got good at war; and a last paranoid period when you could almost taste The World and were constantly afraid again that you weren't going to get there. The folklore of the bunkers was heavy with stories about short-timers who got killed within reaching distance of their departure dates; other grunts got superstitious about being too near them on an operation, and they devised their own ways of minimizing risk. Some wangled fat-rat jobs cooking, clerking or chauffeuring officers back at Lai Khe. Some started throwing away the iodine tablets they were supposed to take every day to keep from coming down ill from contaminated water, and Doc Bowen would look the other way; you did not argue with a man convinced that he was choosing between getting sick and going home in a tin container. Some simply declared their own unilateral cease-fires. Tom Swenticky was out on an operation with some fresh new guys on his last night in the field when three enemy troopers walked right into their kill zone. He let them pass unmolested.

"Have I been dreaming or what?" a guy asked him the next morning. "Did some gooks walk through?"

"You been dreaming," Swenticky answered sharply.

"Why?"

"My last night out and all the new guys around," Swenticky replied, "and I'm going to take a chance on getting hurt?"

Some of the men survived the war by clinging to small symbols of their humanity. Conrad Quezaire, a regular-army sergeant, exchanged artificial roses with his wife when he left for 'Nam. He wore hers on his helmet through the war, against regulations, promising himself that he would bring it home to her. It wound up in tatters, but he brought it home. Taras Popel dug his own private bunkers wherever the company went and furnished them like home, with a hip flask of whiskey, a pinup in that new erotic marvel called a miniskirt, and a library of titles ranging from Desmond Morris's *The Naked Ape* to *The 1968 Porsche North America Parts Catalogue* arrayed on portable shelves. Whenever the company traveled, Popel's paraphernalia traveled with him, on his back; his rucksack got so heavy that he had to lie down on it, slip his arms through the webbing and get two buddies to help him to his feet. Mike Fetterolf had come to the war a bit of a square, an innocent from Kalamazoo who used to wear button-down shirts with his initials on the pockets, but once there, he began cultivating a whole garden of grassy attitudes. His statement on the Army life was the beach chair he hung on the back of his pack, rigged to unfold at a flick of his hand. He would hump it out to an observation post, surround himself with claymores at forty and eighty feet and sit comfortably in the shade reading Ray Bradbury stories to pass the time.

Some survived by suspending their humanity in varying degrees for the duration, hardening themselves to the things they saw and did. A streak of cruel pleasure in the killing seemed to take possession of a few of them. Joe Pentz saw one grunt bowling with the severed head of an enemy trooper, and Peter DeCarlo watched another, stoned on grass, slaughtering an ox for sport—teasing it to death, really, with two clips' worth of bullets, while the ancient Vietnamese who owned it stood by in a fit of helpless fury. There were others who cut off VC ears as trophies, as the VC had done to the American dead, and wore them dried on strings around their necks.

More often, the boys of Charlie Company grew calluses of the spirit; they had been wrenched out of time and place, shipped almost without transition from their car clubs and Pizza Huts into the middle of a war, and they did what their new circumstances told them they had to do. It was said in the bunkers that the Vietnamese believed they would not be admitted to their heaven if their bodies were mutilated, so men mutilated bodies and heaped them up at roadsides for dogs to gnaw at and for the enemy to see. It was said that wounded enemy troopers were as dangerous as rattlesnakes as long as they were breathing, so men learned to hasten death by shooting the dying. It was hard the first time for Bob Mastrogiovanni, a light-year from home in the snug Italian community of Fair Lawn, New Jersey, but he learned; you shot them in the chest, usually, and walked on without a backward glance.

You learned, or were taught by men more expert and more enthusiastic at the job. George Stover, part Shoshone Indian, was brought up tracking elk, deer and bear in the woods around Hoquiam, Washington, and the war for him was more of the same—*hunting gooks*, he thought, instead of game. It was all reaction time for Stover, gliding through the trees with your rifle in your hands, never on a sling, and shooting before you got shot at. He was scornful of the city kids who didn't know how to handle themselves, who froze in their tracks and stared when somebody stopped a bullet. *As long as it ain't me, I'm not worried*, Stover would think. *I can't afford to be.*

Stover was tough, a lean and taciturn man who seemed almost made to fight a hunt-and-kill war like 'Nam, but he, too, had to be educated in just how hard guys could get. He had wounded two Viet Cong with a grenade on an ambush one day on Thunder Road; a fellow grunt cooled one of them with a burst of M-16 fire but the other lay wounded in a ditch, and Stover was reaching down for him when a sergeant came huffing over.

"What are you doing?" the sergeant blustered. He was a lifer, a gung-ho all-Army man who loved killing gooks right up to the day he walked into an enemy machine gun and was shredded.

"Taking him prisoner," Stover told him.

"I'll show you how to take a prisoner," the sergeant said, leveling his own M-16 and emptying a twenty-round clip into the wounded man.

The sergeant walked away. The VC was somehow still breathing. A tank roared up and tried to run over him, but the ditch was too deep.

"For Christ's sake, put that guy out of his misery," a GI riding on the tank told Stover.

The VC's eyes were rolling wildly when Stover drew a bead on him and put a bullet in his head. *That's how you take a prisoner*, he thought; mostly, you didn't.

Some survived by saying no. There were numberless small acts of disobedience in a war in which career soldiers conditioned to obey orders were outnumbered by draftees who routinely questioned them. It was axiomatic in Charlie Company that officers as a class were, with very few exceptions, no damn good. Their complaints echoed the historic grievances of dog soldiers in every war against those men of rank whose caprice could mess up your day and whose mistakes could cost you your life. But the griping was intensified in Vietnam by the shuttlecock arrival and departure of line officers—the career captains trying to prove themselves in six months by the copiousness of their body counts, the fresh-out-of-school lieutenants who seemed frequently to know a lot about military etiquette and dangerously little about the craft of war. "Eight more months and dear old TKB [for Thomas Kitrick Bowen] will be out of the fucking Army," Bowen wrote his father in the spring. "I'm going to hunt for officers when I get out just to laugh and spit in their faces."

If Bowen had published his letter as a manifesto, a major fraction of the grunts of Charlie Company might have signed it. Barracks tales abounded among them about the sins of

their ordained betters—the general who hung a Purple Heart
on a rocket-damaged sign at Lai Khe and thereby debased the
medal's value for men who had earned it with their blood;
the light colonel who ordered an entire fire base floodlit in
the middle of the night so he could chopper out a jump ahead
of a rumored NVA attack; the captain who had hair clippers
and shoe polish airlifted out to some forsaken base in the
bush with orders to the men to use them. Some of the men
had admired Captain Rogers and some had resented him,
but even mixed notices were equivalent to raves for men
starting down the back slope of the war. One of Rogers's
successor COs earned a rather less ambiguous place in their
hearts by requiring them to carry a battery-powered Sharp
television set along on night operations so he could watch *I
Love Lucy* on Armed Forces Television. The men endured
his habit for a couple of weeks, wondering how long it would
take an enemy raiding party to home in on the canned laugh
track and the luminous gray glow of the screen in the dark.
Then the set got broken. *Accidentally broken*, David Brown
remembered, smiling. *Real broken. Permanently broken.*

There were premonitory whispers as well, of rebellions
more serious and reprisals more terminal than totaling the
captain's TV. The incidence of cases of men fragging their
leaders or refusing to go out on dangerous operations did
not reach critical levels until a year or so later, when the
war effort was visibly collapsing and nobody wanted to be
the last American to die in Vietnam. But stories drifted home
from the war with the boys of Charlie Company when it was
safe to tell them. There was, for one example, the time when
Mike Fetterolf by his own account drew a bead on a captain
and was starting to squeeze the trigger when something made
him jerk his rifle off line; there was, for another, the day a
sergeant ordered a grunt to check out an enemy bunker and
the grunt gutted the sergeant with a burst of M-16 fire. And
there was the time two whole platoons refused en masse to
go out on a night operation and got away with it.

The men had been out all that day, sweltering and ducking
sniper fire, and were already rubbed raw when the order
came down from battalion. A platoon from another Black
Lion company had been overrun out on an ambush operation; they had pulled out fast, leaving behind two bodies, a
radio and some unexploded claymore mines. It was Charlie

Company's not uncommon lot to go back and pick up the pieces, except that, this one time, they wouldn't go. The choppers were already on the way to collect them when the men passed the word up through their sergeants and lieutenants to the captain that it was no deal—it was night, the area was hot and the VC were probably waiting in the dark to blow them away with their own claymores. Their view of that prospect, simply put, was *go screw yourself*, Bob Bowers remembered, and the Army accepted it. The drop was put off until daylight the next day.

There were few such general strikes against the war in 1969; the American effort was a composite of private wars and resistance to it was a mosaic of small mutinies. Once, a platoon from Charlie Company was ordered out on a night ambush six kilometers beyond their base in a teeming rain. The men didn't want to go. Their will broke under the CO's threat to courtmartial the platoon and squad leaders, but they won anyway, marching obediently off into the night and hiding in a gully no more than two hundred meters from the perimeter wire. Their respect for authority, and their unquestioning obedience to it, were lower still in the presence of the interchangeable lieutenants who kept appearing and disappearing among them. They husbanded their affection for those who lived and thought like them and who shared their common overriding interest in staying alive. For those who insisted on the style of command and the techniques of war they had learned at OCS, it was commonplace in an army of survival-minded conscripts to have one's orders questioned, politely the first time, more forcefully thereafter. "You dumb shit" was a preferred form of address to brownbars in Charlie Company. "We're gonna go out here and kill us a bunch of gooks," one of them told Omega Harris on his first day in the field, and Harris answered, "You want to kill a bunch of them you go right ahead, but you're goin' by yourself, because my people and me ain't goin'."

The don't-tread-on-me spirit spread with the slow dying of the war and moved men from bitching about it privately to questioning it openly. Bob Bowers was the paradigmatic Charlie Company grunt, wiry, tough and insubordinate, nicknamed Bowser for the bulldog ferocity he brought to a firefight in the bush or a free-for-all with the MPs at Lai Khe. He had grown up in the western Pennsylvania hamlet of

Hardyville, the youngest of three sons of a man who had worked his way up from mill hand to metallographer. One brother grew up to be a teacher, the other a preacher; it was left accordingly to Bowers as baby brother to be the wild one in the family at a time when being wild still meant drinking beer, chasing girls and burning the highways in a hot '57 Chevy. He quit being serious, he reckoned later, after the eleventh grade and busted out of college after four shaky terms. But he went willingly to war nevertheless; he came out of a time and place in which children still pledged allegiance and prayed the Lord's Prayer in public school and in which young pulses pounded at John Kennedy's summons to ask what you could do for your country.

Like most of the young men who answered that summons in Vietnam, Bowers assumed that they were going over to win; the losers were not yet coming home to the Hardyvilles in wheelchairs and body containers, and it took Bowers a while to discover that winning was not what the war was about. Once he did, his soft speech and his cherubic look masked what had become the soul of a rebel. His battle flags were the prescription sunglasses and the rakish bush hat he wore everywhere. He needed them both—the shades because the glare of the sun bothered his eyes and the bush hat because his helmet had been giving him headaches since that day when a misfired grenade had bounced off the back of his skull. But the gear looked to some of his officers like badges of defiance, and they didn't like it.

Bowers was sitting out on a mound of dirt one day when a major spied the sunglasses and called out, "Hey, what's with these?"

Bowers stared silently back at him.

"Hey," the major repeated, pointing to his eyes.

Bowers picked up his M-16 and cocked it. The major went away.

Some of the men who could not similarly declare their independence of the war found their own routes out of it, at escalating degrees of desperation. The Army then was trading early discharges to men who agreed to extend their tours in 'Nam through a thirteenth month. The deal looked good to George Stover, who didn't want to put in six more months in khaki back home, so he signed up and then set out to stall the thirteenth month away out of combat. He had gone ragged in Charlie Company, marinating his frustrations in booze off-duty and on, and had finally transferred out to the 199th Light Infantry Brigade when the Big Red One went home. When his time ran down to those last tacked-on thirty days, he began hanging around the brigade's base camp seeing a doctor one day, a dentist the next, an Army recruiter the next—anything that would sop up another day's survival time off the line. When he ran out of dodges, he reported to the field.

"Get your stuff and go out with this squad," his CO told him, but Stover had deliberately left everything from his rifle to his rucksack back at home base. The CO was furious. Stover demanded to see the inspector general, knowing the request could not be refused under Army regulations, and was on the next chopper out. He was court-martialed for his impertinence and busted a grade, from E-5 to E-4, but the time he bought meant more to him than the stripe he lost. He wound up spending one last night in the jungle, and then it was time to go home.

A less inventive or more strung-out man might take more drastic measures. You could shoot yourself in the foot, the million-dollar wound that could put you back in The World with only a bit of a limp; there was a luckless grunt called West Virginia who tried it, aiming for his toe, but he hit his arch instead and his foot had to be amputated.

Or you could reenlist to come off the line, as Skip Sommer did, or Cowboy Rosson. Halfway through his tour, Rosson had gone off on a gin-soaked five-day tear through Taipei on R&R, trying to appease his fraying nerves. It didn't help; he came back shaky and got shakier when he saw the company, reduced by attrition from 120 to 68 able-bodied men and beginning to clot up with too many raw twinks. Rosson didn't like the feel of it, so he traded three more years out of his life for a job in the rear fixing trucks at Cam Ranh Bay. Once there, he tried to scrape the rust off his rodeo skills by practicing roping a dummy calf. But his competitive edge was already going, and his dream along with it. Most of the time he kept himself dependably anesthetized, waking up to a beer in the morning and chasing it with whiskey and Sprite all night.

Booze was a common anodyne for the boys in Charlie Company; Sea-Tac Olson's family sent him regular refills of

Jack Daniel's decanted into plastic baby bottles to avoid breakage, but usually what was available was Carling's beer or 45 whiskey, a local sauce so violent you didn't even have to wait till morning for your hangover.

Drugs were an alternate and readily accessible route to oblivion. The heroin plague had not yet taken hold during Charlie Company's tour in the war; that came later, in company with the epidemics of fragging, mutiny and desertion, the symptoms of the final demoralization of the American effort. But every ville from Lai Khe to the boonies had a mama-san who would sell you two breadloaf-sized bags of marijuana for $20 when it cost that much an ounce in The World, and sometimes it came laced with opium for its heightened mellowing power. The drift toward harder drugs was welling up, moreover, among the support troops at Charlie Company's rear. The stores of morphine began disappearing from their lockers at Lai Khe, and there were days when a grunt screaming in agony out in the bush would have to make do with Darvon or nothing.

There was the further pain-killer called R&R, for rest and recreation—or, as the men preferred, I&I, for intoxication and intercourse, which composed the usual program. Married men typically rendezvoused with their wives in Hawaii; the unattached headed for various liberty towns in Southeast Asia—Bangkok for the sex, Tokyo or Hong Kong for the bistros and bright lights, Sydney for the society of white people speaking English. For most of them, it was like coming out of a dungeon and blinking into the daylight. *Everything is in color*, Harry Foxwell thought, seeing the sights of Australia; in 'Nam, everything from the foliage to the Army-issue underwear was green.

It did not work out for all of them. Kit Bowen, for one, hired a girl out of a nightclub in Bangkok at $70 for the week and almost immediately regretted his choice. He wanted to shed her. She wouldn't leave. He tried to off-load her on a taxi driver and, later, a bellman at his hotel. She clung tight; to go back to the nightclub without him would have entailed a crushing loss of face. So Bowen unhappily endured her company. They posed for a picture together, a boa constrictor twined around both their necks, but behind his half-lidded eyes and his man-of-the-worldly smile, he was wishing he were back in 'Nam.

A similar pang of displacement pursued Omega Harris through Honolulu, though for considerably different reasons. He was with his Jean with a fat bankroll in his pocket, "ready to buy up this town," he told her, with her on his arm. They did the night spots, all the ladies checking Harris out when he would drop a big bill on the bartender and tell him to keep the change, and one early morning Nat King Cole's brother and his wife bought the Harrises breakfast after their act. It was good, it was nice, but the first time a car backfired behind him, Harris hit the dirt and messed up a new black mohair suit. He didn't like the way people looked at him—*staring at me*, he thought, *like I was a disease*—and he didn't feel right being away from his men. The woman who ran the little hotel he stayed at offered him a beer, and he blurted, "Don't be trying to show me gratitude—think about my troops. I'm *here*. Nobody shooting at me."

But for most it was a sweet time and for some, the sweetest in a lifetime; the only bad thing about R&R for them was that it ended and you had to go back to the war. That journey could be harder even than the flights that had delivered them to 'Nam in the first place, since, this time, they knew where they were going. *A bummer*, David Bean thought, staring dismally at the bulkhead in front of him on the Pan Am jet back from Bangkok. He had hired girls at $12 for twenty-four hours and a cabbie at $40 for a whole week; he had bunked in the no-questions-asked comfort of the Imperial Hotel, screwing all night and lolling in the pool all day; he had dutifully checked out the gold Buddhas on the tourist circuit and had sampled the headier pleasures of a nickel bag of fine Thai weed. It had been a week in a hedonist's heaven, the biggest in his life before or since, and all of it for $300. But the days ran through his fingers like sand, and then he was sitting in a cramped bulkhead seat, feeling scared, depressed and nearly physically ill. *Shit*, he was thinking, *I'm going back. I got to be a fool to go back, I really don't want to go back, but I'm going back*.

Some of the men found peace in prayer and comfort in the feeling that, if they had survived another day and another firefight, God must have been watching out for them. Some found no solace anywhere and finally surrendered to the lunacy they saw in the war. Sometimes it would come and go in little gusts; a guy would jump up on a bunker and scream and rage and throw things, or maybe pick a pointless fight with his best buddy. Sometimes it would gnaw at a man's innards until, figuratively and sometimes literally, he was bleeding inside. There was officially no such illness as shell shock or combat fatigue in Vietnam, the Army supposing that men who had problems in the war had had problems before they came to it. But grunts knew better. A guy would quit eating, Stagnaro remembered, and his eyes would go blank when you were talking to him, and sometimes you would hear him crying in the middle of the night.

Sometimes a man would become the madness of the war made flesh and would explode. Kit Bowen's spoiled R&R wasn't supposed to have been his in the first place; it belonged to a black grunt in the second platoon who had been in-country without respite for eight or nine months to Bowen's three. But Bowen had been overheard once too often bitching about whichever captain was then in charge of Charlie Company. It got back to the captain, and one day a lieutenant told Bowen, "Doc, you got a free R&R going. The captain thinks you should get out of the jungle. It's getting to you."

Because it was a given rather than an earned R&R, Bowen couldn't choose his port of call; it specified Bangkok, and though he preferred Australia like most of the guys, he snapped it up without asking questions. He didn't know it had been spoken for until he wandered into the bunny club at Lai Khe for a beer during a stand-down, and somebody said, "Doc, we're gonna have to tell you this—you took a guy's R&R in platoon two." *Oh, no*, Bowen groaned inwardly; he knew the guy, too, a good guy who had been on the captain's ass at least as much as Bowen himself. He went outside, walked down a couple of hooches and found the dude.

"Hey, man," Bowen said apologetically.

"Doc, it's okay. It's between me and the captain," the dude said. He had been drinking.

"Hey, man," Bowen pressed, "I had no idea—"

"There ain't no straightening it out," the guy said. "The orders are already through. I know you had nothin' to do with it."

Bowen left the dude to his bottle and went back to the club. Some of the boys were drinking coffee and listening to a sergeant major with a government-issue soul doing a dead-serious John Wayne about what a fine group of fighting men they were, and every once in a while somebody would throw a chair or hoot, "God bless America!" They had been kidding for a couple of hours when they heard a sudden chatter of rifle fire close by. Guys jumped up, popping light bulbs to black out the place and running for the door.

They discovered then that the black grunt had tripped out on whiskey and rage, jammed a full clip of bullets into his M-16 and burst into the officers' quarters, looking for the captain and yelling, "I'm gonna blow his ass away!" He had found the captain's door and kicked it open. The captain was off showering. The grunt put his M-16 on automatic and sprayed the captain's empty cot with bullets. Then he careened on to the mail room, grabbed the first person he saw—*this pudgy little mail clerk*, Bowen remembered, *who'd never seen a rifle in his life*—and held him hostage with a gun at his head, demanding the captain as ransom.

The MPs came roaring over to put out the fire, but the men figured it was a family affair; they scattered to their hooches, got their rifles and held the MPs at bay while one of their own, a lieutenant, went inside to talk to the grunt. The grunt trusted the lieutenant and surrendered first his rifle, then his hostage and finally himself. He disappeared after that. The word spread through Charlie Company that he was back in The World doing seventeen years at Leavenworth. Goodbye, war.

"MY DEAR WIFE...
I'VE KILLED"

"My Dear Wife," Bert Kennish wrote in September when the company stood down from a defense position called The French Fort outside the village of Ben Chua. "I love you so much, Faye! This has been a nasty 3 day operation. We have gotten the shaft all the way through. I've been pissed off and so has the platoon, but your wonderful letters have cheered me so that all is well."

Kennish had only been in Vietnam for a month and a half, but he was lonely and the war was chafing at his spirit. He was a son of the conservative West, a chunky man with an open face and eyes that smiled from behind his outsized glasses. He subscribed wholeheartedly to the announced purpose of the war, which he understood to be stopping Communism, and he accepted his presence in it as a test of his ego and his manhood. But it had quit making sense to him almost the moment his inbound jet set down in Bien Hoa, and on the breathless advice of the cabin crew, he hit the ground running for cover in a ditch with the rest of the men. *Shit*, he thought, *I'm going to get it the first day*. It was only later that he learned that the airport hadn't come under enemy fire for months.

That was Vietnam for Kennish, a fantasy war waged against shadows in the South because the constraints of domestic and international politics would not let them take it north and win it. He was a lieutenant, older, at twenty-six, than most of the boys of Charlie Company, and so was obliged by age and station to make the war intelligible to the platoon of grunts under his command. But Kennish could not explain it to himself, and like many of the dragooned civilians who served as junior officers in Vietnam, he felt himself slipping loose from his moorings to the Army's master class. When his men were pissed off, as he wrote Faye, he was pissed off. He was becoming one with them.

The war for Kennish was being assigned forty-four men on paper and counting himself lucky when he could put twenty-seven or thirty in the field. It was hitting the dirt under a hailstorm of rifle and machine-gun fire and discovering that it was coming from another American platoon taking target practice in the jungle a klick away. It was being reduced to a single machine gun because he never had enough hands to carry the usual two and then having the one gun that was available break down for want of replacement parts. Kennish wrote his father in a fury about that, and his father, in a matching fury, scorched their congressman's ear. There was an inquiry, but by the time it labored through the layered military bureaucracy, Kennish had been reassigned off the line as a desk officer and found himself required to compose an official Army answer to his own complaint.

The war for Kennish was a picture he could not erase from his mind or his dreams: the body of a young grunt lying riddled and naked in a trail, bled whiter than the sugary white sand beneath him. He was the first dead American Kennish had seen in the war, the first in a steady trickle of boys who seemed to him to be dying in the service of political leaders who did not dare win and career officers accordingly off on their own personal paths of glory. The kid was from another outfit, a dog handler who had been assigned to work with Charlie Company on an operation. The day had been blistery hot, and the soft, powdery sand had slowed their march to a laborious slog. They had paused for a break, the kid sitting alongside the trail with his German shepherd, and when a hit-and-run party of NVA troopers opened up on them with an automatic rifle, he never had a chance to move.

The enemy was gone by the time Kennish and his men scrambled forward to help. The kid lay in the trail where he had fallen. The dog had stood guard at his side, not letting anyone near the body, until some of the men dragged him away. The medics had moved in then and had pulled all the kid's clothes off to get at his wounds. There were nine of them when Kennish quit counting, each ringed by a little aureole of blood. But what Kennish could not forget was how waxy white the kid looked, whiter than the sand turning red beneath his nude body. All his blood was gone, Kennish thought, feeling numb; there couldn't have been a drop left in him.

"Faye Marie Dreier Kennish," he wrote his wife. "Well, I like that name too. Oh Faye I love you so much!"

He was missing her, badly. In the daytime he was planning their R&R together in Hawaii; at night he was dreaming vividly of seeing her and making love to her again. There had been so little time. They had met while Kennish was working unhappily in a junior personnel management job in Victoria, Texas, and she had been about the only unambiguously good thing that had happened to him there. He had worked his way through Colorado State University and been accepted for the Peace Corps, but a chemical company recruiter had intercepted him. "Leave the Peace Corps stuff to the hippies and the troublemakers," the guy had told him. "Get a job and pay taxes and support those people if you want to do good things for your country." Kennish went off to Peace Corps camp anyway, but he was pure Middle America, the straight-arrow son of a land-leveling contractor from the Colorado farm country, and he felt out of place there. *I guess the guy's right*, he figured after three ill-at-ease weeks, so he quit the corps and signed up with the chemical company instead.

The company posted him to Victoria for a year and a half in what struck him as a pigeonhole job, hiring and firing for a plant under construction there. He was courting Faye when he signed up for the Army's cannon-fodder officer-training program in February 1968, and between his advanced-infantry course and OCS, they were married.

When he went to 'Nam a year later, she moved in with another war wife in Austin and took work as a secretary at Lyndon Johnson's television station. She was safe in The World, but life was as lonely for her there as it was for Kennish in the bunkers. She felt it even among friends, as if Bert's being in the war were a source of embarrassment or pain. *Like when someone in your family dies*, she thought; *people don't know exactly what to say, so they don't say anything.* So she kept Vietnam mostly to herself, saving for their R&R—Bert wanted her to bring $1,400 for the week so they wouldn't have to watch pennies—and worrying whether he was going to make it.

"In my last letter," Kennish wrote, "I may have mentioned that we are supposed to use 'mechanized' ambushes (nice way to say booby traps) now. Well, our first night out Sgt. Ayers and I put one out about 200m from our AP site on the same trail we were on. About 200 hours it blew and 6 [radio code for the captain] wanted us to check out the area for bodies in the dark but decided it was too far from us. I was glad of that! In the morning we found 3 big blood pools, but no bodies. I'm sure we killed 2 and possibly all 3. There were tracks of 2 people leading away—obviously carrying the bodies. So I've killed, but it wasn't like pulling the trigger or pushing the button. I was glad the bodies weren't there. I was rather sick about it, but it would have been worse, if they had been there, because the one who tripped the wire must have been blown to bits. Enough."

He had had enough himself by then. He had seen death and had killed, and he had come to think of the American war machine as a mismanaged and muscle-bound parody of itself—a purposeless enterprise that would scramble a covey of $16 million jets to sink a bamboo boatload of peasant soldiers and granted its real enemy sanctuary behind some artificial border. But there was never enough; it never stopped. He was back at The French Fort one idle afternoon in October, standing barechested and barefoot on a dirt parapet with David Brown and snapping pictures of some F-4 jets pounding an NVA emplacement a mile or so across the river. The jet pilots were putting on a show for the legs, their haughty term for infantrymen; they dropped straight out of the clouds and roared low over the heads of the grunts—so low that one of them sheared off the whip antenna atop The French Fort's fifty-foot-high observation tower.

The plane was *too* low when it loosed a single five-hundred-pound napalm bomb; the men could see it separate from the jet and tumble end over end straight in their direction. *That will never make it across the river*, Kennish thought, surprised at his calm. *I should have gotten a shot of it releasing from the plane*, he thought, still calm. *That bomb is going to hit us*, he thought, and he wasn't calm anymore; he was scrambling for a bunker and peeping out as the napalm blew in a friendly village barely fifty meters beyond their perimeter. A hooch went up in a ball of flame, and a woman and a couple of kids came running out of its suffocating core, the burning jelly charring the soles of their feet black. One of the men hurdled the concertina wire at The French Fort and pulled them screaming out of the fire, but there was no way to put out napalm; it was made to cling to human flesh and keep eating inward until it burned itself out.

"My men," Kennish wrote Faye, "think the war is useless and senseless."

When he spoke of his men, he meant himself, whether he understood that just yet or not; the means and the ends of the war were beyond his comprehension no less than theirs. He had reached that dangerous point in the life-cycle of an officer at which he had begun to think of the Viet Cong not as enemies but as victims, of their own government and his as well. The VC had all but disappeared from the field in Charlie Company's AO anyway, with the progressive North Vietnamization of the war on the other side. Kennish still believed in stopping Communism, but the Communists were in North Vietnam and the Americans couldn't go after them. Instead, he thought, *you got to stop right at the edge and say, "Okay, you guys over there—"* It was bullshit, he thought, a bullshit war and a bullshit Army. Faye had heard about men reenlisting to come off the line and, in her fear for Kennish's safety, had written to ask if he had thought about doing such a deal for himself. He had, he wrote back, but the offer wasn't open to officers and he wouldn't accept it if it were. "I wouldn't put up another day in the army more than I have to no matter how dangerous and tiring this gets. NO WAY."

So he stayed in the line for the five-month duration of his war, an officer by rank, a grunt at heart. On his last day in the jungle he led his platoon out in the wake of the B-2's on a bomb-damage survey, the lieutenant designated to succeed him shagging along with him to learn the ropes. They had walked down into one crater and started up and out when they heard the rattle of AK-47 fire. The men caught in the open jumped back down, all but the new lieutenant. They guessed at first that he had been killed out in no-man's-land, and when they heard him crying during a lull in the firefight, they were sure he had been wounded.

So one of Kennish's grunts, Bill Ayers, went over the top to get him. It was, Kennish thought, the bravest thing he had seen—Ayers lobbing a couple of grenades ahead of him, scuttling into a storm of bullets and hauling the lieutenant's prostrate body back into the crater. It was the bravest thing Kennish had seen, and it was for nothing; the lieutenant hadn't been hit at all. He had frozen in fear at the lip of the crater and had lain there, weeping, with his hands on his helmet till Ayers came for him.

Some of the men wanted to kill him and might have, Kennish thought, if he hadn't been reassigned out of Charlie Company as soon as they got back. Kennish felt sorry for the lieutenant; he remembered how he had got separated from his rifle the first time *he* had come under enemy fire and had tripped on a log and fallen ingloriously on his face trying to retrieve it. But he understood the anger of the grunts; they lived in the mud at the bottom of the war, and, he thought, he was one of them.

"I love you so much Faye!" Kennish wrote. "I probably shouldn't tell you all this stuff. Don't worry about me too much. I keep my head down and my platoon takes care of me." He remembered to praise her for the peanut brittle she had sent and to say they didn't have to spend the whole $1,400 on R&R—he just wanted it there if they needed it. "All my love," he wrote at the end. "Bert."

"PEOPLE DIE IN TECHNICOLOR"

The freedom birds were beginning to fly back to The World by mid-1969, but men were still dying in Vietnam, and still having to live with death as a presence in their young lives. *People die in Technicolor*, George Goldstein thought; it was almost unbearably vivid to witness. Some of them would weep at the death of a buddy, and some would discover that they could not; some vowed never to get emotionally entangled with anyone ever again; some thanked God or blind chance that it had been somebody else who had bought the farm and not themselves. J.C. Wilson wanted to cry sometimes, but there was never time, and his own hard Tennessee boyhood had bred the capacity for tears mostly out of him. When dying and death would crowd in on him, he might jump up and holler a primal holler, or throw a punch at the biggest guy around, or maybe just find Omega Harris or somebody to talk to and work it out. But mostly he tried to blot the sight and stench of death out of his mind. *You try not to think about it*, he mused. *You try to forget what happened to a guy and you try to keep it from happening to you. You got to get a straight head again, 'cause you have to just live from one day to the next. You have to survive.*

Except they couldn't forget; there was too much death, *all uncalled for*, Wilson thought, all without identifiable military purpose or human meaning. In May, Rick Garcia bought it, and while the Army freeze-framed his dying in an attitude of heroism, the grunts who were with him knew it was for nothing. He had sat up in a bunker with Joe Pentz the night before, Pentz smoking a joint and listening to Garcia chatter over the latest news and snapshots from his wife, Sharlene. They had been sweethearts at Live Oak High in Morgan Hill, California, and had married only the June before. "If you want to go to Mexico or Canada, I can be packed in an hour," Sharlene had told him when he was drafted. But Garcia was the macho sort, a handsome blend of his father's Mexican and his mother's Dutch-Irish bloodlines; he had smiled the smile that reminded Sharlene of the young Richard Burton and had gone off to the Army. "Don't be a hero. I'd rather have you home again," she pleaded later, putting him on the plane to 'Nam. He smiled again and was gone.

A bare five months later, Charlie Company was back at Thunder Three, working in tandem with Colonel Patton's Armored Cav. Some of the men didn't much like being around tanks; their noisiness drew the enemy to them, and their bulk made them easy targets. Some didn't like tank crewmen either; they seemed too much into the war, too fond of the blood and the killing. Once, Peter DeCarlo watched a tank gunner train his machine gun on a single enemy trooper and pour rounds into him, hanging his body up on the stream of bullets like a rag on a clothesline. The man's arms, legs and head were flying apart, but his body stayed upright on the stream of lead. The gunner was laughing at the spectacle. DeCarlo felt ill. *How much?* he was thinking. *How much?*

But some of the men liked the tankers and even envied them a little for their swagger—for that hard-drinking, hard-driving, rough-as-a-corncob machismo they brought to what for infantryman was a belly-down, dirt-eating war. They put on a bit of a show for the grunts that May morning, a whole line of them roaring down Highway 13 in an open-throttle "thunder run" meant to detonate any hidden enemy mines. When the way was clear, Garcia and some men from his squad clambered aboard three of the tanks for a slower passage over the same ground. They had covered only a short stretch of roadway when they ran into a storm of rifle and rocket fire. The tank Garcia was on lurched suddenly into reverse, the turret shot around in a 180-degree half-circle, and men were tumbling off into the churned-up dirt along the edge of the highway.

The citation that accompanied Rick Garcia's Silver Star recorded that he had seen another GI wobbling in a daze along the highway and had broken cover under intense enemy fire to knock him out of the way of the tank. He saved his buddy, the Army said, just as a fragment of enemy shrapnel snuffed out his own life. The grunts who were with him didn't see that part. It was Garcia, in their recollection, who had fallen into the path of the tank. They didn't know if he was wounded or not, but they saw him disappear under the treads—*squashed like a bug*, Mike Fetterolf remembered, with his blood splotching the ground red for twenty feet around.

In January 1970, the Big Red One was nearing the end of its 1,656-day run in Vietnam, but Bobby Eugene Jones seemed to know he wasn't going to make it to the plane. Some of his family thought he might have known it when he left for 'Nam in the first place. He came from a large, warm clan, one of eleven children of the police chief of the all-black town of Princeville on the North Carolina coastal plain. The Army had drafted him out of the carton department at Burlington Industries, put him through infantry training and, in July 1969, sent him his orders for Vietnam. His sister Elizatia Andrews threw a barbecue picnic for him at her place the day before he was to leave, but the gaiety was forced and Jones moved through it with his eyes blank and his mind in Vietnam. The next day Elizatia took him to the bus station in Rocky Mount. She was crying. He laughed, but after she left him he called his mother and asked her to send someone for him—he wasn't going that day. *They'll come looking for him*, she thought miserably. She told him to wait for the next bus, and he did.

Jones called her from Tokyo on R&R on Christmas Eve and wrote her every day he could. His letters were usually in the short, determinedly chirpy voice that grunts affected for their mothers—"Hi, Mom, just counting the days before I'll be home"—and sometimes he enclosed part of his pay for her to deposit in his savings account. But one day in January he sent a last note asking her to send him a form card from the bank so he could have the account switched to her name. That night he mentioned what he had done to his buddies James Green and Leroy Pringle; the three of them and a white pal, Barney Cranford, made up a little Carolina caucus in Charlie Company, and they would seek each other out when something was eating at them. What was eating at Jones was an advanced case of point man's paranoia. He had been walking point too long, alone and exposed at the head of a squad. Pringle and Green had been trying to help him get off it, without success, and he was scared. He told them he felt like something was going to happen to him.

Jones was out on patrol the next morning, walking point as usual, when he stepped on a tripwire and set off a booby trap; it blew away both his legs, one above the knee, the other below. Nobody had told him his legs were gone when Green went to see him at the field hospital in Lai Khe. He was conscious and in good spirits, even laughing. All he remembered was having seen the wire too late, and he wanted to know what had happened. Green ducked his questions; he hadn't been there himself, he said, so he didn't know what went down. They said goodbye, and ten days later Green heard that Jones had died in a military hospital in Okinawa. *He must have found out*, Green thought; he found out his legs were gone, and it killed him.

THE DYING OF THE LIGHT

He came in out of the field in his sweat-stiffened fatigues, his cracking combat boots, his crushed bush hat and his brand-new moustache, and his own kid brother Michel didn't even recognize him at first. As far as Sergeant David Rioux was concerned, Private Michel Rioux shouldn't have been in Vietnam at all. There had been a letter that he was trying to talk the Army into sending him over, and when Lieutenant Kennish called David in off a patrol that December morning in 1969, there was a radio message waiting at Fire Base Kien that Michel was in fact in-country. But David hadn't quite believed it; there was the Army rule that two brothers could not be required to serve at the same time in the same war zone, and David had thought Michel safely bound for Germany or Korea instead. He had hitched into Long Binh anyway by chopper, plane and truck to check it out and was hiking toward the receiving center when he felt a tap on his shoulder. He wheeled. Michel was standing there, smiling, and David was sore.

"What are you doing here?" he demanded, and he didn't want or wait for an answer; he was scolding Michel for having come, and lecturing him that one brother in the war was enough, and bludgeoning him with what it would do to their mother to have them both there, and insisting that they march off forthwith to see the judge advocate general's man and get him sent home.

Michel stood patiently listening until David paused for breath. "I'm here for the same reason you are," he said then, and the argument was over.

It was over because the Rioux brothers knew each other and knew why they were in Vietnam; to have pressed his case further, David suddenly understood, would have been to argue against his own most basic beliefs. He and Michel

127

were the second and third of the six children of a Maine carpenter and his wife, born a bare fifteen months apart and raised together in the strongly conservative Catholicism of their French Canadian forebears. Each had grown up thinking that he might have a vocation for the priesthood. Michel, the younger and heartier of the two, discovered in a succession of Catholic boarding schools that he did not; he settled for his diploma and, fourteen days after receiving it, joined the Army. David, the older and more cerebral, had by then made it through a year as a seminarian at Assumption College in Worcester, Massachusetts, but he did not like the liberalizing currents loose in the Church and the seminary after Vatican II—*radical turns*, he thought, *that I don't want anything to do with*. His piety survived but his dream of the priesthood did not. He, too, dropped out, or, more accurately, transferred out to the University of Maine as an English major, and he, too, volunteered for the draft.

It was a decision both brothers took without doubt as to its rightness or hesitation as to what might become of them in the war. Most of the boys of Charlie Company had gone off to the Army and the fighting with some trepidation, and some few felt torn by the arguments of their contemporaries back home that the war was unjust. The Rioux brothers suffered no such torments of the spirit; they went to Vietnam because they believed in the war and were prepared to die for their beliefs. Their certitude was rooted deeply in the patriotism they had learned at home—*If they'd given our father a weapon*, Michel Rioux thought, *he'd be here, to*— and even more powerfully in the teachings of the Church on service to God and to the common good. *You can't separate morality and patriotism*, Michel thought, and the Rioux brothers did not. They had heard the great debate then raging as to whether or not the war was just; they had felt the evidence too inconclusive and themselves too young, David at nineteen and Michel at eighteen, to decide the question, so they gave the benefit of the doubt to their government. For Michel, it was enough that the nation's leadership had committed America to battle. For David, the process of ratiocination was a rather more complex passage to precisely the same conclusion: It was his duty to God and country to serve.

So they left for Vietnam, David in September and Michel

in December, armored by faith and the conviction that the cause was right—that they were there to help deliver the South Vietnamese from the forces of darkness seated in Hanoi, Moscow and Beijing. They understood but were not deterred by the possibility that they could be maimed or killed in the war. "Maybe I won't see any of this again," David told his parents, leaving home in Lewiston and trying to fix the neighborhood in his mind's eye. It was for him a statement of fact, not of fear or self-pity; his duty was more important to him than his life.

His argument with Michel at Long Binh, each urging the other to go home, was accordingly no contest. They wound up standing side by side and shooting a picture of their own boots, David's combat-worn and Michel's brand-new, in token of their decision to stick out the war together. They negotiated Michel an assignment to Charlie Company and served together there. Michel in mortars and David leading a rifle squad, until the Black Lions rotated home early in 1970. They migrated afterward to the Second Mechanized and, later still, the 101st Airborne, the war knitting them closer than they had ever been.

They worried about that sometimes—worried over how one might respond if the other were hurt or killed. They *had* to worry about it the day Bobby Eugene Jones got his legs blown off by a booby trap. They were moving in separate columns. David in the left-hand file and Michel humping a radio on the right, when a second booby trap went off, this one apparently rigged from a 155 mm artillery round with a killing radius of fifty meters in any direction. The force of the blast knocked Michel flying into a crater, his radio a ruin, and in the agonizing time before word came back that he had escaped without serious injury, David had to decide what to do: dash to his brother's side or stay, as duty demanded, with his own men. Duty won; David stayed at his station, praying for his brother's safety and knowing without having to ask that Michel would have approved.

He would have approved, David thought, because they were fighting for reasons larger than their own survival. They were not immune to the frustration rampant among their comrades in arms about the way the war was being fought. *Had we started in the Mekong Delta*, Michel thought afterward, *with the First Division, the Fourth, the Ninth, the*

101st all on line and just walked north, we could have ended the war in a year, and there would have been nothing behind us that we didn't want behind us.

But the war as it was fought took on a discouraging unreality, for them as for the others. Its epiphany was the day Spiro Agnew dropped down into Fire Base Kien in a Chinook helicopter, trailed by the first reporters David Rioux had ever seen in the field. Agnew stood out in the dusty heat in a formal gray suit assuring the men that they weren't alone—that no matter what they read in the stateside papers, "The people back home are pretty darn proud of you and what you're doing over here." The Army had tidied up the base for Agnew's perusal, had ringed it with armor for his security and, as a final precaution, had ordered the men standing guard on the bunkers to leave their ammo below and carry their M-16s empty. The men protested this last and won. But they remained props in a surrealist portrait of the Vietnam effort as it never was; they were at once the defenders of a base so hermetically secured that they didn't need bullets and the prosecutors of a war so unpopular that they could not be trusted with them within range of their own Vice President.

The show struck even David Rioux as cosmetic nonsense, and he believed both in the government and in the war. He and Michel were in fact feeling increasingly lonely in their conviction that what they were doing was right in the sight of God and country; in the armor of their faith, they saw a higher purpose in it that their buddies seemed not to grasp and the Army seemed unable to explain. Bitching about the war had become fashionable among the men, David thought, and he took to probing at their discontent with an improvised foxhole catechism.

"If you feel that way about the war, why are you here?"

"Well, because I don't want to go to jail."

"Why not, if you believe it's wrong?"

"Well, because my parents would have been ashamed of me if I'd gone to jail." Or my girl friend. Or my wife.

So, Rioux thought, they had preferred the risk of war to the disappointment of their loved ones; there was *something* they valued more than their own lives after all, but the military had been unable to raise that impulse from the level of pride to the higher plane of civic duty and national purpose and so had ceded the field to the complainers.

Fashion always governs, he thought unhappily, and he was still rebelling against it when one of the men got a letter from his girl friend's girl friend in Detroit, wanting to strike up a correspondence with somebody serving in Vietnam. She believed in the war, she wrote; it was right and she wanted to thank the men for what they were doing. Her letter passed from hand to hand in David's platoon, the men treating it as a bit of a joke. He was afraid their badinage might find its way back to her, so he wrote her himself saying that he shared her beliefs and that she shouldn't feel that everybody in the war was against it. He didn't sign that first letter to her, since hers had not been addressed to him, but she sought out his name and wrote him again. Their correspondence continued and grew more personal. In those reveries he permitted himself, Rioux began dreaming of settling in Detroit after the war, enrolling in Wayne State University—she was a student there—and exploring whether their friendship might warm into love and marriage.

He could not have known it then, but he would never see her. In April, he and Michel had moved on to the airborne, this time at least temporarily in separate companies; David was still out in the bush, Michel in the relative security of a base known unfortunately as the Alamo on a hilltop high over the South China Sea. They hoped to be reunited, and when they parted at Bien Hoa, David promised to get the paperwork started. Not long after, his new outfit was dispatched north to and perhaps across the Cambodian border—a probe, David thought later, preparing the ground for the massive allied "incursion" that would so divide America a few weeks later. A flight of helicopters deposited them on a hilltop pocked with abandoned bunkers. They were still inspecting the property when David Rioux nearly stepped on a Bouncing Betty mine—a nasty little psy-war contrivance specifically designed to pop up out of the ground on contact, explode waist-high and blow a man's genitals away.

They had been working the area uneventfully for two or three days when, near dusk on a Sunday evening, a lieutenant led Rioux and the other squad leaders into the jungle to assign them ambush positions for the night. Rioux went back to the main body of men for his rucksack, then headed out alone for a closer second look at his squad's spot. The sun was sinking behind the trees to his left, night was falling fast, and he chose a straight route through the knee-high brush into the trees instead of retracing the more roundabout path they had taken with the lieutenant.

He had made it only part of the way when he felt something catch at the front of one leg. *A vine*, he thought at first, but then it came over him that it might be the tripwire of a booby trap. He knew about booby traps; he had set them himself and knew what they could do. He stopped dead still in midstride, left foot forward, right foot back. He understood later that that had been a mistake—that if he had kept on going he might have made it at least a few steps beyond ground zero. But he didn't know in that split second whether he had tripped the wire; he didn't even know for sure that it *was* a tripwire until he stole a glance over his right shoulder and saw a little metal cylinder nestled in the dirt at the bottom of a tree.

He was looking at the cylinder when he heard the blasting cap go off first with a *pop*! no louder than the report of a .22 caliber rifle; then there was an explosion of light, white and blinding, and a deafening roar, and Rioux was flying up and backward through a hail of metal and glass, flying with his sixty-pound rucksack and twisting to the right in mid-air as if it and he were weightless. The jungle was on fire, and his legs were burning though he did not know it; it seemed to him that the great *vavoom* of the blast was still sounding when he sank into darkness.

He came to on the operating table at the big Army hospital at Qui Nhon. He was conscious of a faint, foggy light and a voice saying, "David. David. Move your leg." He asked which one. "Your right one," the voice said, and he felt a hand tap it, but when he moved it he blacked out again, sinking through unconsciousness toward what the Army doctors were certain was his imminent death. He surfaced again later, how much later he did not know, and was aware that Michel was there and that he could not see him. His right eye had been destroyed. His left was damaged and deteriorating. Both his eardrums had been shattered. Both his arms and both his legs were broken. His right hand and right leg were maimed beyond useful repair. He was lacerated with shrapnel wounds. Both legs and one arm were so brutally burned that merely changing the dressings became a surgical procedure and had to be done in the operating room with anesthesia.

They had sent for Michel at the Alamo almost as soon as David was hurt, telling him out of kindness or simply garbled information that his brother had been wounded in one leg. *A cheap wound*, Michel had thought, feeling relieved for David. *A million-dollar wound. He'll be going home*. He caught a ride out on a supply chopper the next morning and hitched the rest of the way across country to Qui Nhon. It took seven hours, and when he got there he couldn't find David at first; he was looking for a leg wound, but when they steered him to intensive care, the ruin they said was his brother was mummified in bandages and plaster casting almost beyond recognition. Michel understood then why they had sent for him. He was supposed to be there when David died.

They hadn't even expected him to make it through the first night, but he had; the doctors hadn't reckoned how strong he was—strong enough in flesh, Michel thought, to survive his wounds and strong enough in faith to go to his death unafraid if it came to that. Michel stayed with him at Qui Nhon for twenty-eight days, officially AWOL at first, then on compassionate loan to the hospital as an orderly when his CO found out about David's situation. The first two or three weeks of that time were a series of crises, David conducting his dalliance with death and Michel nursing him from six in the morning till lights out at eleven at night. He went through ten operations and, ultimately, sixty-six units of blood. He was ravaged with infection and aflame with fever, 106 degrees at its high. He lay sheathed in plaster, unable to move anything except his head, and fogbound by morphine and Demerol. He rallied, faded and rallied again and then, ten days in, developed a bleeding ulcer, the consequence of massive inner stress that could not overwhelm his spirit and so assaulted his body instead. It was Michel who pumped his stomach empty of blood and fed him when he could take food, but he seemed to be wasting away, his sinewy 160 pounds shrinking toward 90.

At low ebb, they thought again that he might die; his father, in Lewiston, negotiated himself a visa for Vietnam to be with him at the end. But David rallied yet again, strongly enough this time to permit his transfer to Tokyo for repair and later to Walter Reed Army Medical Center in Washington for convalescence. His open wounds were sutured closed. His burns were layered over with skin grafts. His left knee was fused. His halt right leg was fitted eventually with a brace. His right eye was irretrievable. His left for a time could pick up light, a gauzy yellow-white haze, and his doctors, first in hope and later in charity, encouraged him to believe that he might see again. The light dimmed and finally died, but David did not rage against the darkness. It troubled his doctors and his rehabilitators that he did not—that he accepted his blindness as he had been prepared to accept death, without anger or tears, as the consequence of having served his God and his country and so having done what he believed to be right.

GOOOBYE, WAR

The freedom birds were flying, and the boys of Charlie Company were going home. Captain Rogers lingered behind, with a new job at division headquarters and the prospect of an early promotion to major; so did Cowboy Rosson, trying to drink his way through his extended run at Cam Ranh Bay; so did Bert Kennish, idling from one dull reassignment to another off the line and wishing he were either home with Faye or back out with the company. But the others were boarding the charter jets one by one and heading back to The World. David Bean limped out in December with the bullet hole that God had given him for Christmas. Goodbye, war. Rick Garcia rode out in May and Bobby Eugene Jones in January in tin boxes. Goodbye, war. J.C. Wilson came out on crutches in September with a gift bottle of pink champagne under one arm, a liter of white under the other and an accidental million-dollar wound in one foot. Goodbye, war.

It was a journey without transition for most of them. American dog soldiers in past wars had come home together in troopships and had had time en route to sort things out among themselves—to swap stories and discover that no one of them was alone in his anxieties or his guilts. But the one-year rotation policy in Vietnam meant they came out singly from the war to The World without company or time in which to decompress. Fewer than seventy-two hours passed between David Brown's departure from the jungle and his arrival in his parents' front parlor in New Jersey; it struck him that the Army had given him a week to acclimate to the heat in Vietnam and not even three days to readjust to the alien psychic climate awaiting him back home.

The trip for some of them was a passage into the unknown as lonely and almost as suspenseful as the flights that had borne them to Vietnam. Mike MacDonald and Danger Dan Colfack left together, MacDonald still plagued by jungle rot; it had even invaded his face and he had grown a moustache to hide it. The war wasn't over for them yet. Their jet was laboring across the Pacific through heavy weather, so violently turbulent that the pilot apologized for it.

"Mike," Colfack said, "I don't like the water."

"Dan," MacDonald answered, "I never thought we were going to make it anyway."

They made it, and the planes kept lumbering airborne with their cargoes of men and pain. *Like a wake*, Omega Harris thought again; the flight cabin was as silent as a sepulcher until the jet leveled off out of antiaircraft range, and then they were all out in the aisles whooping and stomping so unrestrainedly that Harris imagined the plane must be rocking in the sky. The celebration went on for a time, then subsided again as the men drifted back to their seats and to their atomized individual wars. Harris had had a bellyful of his. He felt he had grown to manhood in the war; he had wanted respect so fiercely that his hunger for it overcame his fear in battle, and he felt he had earned it, from his men and from himself. But there had come a day when he had had enough of death and body-counts and had told himself, *Hey, this is not the way for me to die.* He had turned down the offer of another stripe if he would extend his tour in Vietnam for six more months. "I'd rather be a live E-6," he told his CO, "than a dead E-7."

Harris was angry at the war by then and was thinking of leaving the Army when his hitch ran out in eight months' time. He had lost part of the hearing in his right ear, the result of standing too close to his mortar one day when they were firing some high-explosive Charge 9 rounds, but that wasn't it. It was fighting a war so unintelligible that he never understood an operation except the battle for Fire Base Julie, when the Army had used them all as human bait. It was friends dying and being wrapped in their ponchos and loaded on choppers like parcels of freight; it was watching them go and having to tell himself that there was nothing left he could do for them—*they just gone*.

So he walked away from the war when his time came, and as he was going out he met his old top sergeant from Germany coming in. *I'm gonna send your little smart ass to Vietnam*, the Top used to tease him, but now it was Harris's turn. "Well, my good man," he teased back, "do you remember that guff you used to say about sendin' my smart ass to Vietnam? Well, this smart joker leaving, and make sure you duck, 'cause I left a bullet hangin' out here somewhere with your name on it."

But now, flying home in the silence, Harris felt suddenly depressed. His mind was half at home with Jean and half back in 'Nam with his men. He couldn't sleep. *Are they okay?* He didn't know. *Why am I leaving them behind?* He didn't know that either—only that his guilt was chewing at him. He had had them under his wing for a year: Taras Popel, Ed Schweiger, Clyde Garth and the others. He had nursed them along and seen them safely through the war, all but Garth, but now he felt as if he were abandoning them. *Is the next guy gonna take care of these guys*, he wondered, *so they get home?* He didn't know and it hurt. Goodbye, war.

In March it was Kit Bowen, riddled with shrapnel; in August, his chum Don Stagnaro, ravaged by hepatitis. Bowen got it at Holiday Inn, a clearing in the Iron Triangle named for the tranquillity that had reigned there until Charlie Company arrived. Six or seven buddies had clambered up the observation tower, portaging a few beers for refreshment, and were playing with a new starlight scope—a night observation device that borrowed reflected light from the moon and stars and enabled men to see, dimly but usefully, in the dark. "Doc, you gotta check this thing out," somebody called down, and Bowen climbed up after them for a peek.

They were still playing when they heard the first mortars pop beyond the wire. *It's gonna land someplace*, Bowen thought, listening to a round whistle in, and then they were all scrambling down the ladder and dashing for the nearest bunker, and the rounds were walking in closer and closer till one burst practically in Bowen's face. Fragments of metal tore nine holes in him, from his ankle to his ass to his rib cage. He couldn't breathe; he had a sucking chest wound, and he could feel himself going under, with all the other medics working against each other to patch him up. One of them had got out a knife and was ready to start a stab tracheotomy when Bowen, sliding into blackness, remembered that he was a doc too and took over his own case. He ripped a pressure bandage out of its plastic wrapper and threw it away; a bandage was porous and a sucking wound could draw air through it, so instead, Bowen slapped the wrapping over the hole in his chest and was breathing again.

He was still in agony, and it got worse when an out-of-shape medic dropped the litter with him in it on the way to the helicopter pickup zone. They had barely hefted him back up when the incoming fire started up again, and everybody scrambled for cover, all but his pal Stagnaro. Bowen had pasted Stagnaro together at Cantigny; they had become best buddies, and now it was Bowen who was hurting and Stagnaro was crawling toward him in the night, thinking he might crack up if Doc died. *I've got to get to him*, Stagnaro was telling himself. *I've got to say hello—or goodbye.*

They got Bowen out to a MASH unit, the first of seven hospitals in Vietnam, Japan and America that taped and sutured him whole again. Stagnaro stayed behind, humping the boonies and holding himself back from any further entangling alliances. He understood that everybody depended on everybody else, but after Bowen got messed up, Stagnaro got cautious about getting too buddy-buddy with anybody; he preferred loneliness to the pain of saying goodbye again.

He lasted five more months in the war, and when he came out, it wasn't shrapnel that had stopped him but a fistful of tainted ice-cream bars. He had bought five or six of them from a mama-san in a ville one dusty-hot day when the company was out on a run; he knew better, but he was parched and sweaty and he wolfed them down. They straggled back to Lai Khe after that for a two- or three-day standdown before their next operation. Stagnaro felt lousy. He didn't eat or drink a thing for three days because he couldn't even keep water down and couldn't keep his eyes open long enough to do anything else. "Jeez, I'm sick," he finally confessed to a medic when he could no longer deny it to himself. The medic told him to see the doctor. Stagnaro didn't want to; he didn't like the way they were waging the war, but it mattered to him not to be one of those guys who faked being sick to get out of it.

The medic pressed anyway, and it was only when Stagnaro tried to drag himself across the 150 feet between himself and the doctor's hooch that he realized how ill he was. He had to stop every twenty or thirty feet, plunk down on the ground and rest, then get up and do twenty or thirty feet more. It took forever, but finally he was standing across the desk from the doctor. "Okay," the doctor said sarcastically, studying some papers in front of him, "what's wrong with you?"

Stagnaro felt too rotten to speak. The doctor looked up. Stagnaro was gaunt and jaundiced; even the whites of his eyes were a bright piss-yellow. He didn't know it until afterward, but he was dying.

"Man," the doctor gasped. "A medevac helicopter is coming in half an hour. Be over at the pad."

"What about my gear?" Stagnaro asked.

"Don't worry about your gear," the doctor answered. There wasn't time for it; Stagnaro said goodbye to a couple of guys and was gone.

What he had come down with was hepatitis, and it was almost an insult to him; he had never had anything worse than the flu in his young life, and now he was a vegetable, bedridden and shrunken from 175 to 125 pounds. They didn't tell him until after he had turned the corner that his liver had almost quit functioning and that he had missed being dead by no more than a couple of days. By then he was out of 'Nam and back in The World. Goodbye, war.

In June it was Greg Skeels, headed home to Flint and a world he no longer felt he knew. Skeels had been through the human-wave assault on Julie and a half-dozen more bad firefights. He had been a point man, and a good one. Guys liked walking behind him because, it was said, *Skeels can smell gooks;* he could pick that scent of sweat and medicine out of the fetid jungle air and lead you away from trouble. Danger Dan Colfack used to talk about the time they were out in the jungle, hacking through the thick foliage, when Skeels came to a sudden dead standstill. He had caught the scent, but the men didn't know it until they saw him turn, slow and stealthy, and then come tearing back toward them with his face a mask of terror. He was halfway back to his squad when the enemy opened up, but he made it, and the men followed him out of harm's way.

Skeels was good, but after six months in the line he felt himself losing his nerve, wondering how many blizzards of flying metal you could walk through without getting hit. He began thinking that he would rather do anything else, even something as crazy dangerous as being a door gunner in a helicopter. When he caught himself playing with that idea, he knew he couldn't take the jungle anymore—he had to find a way out. Like most of the men, he was losing his heart for the war as well. *This is what we're supposed to do*, he had told himself coming over, but he hadn't been in Vietnam long before he began asking himself, *What the hell are we doing here anyway?*

So Skeels begged off the line and spent his last months in 'Nam working as a company cook in Lai Khe, and now he was finished, waiting on the apron at Bien Hoa for his flight home. He stood watching the new recruits filing down off the plane, raw and innocent of war as he had been a year before. He remembered how he had felt then, walking past the combat vets and feeling their silent gaze. *Now I know why they were shaking their heads*, he thought. He was one of them now, one in a fraternity of boys who looked old at twenty or twenty-one, and he was shaking his head at the new meat too. Goodbye, war.

PART 2

THE WAR COMES HOME

Every time we see something on the news, we're killing somebody, we're running over and taking hostages, we're dealing drugs. Hey, man—we don't deal in drugs. We don't go around killing people every day. We're only ordinary people, have an ordinary job, pay ordinary taxes, and we do our ordinary work every day. And we have a wife and kids and go to school. We do nothing out of the ordinary.

—JERRY DICKMANN, at a reunion of Charlie Company, 1981

GREG SKEELS: "ONE DAY, YOU HAVE A LICENSE TO KILL..."

For Greg Skeels, as for many of his buddies, the trip home was a journey through a time warp—a return that was too fast into a world that was too slow. *Christ, I've just been through part of a war*, he thought, but when he showed up around his old haunts in Flint, Michigan, nobody even wanted to buy him a beer for having risked his life for his country. He bumped into a pal from Ainsworth High who couldn't seem to talk about anything except his car—how he had built a big engine and jacked up the rear wheels and on and on— and Skeels, who had been there, was thinking, *I couldn't give a shit anymore*. He looked up an old girl friend who had sent him a Dear John letter while he was in 'Nam, announcing that she was trading up from him and his '66 Pontiac GTO to another guy with a '67 Chevelle 396. Skeels felt an urge to see her anyway, but when he did he discovered that she was the same and he was different, and he didn't feel anything but lonely.

So Skeels fled for a day to Detroit, just to get away, and spent all of it wandering around the zoo, staring at the animals. He was like them, a curiosity, an alien being who could have come from another continent or even another planet. "It was like I had changed and nothing else had," he reflected years later, sitting in his living room and working on his third bourbon-and-water at two in the afternoon. He had gone away a carefree, gregarious boy out of a world that revolved around cars, girls, radios and six-pack Saturday nights; sin in those days was one brew too many, and the one kid in the crowd who smoked dope was thought to be off the deep end. Skeels found everybody precisely where he had left them, but he had been too far and seen too much

143

and had come home too fast, a stranger. "One day you have a license to kill," he remembered. "The next day a cop pulls you over for speeding. One day you're with people you'd trust with your life. The next day you have to sit in the corner of the bar so you won't draw attention to yourself."

Skeels never did get quite back in sync with The World; his life after 'Nam tacked from job to job, from school to school, and from woman to woman, with a shell of bitterness hardening around him all the while. He went back to the auto assembly line in Flint, this time at Fisher Body; that lasted for eight months. He studied business and basic engineering at a local community college; that lasted for a year. He kicked around from job to job for a while; that filled two years. He went back to college to study heating and cooling, then back to work, then back to college again—this time for a bachelor's in education so he wouldn't feel tied down to any one calling. He was twelve years out of Vietnam by the time he finally earned his license and hung out his shingle as a heating and cooling contractor and sat waiting for his first big payday. It didn't materialize, not right away, but it no longer surprised him that he was out of harmony with time, that his pulse was tuned to the war and not to the far slower pace of The World.

He was like a man trying to walk under water, and for a time he fought it. His temper was as violent and as unpredictable as a claymore mine with a hidden tripwire. He had lived a year in a world in which one solved problems by shooting them, and it had burned his fuse short; he found himself boiling into storms of anger when even small frustrations didn't solve themselves as quickly or as perfectly as he wanted. His girl friend of the moment preserved his sanity, he thought; she would let him rage on and on for a time, "and then," he recalled, "put her arms around me at the end and tell me it was all right." But that relationship came unglued like all his others. He ran through several girl friends and a marriage that dissolved in five years.

The war had made The World too *mundane* for Skeels, too wearyingly tedious; after Vietnam, he thought, "It was hard to tie into thirty-years-and-out in a factory." After Vietnam it was hard for him to tie into anything at all; twelve years on, he was alone, still jumping at street sounds, still afraid to walk in the woods, still brimming with resentment at the war and the damage he felt it had done his life. He imagined that there would be more Vietnams; the daily papers were full of dispatches about the left insurgency in El Salvador and the arrival of the first handful of American military advisers there, and Skeels, like many of the boys of Charlie Company, was seized with a powerful sense of *déjà vu*. No nostalgia attached to the images of jungle war or to the memories they reawakened in Skeels. This time, he said, he would not be there; this time he would be the guy cashing all his chips and investing in the companies that make the guns. "I've been on the shit end of the stick," he said, "and I know how these things work."

He knew how they worked, he supposed, because he had soldiered in the last dirty little war and had come home to a silence he could still hear. He marked with sour amusement that the nation was building a monument in Washington to its Vietnam dead a decade after the collapse of the American war effort. *Making up for lost time*, he thought, and he felt neither a personal stake nor a larger national purpose in it. "We all swallowed our pride for twelve years," he said. "Now, I think there's a national guilt complex emerging over the way they all treated us when we got back. Well, no thanks." He stared past his bourbon at the living room floor. "What's done is done," he said; he wanted only to be left alone, and, a dozen years out of Vietnam, The World was granting him his wish.

OMEGA HARRIS: "I AM NOT BREAKABLE"

Omega Harris always loved a party, but the one his family and his friends threw for him on his sixth day back in The World was more nearly an ordeal. *That year in Vietnam separated me from you*, he thought, looking around the room; it had changed him inside in ways no one there knew and had wrapped him up outside in stereotypes that none of them seemed able to penetrate. A guy was coming on to a girl about how he had fought three or four gooks hand to hand and had broken their necks, and Harris interjected that it didn't happen that way—if you got that close to the enemy, you were halfway dead already. Another dude, a boyhood buddy of Harris's, said he was glad that somebody else was over there dying instead of him. Harris was furious. "Hey, man, wait a minute," he flared. "You and me was raised up together, I knowed you a long time, but let me tell you something—these guys I served with in Vietnam mean more to me than you. If I had a choice between eliminating them and you, you gotta go."

Harris didn't know it yet, but he was fighting the first skirmish in what he came to think of as "my own personal war against society"—a war for the respect he felt was due him and the men he had soldiered with. As a black man trying to make his way in a white man's world, he had always seen his life in the imagery of struggle. He had been fifteen when Martin Luther King had done his I-have-a-dream speech from the steps of the Lincoln Memorial in 1963, and though stirred, he had not believed that the color-blind society King envisioned would ever come to be. *The impossible dream*, Harris thought. *I may never live to see that, 'cause I don't plan to live to be two hundred.* So he was already waging one war when he came out of 'Nam with his Bronze Star and his Purple Heart and discovered that he had to open a second front. He had imagined returning to The World wearing his chestful of ribbons and having somebody come up and say, "Ah, you a Vietnam vet. Good job." But it didn't work out that way. *They sit up there*, he thought, *and they say, "Hey—there's another one them murderers."*

They said that, and it hurt. Harris was coming home with his nerves rubbed raw—*like a damn jumping jack*, he thought later—and his patience with the Army pulled thin. He had been reassigned back to Germany, which he didn't much like, and had heard that one of his first details there would be the NATO war games; having only just experienced the real thing, he didn't like that at all. He toyed with the idea of quitting and might have if there hadn't been a waiting list for jobs at the Post Office. Instead, he came back to his Jean for some leave time alone in Brooklyn, where they had met, and Buffalo, where he had grown up. They were at their own place in Brooklyn just before Memorial Day 1969 when some kids set off a cherry bomb out in the street and Harris, without thinking, hit the floor hard the way you did in the war. "My husband just came home from Vietnam and he can't be dealing with that stuff," Jean yelled at the kids, and they stopped. But Harris, lying there, was thinking that she wouldn't always be around to control the situation. He wondered if people would think he was another Vietnam loony.

He wondered that because he had spent his life encased in one set of stereotypes, about black people, and now was being fitted for another, about Vietnam veterans. There was an uncle who saw through them—who came home from work one evening and found Harris paying a call in his uniform. "Who's that stranger sitting in my house?" his uncle asked his aunt in front of him. "It looks something like my nephew. My nephew, he's a Vietnam veteran, and he be sitting here in uniform because he know how proud I am of him."

Pride was all Harris asked of America, for himself and his buddies, but they seemed to him imprisoned in their media image. VIETNAM VET COMMIT SUICIDE, he thought. *They don't look at what he had to put up with in Vietnam.* VIETNAM VETERAN JOKER ROB A BANK. *Oh, he was a Vietnam vet, hunh?* JOKER O.D. *Oh, he was a Vietnam vet? Yeah, well, we expect that from them guys, y'know—they bizarre anyway.*

It was Jean who got him through the reentry, he figured later; they said a good woman makes a good man, and she was a powerful lady. He had met her through her cousin, a buddy of his at noncom school in 1966. His grandmother had always told him that he would know it when he found the right woman, and she was right; Harris had seen a picture of Jean in his buddy's wallet, and a voice had told him, *Yep, this is for me here.* He wangled an introduction, and in two years they were married. She cried like a baby when he left for Vietnam ten days later, and soon after, she sent him a Temptations album with a song he wanted to remember her by. "When I see her," it went, "I'm gonna give her all the love I've got." He played it on his portable till the grooves wore nearly through. When he finally did go to see Jean, on their R&R in Hawaii, his men told him they were going to break the record in his absence.

When he came home Jean steadied him and eventually

bore him two sons, Omega II and, two years later, Christopher. By then, Harris felt ready. He owed that to Vietnam, he thought. Vietnam had made him appreciate life because he had seen so much young life wasted. But Vietnam had hardened him as well. It had forced him to master his fears. *Somebody in combat have to have the nerve to function*, he thought, *'cause everybody's scared*. It had required him to make life-and-death decisions and left him confident that anything less than that would be easy for him. *I been to combat*, he thought. *I have met the task*. It had burned away the boy in him and left a man of tempered steel. *I am not breakable*, he thought. *No. What is there to scare me? I been shot at. I had bombs dropped at me. I've sat there and seen dead people with their guts blown away. What's left after that?*

Neither did Harris regret what the war had obliged him to do. He thought of himself as a professional soldier; he thought of it as his vocation, his bag, the only job he ever had, and if it required killing of him, he would kill. "Part of my *job* is to be a professional killer," he remarked years later. Nature had fashioned him all wrong for the role; there was no hint of menace in the snapshots of Harris at war, his wide mahogany face lit by the first flicker of a boy's sly smile. But he had contracted to serve his country and to kill if he had to, and he had done so without hesitation then or regret afterward. He wished he had seen some intelligible purpose in it larger than getting himself and his men safely through the fighting. His conscience was otherwise untroubled. "I don't feel bad," he said, reflecting across the distance of a dozen years. "I don't feel ashamed. I don't think I've done nothing wrong. I did what I was trained to do."

Yet the war and the chill of the homecoming had altered Harris in ways that disturbed him. The flip side of his heightened self-reliance was a turning inward, a retreat from the world into himself. He felt that society was measuring him against its inflamed expectations of what Vietnam veterans were like and that he had accordingly to hold himself constantly in check. A reflex still told him *hit it!* every time he heard a backfire or a jackhammer; the rule of thumb in Vietnam was that the more dirt you could eat, the longer you were likely to live, but he learned to contain the impulse after his jangled first months back in The World. *People might think you crazy*, he told himself; just another crazy Vietnam vet.

He thought that Vietnam had revealed something dangerous inside himself as well—something explosive in the presence of threat or provocation. He was out barhopping in Brooklyn one night soon after his return when Jean came down ill. It was two in the morning; there was no place to take her except a hospital emergency room, and here was this dude across the counter telling him he had to have Blue Cross and Blue Shield to get her treated. Harris said he was a soldier just twenty-five days out of Vietnam. "We don't take military dependents," the dude said, and Harris blew up.

"Look," he raged, "I just spent a year of my life dodging bullets so you can have a job, and you're telling me my wife can't get treated here? If my wife suffers complications while you're sitting here fat-mouthing, I'm gonna fuck you up."

A policeman materialized and asked what was wrong. "I sweated a year in Vietnam," Harris told him, "and now this sucker here is telling me nobody gonna look after my wife. I'm gonna fuck him up!"

The dude behind the counter was looking to the cop for succor, but the cop told Harris, "I don't blame you," and walked away.

A woman doctor attracted by the commotion finally agreed to look at Jean if Harris would simmer down. Jean, it turned out, had a bad case of tonsillitis; the doctor gave her something for it, and they went home. But the episode told Harris something unsettling about himself. *I have to keep myself low-key*, he thought. *I have to stay out of things that can provoke what I got within me.*

Harris's response was a strategic retreat from The World. The hearing loss he had suffered in Vietnam became both an instrument of and a metaphor for his withdrawal. The Army refused for years to acknowledge it; it was 1975 before a doctor fitted Harris for a pair of glasses with a built-in hearing aid, and he could hear paper rustling and birds singing for the first time since the war. Till then, he had coped with his partial deafness by vamping through it. It was, he thought, like being black in a white world—that was the hand you were dealt and you had to play it. In company, he would pick up the subject of a conversation and improvise answers he thought would fit. "Yeah, man, that's right, man, I'm gonna do it," he would say, when a lot of the time he hadn't heard anything anyone had said.

A lot of the time, he didn't care; there wasn't much that the world outside had to say to him anymore. He had always been a good-time guy and he partied hard when he first came out of 'Nam. But after a while he lost some of his spirit for it; being in society was like being in the war again, sensing danger down the road, and he began retracing his footsteps out of it. He didn't want to go out much because when you went out you had to meet people. *You meet somebody and they classify you*, he thought, when all he wanted to be was himself. In company, he felt beyond people, marked and apart, separated from them by the war. He felt that nobody except his Jean really knew him, and he couldn't even talk to her about what it was like in Vietnam.

He couldn't really talk to anybody about that except other men who had served there. Sometimes he felt the need to— *everybody need somebody*—and didn't know where to turn. It struck him that he was the kind of guy who always had the right advice for somebody else but didn't have anyone he could ask about things that were troubling him. Psychiatry wasn't the answer; *I don't need a psychiatrist*, Harris thought, *to tell me something he don't know nothing about*. He needed somebody who knew where he was coming from, and nobody knew that except himself. So it was himself Harris turned to in the end. He learned to tuck down his profile and keep himself under control, masking the pain in his soul as he had hidden his deafness behind an air of easy-gaited competence and a sunrise smile. *The worst is behind me*, he thought at last. *As long as I keep it blocked out and it stays out, I'm all right*.

Harris made a hand-carved success of his life and, once past his post-Vietnam crisis of faith in the Army, in his military career. Twelve years later, Sergeant Rock was Sergeant First Class Omega Harris, stationed at Fort Monroe, Virginia, as a postal administrative specialist and awaiting reassignment to Korea in the spring of 1982. He was no longer thinking of leaving the service, not even in 1986 when he would have put in his twenty years and become eligible for retirement. "I'm not a twenty-year-man," he said; the Army was his calling, he was good at it, and he imagined that if there was another Vietnam somewhere, he would willingly go.

But the last Vietnam had never ended for him. He felt doubly marked, as a black man and a Vietnam veteran, and so doubly at war with his own country. "I'm *always* fighting a war," he said. "Why? That's the magic question—why? The war ought to be over with, y'know?" But it wasn't over, not for him. His countrymen seemed to him to have rewarded people who fled the war and pilloried the men who fought it—men like himself—as killers. Harris had been there and he knew it wasn't that way. Men had killed to stay alive; twelve years on, Harris still had no idea what they had been fighting for *except* survival.

JERRY DICKMANN: ORDINARY PEOPLE

We're ordinary people, Jerry Dickmann thought, seeing his old buddies from Charlie Company once again, and so most of them were; so Dickmann certainly was. Twelve years after 'Nam, he was back in Saukville, Wisconsin, where he had grown up, graduated from high school and sweated out the draft working for a heavy-equipment manufacturer. Like most of the men, he had gone sour on the war; its metaphor for him was the flow of Vietnamese who would come to Lai Khe for rice and medicine during the day and surrender them to the VC back in the village after the sun went down. "You could see all our might and all our energy going for nothing," he said, looking unfondly back. "The people just didn't care. What good was all our firepower with that kind of an attitude?"

Still, Dickmann felt he had left the war behind when he came out on Labor Day, 1969. He finished out his Army tour at Fort Riley, Kansas, then came home to Saukville and settled down. People left him alone about the war; Dickmann wanted that, and in a small town, a man's neighbors were sensitive to his wishes without even having to ask what they were. In short order, he met his bride-to-be, Lynn, and married her after a fourteen-month courtship. They had two children, first Angela, then Eric. He was doing work he liked as a troubleshooter for the city water department—*an ordinary job*, he thought, *doing ordinary work every day*. His most vivid enduring grievance about the war was the way the Veterans Administration had shown its gratitude since, refusing to treat him for problems with his hearing and his back and hassling him for a cosigner for a $5,000 furniture loan when both he and Lynn were working. "Stick it up your asses," he told them, until his father-in-law cooled him off and cosigned the note.

We do nothing out of the ordinary, Dickmann thought, and yet out-of-the-ordinary things have happened in his life since Vietnam. There was the passage when the silence came between him and Lynn—when he could not speak to her about things that were bothering him and they finally separated for a while until he could talk it all out. That was Vietnam, Dickmann figured; in Vietnam, you didn't talk about things that troubled or frightened you—you were supposed to be hard and self-reliant, and you worked them out for yourself. And there were the sustained anxiety attacks that still plagued him for six weeks out of every autumn with the approach of Lynn's birthday on November 1. That was Vietnam, too; Dickmann would be thinking about what to get her and watching the days slip by on the calendar and suddenly it would be Julie time again—the anniversary of that October night when he was trapped with his squad in a bamboo thicket with the enemy all around and Larry Samples dying in his arms. It would all flood back on him then: Julie and Cantigny and Junction City, the way stations of Charlie Company's worst six weeks in the war. Those six weeks never stopped being an annual torment for him, a round of jangled days and insomniac nights. He was ordinary people, but he was not yet free of the ghosts of his war in Vietnam.

Big Charlie's Place in Lai Khe. It was said that the VC circulated leaflets offering a reward to any of its soldiers who came back with a shoulder patch removed from a Black Lion. And it was here that the Black Lions took care of the MPs.

(Below) Charlie Company's first platoon the way they were in 1969. The
160 members of Charlie Company
were not really men but boys, nineteen
and a half years old on the average, as
against twenty-six in World War II.
Their object was to stay alive, but few
of them doubted they could have won
if they had been allowed to.

(Above) Waiting to board a Chinook chopper out of Fire Support Base Mahone. (Opposite, top) On Eagle flight. (Below) A Charlie Company patrol follows a mine detector down Thunder Road, Highway 13, north of Saigon.

(Left top) Greg Etzel astride a tank's cannon. Mud was never defeated. (Left center) Five grunts rush a wounded man to a medevac copter. (Below) Tank on a culvert on Thunder Road. (Opposite top) F-4 jets roar in low over Junction City. (Opposite bottom) APCs on the move.

Joe Boxx on the perimeter (top center) and home with his family (below). When he came back, no one wanted to talk about a job.

Frederick V. Suchomel (right) never stopped being nineteen. His parents (below) made their east living-room wall a kind of shrine to the way Fritz was before he died. Along with his high-school trophies and a picture is a prayer: "Oh, God... demand not of them the supreme sacrifice...."

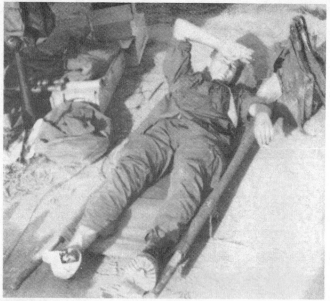

(Top) David Bean's foot stopped an NVA bullet looking for Curtis Gilliland's head. Twelve years later (below left) he still has some numbness in the foot, and he had his first nightmare about Vietnam. He sat straight up in bed and screamed, "Kill him! Kill him! Kill him!"

Taras Popel (right), with foresight he need not have gone at all, but back in Chicago (above), "I have no regrets."

J. C. Wilson (opposite bottom right) was wounded twice, once by enemy shrapnel and once by friendly fire. "I went over to do a job and I done it and I survived," he said (left), "I wasn't ashamed of what I done." But when he limped into line for his plane home from San Francisco Airport, still dragging his crutches, people kept jostling ahead of him as if he were invisible. He knew then where he stood in the hearts of his countrymen.

Clyde Garth (left) before he went to Vietnam. "He always wanted to go out and do the things men did," recalls his sister. He died at nineteen going on twenty. His mother, Katherine (above), was billed later for collecting food stamps and Garth's life insurance at the same time. Although she had eleven other children, she had to pay.

Don Stagnaro (above, in 'Nam, and right, putting on a bulletproof vest before a police raid) realized when he came home that he spent nearly a year of his life with his stomach knotted in fear. He found his future when he passed a test for the Los Angeles Police Department. Not damaged by the war, but disappointed by how it was fought, he reflects, "It didn't seem to matter much our being there."

Doc Johnson (above left, with unidentified GI) was the first of his family to go to college. He was a pre-med student, but a twenty-six month tour in 'Nam was the closest he got to doctoring anybody. Although he won the Silver Star, his dream of medical school died. With girl friend Donna (right) and a degree in geology, he is now ten years behind where he should be at thirty-four. "My life has been a series of adaptations."

Jerry Dickmann (above right, with unidentified GI) and at home today (left). "You could see all your energy going for nothing."

The war began for Greg Skeels (above left) the moment his plane touched down at Bien Hoa, in June of '68. As for coming home, he says, "One day you have a license to kill. The next day a cop pulls you over for speeding." With his lady in Detroit (above right), he says, "What's done is done." Mike MacDonald wore his decorations (below left) but turned down a battlefield commission. He came home thinking his medals were as worthless as the war. Living now in Minneapolis (below right), he still believes the country owes him, and a million others, a parade for what they went through.

One of the first laws of survival in Vietnam was to be buddies with everyone, because you needed buddies to look out for you, and close friends with no one, because it hurt too much when a close friend died. (Top) Stagnaro, Vittorini and Bowers in 'Nam. (Below) at the reunion in Florida.

DCSDOC
DEPUTY CHIEF OF STAFF
FOR
DOCTRINE

Omega Harris (top left) with unidentified buddy, and (below) on active duty today. "I have met the task. I am not breakable."

(Right) Captain Richard Rogers (seated left) did not rue his service time. "I asked God not to let me be a coward." His men thought he cared for them and he did. But he gave up a promising Army career thirteen years out of Vietnam and retired to the corporate life.

Frank Goins (left) in 'Nam, and with his family (below left) Lajanda, Frank, Jr., Steffanie, wife Mattie, and Katherine Tameka. "There was no such thing as color in Vietnam," Goins says. "We would eat out of the same pan. We all shared boxes and stuff. Everybody was trying to make it home alive." But in the real world nothing had changed: The Silver and Bronze Stars and the Purple Heart he brought home still counted for less than the color of his skin. "When we got home they still didn't want us to go into Mr. Charlie's cafe by the front door.... If you was black, you had to go round to the back." So he locked away his memories with his medals and built a new life for himself and his family, from the ground up.

Kevin Abbott (above) with two children orphaned by war. He had been the hero of Cantigny, and later was a victim at Luke's Castle when a new lieutenant mistakenly called in Charlie Company's mortars on his own troops. Coming home to Brooklyn (right), Abbott reached out for his small portion of the American dream. Because of inflation he could no longer afford it.

(Below left) the Rioux brothers, Michel, eighteen (left), and David, nineteen, before David was severely wounded by a booby trap. Michel nursed him in the hospital from 6:00 A.M. to 11:00 P.M., but David was blinded and his right hand and right leg were maimed beyond repair. (Top) Michel plays the guitar for David in the ward. (Below right) David today says, "Being blind is horrible." But the tragedy of the war for both brothers was instead its unhappy ending. "We left real people back there": To abandon them to a Communist bloodletting was an act of treachery.

Curtis Gilliland, Jr., with an ARVN (above) and with a Vietnamese friend, Tri Huu Truong, back home in Kentucky (below). "We didn't understand them. We made no attempt to. We just killed 'em."

Kit Bowen (above left) and Don Stagnaro (above right) were best of friends. Kit kept Stag from dying at Cantigny, then nearly bought it at Holiday Inn and Stag thought he might go crazy with sorrow. Bowen came home riddled with shrapnel. Bowen (left) now says, "'Nam was a total mistake."

(Above) David Brown (left) with unidentified GI, and (right) at home in New Jersey. There his uniform was not a badge of honor but of shame. *As if,* he thought, *we carried a plague.*

Harry Foxwell with a grenade launcher (left) and at home teaching his son Andrew how to use a computer (below). "That really wasn't me over there. That was somebody else. I'm not the same person now...."

David Spain (right) on bivouac before shipping out. Now, with his children (below), he remembered that long-gone time when he sort of liked the Army. Thirteen years later, he blames it for having made him the man he is today.

McNamee © *Newsweek*

Denny Pierce (left) with a Vietnamese villager. His wife, Betty (below), worried that he'd bring home the war. But he came back whole, his spirit unscarred. Later, an industrial accident damaged him more sorely than did combat.

(Top) Bert Kennish, left, with unidentified fellow officers, and (below left) at work near Denver. "What we lost in Vietnam was something more than a war." Lloyd Collins (right) with his wife, Nancy, in their wedding photo. He never revealed to her the open wound in his soul.

Roy Rosson (above) outside Charlie Company's club in Vietnam, and (right) at home in Ranger, Texas. He went to war a stringy farm boy raised to believe in his country. Now he says, "We really didn't do much good there. My friends died and they didn't have to. The war was for nothing."

Mike Fetterolf (left) went through the war with a folding chair and a rebellious attitude. Now (below) he chops wood for his cabin at Star Meadow on a Montana mountain.

(Top) Skip Sommer reenlisted to get off the line, and then deserted, living three years on the lam. (Right) Bob Selig went back to Northern State University, where a girl asked him, "Did you shoot women and children?"

Jim Soike returned from his bunker (top) and went to church thinking, *They believe I committed all kinds of atrocities.* Finally, he kept going back, and did not feel lost anymore. He works today (left) as an arborist in Milwaukee.

(Right) Charlie Company's mortars in action.

The enemy dead lay where they fell after a human wave assault on Fire Base Julie. Counting the dead became a proof of merit for ambitious career officers, a measure of success for the tacticians in Saigon, an instrument of persuasion for the leaders in Washington. *This is their only opportunity to have a war,* Bert Kennish thought, surveying the lifers among his fellow officers. The men in Washington set great store by these numbers. The boys of Charlie Company did not.

RICHARD ROGERS: "I ASKED GOD NOT TO LET ME BE A COWARD"

Richard Lee Rogers came home from Vietnam a major, with his chest rainbowed with ribbons and his prospects as an officer plated with gold. He had done what he had sought to do in the war and had affirmed what he had gone to find out, that he was not a coward. He had put his skills, his patriotism and his mettle to the ultimate test, he felt, and had passed in the Army's eyes as well as his own; one of his immediate superiors at battalion headquarters said afterward that Rogers was the finest company commander he had seen in Vietnam. Rogers accordingly returned to those great expectations due an upwardly mobile career officer who had achieved a combat command and had executed it with distinction. Twelve years later, at forty-one, he was a lieutenant colonel with a post suited to a soldier on the rise, as a staff leader at the combined armed services staff school at Fort Leavenworth, Kansas.

But a restlessness he had experienced before and resisted was stealing over him again—a progressive unease with the new Army and a subcutaneous itch to seek his fortune in civilian life. It wasn't Vietnam that was bothering him at midlife; on the contrary, his only regret about the war was that the military was not allowed to win it. It had struck him during his first tour in 1965, when the great escalation of the war was only just beginning, that Vietnam was near anarchy. The danger then, it seemed to him, came less from a coherent Communist guerrilla movement than from plain brigands and banditos pillaging the countryside like Quantrill's raiders during the Civil War. "Freedom was being able to drive down a road and not getting beaten up or having your wife raped or your child mistreated," he remembered. The American

153

presence had brought something nearer to order by the time he left in 1969, he thought, and the Vietnamese appeared to him to be grateful for it.

Neither did Rogers regret his own participation in the war. The duty-first ethic of the Big Red One, and by extension any army at war, caused stresses in his marriage. His personal trinity of values was God, country and family, and his wife, like the wives of many of his colleagues in the officer corps, was not always happy with where that placed her and their son among his priorities. He understood that there were strains between him and some of the men as well—between his commitment to prosecuting the war and theirs to surviving it. He had felt close to them, not as a man feels toward his friends but as a father feels toward his children. He had lived and fought alongside them for six months and had felt responsible for them. He presumed each of them had disagreed with some decision of his and that some held him to blame when a buddy had died in combat. He had tried in each case to do what was tactically sound and was persuaded that what was sound had been safest for the men. But he knew that he had not always been right—nobody could be—and that men might have died as a result.

Twelve men in all had died on his watch; twelve times he had written letters home to grieving families, and each had caused him pain. Some of the men, at least, had seen that and knew he cared about them. He remembered the day early in his tour when he had choked up trying to eulogize Sergeant Williams, the first man to fall under his command, and had felt ashamed before them. His embarrassment had lingered with him for months; an officer was not supposed to show emotion before his men, and Rogers thought of it as his weakest moment in the war. But when he brought the company down to Lai Khe to mend after the battle for Fire Base Julie, some of them invited him around to their club for a toast.

"Sir," one of them asked, "do you know why we think you're great?"

Rogers straightened up and smiled, preparing to be complimented for his tactical gifts, perhaps, or his leadership under fire at Julie. "No, why?" he asked.

"Sir," his radioman said, "do you remember Sergeant

Williams? That day at the memorial service, we knew you cared."

Rogers was secretly pleased. He understood and to some degree shared the frustration of the men at the way the war was being fought in the field and, in their view, undermined by politics back home. He had himself been shocked when, during his first tour in-country, the North Vietnamese air-dropped leaflets quoting a number of prominent Americans in opposition to the war. "It was hard for me to believe they would not support their own Army," he reflected years later. The constraints of a limited war had likewise chafed at him, as they had at the grunts in his command. He believed that the American forces could have taken Hanoi in a week had they been allowed to, but the rules of play forbade their pursuing the enemy to his lairs in North Vietnam and Cambodia; it was, Rogers thought, as if they were policemen who could chase a criminal up to the city limits and then had to stop. He understood what the men felt when they were obliged to fight for a position, then walked away from it and had to take it all over again two weeks later. "I was tired of having my hands tied and being so restricted in what we could do," he said, "and the apparent lack of orientation on destroying the—" He checked himself, then resumed: "On ending the conflict, I should say, in a positive way that the people of Vietnam would have a chance to control their own fate."

So acute was his irritation with the limits imposed on him that he thought of leaving the Army after his second tour in Vietnam. He stayed instead out of a lingering sense of obligation to the cause he had served. He believed that the war was a just one and, even after the fall of Saigon in 1975, did not accept that America had lost it. "The American spirit is the offensive," he said. "As long as we are moving and the soldiers feel that they are accomplishing something, it will work. We tie so much in our society to attaining quantifiable goals." His own professional military opinion was that the war worked anyway, better than his men saw then and better than the nation appreciates now. "There's a feeling in the country that we didn't win the war, and that because we didn't win, we lost it," he said. "And I'm not sure we did lose in Vietnam. Did we lose the freedoms that we enjoy in America? Could it be that the confrontation in Vietnam prevented something from happening closer to the United States?

In South America? Mexico? Maybe that's what we won—
time. Time to develop our nation. Time for smaller countries
to get a hold on things so they could better defend themselves."

What troubled Rogers instead was the course that the
Army—*his* Army—had taken after Vietnam. It had, for one
thing, become an all-volunteer army. The Charlie Companies
that soldiered in Vietnam had been products of the draft and
were thus collective ventures of the American people in all
their great diversity. A volunteer army, by contrast, turned
soldiering from a commitment into a job, and in Rogers's
view, no wage, however high, was enough by itself to persuade a man to die for his country. In the Age of Reagan,
he felt surrounded as well by a new breed of officers whose
impulses were less military than managerial and whose appetites for the money Reagan proposed to throw into exotic
weapons systems were boundless. Rogers's own bent was
toward the philosophy and strategy of armies as against their
tables of organization; he felt that Reagan's trillion-dollar
defense build-up ought to be measured by what it would buy
for America's national security and not by what careers it
might advance.

He had discovered, in sum, that he no longer felt at home
in the Army, and when he realized that, he finally submitted
to his old, repressed impulse to put in his papers and retire
to private life. He left the military and, in the summer of
1982, went to work as a vice-president of a taco-making
company called Mexican Originals in Fayetteville, Arkansas.
He had served in Fayetteville before, as head of the ROTC
program at the University of Arkansas, and had made some
good connections. It was not outside the range of possibilities he imagined for himself that he might some day run for
public office, with his insider's skeptical view of the bal-
looning military budget as a central campaign theme. He did
not rue his service in Vietnam or feel damaged by it; he
believed that the experience of war revealed what men were
made of and that those who came out badly had usually had
problems going in. He was not unpleased with what Vietnam
had told him about himself. He felt that it had in fact made

him a stronger man by deepening his commitment to Christ and helping him, through prayer, to master the fears he sensed in himself and saw in other men. "I asked God not to let me be a coward," Rogers said, and He did not.

LLOYD COLLINS: THE DEATH OF THE HEART

Lloyd Collins came back to Peoria looking much as he had when he left for Vietnam, a big, roistering son of Middle America who loved pretty girls, fast cars, low lights, six-packed beer and the Chicago Cubs. His old running buddies didn't think the war had changed him at all. But behind his smiling mask and his lusty good-time appetites, the war had disfigured Collins in ways they could not see. He never talked about what he had seen and done in 'Nam, not to them, not to his mother, not to his girl Nancy; he never spoke about the hell they had caught at Julie and Cantigny or about his own sudden blood binges, shooting up the bodies of dead and dying Vietnamese in the aftermath of battle. His best friends didn't know he had won a Bronze Star for his valor in action. The mask stayed in place, the silence un-breached. Collins was still a million laughs; it was only when he would wake up screaming in the middle of the night that Nancy would know he had been back in Vietnam in his dreams and had seen things there that he could not speak about even to her.

His mother, Doris Wilson, had been the first to see that he really wasn't the same fresh-faced, sports-happy innocent she had sent off to the war two years before. She knew it when he enrolled at Illinois State and didn't even go out for baseball. *Something's wrong*, she thought. *Really wrong*. His nerves were shot. He had high blood pressure. He wasn't sleeping. He couldn't get along with anybody except the crowd he caroused with. He flew into rages—"sudden, incredible rages," Mrs. Wilson recalled, over next to nothing. Once, not long after his return, he was sacked as coach of a Sunday morning baseball team for dressing down his players in uncontrolled fury before a bleacherful of fans. He was smoldering inside, and no one knew how to reach him. He told his mother that no boy of his would ever be in the Army. He told her that he hated everyone over forty—"It was the people over forty, you see, who made him go to Vietnam."

He managed to slide through college and a succession of jobs with insurance companies, the longest lasting three years. But his life was falling apart around him. He was drinking too hard and driving too fast; his license was lifted for speeding, and when he got it back he was busted again, this time for leaving the scene of an accident. Nancy was frightened by his bad dreams and his benders, but after five years commuting between her place and his, they married in 1975. It lasted nine months; Nancy watched him soak up booze by the bottle and beer by the twelve-pack and knew it was over when she found herself praying that he would pass out before his rage took possession of him. In desperation, she went to a priest for counseling. Collins wouldn't go; he didn't think he had a problem, and neither did the guys he was drinking with at the time. "Lloyd was just a jolly guy," one of them said. "A carefree, pretty well self-centered guy. He loved to dance and he loved his women and he loved high speed. He loved to have fun, no matter what the cost."

When the cost finally got too high for Nancy—when their marriage was drowning in alcohol and unpaid bills—she walked away and divorced him. "It killed me to have to do that," she remembered years afterward. "He was so handsome. He looked so good. I was so incredibly in love with him. I still am." She loved him, but, as she had discovered, she did not really know him; he had never revealed to her the open wound on his soul that he had brought home from the war.

They stayed friends after they parted, and one night in August 1978 their eyes met across the room at a Peoria nightclub called the Second Chance. The band played their song, "Colour My World," the theme from their wedding, and they were out on the floor one last time dancing to it:

"As time goes on, I realize just what you mean to me...."
They never saw each other again. Collins went home to his
place, an apartment stripped bare except for a bed and a few
appliances; everything else had been sold to pay the bill
collectors. There wasn't even a television set for company
when they found him there the next morning.

Collins had known for five years that he had a heart condition. He had wakened with chest pains one morning; his
mother had insisted that he see a cardiologist, and he had
gone, but he quit taking the pills the doctor prescribed after
a month. "He didn't seem to care," his mother said, not after
Vietnam; and that night in August his aorta finally exploded
like a road-worn tire, flooding his heart cavity with blood.
It was, said Phillip Immesoete, the doctor who performed
the autopsy, the kind of attack you expect to see in much
older men—men say, of seventy-five. Lloyd Collins was
thirty when he died.

DAN COLFACK: A KILLING GROUND IN HEAVEN

It was a hot August day in the Colorado mountains, but,
sitting in the kitchen of his mobile home, Dan Colfack was
shivering. A visitor had asked him about the day the rookie
lieutenant had called down the mortar barrage on his own
position and decimated Colfack's platoon. "I don't want to
talk about it," Colfack said. He was staring at the kitchen
table, his jaw set in a tight, angry line. The visitor asked
why. "Because it was all sick and unnecessary, that's
why," he said, his voice a hoarse bark that cut off further
inquiry. "You spend a lot of time trying to forget about things
like that. That was part of the incredible stupidity of that
war and the people who were running it. If I talk about it

and think about it, I get mad, because it never should have happened. It was stupid."

Colfack had spent a lot of years and a lot of psychic energy interring the war in the deeper recesses of his mind. He was a man of the West, tough and self-reliant, born in the hamlet of Belgrade in Nebraska's Platte River country. It was hard, bitter land, settled in the last century by immigrants from the chillier middle and northern reaches of Europe; Colfack's own parents were Danish-American, and they raised him to believe that a man must take care of himself and his own. He had gone gamely off to the Army in 1968, one year out of high school and barely two months after he and his Mary were married. She wept over Thanksgiving dinner when he left for 'Nam, but he saw it as his duty, and he soldiered well in a war he never figured out. His buddies called him Danger Dan, because trouble seemed to trail him around and he did not run from it.

But the war was a bitter canker in the bottom of his consciousness a dozen years later, a sore spot that could set him shaking in the midsummer heat as if it were February in the mountains. He had gone home to a job in the power plant at Grand Island, Nebraska, after the war; a guy there had called him a baby killer, and Colfack had had to suppress a powerful urge to strangle him. He migrated after a time to Craig, Colorado, in search of a better livelihood for himself, Mary and their young son, and had found it as an assistant shift supervisor for the local electric company.

Colfack was not one of the walking wounded; he was making a go of his life and was impatient with those fellow veterans who felt entitled to some larger claim on America than a chance to make a decent living. But, twelve years on, he was still trying to distance himself from Vietnam, hiding the souvenirs of war out of sight and out of mind. "You try not to think about it," he said. "You bury a lot of memories and carry on." His Bronze Star lay at the bottom of a drawer, an object as devoid of meaning to him as the war itself; he felt neither pride nor shame looking at it, only emptiness. A photograph lay with it, a landscape of a flat, grassy sweep of Vietnam without swamp or jungle. Colfack had kept it because, long ago, the vista had reminded him of the Nebraska flatlands stretching out from the Platte in the spring. "It was like heaven there," he said, or had been until they chose it as an ambush site. They had made a killing ground of the only place in Vietnam that looked to him like home.

ROY ROSSON: LOOKING FOR SOMETHING ELSE

Fresh out of Vietnam but still in Army khakis, Roy Rosson II headed for his parents' new home in Arizona and arrived at the door in a brand-new pickup truck he had bought out of his savings. They embraced, kissed and clasped hands, and then Roy Sr. sent Rosson back out in the truck to fetch a celebratory six-pack of beer. Rosson bought two six-packs instead and had drained three cans by the time he got them home. "You learned to drink while you was over there, didn't you?" his father said, eying him appraisingly.

"Yeah, a little bit," Rosson answered, but he didn't quit; he kept popping tops and chugging beers till most of them were gone.

Rosson *had* learned to drink in the Army, idling out his last months at Cam Ranh Bay with his dream of making it on the rodeo tour receding farther and farther out of reach. By his own assessment, he had become "almost an alcoholic" in that blue period, mixing $1.65-a-bottle PX whiskey with Coke or Sprite in a cooler jug and sponging it up all night. He wasn't exactly drunk all the time, but he was always drinking. He told himself at the time that it was because of what he had been through, an anodyne and a reward for the hundred days in the bush in which he had never seen a bed and had had maybe one hot meal. But there was a quality of melancholy about his boozing as he described it a decade later—a sense of loss attached to the two years he had been drafted for and the three more he had agreed to serve as the price of coming off the line. "It took the better part of my youth," he said, and, with his youth, his dream.

He had gone off an Okie from Muskogee, a stringy farm boy raised up to believe in his country, right or wrong. The war bleached the red, white and blue mostly out of him. He had been wounded twice and had lost two front teeth; he had killed and seen buddies die, Fritz Suchomel and the rest, and had grown thick calluses over his spirit. There was a medic in the company who used to throw things at little Vietnamese children to keep them away from him. *Man, that guy's cruel,* Rosson had thought, but then he heard about the five-year-old girl who had taken out a tank with a hand grenade, and he started throwing things at kids too. He learned to inflict death without feeling, writing it off in his consciousness as a simple necessity of survival. Once, he was out on a patrol with his buddy Rabbit and the company's new top sergeant when they came across a fallen enemy soldier.

"Hey, here's one laying," Rabbit said.

"Is he dead?" Rosson asked.

"I don't know. We'll shoot him and find out," Rabbit answered. He pumped three or four rounds into the body. The new Top stared at them, dead silent. *He thinks we're crazy,* Rasson supposed. *I been over here long enough where maybe I am.*

There was a shadow across Rosson's easy Marlboro-man smile when he came back to Fort Hood, Texas, to finish out his extended tour and to reconnect with his roots in Oklahoma. On one trip home, he rekindled his acquaintance with his schoolmate Connie. He had been one of twelve boys and she one of twelve girls in their graduating class at Ripley High, and when she married him during the spring break in her senior year at Oklahoma State University, she still imagined that he was the shy, loose-gaited country boy she had grown up with. It was only afterward that she began to see how tightly Vietnam had wound him. They were watching fireworks from the porch at her family's place on their first Fourth of July together; one went off close to them, and when Connie turned to say something to Rosson, he was flattened out face down on the ground.

His bad dreams and flashbacks trailed them to Belton. Texas, where they lived while he was soldiering at Hood.

Their first night there, he came up screaming in his sleep: "Get down! Get down!"

"Why?" Connie whispered, terrified.

"I told you to get down!" Rosson shouted. Connie looked at him, saucer-eyed. He was still asleep.

The drinking and the nightmares eventually subsided. The wandering never really stopped. When the Army finally turned him loose in 1972, Rosson headed straight for the rodeo circuit and found that men he used to beat riding bulls had left him behind. "They were tough," he recalled afterward, "and when I came back, I couldn't cut it anymore. Couldn't ride the bulls like I could." He switched specialties from riding to roping and kept on haunting rodeo rings wherever he found them on his nomadic course. But the dream was dying, and inside, Rosson knew it.

He couldn't raise the money to buy a farm either, so, discouraged, he began drifting across Oklahoma from town to town and job to job as a truck driver, a construction worker, a feed-lot hand, a roustabout in the oil fields—anything within roping distance of a rodeo. *When I get out of this*, he used to tell himself in the straitjacketed life of the Army, *I'm not taking nothing off nobody*, and he did not. He bopped through twelve jobs in his first year alone; some lasted no longer than a few days before he shambled on to the next gig in the next town, and none then or later held him for even as long as a year. It wasn't like him, he kept thinking; as a kid before the war, he would start something and see it through, and now it seemed he could hardly set foot in one place without getting sore or bored or itchy and wanting to move on to the next. "I never been fired," he said. "I'd quit. Somebody'd give me some guff, say something I didn't like, I'd just move on."

The day he touched bottom, Rosson walked out on Connie too. He had never really talked to her about the war beyond a slightly bowdlerized account of his five-day drunk in Taiwan on R&R; she never heard the stories gnawing at his innards until years afterward, when a reporter came to ask about them, and even then she had to stand out in the hallway eavesdropping to hear them. She had been mystified when he talked about throwing away his two Purple Hearts and his Soldier's Medal; she had wanted him to be proud of his service and felt shut out by his brooding silence about it. Once, they were watching a TV movie about a Vietnam veteran, and when the veteran in the movie started having flashbacks, Rosson did, too, and left the room. Connie had learned by then not to ask too many questions. Instead, she endured Rosson's silence and followed along in his rambling Willie Nelson wake, telling herself: *It's like he's always looking for something else*.

And then one day she came home and he wasn't there. She had always feared that; they had waited five years to have their first child because she was never sure Rosson was going to be around very long. It was in fact only nine months after their Blane was born in 1975 when Rosson headed for the door. He had been failing in one last try at rodeoing full-time; for a year he had been competing six nights a week for $200 and $300 purses and, with the expenses of the tour, was only barely breaking even. Connie had gone back and finished college by then and had gone to work as a schoolteacher. It wasn't easy; they had moved four times in her first two years teaching, but she was making enough to keep them going while he pursued the last will-o'-the-wisp remnants of his dream. Only Rosson couldn't take it anymore; his wanderlust was coming over him again, and this time there was no room in his train for her. "It just seemed like everything was closing in," he remembered. "One day, Connie went to work and I packed my clothes and left."

It took some time and some straightening out, but Rosson came home. They migrated to Nebraska for a while, Rosson rodeoing through the spring and summer and shivering miserably through the prairie winters, and then headed south again. They had come to roost, twelve years after 'Nam, in a pink slate house on Highway 80 in Ranger, Texas, with a miniature saddle on the mailbox—Rosson's touch—and five horses grazing the ten acres out back. He was working pumping oil, and was breaking and training horses on the side; she had a good job with the Farmers' Home Administration. Blane was six years old then, and their daughter, Bana, four. Their world seemed almost stable, or so Connie dared dream. "We're very pleased with what we have here," she said. "It's been quite shaky, but he's never mentioned leaving again."

But Roy Rosson's children would not be raised in that

unquestioning patriotism that Roy's parents had imbued in him. His impacted memories of Vietnam had left him bitter toward the war and toward the country that sent him into it. His own father had referred to it offhandedly as a "police action," as if, Rosson thought, the euphemism could make the outcome somehow less humiliating. "Police action, hell," he had flared, "that was a war." It had turned out, in his view, to be a war for nothing, and he blamed the country for that. "Don't think that much of it anymore," he said. "I never have registered to vote, and I'm not going to. I don't think that much of the country *to* vote."

He was watching the television news the day South Vietnam finally fell in 1975, looking at pictures of his old base at Cam Ranh Bay stripped bare and abandoned. He remembered when it had been alive with men and machines; now it was empty, the symbol of America's loss, and Rosson, staring at the images, was thinking: *We really didn't do much good there, did we? My friends died and they didn't have to. The war was for nothing.* He remembered how, when he was drafted, his father had bridled at his little joke about running away to Canada and had insisted that he go do his job. *I'll fight them here*, he thought, but he wouldn't serve in another Vietnam, and his boy Blane wouldn't either. Should that day come, Roy Rosson thought, he would send *his* son to Canada.

ANTONIO RIVERA PARILLA: A PETITION FOR HELP

From the serene distance of his home in a suburban condominium complex overlooking San Juan, Puerto Rico, and the Atlantic Ocean, Antonio Rivera Parilla could think of Vietnam as having been little more than an "interruption" in his life. The interruption, to be sure, had run for five years—two in the Army and two on unemployment wrapped around one year in a treadmill job as an office clerk. It had its scary moments as well, for him and the close, stable family of working people he had left behind. Once, in the Iron Triangle, a mortar round hit near his machine-gun emplacement and a piece of shrapnel lodged in his head. The letters home had stopped coming, and his mother, sensing that he was in danger, had gone to church and inched on her knees from the entrance to the candlelit altar to pray for his deliverance.

That he survived the wound and the war remained Rivera's proudest achievement in Vietnam. He had fought against going there in the first place, on the ground that he was an only son, and had resisted going out in the field again after his head injury until the CO threatened him with a court-martial. He was almost as unhappy off the line as he was in it, brimming with resentment at the racial mores he saw in the Army. His own squad leader for a time was a white southerner who seemed to award all the worst details—*the shit work*—to the blacks and Hispanics. Once, as they were slogging wearily in from a three-day ambush run, the sergeant gave Rivera a particularly onerous chore. "Find somebody else," Rivera snapped. They jawed at one another all the way back to the barracks, and by the time they got there, Rivera was stoked so hot that it took two or three men to keep him from going after the sergeant with his M-16. "From then on," he remembered mildly years later, "the duties were divided up more fairly."

Yet, more than most of his buddies, Rivera saw some purpose larger than survival in what he was doing in Vietnam. "The Vietnamese used to say, 'GI Number One,'" he said in his first and most comfortable language, Spanish. "I looked at the poverty around me there and saw that phrase as a petition for help." He had himself witnessed poverty all around him in his boyhood and, like his parents, was steeped with a striver's determination to fight free of its embrace. After his first low-gear years home, he found a place with Kodak Caribbean, Ltd., at a Veterans Administration job fair in 1973 and stayed on, with a night-school bachelor's in business administration and a desk in the accounting department. He lived in something like comfort with his wife, Yolanda, and their two boys in their condo above the sea.

The headaches that kept recurring had been competently diagnosed as the result of tensions on the job and not the time-fused stresses of his services in Vietnam; he felt a world away from the lurid tabloid tales he read about veterans going berserk ten and twelve years out. "People see me tranquil and normal," he said, "and they don't believe I was in the war."

FRITZ SUCHOMEL: "BRING THEM SAFELY AND QUICKLY HOME"

Frederick V. Suchomel—Fritz to practically everybody—used to dream a boy's dream of what he wanted to do when he came home from the war: buy himself a motorcycle and go see that vast America beyond the rolling Wisconsin hills. He never got to do it, but he never stopped being nineteen in the farmhouse just outside Sun Prairie where he grew up. His parents made the east living-room wall a kind of shrine to the way Fritz was before he suffocated at the bottom of a well in Vietnam. Over the mantel hung an oil portrait of him in uniform; the painter who copied it from an ID photo gentled the solemn soldier face with the hint of a boyish smile. His baseball and wrestling trophies from Sun Prairie High were clustered below, along with his picture and a "Prayer for Those in Service" set together in a folding frame. "Oh, God," the prayer said, "...demand not of them the supreme sacrifice, but bring them safely and quickly home to their loved ones."

The American flag hanging beneath the mantel, folded in a funereal triangle and sheathed in clear plastic, bore witness that the prayer had not been granted to Rudy and Janet Suchomel. They had known that without asking when somebody called from their priest's house on an April Sunday in 1969 asking to see them. From their kitchen window they had watched the two cars coming west down the road from town and had seen the men get out, first the priest, then two Army officers. "Nobody had to tell us," Rudy Suchomel, a sheet-metal worker, remembered. "We knew." The other five children were out of the house. The Suchomels were alone with their grief. "We both went all to pieces," Suchomel said, rubbing one grizzled cheek. "What else could a guy do?"

The Army was kind to them, and so were Fritz's buddies in Charlie Company. There were telegrams announcing that the mortal remains of Frederick V. Suchomel were in transit home, totting up the pay still due him as of the morning in April when he died and advising that, because he had died in a war zone, the government would pay for the funeral. The officer who told them about Fritz, a Captain Richardson, came back to see them whenever he was in the area and left his address and number when he was transferred to another part of the country; the slip of paper was still tacked to the Suchomels' kitchen bulletin board a decade later. Somebody wrote from Vietnam that Fritz had received the last rites of the Roman Catholic Church; the Suchomels were deeply religious and that meant a lot to them. Tiny Scott had wept when Fritz died, the only time in the war when he had let himself go, and he sent the family a letter saying how terribly sorry he was. Mike MacDonald drove down to visit them when he got home. So did Littlefellow Fahrner. An honor guard came; there was a soldier's funeral, and Fritz was buried.

Then they were all gone, and nothing survived of him except the reliquary wall in the living room and some memorabilia in an old cardboard carton—the blue braid circle from his dress uniform; the empty cartridges from the rounds they fired over his grave. His letters reposed there for a time, too, until the Suchomels could not bear to keep them any longer. "It hurt too much," Rudy Suchomel said, and they threw them away.

It was pain they still felt twelve years afterward, not bitterness; they were people of stolid and pious German stock, and they did not question the ways of God or the duty of young men to fight for their country. But their sorrow and their sense of loss survived, as vividly as on the day the cars had first appeared in their driveway. "You know, I got wounded back in the last war, in France," Rudy Suchomel said, standing with a visitor in his barnyard. A stiff wind was rising out of the south, and his eyes, gazing into it, were moist. "Maybe if I'd gotten it for good back then," he said, "none of this would have happened." The visitor protested. Suchomel smiled wanly and shrugged his shoulders. Then he turned and walked back into his house.

KIT BOWEN AND DON STAGNARO: THE BEST OF FRIENDS

One of the first laws of survival in Vietnam was to be buddies with everyone because you needed buddies to look out for you, and close friends with no one, because it hurt too much when a close friend died. For a time in the war, Kit Bowen and Don Stagnaro flouted that rule; they were Doc and Stag, the medic and the radioman, fused together under fire in a friendship that looked as if it would last forever. It was a comradeship born in blood, when Doc kept Stag from dying at Cantigny, and annealed in pain, when Doc nearly bought it at Holiday Inn and Stag thought he might go crazy with sorrow.

Yet even the thickest friendships were not made to survive the journey home from the bunkers and the need to forget Vietnam. The two of them came back to The World, Stag gravely ill and Doc riddled with shrapnel, and back to their separate worlds. They were Bowen and Stagnaro again, their friendship left behind with their *noms de guerre* on the far side of the planet. Even in the years in which they lived a short drive apart in Southern California, they barely stayed in touch with one another.

Stagnaro had the smoother reentry, though it took a little time. He realized when he came out of 'Nam that he had spent nearly a year of his life with his stomach constantly knotted in fear. He hadn't eaten enough because he was never hungry and hadn't slept enough because, in the war, you took your sleep in catnaps. He had lived planning where he could run and hide if the shooting started and had gone through firefights wishing he could burrow into the ground and pull a rug up over his head. He had finally almost died of hepatitis, his liver function two-thirds shut down. So when he first came back to San Pedro, he didn't want to do anything much except have a few drinks and collect unemployment. He looked for work but not too hard in those first months. He didn't feel ready yet.

He hunted up his old car-club buddies first thing and discovered how little he had in common with them anymore. He had been living out at the edge for a year, in a world whose only law was kill or be killed; it had been both a humbling and a maturing experience, he thought, and he suddenly felt, among the old crowd, like a man among boys. He didn't want to talk about cars and they didn't want to talk about the war, except to ask Stagnaro how many gooks he had killed. The answer was two, so far as Stagnaro knew, but he slid off questions like that and his pals seemed uninterested in pressing further. It was, he thought, as if they wanted to bury Vietnam—as if it didn't exist for them except as a nightly series of film strips on the six o'clock television news. For him, it was a vivid ongoing reality. He couldn't even bring himself to tag along anymore when the guys wanted to go out hunting deer or rabbit; after the war, he valued life—any life—too much to take it.

His family instead was his bridge back to The World. He would go out drinking until two or three in the morning in his first months back; when he came home, his father would be waiting up with a pot of coffee brewing on the stove, and they would sit in the dark in the living room talking, father and son, closer than they had ever been. The old man had almost died of high blood pressure when Stagnaro was wounded, and Stagnaro was careful to drain most of the blood and guts out of the few war stories he told. Mostly, he sat in the night and listened to the family past—how his grandfather had jumped ship in Florida on the voyage over from the old country and had migrated across the continent to San Francisco just in time for the great earthquake; how his father had followed his grandfather onto the boats out of

San Pedro and had seined a precarious living out of the sea. Stagnaro heard the stories and was touched. *It's as if he's trying to pass on his life to me,* he thought. *As if he was writing a book and maybe this is the end—this is what it's about.*

He found his own future the day he took and passed a test for the Los Angeles Police Department. He brought no deep sense of vocation to the job; it was available when he didn't feel ready to go into business for himself—*to be an individual,* he thought—and didn't have schooling enough to support a very much grander dream. "I didn't know what I wanted to do," he reflected years later. "I just kinda latched on to the police department." There were moments when he wondered whether he should have; his first assignment was to his old neighborhood, and he found himself obliged to bust some of his boyhood car-club pals—"guys I used to get drunk with"—for sins not much graver than they had committed together in the old days. He was looking at his own youth from the back side of a badge, and he wasn't sure he would ever learn to enjoy the view.

It was only after he transferred out to the ghetto watch in Watts that he discovered a sense of calling to police work and began a ten-year climb up the ladder to a prince-of-the-city assignment as a narcotics detective. Police work meant being around guns and danger again; once, Stagnaro had to draw on a man involved in a violent domestic quarrel, and once, a suspected narcotics dealer drew on him and some buddies before they took him by superior force of arms and numbers. But Stagnaro found himself liking the echoes of Vietnam—the experience of being men together, living out at the edge again, bound to one another by their mutual dependence in life-and-death situations. Being a cop, like being a grunt, meant developing a sixth sense for danger and responding to it without skipping a heartbeat; Stagnaro had learned that in Vietnam. It meant being a team player with your partner or your squad as you had been with your platoon in the war, and Stagnaro had learned that in Vietnam, too. It struck him that what men felt for one another there had been stronger even than the love most men feel for their wives.

Stagnaro learned to live with those ghosts of war that survived in his life. He had nightmares about it for his first year or two home, dreams vivid enough to bring him snapping upright in the dark, the bedclothes drenched with his sweat. He discovered as well that he was not yet out of reaching distance of death. He got a letter, not long after his return, from an old buddy named Dave Reid. They had played in a rock band together in the old days, Stagnaro with the stamina on piano and organ, Reid with the talent on guitar, and then they had both gone off to the war. Reid was still there after Stagnaro came home, still walking point and coming down with point man's paranoia. "I've been over here a long time," he wrote Stagnaro. "I'm getting short and my CO won't let me off point. Could you do something?"

Stagnaro sent word back promising, without much hope, to write Reid's CO himself and see if that would help. He had barely put the letter in the mail when the phone rang one evening at his parents' place. "It was about seven o'clock," he remembered long afterward, "and it could've been anybody, but my heart started beating. I knew. My mom answered it, and I knew it. My heart was beating, and I turned around. My mom was crying and she said, 'David's dead.'" *David*, he thought; he was getting short and he got it, right through the head, and was gone. His parents used his insurance to buy a house and hung a plaque over the front door. THE HOUSE THAT DAVID BUILT, it said; there was nothing left of them but that.

Stagnaro was still dreaming about the war ten years later, and still flashing back to it whenever something in The World wakened a sense memory of 'Nam—the smell of diesel, the sound of a machine shop, the look of a field or a mountain path. But the dreams and the reveries were no longer torture for him; he accepted matter-of-factly that they were and probably always would be a part of his life. For a time he was victim, too, to that silence that enveloped many of the men who served in the war. A first marriage dissolved in part because of it. He had not spoken to her very much about Vietnam, and she had not asked about it, out of what he later understood to have been a delicate concern for his feelings. They had long since gone their separate and still amicable ways when she read the story of Charlie Company's war; if she had known about it before, she told Stagnaro over lunch one day, they probably would still be together.

He had remarried by then and had settled with his new

wife, Michele, ten years his junior at twenty-three, in a new house in a new subdivision in Orange County. When they gave a housewarming in the summer of 1981, sixty friends came to feast with them on quiche and spicy meatballs. Stagnaro had always dreamed of retiring from the force after twenty years and trying something else—opening his own restaurant, maybe, and setting up drinks for his friends at the bar. When Michele got pregnant with their first child, twenty-five years began to seem more realistic than twenty, but a kind of settled contentment suffused Stagnaro's life nevertheless.

He did not feel damaged by the war, only disappointed in how it had been fought and how it had come out. America's commitment to Vietnam, in his view, was like a man's commitment to help his neighbor out in trouble. You didn't back down just because you might get a bloody nose. But America *had* backed down, he thought. They could have bombed hell out of North Vietnam and taken it in no time; instead, guys fought and bled and died piecemeal in a treadmill war that had been going for years when they arrived and was still going years after they left. He remembered how they used to slog through a ville and see children starving to death along the trail. *Are we helping them?* he would wonder. The answer irresistibly was no. "It didn't seem to matter much," he said, "our being there."

Kit Bowen's way back was bumpier. He started home at roughly the same time as Stagnaro, but it took him nine years to feel he had got there. Where Stagnaro had griped about the conduct of the war, Bowen had raged through it, his soul tumescent with anger and his fatigues encrusted with the blood of his buddies. "I was pissed probably from the word go," he remembered and, remembering, was pissed again. It had been crazy, *a dog chasing its own tail*, he thought. He had been nineteen then, innocent of geopolitics, and he didn't understand why they hadn't told Ho Chi Minh to fold his hand in forty-eight hours or kiss Hanoi goodbye. He figured later that he had survived in part because he *was* a medic, ministering to the wounds and the anxieties of boys at war; he was no older than they, but he thought of himself as an open and loving person, an Irish Sea of emotion, and in 'Nam they brought it all to the Doc. He patched bodies, calmed nerves, cursed officers, chugged beer, stanched bleeding and envied the enemy dead their apparent blood-lessness. *Like wax mannequins,* he thought. *They're all shredded and they don't bleed.* Americans, he thought, bled too much. Way too much.

He spilled his own blood on the patch of Vietnam they called Holiday Inn and was processed home through three hospitals there, one in Yokohama, one in Oakland, California, and finally one at Fort Lewis, Washington, whose principal restorative power was that it was close to his home in Portland. When he was sufficiently sutured together, they turned him loose on leave and he spent it with his old crowd, "drinkin'," he recalled later, "and gettin' crazy." But, like many of the men who fought in Vietnam, he still owed the Army a year when he left the war, and like most, he resented it—resented the KP and the guard details, the dress code and the war games, the chickenshit and the Mickey Mouse, and most of all the hazing at the hands of lifers who had never been near the war.

The year was the unhappiest of Bowen's young life. He fell out wearing his medals, his patches and his pride in his first days at Lewis, and his top sergeant didn't like it. A Cool Hand Luke *thing,* Bowen thought; *he's never seen combat and, by God, he's going to humble my ass.* It was a near thing. The orders promoting Bowen to sergeant, cut in Vietnam, got mysteriously lost in The World. He stood guard. He scrubbed dishes. For a time, until he couldn't take it anymore, he served as a kind of professional mourner—a member of one of the roving honor guards the Army sent around to bury its dead.

Once, he was sitting in the front row at a funeral for a boy who had been killed in Vietnam; the kid had practically come home in a Baggie, there was that little left of him, and the father was staring at Bowen, muttering, "Why the fuck is my son there and you're here?"

Another day, they buried a thirty-year veteran sergeant who had wigged out, tried to fly a homemade helicopter and wound up Jell-O on the pavement of a Safeway supermarket parking lot. The ceremony required Bowen to stand rigid through the twenty-one-gun salute, then turn and face the bereaved family. As he did, the sergeant's widow saw his Big Red One patch. "Oh, my God, my husband was in the First Infantry," she cried, and then she was weeping and clutching at Bowen, with her two sons trying to tug her away, and he was standing miserably at attention, frozen as an ice carving, wishing he could fold her in his arms and comfort her.

In that moment, the top sergeant had found and crossed Bowen's threshold of pain. *I had too much of this over there*, Bowen thought. Next day, he went smashing into the Top's office, hot enough to walk through doors, and told him enough was enough—he couldn't take the death watch anymore. The Top looked appraisingly at him. Bowen was, militarily speaking, a mess. He had let his hair grow long. His hat, to accommodate it, was two sizes too big. He had been fooling with pills to get through the days. Even his act of defiance was a capitulation of sorts, Bowen crying uncle. He never had to do the burial detail again, but the Top had won.

Bowen came out of the Army in 1970 and went back to The World, as he put it later, "in a coma"—a long, shambling second boyhood recapitulating what he had lost of his first. "I was always the wilder one on the block," he said, not unhappy with the role; it was a family joke that, when he was born, the hospital dropped him twice and caught him once. When the military turned him loose, he accordingly hit the ground careening. He drew unemployment and did odd carpentry jobs for two years to keep himself fed and fueled. He tried college for a year in Oregon and dropped out. He packed his clothes, his dog and his grandmother's bed into the back of a 1950 pickup and headed south into the California sunshine for a long passage alternating doing little with doing nothing. There was a two-year second try at college, mainly so he could draw GI benefits and live on the beach. There were passages working for a machine shop, a body-building equipment company and, when he was really hungry, a restaurant in Newport, California, as a busboy. At low ebb, he walked out of a grocery store with a bag of groceries for himself, which he had paid for, and a fifty-pound sack of food for his dog, which he had not. The manager chased him out onto the parking lot and accused him of shoplifting. "You think I'm so down I'm going to steal dog food?" Bowen blurted, handing over some money—but that was in fact how far down he had slid.

It was 1979 and Bowen was ten years out of Vietnam before he felt ready to come home to Portland, with a beard, a thick mane and fifty-five new pounds of muscle from pumping iron. His gyroscope had steadied a good deal by then; he tucked down his profile, took a bachelor apartment on Lake Oswego, just outside town, and went to work, first running a distribution area for the daily *Portland Oregonian*, later returning to the body-building equipment business. "I guess there was something subliminally that I had to get out of my system," he said, reflecting on his nine-year walk on the wild side. He did not feel scarred inside and did not recognize himself in the media imagery of Vietnam veterans stressing out a decade after the war, waking up screaming and kicking the cat. He saw some vets like that on a television panel once and thought: *They look like they were woken up the last ten years by putting a starting pistol to their heads. They're definitely sideways.* That wasn't Kit Bowen, he thought, and it wasn't 97 percent of the Vietnam veterans he knew; they were coping. Maybe he *had* lost some years, and maybe he wasn't pulling down much better than a C-minus in life so far, but it wasn't the war that had cut him adrift, he thought—it was the lost time. "Hell," he said, looking back on it, "I was a young buck. Maybe I was grabbin' those years when I wasn't in the frat house raising hell, y'know?"

There remained in Bowen a wide streak of the roustabout—*the rabble-rousin' loose goose*—he had always been. His life on the lake was settled but not too settled; he thought of himself as still searching and caught himself still dreaming of something else to do: running a tavern, say, or working on a tugboat. He still liked a laugh, a drink and an audience for his bravura gift of gab, but at least once a month he attached some redeeming social purpose to those appetites. With his kid brother and sister and some of their old pals from Beaverton High, he turned a casual one-time reunion into a monthly pub crawl for charity, the revelers anteing $10 apiece beyond the price of the drinks for one or another good cause. The group tried on various acronyms, discarding SPILL (for Society for the Preservation of Ignoble Lowlifes) in favor of VACO (for Vista Avenue Castoffs, or, in certain conjunctions of the stars, Vanquished Americans Crawling On). The humor was of the Laff Riot school, as foamy and as perishable as the head on a glass of beer, but the impulse was pure Bowen: a smile, a brew and leave the change on the bar for the Lord and the people.

He had been like that in the war. One day he was out in the bush with his bandages and his rage; the next, he and a buddy were caught crawling under the base-camp barbed wire in search of a piece of ass in Lai Khe, knowing there were VC in town and thinking boozily how glorious it would be to die in the saddle. But twelve years out, he had pushed all that to the back of his memory, the laughs along with the blood. His Vietnam was the private anthology of horror stories he hadn't been able to tell his own father—the night he lay listening to the moans of the grunts who died outside the wire at Cantigny, the day the rookie lieutenant called down the mortars on their own heads, the time the Top died in Bowen's arms with his brains in his mouth. "Vietnam," he said, looking back in anger. "That's in the past—why talk about it now? It was shitty. I'm not proud of it."

The old rage lingered close to the hearty surface of the new Kit Bowen. The war had deeply corroded his patriotism and his family's; his father had been a hero bombardier in World War II, but on what he knew of his Kit's experience, he said, he would never send another child of his to war—he'd see them off for Canada first. Bowen felt similarly disposed; all that remained of Vietnam for him was the 30 percent disability check he still drew for nearly having died in a war he had never understood and had come to despise. "It was a total mistake," he said. "I mean I have no—absolutely no—respect for my government."

A dozen years after the war, his old pal Stag ventured that, for all Doc's bitching, he would not have missed Vietnam and would do it again if it came to that. Bowen was amused, hearing that. "He's dead-ass wrong," he said; it was the cop in Stag talking, he guessed, the don't-fuck-with-me officer of the law. If the Communists were hitting the beaches of Oregon or the piers of Manhattan, yeah, maybe, he would be back patching up grunts, he thought, and spitting at lieutenants. But there would be no more Vietnams for Bowen. He had seen too much blood already.

JOE BOXX: "IT WAS THE YOUNG BOY YOU KILLED"

"You've got to understand," Nancy Boxx was saying. She and her husband—Michael J. Boxx on his dog tag but Joe everywhere else—were sitting at the pine dining table in their double-width mobile home outside Ottumwa, Iowa, trying to explain to a stranger and codify for themselves what it had been like when Joe came home from Vietnam. "You've got to understand," Nancy was saying. "He had a chip on his shoulder when he got back. He was a boy when he went in, a hard man when he came out."

"That's right," Joe agreed, taking another swig of Budweiser from the long-necked bottle in front of him: those had been bitter, brawling days. He had gone away a big, quiet boy of twenty, a welder's son who had dropped out of school after the tenth grade because he hated it and went to work at Proctor's Standard Station for $60 a week to support his own car. When the Army snatched him up out of Ottumwa in 1968, he had never before been farther from home than Missouri, once. Neither had Nancy until she came south to El Paso to marry him; he was in training there, and she was carrying their firstborn, Kenny. Joe was out on bivouac five minutes after the ceremony and in Vietnam before the year was out, never questioning that that was his lot. "A lot of people had gone before me, and I was no better than them," he reflected, toying with the Bud bottle. He decided only after he had been there for a while and then had come home to nothing that it had all been a crock—that 55,000 guys had died to make some ammo plants and tire companies rich.

"He was mad at everybody," Nancy said, trying to explain.

"Hell, I still am," Joe said, only now he was smiling. He wasn't then—not when he came back to his wife and kid and discovered that nobody even wanted to talk to him about a job making more than a buck and a quarter or a buck seventy-five an hour. He went around to Proctor's Standard, where he used to work, and found a kid in his old job at better pay—a long-haired kid who hadn't even been in the Army. He took a job in a foundry for a while at $1.65 an hour and could hardly get out of bed the morning after his first day. He bought into a gas station, and his $1,400 nest egg disappeared like water down a drain. He drove a truck for three months and put up prefab housing for ten. He canvassed everywhere and couldn't find anything—nothing he liked and could raise a family on—and his temper was rising. "I'd put my applications in," he said, snuffing out a Marlboro, "and they wouldn't talk to me. Bein' a Vietnam vet didn't mean shit."

"He hardly drank or smoked before," Nancy was saying. "He wasn't the type to hurt people. It changes a man—the war does; the Army does."

It seemed to change Joe Boxx. The fresh-faced boy who went away had come home a red-eyed giant roaming the joints in town, knocking back drinks, breaking up bars and getting into fights with buddies. The whiskey he was drinking to quiet his ghosts was wakening them instead, and he needed more whiskey to make them go away. "I'd relive it," he said. "Every time I'd get to feelin' good after some drinking, all I'd talk was Vietnam, Vietnam, Vietnam, and then when I'd go to sleep I'd get the nightmares. Sometimes I'd wake up in the middle of the night and think I'm there."

Nancy nodded. She had been through a lot with her Joe in those early years, the binges and the bad dreams, waiting for him to come home from the joints and wondering whether he would be in one piece. "See," he said, draining another draught of Bud, "I used to drink a jug or two of bourbon and not know where I was for two or three days." He got involved in so many fights and splintered so much saloon furniture that his outstanding fines ran up to $2,000 at one point and he couldn't afford to pay them. An old buddy from town was teasing him a lot about Vietnam. It was friendly for a while, but then the two started snarling at each other when they met at bars, and one night Boxx called his buddy's game. His buddy showed up but brought another guy with him. Boxx wound up in the hospital, uninsured, for five days.

"You've got to understand," Nancy was saying. "It wasn't like him—killing people, I mean. It bothered him a lot. Still does."

"That's right," Joe said.

"Even today, he's really jumpy," Nancy said.

"That's right."

"He was just a boy when he went into the Army," Nancy said. She was silent for a moment, staring at a lamp. "I think it was the young kid," she said.

Joe looked up from his ashtray. He was on his third Bud.

"The young boy you killed," Nancy said.

Joe Boxx had been there that Christmas Eve when they popped the ambush out of Junction City, the NVAs walking right into their claymores and their machine gun, and he and another guy had to shoot one of the last people left alive on the trail. "He was just a boy, really," he remembered, the image still painfully alive. "Maybe he wasn't killed—I don't know. He wasn't there when we went out for body count. But I saw him go down. I think I killed him, but I don't know. That's part of the trouble."

It was a long time before he could co-exist with his memories. "I was pretty messed up for about five or six years," he said. "I resented a hell of a lot of things. Like Nancy says, I had a pretty big chip on my shoulder." His rancor had not entirely deserted him. He felt used in the war—"And for what?" he wondered bitterly. "For nothing. There are a lot of guys paralyzed and killed and vegetables. Was it worth it?" His anger had been reawakened, as it had been for many of the boys of Charlie Company, by the yellow-ribboned festival of welcome America threw for the fifty-three hostages ransomed from Iran in January 1981. He sat watching the TV images, remembering Cantigny and Junction City and the kid dying on the trail on Christmas Eve. *What a crock*, he thought. *They get the hero treatment and we get treated like dirt*.

But his life had gentled over a decade, and that was Nancy. "If it hadn't been for her," he told the stranger across the dining table, gesturing with his beer bottle, "I'd have been a real mess." He was still drinking a lot of beer and smoking a lot of Marlboros, but he was doing it at home now, not at the joints in town, and that was Nancy too. His father had fixed him up with a welding job at John Deere Tractor, and he had been working steadily for eight years. There had been two more children, both girls; Boxx was building a new family room off the dining room to accommodate the overflow. The war was finally ending for him.

"He's a lot calmer now," Nancy said. The girls were coming in from dance class; the kitchen was a maelstrom of swinging doors, shucked boots and wrinkled tights, and Joe Boxx sat serenely in the middle of it, sipping a Bud, smoking a Marlboro and smiling.

DENNY PIERCE: ALL THE WAY HOME

Betty Pierce was scared when her Denny came back to Lima, Ohio. She had seen people on Merv Griffin and some of the other talk shows discussing all the problems that combat veterans were bringing home from the war, the night sweats and flashbacks and explosive rages. Would Denny be like that? She didn't know. She didn't know him, not really, not in that intimate way in which married couples learn one another. There hadn't been time. He had come home on a ten-day leave to marry her before he went to Vietnam and had sent for her for his week's R&R in Hawaii, and that was it. He had soldiered through some of Charlie Company's worst days in combat; he had been baptized in blood and fear at Cantigny and had been wounded by shrapnel the day the green lieutenant called down the mortars on his own men. The people on the talk shows were saying it could change a man, seeing things like that, and Betty Pierce was worried.

Her fears dissolved almost as soon as she saw him. He had come back whole from Vietnam, his spirit unscarred, his sleep untroubled by nightmares, his temper as resiliently good-humored as ever. His return was a kind of delayed honeymoon; his first year back was the best of their lives, and that was saying something, Betty thought later, because the years since had been good to them too.

Peace had damaged Pierce more sorely than the war ever did. It was October 4, 1977—he remembered the date because it was National 10-4 Day on citizens-band radio—and he was working a grinder at the Teledyne Steel plant just outside town. A chain snapped under the weight of an enormous roll of steel and lashed out wildly, a deadly whip of four-inch-thick metal links. It caught Pierce full in the head, gouging out his right eye and breaking every bone in the right side of his face. A Lima hospital took two months putting him back together again.

Yet he took the accident in the same accepting spirit he had brought to the war; he went back to the three-to-eleven shift at Teledyne with his glass eye, his reconstructed face and his uncomplaining manner. The bad news was that he had to quit the local softball team, but he hadn't exactly been all-league anyway; the good news was that he didn't have to wear glasses anymore, because his lost right eye had been the bad one. He had been married for thirteen contented years by the autumn of 1981, and had fathered two boys, Andy and Eric. Vietnam was a faded memory for him, a source of puzzlement as to why he had been there but no visible pain as to what he had seen and done. He had concluded after Cantigny, his first firefight and his worst, that his number wasn't going to come up and had made it his principal war aim thereafter to reassure Betty that he was right. "I think she was more scared than I was," he said. She was, and she never quit being scared until she saw him and knew that he was all the way home.

SKIP SOMMER: ON THE RUN

The day he signed his reenlistment papers as the price of coming in from the heat of combat, Skip Sommer thought he might be cracking up. He knew that some men less desperate than he were looking at him sideways for trading away three more years of his life; he himself loathed everything about the Army, but he hated the war more and was afraid that he would never get out of it whole in mind or body. "So I did it," he said years later, sitting spare and taut over a coffee in the Connecticut exurb where he had come to ground. "I guess I was maybe half-insane at that point. All I knew was that I was surviving." He signed and came off the line, just as the Army had promised; he marked time for a few more months in a safe billet at Bien Hoa, assigned to a company processing new twinks into the nightmare he had just escaped. Then they sent him stateside to Fort Lee, Virginia, and John G. Sommer, a twenty-one-year-old son of the flag-flying, God-fearing, law-abiding conservatism of affluent America, discovered just how close to the edge he had been driven by the war.

He discovered, by his own later reckoning, that he had gone from maybe half-insane to "more or less crazy." His days were a torment of sustained anxiety, his nights sweaty with flashbacks to the war. He had a premonitory angst attack the first time he fell out for a formation, standing in his wrinkled dog-soldier fatigues in a line of men with razor-creased pants and spit-shined shoes, and he spent the weeks thereafter weaving a jagged course between simple tension and abject panic. The moaning of women and children dying on a jungle trail on Christmas Eve echoed through his dreams, and he would snap awake with his body drenched and his heart pounding. His weekends home in the sheltered suburban world of Ardsley, New York, were blue with dope smoke and red with blind, violent rage. The Sommers were a close and stable family; they had accepted the rightness of the war on faith until they saw how it had damaged him, and they had suffered under his sudden, profane attacks on them. They knew then that their son meant more to them even than the flag they revered, the laws they honored and the cause they had sent him off to serve. When he became an outlaw, they became his willing accomplices.

It had been at the back of Sommer's mind from the moment he re-upped that he could not endure his extended tour in the Army, and his jangled days at Fort Lee only confirmed his suspicion. *I got to get out,* he thought, the urgency of it consuming his days. *This is crazy.* Out of a sense of obligation, he tried it his parents' way first, submitting to examination by a succession of psychologists and psychiatrists and presenting their findings to the Army in support of his application for a medical discharge.

But military psychiatry no longer recognized combat fatigue as a disabling emotional illness; the new orthodoxy held that catering to the symptoms of battlefield stress would only make them worse and that it was best all around to return a man to duty as quickly as possible. The Army accordingly told Sommer no, and, with a certain Kafka-esque genius for fitting punishments to crimes, assigned him to duty close to the heart of his own nightmares: helping to restrain out-and-out psychotics on the ride from Lee to Walter Reed hospital in Washington for treatment. *They're saying this is what we're going to do to you, buddy,* Sommer thought. *They're saying if you continue with this nonsense, trying to get out on psychological reasons, we'll end up putting you in the nut house.*

He was in fact near the end of his string, feeling himself chip and crack, hating everybody around him. When he couldn't take any more, he went AWOL on a weekend home, then slunk back to Fort Lee a day late and took the obligatory slap on the wrist. The next weekend he went AWOL again, this time for a week. The local police were notified, and a friend on the force called Sommer's big brother. "Look," he said, "we know he's there. I don't want to do anything, but we're legally bound. Could you please get him back and work it out?" So Sommer headed south one last time, this time in company with his father, his mother, his brother, and his misery. His brother, who had served as a peacetime sergeant in Korea and knew the language, went with Sommer to see a captain about getting him out legally. The captain was polite and unencouraging. While they were inside, a sergeant in the outer office, large and flat-topped, offered Sommer's father the personal view that Sommer was a coward and belonged in jail. Sommer's father, equally large, had to restrain himself from throwing a punch in reply.

There was little in the visitation to invite hope, and Sommer abandoned it entirely soon afterward. A captain assigned as his counsel warned him man-to-man that he was undertaking what would surely be a long, hard struggle; the odds were a discouraging 70–30 against his getting out even then, and the Army had ways to make his life uncomfortable in the meantime. A vision of permanent assignment to the nuthouse detail was flittering through Sommer's mind. In despair, he left the captain's office, climbed into his roadworn VW, headed north for Ardsley and didn't come back to the Army for three years.

By instinct, Sommer went home first. The fact that he could was itself a measure of how deeply support for the war had eroded in what had been its core middle-class constituency; his family and friends saw in him what Vietnam was doing to their America and harbored him in knowing defiance of the law. He lay low with his own family for a time, smoking dope and, as he ruefully recalled later, putting his mother through hell with his storms of temper. He felt caught between his dependence on his parents and his uncontrollable fits of anger toward them. He grew long hair and a beard, the badges of his estrangement from them and from the world. He yelled. He threw things. He spouted obscenities at the most trivial provocations. He was, by his own catalogue, mad and frustrated and paranoid and scared—scared of what might happen to him if he got caught and scared of what was already happening to him inside.

His furies boiled over one day when he was working at a bicycle shop not far from home. He was officially a deserter by then, a fugitive from the law, but a sympathetic friend had hired him off the books and left him to tend the shop alone. A customer had come in, a local lawyer, and asked a perfectly innocuous question, and suddenly Sommer was screaming profanities at him, calling him asshole and cocksucker and motherfucker—*verbally destroying him,* he thought later, as he had seen men physically destroyed in Vietnam. He was out of control; he kept screaming until the curses gave way to great, heaving sobs and all he could do was yell through his tears at the terrified man to get out. Sommer was alone in the shop then, the tears spilling down his face. When he could speak again, he called the shopkeeper and told him, "I'm leaving—I can't handle it anymore." He found out only later that the customer had reported him to the sheriff's office. By the time a deputy arrived, Sommer had locked up the shop and was gone.

He lived in flight thereafter, moving in a widening orbit from Ardsley to New Jersey to Cape Cod, seeing or imagining federal agents shadowing him every step of the way. The FBI's interest was nearer surveillance than hot pursuit, as an agent once acknowledged to Sommer's father; there were too many cases like Sommer's in middle-class America, and too great a damage potential in prosecuting them at a time when even the most conservative communities were losing their appetite for the war. But the unmarked cars kept pulling up at the Sommers' house, once or twice every month, the cat making its presence known to the mouse. Once, Sommer was there, hiding in a bedroom, when the agents showed up and asked his mother yet again where he was. She said she didn't know. *She's sitting there lying, and they know she's lying,* Sommer thought. *They know I'm in here.* He sat for twenty minutes and felt twenty years come off his life, waiting for the rap at the bedroom door. It never came.

For months that stretched into years, Sommer roamed the East Coast in his old VW, camping out, crashing with friends, working at odd jobs to supplement the money his parents were giving him. He never strayed too far from home—"I needed all the support I could get," he said—but never lit there long either; he kept seeing the plain cars with the black sidewalls and the men in the uniformly cut three-piece gray suits. He felt his paranoia taking control of his life and was trying to quiet it with dope, drink, tranquilizers and constant motion. *Like a man without a country,* he thought, a bearded spiritual DP living in flight and fear of discovery. Once, he was stopped for speeding in Ossining, New York, almost in the shadow of Sing Sing prison, and the cop held him up for a computer check of his record. Sommer sat shaking in his car for forty-five minutes, sure the computer would spit up a WANTED-FOR-DESERTION next to his name and planning which way he would run if it did.

The Sommers begged him all the while to turn himself in. For a long time the mere suggestion was enough to bring down one of his fits of screaming abuse on their heads. A psychiatrist friend of the family urged them to be patient with him, to recognize what he had been through and why he was being so crazy and to wait until he was ready to go back. They did, and the day came when Sommer was ready. "I got to the point where I said I can't handle this anymore," he recalled. "I was a sick person. I just could not emotionally handle it—I had to get my life straightened out." He felt he could not keep on running; he told his family that, with the right lawyer and the right psychiatric documentation, he would go back to the Army.

His mother found the lawyer, a six-foot-four giant in cowboy boots and aviator glasses who had learned military law in twenty years in the Navy, and they set a date for Sommer's return. Sommer couldn't sleep for three nights before, but when the day came he shaved his beard, packed his ditty bag and, quaking with anxiety, presented himself at the lawyer's office in Lakehurst, New Jersey. The lawyer, as a precaution, had brought along a friend as big and massively muscled as he in case Sommer changed his mind en route. He didn't. His marathon run was over. He rode silent and shivering between the two men to Fort Dix, New Jersey, and was parked in a detention room in the stockade while the lawyer went off to barter with the Army for his future.

He sat in the room for most of the day, alone with his demons. At a point, he peeped out the window and saw the lawyer and his associate pacing the grass with an Army major, deep in conversation. *He's doing something,* Sommer thought, but it was more wish than hope; he had heard that you automatically got stockade time if you were gone longer than one thousand days, as he had been, and he felt sick with fear that he was going to wake up the next morning behind bars.

He was still shaking when they haled him before the captain sitting in preliminary judgment on him. The captain looked up at Sommer, standing before him in his civilian clothes.

"If it was up to me, you'd go right to the stockade," he said, "but apparently it isn't up to me."

Sommer stole a glance at the captain's desk. There was a note with his name on it and, at the bottom, a major's signature—the major, Sommer guessed, who had been talking to his lawyer on the grounds outside the stockade.

"Apparently it isn't up to me," the captain repeated, not bothering to hide his displeasure. "I'm going to put you in A Company, but if you make one mismove—if you mess up one effin' time—I'm going to throw your ass inside the stockade so fast you'll never get out. You're dismissed."

Sommer reported to A Company, a detention unit that bunked in open barracks next to the stockade and did scutwork details around the fort. He stayed four months, through the summer of 1973, and made no mismoves; he worked hard, followed the rules to the letter and, when they finally trusted him with a weekend home, made sure he was back bright and early Monday morning. He never knew what had passed between his lawyer and the Army; but there was no attempt to prosecute him or even to charge him formally with having deserted. Instead, in September, he was processed out of the Army with an undesirable discharge. It was bad paper, but it meant nothing to him as against his liberation. He could feel a great weight lifting from his life. He was free.

He had fallen in love with Cape Cod during his fugitive years and, on his deliverance, headed there with his lady of that moment, his best friend and his friend's wife. The men pooled their money and opened a bike shop, and the women took jobs as waitresses to help pay the bills. The enterprise didn't work out. Sommer's lady fell in love with somebody else. His friend, a Vietnam veteran nearly as haunted as he, was drinking too much. The bike business teetered and then collapsed; Sommer bought out the stock, packed it in a truck, drove it back home and put it in storage. It languished there for a time while Sommer, freshly pressed and barbered, took a job days and went to school nights. But he wanted independence and he wanted the quiet that had deserted him in Vietnam. With $2,000 borrowed from his mother, he bailed his stock of bikes and parts out of storage, moved to a leafy eighteenth-century town in Connecticut and, in the spring of 1975, opened a shop of his own.

His life further improved when, five years later, a doctor friend with a practice next door to Sommer's shop half-dragged him to a Halloween costume party on the promise that there would be some single women there. Sommer had resisted. He had always been a shy sort, and since Vietnam, he was having a harder time than ever connecting with anyone. There was the war, for one thing, lying between him and other people—between him and his own family—like an unclosed wound. There was his mother's death of cancer late in the 1970s, for another; it had added a fresh layer of guilt to the guilts Sommer already felt for the war and the tumult he had caused his family, and a relationship he was having then with a woman broke up under the strain.

He was still feeling raw and jumpy that Halloween, and ten minutes before the party he was ready to say no. But his doctor friend nagged and tugged and prodded, and Sommer, to appease him, plopped on a cowboy hat—his minimalist concession to the costume requirement—and went along. He headed straight for the beer, needing one to calm his nerves, and sought shelter among some friends. There was a girl hidden inside a bumblebee costume who kept saying hello to him, but he didn't pay much attention until it was midnight and everybody unmasked. Sommer turned and saw her standing across the room. He went over and asked her name. "Janet," she said. They chatted, and started dating, and the following summer they married.

That he could let anyone so close to him was an important station on his journey home; his liberation from the Army had not accomplished his deliverance from Vietnam. He was still having nightmares twelve years later, still hearing the moans of children dying on a jungle trail. He no longer thought consciously about the war, he said, "but it is always in my mind." He had not yet conquered the flash-fire anger he brought home from Vietnam or the paranoia that haunted him in flight. He could not stand the city because its noise and its violence reminded him of 'Nam. "I got to be in stability like in this town," he said, and even then he and Janet were thinking of moving deeper into the countryside than their placid community of 19,000 souls—somewhere, he said, where there weren't so many people around. He remained prey to sudden terrors. Violence frightened him, however safe his distance from it; a murder in the morning paper or on the nightly television news was enough to ignite an anxiety attack, and the images of the mass suicide of the Jonestown cultists in Guyana in 1978, their bodies bloating in a jungle clearing, set his nerves screaming for a month.

He was only just beginning then to come to peaceful terms with his past. He still thought the war insane—"It was lost," he said, "the day the first American landed"—and still did not repent his flight from it. The charity of Gerald Ford and Jimmy Carter toward war resisters had wiped his desertion from the books, upgraded his discharge and restored him to the company of certifiably honorable men. He did not want or need their accreditation; he felt that his experience of Vietnam had formed him as a person, and twelve years afterward, he was not unpleased with what it had produced. His pity was for the dead and the maimed, the men who could not walk or see or have sex, not for himself. "I cry for them inside," he said.

Yet Sommer had himself been one of the walking wounded of Vietnam and was not completely healed. He was still in flight from the war, still pursued by the anguish of what it had obliged him to do to stay alive. "I don't remember anything I really am ashamed of," he said, "besides the fact that I survived."

BILLY JOHNSON: THE WAY LIFE IS

This is the way life is now, Doc Johnson used to tell himself on bad days in the war, ducking shrapnel and trying to paste dying grunts back together with pressure bandages; this was now, and you had to think about what would come later, after Vietnam. Later had seemed rosy with promise when, as Billy Johnson, he left The World for the war at twenty-one. He had been born into an inheritance of poverty and hard work; he had picked cotton as a boy when his daddy was cropping shares in the Missouri Bootheel and had worked

in a drugstore in Rockford, Illinois, from fifteen on to keep himself in high school and junior college. But Johnson dreamed then of being a doctor and kept plugging stubbornly on in pursuit of his dream. He was working his way through Drake University in Des Moines as a part-time pre-med student, the first of the Johnsons ever to get as far as college, when the Army caught up with him early in 1968. *Somebody's got to go,* he figured, indomitably stolid. He went, and his extended twenty-six month tour in 'Nam as a medic was the closest he ever got to doctoring anybody.

Twelve years later, the promise had worn thin nearly to the vanishing point. At thirty-four Johnson was still the shy, straw-blond young man the Rockford paper described when he clubbed a North Vietnamese trooper to death at Fire Base Julie and won the Silver Star. But the old dream of being a doctor, or if not a doctor, a dentist, or if not a dentist, a pharmacist, had died. Johnson had lost three years in the service and three more as a construction worker before he could flog himself back to college. "I wanted to go back," he said, nursing a beer in his girl friend Donna's cramped mobile home outside Lafayette, Louisiana, "but after two years in Vietnam, I couldn't face the strictness—having to get back into a rigorous routine again." When he finally did enroll at the University of South Florida in Tampa, it took him two tries just to get a C in organic chemistry. He knew then that he wasn't going to make it to med school, so he changed majors to geology and got his bachelor's in 1976.

As he soon discovered, he was graduating into a world that didn't need him, no matter how many lives he had saved or medals he had won in the war. He had gone away in flush times and returned to the job market in a pinched economy; he was pushing thirty when he graduated, and in a buyer's market the oil companies were shopping for younger men with master's degrees and two or three years of experience. Johnson started well enough as a soil analyst in the Florida peanut fields, but the agricultural company he was working for folded under him in six months, and no one else seemed interested in his bachelor's in geology. He knocked through a succession of jobs thereafter as a construction worker again, a carpenter, a sign company employee and, finally, a mud engineer monitoring drilling and analyzing samples on an oil rig off the Gulf Coast of Louisiana. The last was the closest thing he had yet found to entry-level work as a geologist and in the recession of 1982, he was laid off.

He was thus, by his own calculation, ten years behind where he should be at thirty-four and still toiling along with no certain prospect that he could ever catch up. "Face it," he said, as matter-of-factly as if he were sitting on the other side of the personnel man's desk, "my résumé stinks." He remained, as he had always been, a man of soft speech and uncomplainingly stoic temperament; he blamed his difficulties accordingly on hard luck and lean times, not on Vietnam. "I suppose I could go into one of these oil companies down here and throw my Silver Star down on the desk and say, 'Give me a job,' " he said, "but I'm not that kind of person." He carried no enduring scars of the war, none, at least, that he could see or feel—no binges, no night sweats, no sudden Vesuvian eruptions of anger. The memories had come flooding back whenever he went out to the rig, flying low in a chopper over a *déjà-vu* landscape of rice fields and bayous, but Johnson accommodated himself to that as he had to everything else. "My life has been a series of adaptations," he said, sipping at a beer. Twelve years out of Vietnam, he was still telling himself that this was the way life was now and still waiting for things to get better.

ALBERTO MARTINEZ: "THEY BURNED MY MIND UP"

Alberto Martinez stood on an overpass on the Miami airport expressway in the lowering twilight, watching the thinning traffic stream south on Okeechobee Road below him. He had never wanted his death to be messy. He had tried ODing on Thorazine a couple of times, and once the police found him high in the superstructure of a bridge over the Delaware River with a suicide note to his sister Nancy in his car. He was throwing pennies down. The cop who finally talked him down asked him why. He said he was trying to see where they hit—he wanted to be certain that, when he jumped, he would land in the water and not on the bridge. He had always wanted it clean and sure, only now, standing on the overpass, he didn't care anymore. He believed, in his long passages of madness, that "they" were destroying his mind and saw in his shortening intervals of lucidity that they had succeeded. "Mom," he had told his mother a couple of days before, "I just can't live like this. I will never ever be well again. They've burned my mind up and it's gone."

By then, his own family barely knew him. The Martinezes had carried him up from Cuba in their arms when he was four, and had reluctantly sent him off to the war in 1966, when he was a sunny and outgoing young man of twenty-two. They had hoped he would be spared because of his Cuban citizenship; even after the family emigrated to the mainland, Mrs. Martinez had returned to pre-Castro Cuba to have her babies because she didn't want them fighting in *yanqui* wars. He might similarly have pleaded for a medical exemption on the strength—or, more accurately, the continuing weakness—of the arm he had mangled in an auto crash just after his graduation from high school. But he told the family that America was his country and that its war was his war. His father, by then retired from riding to training racehorses, proposed moving the whole clan to Canada to keep him with them. Martinez said no—the war was his duty.

So far as they could see afterward, it had been his destruction as well, the beginning of a journey into a private hell that might have been designed by Franz Kafka with incidental effects by Joseph Heller. Martinez had fought for a year, valiantly enough in the Army's eyes to have merited the Bronze and Silver Stars, and had witnessed much death and dying, yet in all that time and all that fighting, he had seen only one man he could surely identify as an enemy soldier. *Catch 22*. He was not paid for much of his tour because the Army had mislaid his papers and so did not formally acknowledge that he was in Vietnam at all. "If there's no record of you being there, then you belong back here," his father wrote when he sent home for some spending money, but Martinez stayed. *Catch 23*. His bad arm was bothering him, the bone afire with infection, but he couldn't make the doctors believe the pain was real even when the arm was oozing pus. His medical records, retrieved by the family years later under the Freedom of Information Act, confirmed that he had been dosed with Librium for his nerves and sent back out into combat. *Catch 24*.

He had passed those last twenty-four hours in 'Nam pinned down in a foxhole with a dead buddy and had come home a psychic ruin. His first stop was his sister Nancy's place in Hagerstown, Maryland; he spent his days there alone staring at nothing and his nights lying sleepless in the dark with the stereo drowning out thought. Nancy got him out to a picnic with some people. His arm was puffed and hurting. "That looks pretty bad," one of the picnickers, the local sheriff, told him. "You should go see a doctor." Martinez was afraid of doctors and hospitals after 'Nam. By the time the family finally jollied him into going, the arm was ravaged by osteomyelitis and needed immediate surgery. A doctor told the Martinezes afterward that they had scraped the bone nearly to the diameter of a cigarette and that Martinez shouldn't use it for a year—that if he so much as shook hands with somebody, the arm might break.

It was a sit-around year for Martinez, idling between his sister's home and his parents' place across the border in West Virginia, walking and gazing at walls until he mended. Then, when he felt up to it, he began his delayed reentry into The World and discovered that he was not yet out of Kafka's thrall. He took a test for a postal job in Washington. The people there told him they were very sorry—he had done well and they needed somebody, but they couldn't hire him because he wasn't an American citizen. "You mean I can go out and fight for this country," he raged, "but when I come back I can't work for them?" That was the law, the person behind the desk told his retreating back. *Catch 25*. He couldn't find another job and couldn't afford not to work. The government had begun whittling back his disability benefits from 100 percent to 60 to 40 to 20 percent, a skinny $92 a month, and when he protested that his arm wouldn't have got infected if he hadn't been in the war, they told him he had missed the deadline for claiming a service-connected disability. *Catch 26*.

He was still idling and still jangled when his father took him on to help train horses. It seemed to go well for a time;

Martinez even scraped together a little money to buy a horse of his own, and was racing it with some success. But then he had the first of what his family came to call his breakdowns—fits of nerves and depression that were disabling from the start and ultimately became delusional. He had had an episode of paranoia at the track, a seizure of terror in which he imagined everybody coming at him. He checked himself into a VA hospital. He was coherent when he went in, Nancy remembered, and "completely out of his mind" when he came out.

"I was drugged," he kept saying. "In Vietnam I was drugged and when I walked in that veterans' hospital, they gave me drugs." He couldn't eat. He couldn't hear people talking to him. He went outside for long passages, sitting on the grass and staring at nothing. One day he borrowed his brother Fernando's car and disappeared. The family waited for him, their anxieties tearing at them. The phone rang at Nancy's house. She felt a stab of fear picking it up and hearing Alberto's voice. "I'm at the White House," he said, "and I want some action. Why are they doing this to me? I want something done."

Nancy was at the White House with a girl friend, frantically looking for him, when he called her husband, Jesse Davidson, at their new home in Laurel, Maryland. Davidson asked where he was. Martinez said he didn't know. Davidson asked him to come home. "Well," Martinez answered, "if I come home, are you going to put me away?" Davidson promised they wouldn't, and they finally found him lost in Hagerstown, looking for Nancy's old place.

They took him to a better VA hospital in Washington this time, one with a psychiatrist instead of a psychologist. While they were waiting to get him admitted, another young veteran asked Nancy how many times Martinez had been there.

"This is the first time," she answered.

"Well, this is my tenth," the kid told her, and her heart sank.

She could not have known it then, but her brother was starting his own long downhill slide into madness—a toboggan plunge through one or two breakdowns a year to a point where, some years, he was spending more time in VA hospitals than outside. The episodes seemed connected with flare-ups of his osteomyelitis, though whether the pain produced the madness or the madness brought on the pain was no longer clear to the Martinezes. When he was feeling well, he was still something like the Alberto they remembered, a smiling young man who loved children and always remembered everyone's birthday. When his sickness was upon him, he would head for Nancy's house, the only safe haven he knew. Sometimes it would take him days getting there; he was sure the government had changed the road signs to confuse him. He would never announce himself in advance; there would be a knock at the door, and Nancy would peep out, see him and know he was in trouble again.

Once, at his parents' house, he swallowed a whole bottle of the Thorazine the government had prescribed for him. Nancy took him to a doctor and got him a shot of something, but the injection made him sicker, and the Davidsons raced him to Washington at ninety miles an hour, Martinez howling and babbling incoherently in the back seat until he finally hit on numbers. He started counting, *one-two-three*, up to two hundred or so, and it seemed to pacify him, but then he got stuck and was screaming again. They got him to the VA hospital at 9:00 P.M., waited until 3:00 A.M. to get him admitted, then were told to come back at 6:00 because there were no beds for him. Martinez catnapped on a couch at the Davidsons' for a couple of hours, and when they brought him back to the hospital he wouldn't stay. He seemed in okay spirits, even laughing about it. He was just tired, he said; he couldn't work with horses anymore, his arm was bothering him and it had gotten to be too much for him.

He headed south for Miami next to go to electronics school and learn TV repair. That seemed to work out for a while, too, until the night the cops called Nancy from Delaware about how they had found him on top of a bridge pitching pennies down to see where he was going to land when he jumped. He spent two months in the hospital that time, then went back to Miami to finish school and find a job. He found one but couldn't handle it. He couldn't keep his eyes in focus when he took the pills the VA gave him and couldn't pacify his nerves without them. *Catch 27*. He couldn't pick up television sets because his arm was still hurting and he still couldn't persuade the government's doctors that there was anything seriously wrong with him. *Catch 28*.

For nine years the knocks kept coming at Nancy Davidson's door, and Alberto would be back in the hospital again, sometimes for eight or nine months of the year. Just checking him in through the mazy bureaucracy became a recurring nightmare, for her and for him; the hours would stretch out end on end, and he would start boiling up, tugging at her to take him home. "Let's go," he would tell her, his urgency rising with his anger. "They messed up my mind and now they don't want to do anything about it." Once, they had waited ten hours, from one in the afternoon to eleven at night, to negotiate the bureaucratic channels, and Alberto was muttering about wanting to kill a few people. Nancy was scared, and when they finally got to the admissions lady and were told there was no room for Alberto, she boiled over.

"We don't have to take him if we don't have a bed," the admissions lady said. *Catch 29.*

"Look," Nancy raged, "he didn't want to go to Vietnam and you took him. Now he's sick, and you're going to take him!" She turned on her heel and left him sitting there, smoking a Marlboro and thinking homicidal thoughts. They took him.

But the storm warnings in his black periods were getting closer together and more frightening. "Blood they want," he would say, "and blood they'll get." The patriot who had gone willingly off to fight Communism in Vietnam began talking about leaving the country, for Cuba or anywhere else that would have him. "They burned my mind up; I don't need this," he would say, and Nancy began fantasizing his trying to skyjack a plane just to get out. One day he called the family from federal jail in Miami. He had gone to the passport office, so desperate to begin his breakaway that he had left his car out at the curb with the motor running. There had been a line for passports; he had made a scene—"I want to get away right now!"—and had swept some papers off the counter onto the floor in a desperate rage. A guard had come over to quiet him, and Martinez had shoved him roughly out of the way. The next thing he knew, he was in jail, due for trial two days later for assaulting a federal officer. Nancy flew south to fetch him, accepting a deal under which he would plead guilty and she would get him out of the state and into a hospital within forty-eight hours.

She flew him back north that time, popping a pill into him

every time he began getting jumpy, and cajoled him into a hospital—"for me," she told him—and he went yet another time. But the strain of violence in his talk and his fantasy life was darkening, and Nancy was frightened by it. He said he wanted a gun; she and her husband hid the family hunting rifles and told Martinez they had got rid of them. He said he wanted to go to the White House; he sent the President an anguished plea for help, enclosing his honorable discharge, and when it came back unopened and unanswered, he was furious. He said that maybe if he killed a few people he could get some attention, and Nancy was afraid that he meant it—that he might go to the White House and hurt somebody. She called the police; they told her they couldn't intercede until Martinez did something. *Catch 30*. She called his doctors; they were no help. She tried to have him committed to a state mental hospital; her husband took him there, looked around at the squalor and didn't have the heart to leave him.

So he kept drifting in and out of VA hospitals, four of them in four states, undergoing drug therapy and later shock treatments. Between stays he tried to work, poring daily over the help-wanted ads, but couldn't hold a job because of his arm and couldn't get treatment for it—not until his elbow swelled up to the size of a softball and they finally operated. *Catch 31*. The government raised his disability back up to 40 percent then, good for $232 a month, and then proceeded to dock his checks by $1,000, on the claim— disputed by the Martinezes—that he was delinquent on a GI loan for electronics school. *Catch 32*. He studied the pharmacopoeia, learning the properties of all the medication he had been given and seeing in it a conscious attempt to destroy his reason. He watched television, listening to the prattle and concluding that the set, sometimes overtly and sometimes in code, was talking to him.

On the day after Christmas, 1981, he took an overdose of Thorazine again. His father got him to a hospital in Miami this time; he was in intensive care for three days, then moved to a psychiatric ward. It was supposed to be locked, but in mid-January he walked out and materialized at his parents' place. He was there for most of a week, sitting immobile in the living room, staring, smoking, complaining that the government had sent him to the war and then cheated him of his mind. The family began proceedings to have him committed, to a VA hospital this time. "We didn't want him to die," Nancy said later. He agreed to attend the hearing, but for perfectly correct bureaucratic reasons, it never came off. *Catch 33.*

On a Friday night, Nancy called from Maryland. "How are you?" she asked.

"All right," he said.

"Are you taking your medication?"

"No, I don't need any more medication," he said.

"Albert," she said, "you should take the medication or you'll get sick."

"No, the only time I take it is when my stomach starts to jump, and then I take one. But that's it. I won't need it anymore. I'm okay."

He had been hovering around his mother through that week, kissing her, almost as if he were trying to say goodbye. On Saturday he told her he loved her. "I just can't live like this," he said. "I will never, ever be well again. They've burned my mind up and it's gone." That afternoon he stuffed his life savings—$1,094—in his back pocket and drove off; he was going to Washington, he said, and then leaving the country for good. His parents assumed, or prayed, that he was headed for Nancy's place, where he usually sought haven when he was ill. Instead, he turned up at a VFW post in the Miami area, parked outside and encamped for two days. Mostly he sat in the car. Occasionally he would come inside and ask the barmaid for a glass of water, telling whoever would listen that he was fed up with his country and was going to starve himself to death. No one seemed interested, not even enough to call his family to come get him; the post chaplain told the papers later that they had considered him a pain in the ass. *Catch 34.*

When he hadn't gone away by the third day, he began making the post officials nervous, and they called him in for a talk, a tape recorder running as a precaution.

"What seems to be the problem?" the post commander asked.

"I'd like to leave the country," Martinez said.

"So you don't believe in the system anymore?" someone else asked later.

"The system broke down," Martinez answered.

They talked some more. Martinez told them how he talked to the TV and how the TV talked back to him. "The first time, I thought it was just my mind going crazy," he said, "but I see that's not so." His eyes were rolling. He looked crazy. The VFW people took him to see the Disabled American Veterans people and, in tandem, tried to persuade him to go to a hospital. "I don't want to go to the hospital," he said; he had had enough of hospitals in nine years, and he drifted back to his vigil outside the VFW post instead.

They called the police this time. They came and found him still sitting in his '74 Chevy. He said he needed help. They thought he was begging money; he was pleading for the restoration of his soul. They spoke with him, reassuringly. He seemed to calm down. He told them he hadn't had any food for two days and was going off to get something to eat. It was ten past six on a Monday evening.

He drove out along the Miami Airport expressway in the fading light and came to the overpass over Okeechobee Road. *I just can't live like this.* He parked and looked down over the rail at the pavement below. *They've burned my mind up and it's gone.* He had never wanted his death to be messy. *Catch 35.* He plunged head first off the overpass, and his broken body lay for two hours in his puddling blood before they took him away.

EDMUND LEE VI: AT HOME ABROAD

The best thing that happened to Edmund Lee VI in Vietnam was leaving it for a week in Australia. The war otherwise was not his thing. He was a direct descendant of Richard Henry Lee, a signer of the Declaration of Independence, and cousin at some forgotten degree of consanguinity to General Robert E. Lee. But he had neither his cousin's flair for command, preferring taking orders to giving them, nor his ancestor's eagerness to pledge his life, his Fortune and his sacred Honor to what was then the new American nation. He had enlisted in the Army one lazy summer out of prep school in the hope of becoming a combat photographer and had thought fleetingly of bolting to Sweden when he got his orders for 'Nam as a grunt instead. He was deterred mainly by the stiff penalty for desertion and the possibility that he might never be allowed to return to the United States. It occurred to him only after he had seen Australia on his R&R that he might not be going back to stay anyway.

The war for him was less an ágony of the soul than a thorn in the flesh and even, in the slack months before the battle for Fire Base Julie, a bore. His most vivid memories of it, apart from his R&R, were the mellowness of the dope and the intensity of the sex in the massage parlors. He was four or five years older, at twenty-four, than most of his comrades in arms, and a bit of a loner besides. He made his own way through the war accordingly, resisting responsibility for anyone else and volunteering for machine gunner because it gave him a kind of independence "out of the table of command."

The war made as little sense to him as it did to most of Charlie Company. On his very first operation he asked a villager what he felt about the American presence, and the villager answered, "Everyone should go home and leave us alone." As a bit of a history buff, Lee knew that the Vietnamese had been fighting for a thousand years, more or less, before the Americans came. "I never really saw how we'd make much difference," he said. "I never thought we'd do any better than the French."

His war objective instead, as for most of the others, was to stay alive. His first reaction when he got hit with shrapnel at Julie and saw the blood soaking the front of his fatigue pants, was *Oh, damn—not me!* His second, after he came to and satisfied himself that his vitals were all present and accounted for, was that it was at least a half-million-dollar wound—a ticket out of the war for a while if not for good. He was sent to Cam Ranh Bay to recuperate and stretched out his stay there for six weeks by going swimming in the salt water at two or three critical points in the healing process. He had been back with Charlie Company for less than a week thereafter when he was transferred, at his own request, to a VIP helicopter unit at Long Binh; his assignment there was door gunner, but the milk runs he flew seemed never to get within range of anything worth gunning.

He came out in the autumn of 1969 and crashed for a time at his family's apartment on Park Avenue in Manhattan. It was, he remembered later, like living in a dream, as if he had struck out on a path in some new direction while everyone else he knew was slogging along on the same course as ever. His first weeks back were numb with booze and dope smoke, but his father understood both war and loneliness; he had himself served as a deputy to Wild Bill Donovan in the OSS in World War II and had been red-baited in the anti-Communist hysteria afterward, without supporting evidence, and he was content to wait while Lee exorcised his devils on his own. Lee had nightmares, but they went away after two or three months. He had trouble dragging himself out on the job market, but his father took him on at his insurance office as a computer programmer. "I reached a point where I just cut out the crap," he said, dealing with his memories of Vietnam by blanking it out of his mind.

Vietnam but not Australia; he had loved it enough at first sight to go back, at least for a long look, and the paperwork required to get there put some direction in his otherwise unanchored life. "Going to Australia was like starting out on my own for the first time," he said. He had contracted for two years as an "assisted migrant" when he left for Sydney in 1971 and had stayed for ten. He had gone back to the States once on a brief visit in the latter 1970s, but had no plan or desire to return for good. He had worked as a programmer, a produce-truck loader, a record warehouseman and, for five years, a brakeman on the New South Wales state railroad. He had lived for several years with a beautiful Maori named Tania and had fathered a daughter, Ishbel. His American accent was layered over with the idiom and the inflection of Australia. He stayed in touch with the news from America and, in the dawning Age of Reagan, wasn't liking it; the dispatches on the arrival of the first few United States military advisers in El Salvador reminded him uncomfortably of Vietnam. "When I read about all that crap in the States, I don't feel like heading home," he said. The heir to Richard Henry Lee's name and bloodline felt by then that he was home already.

KEVIN ABBOTT: "THEY WANTED US TO GO AWAY"

Kevin Abbott had been the hero of Cantigny, defending a whole besieged bunkerful of grunts with a machine gun, a grenade launcher and a regiment's ration of guts. He had been a victim at Luke's Castle, his back laid open by shrapnel the day the new lieutenant called down Charlie Company's mortars on Charlie Company's troops. But when Abbott came home to Brooklyn in 1970, it was as if his Bronze Star were for nothing and the friendly fire were still raining down around his ears. He had expected to be welcomed home as a soldier, if not a conquering hero, with honor and pride. Instead, people said, "Hi there, how are you?" and left it at that—*as if*, he thought, *I was coming back from a year in California*. He had dreamed the American dream, while he was away, of a house of his own in the suburbs. Instead, he walked back into the devouring inflation ignited in part by the war, and when he was ready to reach out for his small piece of the dream, he could no longer afford it.

It hurt all the more because Abbott felt he had paid his dues—had served his country in a war he never understood and had been brought to tears by the carnage in which it had immersed him. He had grown up in a striving middle-class Irish family in Brooklyn, first Bedford-Stuyvesant before it tipped black, later in the house his father bought in Flatbush by working two jobs. The breakup of his parents' marriage when he was thirteen forced a kind of precocious independence on him, and the city bred its pavement toughness into him. But none of it quite prepared him for Vietnam—for the sudden, sickening feeling of having to put a bullet into another man's head before he could put one in yours; for the sight of a kid GI blown to bits outside the wire at Cantigny, with a photo of his girl lying incongruously whole among the fragments of his body. Abbott had soldiered well, with deadly efficiency when he needed it, and had worked his way up from scared point man to seasoned squad leader. But he never got used to the blood. "I cried a lot over there," he said long afterward. "I mean how much did they expect you to give? There were times when I just sat in a bunker and cried."

He dreamed about it for a time when he came home, sweaty nightmares pierced by the cry of *incoming!* and the shrill howl of mortar rounds screaming toward him. Like many of the boys of Charlie Company, he sought shelter in drinking for a time, but it was happy drinking, mostly, the glow of whiskey and the laughter of old pals holding Vietnam at a safe distance. Neither the dreams nor the drinking lasted very long. An employer was obliged to give a Vietnam veteran his old job back if he applied within ninety days; Abbott waited eighty-nine, then presented himself at Morgan Guaranty Trust on Wall Street for reemployment as a clerk. He did not feel damaged inside by the war as he knew some veterans had been; its emotional residue for him was less pain than anger. "I was fortunate enough to come back with a pretty clear head," he said. "But to go over there and kill people and then come back into the society we came back into without any kind of special recognition and try to act normal—that's really tough."

His anger tinctured the patriotism he had carried into Vietnam. His Catholic boyhood had been centered around home, church and the presumption that if your country was in trouble, you went to war for it. His further supposition— "a little naive," he came to think—was that when you went to war, you fought to win. Since they didn't even try, he finally concluded that there was no reason for them to be in Vietnam at all. "I mean, we *lost*," he said. "I'm not going to say that we were used as pawns, because that's kind of a rough thing to say against a country, but I was kind of disappointed. I thought if we had been intent on winning, then we would have won the war."

Abbott accordingly came home "a little militant," more nearly in sympathy with the antiwar dissidents than with the co-workers who regularly abused them during coffee breaks in the Morgan Guaranty cafeteria. He wasn't about to go peace marching, and he didn't agree with everything the movement said, but when guys he worked with did their love-it-or-leave-it number on the demonstrators, Abbott would flare up at them. *These people have no idea of what war is really like,* he thought. *These people have never experienced the fright of laying in a bunker and hearing mortar rounds come down on top of you or seeing a friend of yours blown apart.* He had experienced that, all of it, and he would rattle the coffee cups with his anger. "If they were attacking our shores, it's a different story," he would say. "But I don't really know what we were doing over there. I experienced it and I would never do it again."

His days of rage subsided with the waning of the war. His sense of grievance at what he felt was America's ingratitude toward the men who had waged it never stopped. He had worked his way up to investigator at the bank, a decent enough job, and was studying nights for an associate degree at the American Institute of Banking to better his and his family's lot. But he felt stalled in his work and straitened by life in a four-room apartment on Staten Island, New York's fifth borough, at $340 a month. He had married late, at thirty, and had fathered two boys, Matthew and Christopher; when the second was born, his wife, Debbie, quit work, and the additional income that had made a little breathing space in their lives stopped coming in. When it stopped, their savings stopped, too, eroded by bills, rent checks and inflation. Money quit going into the bank and started flowing out.

The symbol of Abbott's frustration was the house he almost bought in New Jersey and couldn't. The inflation begotten by Lyndon Johnson's guns-and-butter attempt to finance the war and the Great Society at the same time had priced much of the housing market out of Abbott's reach. When he finally found one he liked and could afford, in New Jersey, the interest rate on the mortgage rose from 11.5 percent when he signed to 13.5 percent and rising at closing time, and he had to back out; the money wasn't there, and the government wasn't there to help. So he was still stuck in his flat on Staten Island when the hostages came home from Iran to a welcome that seemed to him a cruel joke on himself and a million men like him. *Ticker tape parades and the country going overboard,* he thought. *They can write their own ticket. They'll do books and probably never have to worry where their next buck is coming from, and here I am sweating out the phone bill, sweating out the gas bill, sweating out where I'm going in my job, sweating out trying to buy a house. Will I ever be able to afford a house? It's scary.*

Abbott thought America owed those of its sons who fought in Vietnam something rather better than that—not a handout but a handhold on the dreams they had deferred to go off and wage a thankless war. He had come to regret his own service in that war and would think twice, he said, about committing his own sons to another like it. It wouldn't be the way it was for him in 1968, when it was simply assumed between his father and himself that he would serve without question. Abbott had spilled blood and tears in Vietnam and had come home to indifference. "We lost the war," he said, "and they just wanted us to go away."

DAVID AND MICHEL RIOUX: ON HIS BLINDNESS

"Being blind is horrible," David Rioux said, as tonelessly as if he were talking about a bad spell of weather or an unlucky day on the market. A caller had come to the home Rioux shared with his sister and brother-in-law in a hilly subdivision south of Santa Barbara, California, the front yard riotous with bougainvillea in full bloom. Rioux had emerged from a darkened hallway to greet him, thin and pale, feeling his way along the wall and the edges of the furniture toward a chair. One arm dangled at his side, scarred and mottled by multiple skin grafts. One leg was in a brace, making his progress slow and cautious. His sightless eyes squinted behind heavy dark glasses.

Yes, he said, blindness was a terrible thing, frightening to those who have never experienced it and to those who have entered upon it; it had narrowed all his options, aborted his dream of marrying the pen pal in Detroit he had never seen and sentenced him to a life lived in the dark. Yet his reserves of faith, patriotism and intellect seemed to armor him against bitterness toward the war or self-pity at what it had done to him. He bore his wounds so calmly, indeed, that some of the kindly VA counselors assigned to rehabilitate him thought he must be crazy.

His father had brought him back from Tokyo to Walter Reed Hospital in Washington a physical ruin, wasted away to an emaciated ninety pounds; his brother Michel followed on compassionate leave a short time later. The doctors at Reed were gentle with David to the point, he thought later, of uncandor in their solicitude for what they presumed he was feeling. They were slow to tell him that he would never recover the vision in his left eye, a reticence that continued until the last haze of light went out four months after his arrival. "Look," he asked then, "what's going on? Why don't you tell me what's really the case—that the eye's been deteriorating."

It was then they finally told him yes, it was so, he would never see again. It looked to Michel for a time as if David would never walk again either; as if he would vegetate in a wheelchair, crippled and blind, for the rest of his life. A sorrow fell over David at that, not for himself but for his father and mother. "It seemed to me that I was going to have to depend upon my parents again," he remembered years afterward, "and that made me sad. It seemed to me that now it was my turn to do things for them."

Rioux began at that point to examine with a cold clarity what had happened to him and how he could make do with what the booby trap he had tripped in Vietnam had left him of his body. He had dreamed of going to college in Detroit to witness for the war against a generation of students clamoring for an end to it and to find out at first hand whether his chaste airmail liaison would blossom into love and marriage. That no longer seemed realistic to him. He knew he would never see his wife or children; he could not be sure how his blindness would affect the way she, or the world, saw him. "It seemed to me most prudent," he said, "just to wait and see what would develop—to let time discover to both of us whether or not what had happened would change our feelings for one another."

What time discovered to them was that their unborn romance was gone. They remained friends, "as much as we can be friends across such a distance," Rioux said. They stayed in touch, but when she came to visit him in the early 1980s, her husband visited with her.

Rioux resisted anger or depression to a point where his counselors feared for his sanity, and his own brother, even knowing the answer, wondered how he could handle so catastrophic a maiming with so little bitterness. Michel Rioux understood that David was sustained first by his interwoven faith in God, country and the justness of the cause they had both served. "What he suffers, he suffers for good reasons," Michel said. "If he didn't believe in anything—if he were an agnostic or an atheist—he'd have pretty good reason to commit suicide. It's this faith that gives him the strength that he needs."

Yet Michel, sharing that faith, wondered whether he could have borne David's wounds as well, and Michel more than David was afflicted with a sense of what a waste it had been. His own faith in the ability of his country to govern with justice was shaken when he heard the bells at Saint Peter's Church in Lewiston, Maine, tolling for the final withdrawal of America's forces from Vietnam and the dying commitment of Congress to help the South Vietnamese defend themselves. *Well, we finally did it*, he thought, and he was angry. It wasn't just David; it was all the wounded and all the dead—*absolutely for nothing*, Michel thought, hearing the bells. *If I had known what we were going to do at the end of Vietnam, I would have gone to jail.*

David shared Michel's anger at what they saw as the abandonment of Vietnam to a Communist bloodbath, but not his sense that American lives and treasure had been entirely squandered. He regretted nothing in the war except its outcome and, having gone prepared to die in the service of God and the flag, was prepared to accept the lesser death of his sight. The psychologists and sociologists at the VA's center for the blind in West Haven, Connecticut, hovered attentively over him, assuring him that he had not yet suffered what their manuals identified as the shock of blindness and waiting for the first confirming signs of depression to set in. Rioux disappointed their expectations, largely, he imagined, because they didn't know him or the depths of his belief. "I didn't *have* any shock or depression," he said. "I feel bad about it. Blindness is very severe and discouraging; you want to see and be able to do what sighted people do. But I sat down and I said, 'All right now, this is what remains to me, these are the faculties I still have, this is what I can do with them and these are the steps I am going to take.'"

What he found undamaged in his inventorying was his mind, an instrument of rigor and clarity undergirded by the certainties of his politics and his church. Where Michel had grown up robust and hearty, a carpenter like their father, David had always had a bent for literature, philosophy and theology. If he could not see, he could still think, study and write. When he understood that, he knew what he wanted: to go back to school and prepare himself to lead a life of the intellect.

His remaining problem was to persuade the VA, through its suffocating kindliness, that he knew what he was doing. What he wanted of his rehabilitators was training in mobility so he could get around and in one-handed typing so he could set his thoughts on paper. The VA offered both but insisted on packaging what he considered necessary with what he considered superfluous—woodworking, belt making, rug weaving, even—as encouraged electives—golf and bowling for the blind. Rioux understood the importance of developing dexterity for a life encapsulated in darkness, but he considered the course of instruction unnecessary for himself and potentially damaging even for those with a less clear singleness of purpose than his.

Exhibit "A" for him was teaching a blind man to "play" golf by having a sighted person line him up with the ball, aim him at the cup and tell him to swing. "That is not playing golf," Rioux said. "If anybody knows they can't help themselves, it's the people who are in this mess. But people keep telling you you can do it, you can help yourself. These blind people are surrounded by people who humor them, who deceive the blind person into thinking he or she is independent, just as they are led to believe they are really playing golf when they cannot see to aim their shots. They are finally made to live in a dream world instead of being led to acknowledge the reality that they live in: Here you are blind, and blind people are *not* like everyone else. Blindness is just a terrible thing, but it's really a worse thing to lie about it."

Rioux understood that there was nothing malicious in the lies—that they were in fact motivated by a kind of misdirected pity. Pity is a virtue in the sight of God, Rioux thought, but real pity meant facing facts and seeking realistic solutions. He submitted for nine weeks anyway, progressing to the point of mobility training outdoors and fumbling unhappily at belt making as the price. Then the weather at West Haven turned wintry; because of the extensive vascular surgery he had undergone as part of his repair, Rioux could no longer acclimate well to temperatures outside a range of sixty or seventy to one hundred degrees, so the center sent him home until spring.

When he returned in April, he told his comforters as forcefully as he could that he knew precisely what he wanted in his life: to study and write. He would therefore appreciate it, he said, if they would stick to mobility training and forget about the woodworking and the weaving. "They didn't want to hear that," he said; they were insistent on the entire curriculum. He was equally insistent that he did not want it. It struck him that, as government people, they were bound by law and habit of mind to secular and not religious courses of treatment. Their manuals told them nothing about that solace of the spirit known as grace; when they looked up what was ailing Rioux, they concluded and announced to him that he still hadn't experienced the shock of blindness and was accordingly afflicted with a case of passive hostility toward them.

So Rioux finally left—went AWOL, in the eyes of his benefactors—and set out into a darkened world to find his way on his own. *These people don't even know me, and they're presuming to tell me what I should do with my life*, he thought. That he should prefer trust in the grace of God to a claustrophobic dependency on the government made him an anomaly in the experience of his counselors, and that in turn made them an encumbrance rather than a help to him. He went home to Lewiston first, to write a few practice stories and shop around for a college suited to his thirst for a conservative Catholic education. He found one in Thomas Aquinas College near Los Angeles, then a brand-new institution with an old-fashioned Great Books curriculum melded with the philosophy of Aristotle and the theology of Saint Thomas, and enrolled in its first class in 1971. The VA was unhappy with that, too, since the school was too young to have been accredited and he hadn't cleared his plan with them. They told him he couldn't go to Aquinas. "All right, you can't let me go there, fine," he answered, *but*, he thought, *I am going.* The VA finally dispatched a committee to look the place over, concluded that it was good for him and reinstated him to the VA rolls. They sent a social worker around at intervals thereafter to see how he was doing but otherwise left him alone.

He took his bachelor's at Aquinas and worked at creative writing, then pursued his studies in philosophy at Université Laval in Quebec. His doctoral dissertation dealt in important part with the relationship between art and morality, and was entitled *Arthur and Aristotle, Poetry and Prudence*; it was under review there in the summer of 1982. Rioux was guarded about his plans beyond his Ph.D., only insisting that he *had* plans and intimating that they involved writing. "I'm not in limbo," he said, nor did he feel helplessly dependent on his family as he once had feared. His brother-in-law had followed him to Aquinas as an admissions officer, and they had pooled their money to buy a house. Rioux had hoped for attached but separate quarters of his own. That did not work out, for a tangle of reasons having to do with zoning codes and interest rates, but Rioux had made his own space in the world anyway, at once a member of the family and a man apart, cool and ascetic, passing his days in the cloister of his mind.

Michel Rioux had made his separate peace back home in Lewiston, a continent's breadth away. He had assumed he would be returned to Vietnam once David was safely home, and had hoped to be reassigned to orderly duty in the massive-trauma unit where he had nursed his brother through the shadow of death for twenty-eight days. But the Army kept him stateside, and he Mickey-Moused through the last months of tour as a chaplain's assistant at Fort Devens, Massachusetts. When he came out he had lost any last sense of calling to the priesthood and any further interest in school; he married a high-school friend, fathered six children and worked as a self-employed carpenter.

He was earning a spare living ten years out of 'Nam, but he valued his own independence more than a larger fortune. There were, he thought, "too many things to compromise" to achieve material success. Neither did he have much sympathy for those among his fellow veterans who, in his view, used their experience of the war as an excuse for their own failures. "The Vietnam veterans didn't go through anything that any other man in any other war didn't go through, all the way back to someone with a club and a sword," he said. Those who were strong in faith and spirit, as David was, and were fighting for good and clear reasons, as David had, survived the war and the silence of the homecoming. The single consequence of David's blindness, in Michel's view, was that he could not see.

The tragedy of the war for both brothers was instead its unhappy ending: It became an unjust war for them only when America abandoned it and allowed South Vietnam to fall victim to a Communist bloodletting. "We left real people back there," Michel said. To have done so, in his eyes, was an act of treachery promulgated by Congress for political reasons; it hardened his own view, widely held on the American right, that the United States was a republic deteriorating into a democracy governed by majority whim rather than the wisdom and the conscience of its best men.

It influenced David's graduate studies as well, in his explorations of the impact of art—including the arts of rhetoric and propaganda—on the emotions and the vulnerability of the will when the emotions are excited. He recognized that rhetoric itself was a neutral vessel, available for exploitation for good or evil, for charity or greed. But it seemed to him that Soviet Communism had developed it to a particularly polished art and, in the moral vacuum he saw in the America of the 1960s and 1970s, had used it to influence a generation against the war. "Young people, because they are young, are more apt to think that they know more than they know," he said. "So when they were told that there was a civil war in Vietnam, and that there were great atrocities going on there, they believed those things. They didn't even realize they were only believing them—they thought they *knew* them. The antiwar movement stemmed not from reason but from emotion."

That their dissidence ultimately prevailed was the only

grievance David Rioux felt, or acknowledged, about the war; he seemed utterly without sorrow as to his participation in it, or what it had done to him. Like Michel, he did not like to tell war stories, though both of them had stories to tell out of their own ample and vivid experience of combat. David understood the impulse among some of his comrades to describe what they had seen in all its lurid detail; they hungered for the appreciation they deserved, in his view, and sought it by trying to make people understand what it had been like in Vietnam. They sought, in the only way they knew how, the praise denied them on their homecoming by an ungrateful America. His own feeling was that a soldier does better to keep his stories to himself—that men fought abroad precisely to protect the people back home from the experience of war, real or vicarious.

It was quite enough for the Rioux brothers that they had served in a cause they felt they understood and believed to be just; they did not seek appreciation for it. "Michel and I saw clearly a lot of things that other people didn't see," David said. "We both knew why we were in Vietnam, and the men around us didn't, for the most part, or saw it only confusedly, but we saw why we were there and we were proud to be there, defending a people who were being oppressed by Marxist Communism. We were doing something that was commendable, in the eyes of God, our country and our family."

He was as prepared to live in darkness as he had been to die for that belief. The shock of blindness so confidently prophesied in the rehabilitation manuals had never been visited on him. A large, brightly colored figure of the Queen of Heaven loomed above him as he spoke, gazing down protectively from the living room mantel. David Rioux in his blindness had plainly found shelter in her sight.

TARAS POPEL: "I HAVE NO REGRETS"

The good news for Taras Popel, back home in the little Ukraine on the West Side of Chicago, was that his war in Vietnam was over. The bad news only began with the discovery that with foresight, he need not have gone at all. He had been barely eighteen when he signed up voluntarily, under what amounted to a fire-sale offering of enlistments of two years instead of the usual three. He had endured his baptism of fire at Junction City, praying God to stop the noise and the light show, and had humped through the war thereafter stewing at officers and staying alive. He had endured six further months at Fort Carson, Colorado, on dope smoke and fantasies, the most desperate of them involving re-upping for Vietnam just to get out of the chickenshit routines of the stateside Army. His mother was on him to go back to college. His girl had got pregnant by and married to another man and had dropped Popel. His sister had sold his car. His bank balance was zero. But what hurt worst of all was the day they inaugurated the new lottery system for the draft and his birthday came up No. 328—a sure ticket out of the Army and the war if only he had waited long enough to seize it.

He hadn't, and the nagging knowledge that he need not have gone to 'Nam at all did not ease his reentry into the world he had left as a street-corner wise guy two years before. He was Sgt. Taras Popel, U.S. Army (ret.), enrolled at the University of Illinois's Chicago Circle campus—his mother had won—and isolated by experience from the anti-war movement still roiling among his classmates. He argued bootlessly with them that the intent of the war was right, even if its execution was wrong; the Russians had only $30 billion a year for military purposes, he would say, and it was better to keep them spending it off in Vietnam than some place closer to home. Geopolitics got him nowhere, so he resorted to his own counterinsurgency tactics. A student handed him a flier for a get-out-of-Vietnam rally one day, and Popel started rapping on his own shinbone, having discovered that if he hit it hard enough, it sounded like wood. "That's what I invested in my country," he shouted in a bravura fury. "What have you invested? Just your mouth, that's all!" The student fled in horror.

Mostly, through his first years home, Popel felt adrift, staying in school mainly to please his mother and working full-time as a campus cop to pay those bills not covered by his meager $130 monthly stipend under the GI Bill. He began to entertain other, less strait-jacketing dreams—moving to Seattle for the seafood, for one; buying a boat and sailing the Caribbean, for another. But then he racked up his sporty new Lotus on Michigan Avenue and wound up in the hospital instead, with no insurance and no way to pay his bills except by getting serious. Necessity thereupon became the mother of his intentions; he dropped out of school for the last time and went to work, first as an assistant manager for Duraco, later running a custom machine shop in partnership with his father. He found a new lady, Sheri, and was still living with her seven years later. He found a new calm as well, having discovered in a real war that he wasn't the tough guy he imagined himself to have been as a kid in the streets. "I'm very comfortable, very happy," he said, surveying what he had made of his life. "I have no regrets."

He was not without complaints about the lot of being a Vietnam veteran. He had had his own imbroglios with the VA about the treatment of an arthritic right knee. "They won't help you with anything unless whatever it is you want them to help you with is missing from your body," he said. He was in the operating room at last for surgery when he noticed the attendants dressing his healthy left knee instead of his lame right; he corrected them, but when the anesthesiologist administering the ether asked him to count backward from one hundred, Popel made it to twenty-eight before he went suspiciously under.

But he had largely assimilated the war experience and had retired it to that storehouse of memories people think of as

formative experiences. Only the dispatches from new guerrilla battlegrounds reawakened the old, bitter aftertaste in
his mouth. "El Salvador is Vietnam in 1958," he said in 1981,
and this time they would fight it without Taras Popel.

FRANK GOINS: IF YOU'RE BLACK,
GET BACK

Like so many of his comrades in Charlie Company, Frank
Goins simmered in anger watching the national homecoming
party for the fifty-three hostages America ransomed from
Iran in 1981. *Man,* he thought, seeing the flutter of yellow
ribbons, *those suckers knew what they were getting into
when they took that job. Didn't nobody lay out a red carpet
for me, and I like to died over there.* Goins had come home
to Quitman, Georgia, in 1969 with his nerves shot and the
leg he nearly lost at Fire Base Julie still hurting after three
operations. He thought people would welcome him—shake
his hand, maybe, and say, "Glad to see you made it back
alive"—but they didn't. They didn't want to hear anything
about 'Nam at all except how many gooks he had killed,
which he didn't know and didn't want to talk about anyway.
There were no yellow ribbons for Goins, no presidential
proclamation of thanksgiving. There was only the key chain
the Red Cross gave him in Japan, telling him, WELCOME
HOME. YOUR COUNTRY'S PROUD.

The irony in the inscription had particular bite for a black
man coming home to deepest South Georgia and its racial
folkways, still incompletely reconstructed for all the civil-
rights crusades of the 1960s. In the war, the common danger
of death had imposed its own democracy on combat outfits
like Charlie Company. "There was no such thing as color in
Vietnam," Goins recalled years later. "We would eat out of
the same pan. We all shared boxes and stuff. Color didn't

matter to nobody. Everybody was trying to make it back home alive." In The World, nothing had changed; the Silver and Bronze Stars and the Purple Heart he brought home from Vietnam still counted for less than the color of his skin. "When we got home," he said, "they still didn't want us to go to Mr. Charlie's café by the front door and sit down with them white folks. If you was black, you had to go round to the back to get a sandwich if you wanted one. When wartime comes, you're just like brothers, and then, as soon as everything is over, it's 'Hey, boy, you get back in your class now.'"

The medals were buried out of sight in a bureau drawer twelve years later, mementos of a war Goins would just as soon forget. He had been raised by his grandparents in Quitman and had gone off to war fresh out of high school, a slab-muscled kid with an open manner and a face of polished ebony. When he came home he was different, jumpy as a cat and unable to talk about why—not even to his own wife, Mattie. He totaled his mother-in-law's car, then his own mother's. He had vivid nightmares and explosively raw nerve endings. "When he was laying down," Mattie said, remembering those days, "I couldn't even go up to him and touch him. He'd knock you down. I had to stand off from him and then call his name." She stood large and patient on the outside of his dreamscape, feeling helpless and alone. "I mean he just shut me out of everything, you know. He never did sit down and talk about what was on his mind. I knew there was something bothering him, but I just couldn't picture it, and every time I would ask him, he would say, 'Nothing.' I probably couldn't understand some of the things that happened over there, but I believe I could have understood some of it, you know. But he never did sit me down and wanted to talk about it."

Instead, he locked away his memories with his medals and built a new life for himself and his family, from the ground up. He took a technical-school course in auto-body repair, then went to work for a Chevrolet dealer in Valdosta as a body-and-fender man and later a bakery in Thomasville. He and Mattie were married in 1970 and began having children, first Lawanda, then Stephanie, then Frank Jr. and Catherine. The bills were stretching his wage and his $287 monthly disability check, so he joined the National Guard for a little extra money. He had served ten years when they told him he could no longer draw both his Guard pay and his disability compensation at once. The prospect of losing the supplemental income hurt his pocketbook but not his pride in the life he had built for Mattie and the kids in a neat brick house in the piney woods off Highway 84 in Boston, Georgia. "People around here know I'm a Vietnam veteran," he said, "but I think most people want to forget that war. They kind of respect me for what I am, not for what I did when I was in service. They know I'm a good provider for my family."

A decade and more after the war he was still prey to occasional nightmares, fearful enough to bring him upright in bed in a cold and shivering sweat; once again he would be back in 'Nam, with Mattie at his side in her own torment of wonderment at what he was seeing there. By then he had come to accept his bad dreams as part of his life and had learned to live with them. "I've got myself adjusted now," he said. "I'm on the mend." But he remained bewildered as to why America had been in Vietnam in the first place and why, having gone, they allowed the other side to dictate the rules of warfare instead of going all out to win. "If I know poker's your game," he puzzled, "why am I going to try and beat you at it? There's no way I can win. We lost all those people playing their game."

He is persuaded accordingly that there will be no more Vietnams—that the next war will be nuclear and that America will lose it, too. "We'll lose," he said, "because half the people would die from shock—from feeling the ground trembling at their feet and seeing a shell hit and blow a hole in the earth, bodies flying through the air..." His scenario for *Apocalypse Then* trailed off in mid-sentence. He imagined, he said then, that Vietnam veterans would get through it alive. They had lived nightmares like it already, and they knew how to survive.

DAVID BROWN: WHAT THE ARMY TAUGHT ME

Just home from the war, David Brown put on his Class A's, picked up his old girl friend and set out on what he thought was going to be a nostalgia trip to Trenton State College. The campus had been a second home to Brown all his life; he had biked there and bought ice cream in the student cafeteria when he had been a boy growing up in Trenton, New Jersey, and he had studied two and a half years toward a degree in education there before he got caught in the draft. He wanted his girl with him because she, too, was part of where he had left off. He wore his uniform because his civvies no longer fit him but even more because he was proud of it; it announced to the world that he was due that respect owed to men who have served their country at war.

But his girl, as it turned out, was not his girl anymore—she had taken up with his best friend—and his uniform was not so much a badge of honor as a mark of shame, *as if*, Brown thought, *we carried a plague that was contagious*. He said hi to some old classmates; they fell silent and turned away. He took his date to a gymnastics meet; when they found seats in the bleachers, the kids nearest them scowled at Brown's khakis, got up and moved off. He walked out on the meet, went on to the cafeteria and found himself at the edge of a crowd of antiwar activists listening to a lecture on how to make a bomb. His girl was telling him to keep quiet, but the lecture offended both his loyalty to the country and his sense of craft. "You follow those directions," he blurted, rising to his feet at the back of the room, "you're all going to blow yourself to hell." Heads swiveled his way; there were oohs and ahs, and then people were spilling out of the cafeteria, yelling, "Spy! Spy!"

He felt in that moment, and for a long passage thereafter, that he no longer knew where he was. *I just did what I was told I was supposed to do*, he thought. He had fought bravely, under enemy and friendly fire, in a war he never understood; he had killed five or six men that he knew of, each because it was necessary, each without remorse. They had hung a Silver Star and two Bronze Stars on him and, thanks to a paper-pushing snafu, shipped him from the war zone to The World with no decompression time whatever—not even the usual four or five days off the line awarded a man as a kind of farewell present at the end of his year's tour. One day he was riding out of a hot LZ on a light helicopter, the pilot flying so low they had to climb just to clear the concertina wire. The next night he was in San Francisco, out breathing the evening air, when a stranger laid hands on his back in the dark, and Brown, who had once beaten an enemy soldier to death with his bare hands, flew at the man in a violent fury. "You don't touch anybody at night," he said years later, without apology. He never knew who the stranger was or how much damage he caused him; he knew only that the Army had to clean up after him and process him home to Trenton in what he imagined was record time.

He was still coiled tight when he got there, still not quite out of Vietnam. He had written his family that he wanted his homecoming quiet, and it was—*dead quiet*, he thought, *like I hadn't been anywhere*. In his sleep, he had not yet left the war. His kid brother, Bob, two years his junior, tried to shake him awake on his first morning back, and Brown, ninety hours out of combat, sent him crashing against the bedroom wall with a swipe of one powerful arm. In his waking hours he was smoldering with angers and anxieties that he could not talk about, not then and not for years afterward, even if anyone had seemed interested in listening. He felt himself a stranger, wrenched out of time and marked as if by stigmata. "We were brought back too suddenly and forced to take everything into ourselves," he reflected a decade later. "If only they had brought us back as units with mutual support from each other and given us a couple of months to get acclimated again. I mean they gave us seven days just to get used to the *weather* over there. I don't think they gave us seven hours to get used to The World, and it was very poor psychological weather for us to walk back into."

What he discovered starting that day at Trenton State was that America wasn't the John Wayne country he thought it had been when he had left two years before. "Okay," he said, remembering those days, "I come home with two Bronze Stars, one Silver..." His voice trailed off into a silence echoing the silence that had greeted him. Nobody cared about his medals or wanted to hear his memories of war. He was ignored and, worse than being ignored, was shunned; old buddies he thought might be proud of what he had done acted ashamed of him instead. He had done what his country had asked of him. Now the country was saying he had been wrong, and he was angry.

"We shouldn't have been in Vietnam," somebody would inevitably say if the subject came up at all.

"Maybe we shouldn't, but the government said we were supposed to go, and we're still American," Brown would answer, and the conversation would abruptly die.

At a point, Brown began to think he liked the silence better. For a year or maybe two—time washed out for him in a blur of alcohol—Brown sought shelter in an out-of-the-way saloon called the American House Tavern in an out-of-the-way town named New Egypt, New Jersey, alone in a crowd of people who didn't know him and didn't know he had been in Vietnam at all. There, nightly, he would occupy a stool in what he called "my own little corner" of the bar, anesthetizing himself with Scotch, tequila, zombies and, in one epic chug-a-lug contest with the owner, the winner's share of thirteen bottles of champagne. The corner was his bunker, his refuge from The World; he sat in it sometimes gripping the bar till his knuckles were white, thinking bitterly that the war had been for nothing after all. Once, there was a commotion in the bar; Brown ignored it until it invaded his corner and somebody shoved him. They told him later that he had picked the man up, hauled him outside, beaten him bloody, then come back inside to his corner and ordered another round. "I mean," he wondered long afterward, "what else had the Army taught me as far as emotions and things like that?"

What the Army never taught him was why he had been in the war at all. He kept the notes he had taken in the appropriate course at NCO school, all about how Vietnam was the biggest exporter of rice in the Far East and the source of something like a third of the world's rubber. But in the boozy depths of his anger then, and in the lees of bitterness left behind when he sobered up, the statistics explained neither the strategic purpose nor the snark-hunting tactics of the American mission; he began accordingly to suspect that the Army hadn't understood it either. "We weren't trying to *take* anything," he said. "We either won the battle or lost the battle. Then everybody moved on and nobody stayed there. They didn't want it; we didn't want it. So what were we fighting over?"

The answer he found irresistible was: nothing. "We could have blown that whole country to hell," he said, eleven years out. "We didn't even have to set foot on it. But we sent thousands of GIs who didn't come home, and what do we have to show for it?" His unspoken answer again was: nothing. He found an acid drop of irony in the fact that the proposed monument to the war dead in Washington, as originally planned, was to list only the names of the fallen with no reference at all to Vietnam. "Everybody's name but no place," Brown said. "Probably sections of history books will be erased so we will never have to admit it ever happened."

His bafflement and his anger never left him, but the day came when Brown dried out, walked away from the American House and began reassembling the pieces of his life. It wasn't easy. When he went job-hunting, personnel officers noted his two and a half years at Trenton State and presumed that he only wanted to raise enough money to go back. Brown had no such intention at the time, but when he tired of hearing it as a reason for rejecting his applications, he finally did reenroll to pursue his degree in education. He had to work three part-time jobs to pay his way, on a schedule that theoretically left him no time for either study or sleep. He went to school from 8:00 A.M. to noon, sold auto parts from 1:00 to 6:00 P.M., then patrolled a rubber-goods plant from 7:00 to 11:00 P.M. and a mental hospital from 11:00 to 7:00 the next morning.

He got his degree and discovered only then that it had prepared him for the realities of public education about as well as the Army had prepared him for the realities of Vietnam. His enlightenment began in a year's student teaching in an exurban Pennsylvania district divided body and soul between wealthy whites and poverty-ridden blacks. The school had been shut down by a baby race riot the day he arrived—*one war*, he thought, *into another*. Brown came to think that the source of the tensions lay in a double standard for discipline in the school, a reverse-racist code that seemed to him tough on whites and slack for blacks. He set forth his views in a term paper and got a passing grade, but when he asked for the paper back, he was told the school district had it and didn't want it out.

He lasted one more year thereafter teaching industrial arts in Jackson Township, New Jersey, and decided he couldn't live with the permissive fashions of contemporary public education—the no-flunk classes, the rampant truancy, the loose attention to the basic three-R skills. "I had kids as seniors who could not read," he said. He attempted a one-man revolution, flunking a fourth of the class, but the guidance office readjusted some of the grades upward. "They'll only fail students whose parents have given permission to fail them," he said. *Nice*, he thought. He quit.

His next stop was a discount chain store. He applied for the management-training program and, as he recounted it later, was told he was too old at twenty-four. *What do I do now?* he wondered. *Sit down and crumble to death or something? It wasn't my fault I had to take a forced vacation*. But somebody in the chain's automotive section noticed his résumé and hired him as a mechanic. He stayed with the chain for nine years till he was cast adrift again in 1982 and worked in thirteen stores around New Jersey, graduating from the garage to sporting-goods manager in Matawan. He met his bride-to-be, Cherie, behind a toy counter and courted her in violation of company regulations against fraternizing with the female help until they were spied hand-holding on the boardwalk at Seaside. He survived the subsequent inquiries. She did not. But they kept seeing each other and, in 1976, were married.

Time and distance from Vietnam gentled Brown's life and tamed his furies. He lived with Cherie and their little boy in a modest ranch house in Lakewood, New Jersey, and found work with the state placing veterans in jobs. The only fights that concerned him twelve years out were making up the ground he had lost in the war and guarding his diminished piece of the American dream against the ravages of inflation and recession. But he still had nightmares of the war, vivid with images of heat and death; in them, he could still see the first enemy trooper he had killed, his head exploding in a stream of submachine-gun rounds, and the last, his skull caving in under the impact of Brown's bare fist. *They keep coming back at me*, he thought, the more so when he was under pressure in his daily life. It was as if their ghosts had it as their posthumous mission to add to the sum of his miseries. He would wake up in a sweat seeing them. If he was lucky, he might have drifted off to sleep with the television on and, seeing its glow, would remember where he was. If he was unlucky—if there was only the darkness—he would be in Vietnam again.

He felt afflicted as well by a certain hardening of the spirit with the scar tissue of those days when he had had to kill people to survive. Once he stopped telling people he was a veteran, he felt able to assimilate the Vietnam experience and began to think of it as having been a necessary and even valuable part of his passage to manhood. Yet he was haunted by it still and by what it had discovered to him about himself. "I could sit here and watch television, walk outside, shoot somebody and come back in and watch television," he said. "It would not faze me in the least. I would come back and cry over some movie." He did not mean that he *would* do it; he had left the impulse to hair-trigger violence behind the day he had walked out of the American House Tavern for the last time. But there remained a formless dread in him, an angst whose source he could not identify. "It's just stark fear," he said, and it troubled him, because he had learned in Vietnam what a man can do when he is afraid.

CLYDE GARTH: HE WANTED TO DO THE THINGS MEN DO

There was a rapping at the door of the worn frame house in Aberdeen, Mississippi, where Clyde Garth, Jr., had lived until, at nineteen going-on-twenty, he came of dying age. His sister Daisy, then seventeen, answered the knock. She saw her father, who had left home, standing there with an Army man, and she knew. *Clyde*, she thought. *Something happened to Clyde.* Her eyes were already flooding with tears and her mind with memories of the last time they had seen him, the day he left Aberdeen for Vietnam, rough-housing in the dust with two of their kid brothers—a boy saying goodbye to boys and to boyhood at the same time. *He always wanted to go out and do the things men did*, she thought, seeing her father and the Army man in the doorway, and now he had finally done it. He had gone away to Vietnam and had died.

It had frightened Daisy when he left, but he had smiled and told her, "I know I'll be coming back." Clyde had always been that way, always smiling, always sure and always impatient. It was as if, being the eldest boy in a suddenly fatherless brood of twelve children, he couldn't wait to grow up—to go out and do the things men do. He had dropped out of school at sixteen and again at eighteen, though his grades were good and his football skills superb, to go to work cutting meat at Smith's Grocery; then he had dropped out of Smith's, though both the boss and the customers liked him, and volunteered for the Army. He was already the daddy of one baby girl of his own by that time, and his lady, Leome Heard, was carrying their second child, when they were both nineteen. Garth had picked up all the bills, and they had an understanding that they would marry when he came back. But all that remained of the dream after that October morning in 1968 was the two mail-order diamond rings that came home to Aberdeen among his personal effects.

Garth left little else to either of his families, the one he had been born into or the one he had begun. His death had been almost banal in its randomness, a chance encounter between a vagrant speck of metal and a boy's skinny chest at Fire Base Julie. The Army, with a sort of cumbersome kindliness, tried to attach some meaning to it; in its accounting to the family and its press release to the Aberdeen paper, it painted Garth at the center of a tableau of heroism manning his mortar under intense enemy fire and helping to beat back one assault wave after another. The family clung gratefully to the story and to the posthumous Bronze Star that certified its truth. His medals were nearly all that remained to them of him—those and his faded photograph in dress greens, his write-up in the Aberdeen *Examiner*, his GI gravestone in an all-black Mississippi cemetery and the memory of how empty they all felt when they heard he had died. His brother, Cloyd, then ten years old, had wakened that morning to a houseful of people weeping and had never made sense of it, not then or ever. "I look at it like a man wasted his life because the heads of two countries didn't get along," he said, "and after it was over, it was like nothing had ever happened."

The emptiness curdled into anger when, two years later, the local food-stamp office discovered that Garth's mother had been drawing food stamps and benefits from his government life insurance at the same time. They presented her a bill for $298. She protested that her son had lost his life fighting for his country. "He wasn't the only one," the person behind the desk answered, "and you're going to have to pay the money before you can get any more stamps." Mrs. Garth had no husband and eleven surviving children; she scraped together $100 of her own, borrowed the rest from a friend and paid.

The episode only sharpened the family's puzzlement over what it was Garth had died for. His girl, Leome, had been too desolate even for tears when she had heard the news. "People said cry," she remembered years afterward, "but I was too full. I just walked and walked." It was ten years before she could bring herself to see another man. Even then, she still kept Garth's picture on her wall and still took their two daughters to the cemetery to leave some flowers on his grave every Father's Day so they wouldn't forget him. But when they asked why he had been in Vietnam and why he had to die, she could not answer.

BERT KENNISH: A QUESTION OF SELF-ESTEEM

The homebound jet banked in over the California coastline toward Oakland, and Bert Kennish gazed out at a landscape of parched brown grass sliding past beneath him. *Son of a bitch, it's so pretty*, he thought; he was coming from a place where he had felt dirty all the time and afraid a lot of the time, and even dead grass looked good to him as long as it was home. He had eased the transition by meeting Faye in Tokyo for three weeks of sight-seeing and second-honey-mooning, an interlude that buffered him against the culture shock so many of his men experienced in the twenty-four-hour passage from free-fire zone to front parlor. Kennish was feeling good, at ease in his skin and his experience of the war. He knew that the economy was souring and that he would be pushing twenty-eight when he got back on the civilian job market after three lost years, but it wasn't what Vietnam had done to him that troubled him; it was what he felt Vietnam was doing to America.

Kennish was nonetheless happy to have it behind him, even with a tail-of-the-dog tour still to serve at Fort Sill, Oklahoma. He had spent five months in the field chafing at the rules, the politics and the conduct of the war and seven months in the rear wishing he were back in the field with his fellow grunts. He had moved from one paper-pushing executive-officer's billet to another, each confirming his feeling that the war was meaningless. In his last weeks in the bush, he had written up one of his men for the Silver Star; he was an XO in Lai Khe when the medal came through, and by then the man was being court-martialed for resisting his new lieutenant's orders. *A pointless situation*, Kennish thought. For a sad time, he handled payouts to those *chieu hoi* scouts who had been disabled in the Big Red One's service; he issued a $200 compensation check to one man who had lost both legs and wondered bleakly what would become of him after the Americans went home. *Real pointless*, he thought. For a longer passage, he idled through a psy-war assignment with the Ninth Division in the Mekong Delta, one of five lieutenants divvying up a job that any of them could have handled alone. *Very pointless*, he thought; even the do-nothing terminal assignment they gave him at Fort Sill was exciting by contrast.

And then he was home in Denver with Faye, bobbing along jobless for a while in the tides of inflation loosed by the deficit financing of the war. He felt largely unscarred by Vietnam, once he got over hitting the ground whenever a car backfired and dreaming of the first dead GI he had seen, bled white and naked on a field of bloodstained white sand. His problems had to do with the time he had lost—"Three years of my life had gone away"—and the altered economic terrain he found on his return. The corporate recruiters had courted him ardently in the flush times before 'Nam, when he was fresh out of Colorado State, but now he was older, the market was tighter, and the headhunters had disappeared. For a long time Faye was working and he was not. The situation was a strain on their couple of thousands in savings and an affront to Kennish's pride as well—to what he later recognized as the male-chauvinist notion that it was not in the natural order of things for women to be breadwinners or for men to stay home.

He finally found work with a World War II veteran who seemed to care that he had served in Vietnam and hired him as office manager at a Denver cemetery. He spent a year there in a state of spiritual dislocation; his command had dwindled from a platoon of grunts to four or five little old ladies, and his feelings were numbed to the tears of the aged widows who penetrated their defense perimeter. *She's weeping over the death of a husband she's lived with for forty-*

five years, he would think, *and just last year I had a good friend blown away who was nineteen years old*.

He was reprieved when something opened up at the computer-products office where Faye had been working, just as she was about to leave to bear their baby son. Kennish spent a year there, then moved on to selling life insurance and, later, real estate. He lived with Faye and their boy, Kendra, in a comfortably big ranch-style house on a windswept rise outside Castle Rock, Colorado, fifteen miles south of Denver. The view from his hilltop was a serene one, a deferred contentment at the way his life was turning out.

He felt in fact that his experience of the war had played a vital part in that contentment—that it had both shaped and comfirmed him as a man. He and Faye had taken a marriage-enrichment class at their church for a year or so, and one of the things he had discovered about himself was that he had always been in competition with his father. "Everything my dad had done," he said, "I had wanted to do better. He did this, and I would do this plus this. He had a high-school diploma, I had a college degree. He was in the military as a grunt, I was a grunt officer. In everything I had ever done, I had wanted to surpass what my dad had done in order to get some recognition and some self-esteem." His preacher had brought him up short with that realization. With your attitude, he told Kennish, just think what you're going to do to your own kid, and Kennish resolved to get off the racetrack then and there. He saw in the process that he didn't need the racetrack anymore—that his service in the war had brought him that self-esteem he had been chasing so hard so long.

He felt that Vietnam had been a kind of trial for him, and that he had passed. It did not trouble him that most of the people he encountered back in The World didn't want to talk about the war, or that those who did seemed moved mainly by a prurient interest in its gorier details. Kennish didn't much want to talk about it anyway and, unlike many of the men he soldiered with, didn't feel the need to. "One of the biggest tests for a man's ego, I suppose, is being under fire," he said eleven years out of 'Nam, "and I made it. It was a test that said Bert Kennish is okay. He is a man." He had not been shot up or scarred emotionally; he had not flinched from combat and yet had not lost a single man in his command. "In my own little capsule here," he said, "I did pretty well. No problems at all, really, that are going to afflict me for the rest of my life. I think I gained more from my experience in the military and in Vietnam than I lost."

Yet if he felt better off for his service in Vietnam, he thought the country worse off for having committed to a shadow war there and failed. Kennish never stopped believing that the cause of stopping Communism had been just and that the fatal flaw in America's strategy had been its timidity about hitting the Communists literally where they lived—in Hanoi. Its objective had been to stalemate the Communists instead of defeating them, and as a consequence, in Kennish's view, America's spirit for the enterprise withered and finally died of exhaustion. "By the time I got there," he said, "it was already an old war. It had been going on for nearly ten years. So nobody really cared. It was clear there was no threat of an invasion and no real concern with world war, so it really didn't matter to anyone. The only people it mattered to were the people who were making a profit and the few people—few in relation to the number of people in America—whose family members were killed or mutilated."

The outcome accordingly became a self-fulfilling prophecy. "We lost a war," Kennish said, "and there was no major consequence to losing, and now nobody really gives a rat's ass whether we won or not. I think that's bad." He followed the 444-day captivity of the American hostages in Iran with a sinking heart. His grievance was not over the festival of welcome attending their homecoming, in contrast to the embarrassed silence that greeted the veterans of Vietnam. It lay instead with what the crisis said to him about the debilitation of the nation's muscle, will and plain old Yankee gumption in the ashy aftermath of Vietnam. "What we lost in Vietnam was something more than a war," Kennish said. It struck him that America had lost its self-esteem on the faraway battleground on which he had found his own.

BOB BOWERS: "SNEAKING IN THE BACK DOOR"

It was, Bob Bowers thought, remembering his return to The World, *as if we were sneaking in the back door of the country at night.* He had gone off to the Army and ultimately to Vietnam feeling proud to be a soldier, asking what he could do for his country and not what his country could do for him. "Keep your head down. Don't volunteer," his father had told him gruffly the day he left, and later, seeing him off at the airport, the old man had burst into tears. That had scared Bowers a little; his father had been in combat in World War II and so knew with the terrible clarity of experience what Bowers was getting into.

But he had boarded his plane, flown off to 'Nam and buzz-sawed through his 365 days in the war on faith, guts, adrenaline and Carling Black Label beer. He bad-mouthed officers, brawled with MPs and tracked gooks in the jungle as he had stalked deer in the western Pennsylvania woods; he was nicked by American shrapnel and knocked cold by an unexploded American grenade; he bridled at military etiquette, breached the Army dress code and bristled at the rules of limited war. But it wasn't until he got back to the States that Bob Bowers really got sore.

He had gone off, so he believed, to defend democracy— *the same as my father fought for,* he thought—and had imagined that there might be some show of welcome for him and his brother grunts when they deplaned in Oakland, California. There was none. The freedom bird set them down on a military reservation in the middle of the night, as if they were objects of shame, not pride, and had to be smuggled back into their own country. He had supposed that the Army, at least, might have laid on a steak dinner as a thank-you for

231

their service. There were no steaks or toasts of gratitude; Bowers couldn't even buy *himself* a drink in a bar because he was not yet twenty-one, and having served in Vietnam was insufficiently heart-tugging to persuade a barkeep to bend the rules. He had expected to be received with honor, as soldiers in past American wars had been. Instead, he saw a welcoming party of his countrymen spit on a couple of his fellow returnees and call them baby-killers. Thus forewarned, Bowers ducked into a men's room of San Francisco International Airport and changed out of his uniform into civvies for the rest of his journey home.

That journey was a hard one, made harder by the wounding feeling that the mark of Vietnam was upon him like an indelible stain and that he was not wanted. He had five months left to serve at Fort Knox, Kentucky, and made the mistake of falling out for his first formation with his First Infantry patch and his chestful of decorations. They attracted the notice of the inspecting colonel, who had served with the Big Red One in the war; he paused to chat with Bowers. His captain and his top sergeant seemed to resent the special attention and let Bowers know it, hazing him with chicken-shit routine for the rest of his tour. He commuted home to Elwood, Pennsylvania, when he could, each time using airport toilets as his changing room to get into civilian camouflage, but he was having problems at home too. His lady Pat had written him in 'Nam suggesting that they each see other people when he got back. It wasn't a Dear John letter of the sort that seemed to paper Vietnam at high cost to morale in the field; it was just that she was seven years older than he and thought they shouldn't jump into anything without his having dated girls his own age just to be sure.

Bowers pursued and finally won her his first summer home, but their courtship had to bump through a passage of clear-air turbulence. As the youngest and wildest of three brothers, he had always loved a beer and a fast car; before he went off to war, he had partied his way onto probation for four straight semesters and finally out of college entirely. When he came back he was putting away three beers with breakfast and a six-pack every night. "For a guy who weighed only a hundred and twenty pounds," he said, "that's a hell of a lot of beer. I was dangerously close to becoming an alcoholic."

The issue, for a suspenseful period in his postwar life,

was whether he would live long enough to get there. He had bought a 455-cubic-inch Buick Prix and was letting it out on the back roads, mashing the accelerator to the floor to see how suicidally fast he could go. "I missed that sensation of danger, that sensation that was always with you in Vietnam," he guessed later. "Even though you feared it, you missed it. Your adrenaline would start to flow when you were near danger. It was like a high. You liked that feeling, face it. You'd volunteer for things to get more of it. And then *boom*— it's gone, and it's very tough to do without it."

His marriage to Pat helped sober him up and slow him down, but even then he had a time of trouble finding his way. He couldn't afford to go back to college; the GI Bill for Vietnam veterans would barely have paid for his tuition and books, with nothing left over to live on, and his anger grew in inverse proportion to the stinginess of the benefits. He knocked around from job to job, as a house painter, an insurance salesman, an assistant manager in a jewelry store. Four years had slipped away before he joined the labor gang at Armco Steel, where his father had worked before him, and began a six-year climb up the ladder to foreman and, later, industrial engineer. It had taken him that long, he reckoned afterward, to settle back into the slow pace and the daily aggravations of The World. "When I didn't get promotions or when I got too much bullshit, I quit," he said, remembering those years. "Over there, I led a squad. You come back feeling like a leader and there's nothing here to lead. Over there, you learn not to put up with the bullshit. Back here, you have to."

He had to learn to quiet the ghosts of war as well. He had been home for two years when he went deer-hunting for the first time and the last. They set out into the woods where he had grown up, Bowers moving through a valley, his father walking a high ridge to flush the deer down toward him. His dad sighted a big buck and fired a single shot, and suddenly Bowers was back in 'Nam, ramming a clip into his rifle, dropping belly down into the dirt and drawing a bead on his own father. He snapped back to The World in a cold sweat before he could squeeze off a shot. After that, he never went hunting again.

But he never quit dreaming about the war, the images still vivid enough twelve years out to wake him up screaming in the dark, and there was a time when a particular nightmare called Agent Orange intruded on his days as well. The defoliant contained dioxin, a toxic contaminant suspect in a wide range of disorders ranging from acne to headaches to cancer, liver damage and birth defects. For a brief while in the Carter administration, the Veterans Administration conceded those possibilities; then, in the Age of Reagan, it fell back behind the contention that a link between dioxin and certain "delayed health effects"—discreetly unnamed in the VA's latest pamphlet on the subject—existed only in theory. But Bowers knew that Agent Orange had been used in Charlie Company's area of operations and was haunted by the memory of a C-111 lumbering low overhead, spraying *something* right on them. He thought about that when he read the Agent Orange stories in the papers and connected them with some disquieting symptoms of his own. He was losing his hair prematurely. He developed eight or nine fatty tumors on his knees. He discovered in a checkup that his sperm count was abnormally low; after years of trying, he and Pat despaired of having a child of their own and adopted their daughter, Casey, in 1977. He understood that each of his problems could be innocent and unconnected in origin. He knew as well that each of them had been connected in the literature with Agent Orange, and he was scared.

His anxieties were at least partly allayed when his son, Justin, was born whole and healthy in 1980. His sense of grievance with his government was unappeased. "I fear for myself—of course I do," he said, "and for my children, for what they might be getting hereditarily from me. But it's the people affected right now, where you can actually physically *see* what it's done to them, and here's the government denying everything and covering it up and not helping those people." The government's penny-wise counterclaim was that putting Agent Orange poisoning on the books as a disability would be an invitation to freeloaders with a whole variety of real or trumped-up problems. Whatever patience Bowers might have felt for that argument evaporated the day a man his own age at his own plant died with the symptoms of Agent Orange written all over him. "What scares me is that these victims are all going to be gone before any help comes through," Bowers said. "It's just another slap in the face for Vietnam veterans."

Bowers otherwise had fought free of Vietnam. The experience of the war and the homecoming ached sometimes, like an old wound, but it no longer held him in its thrall. He thanked God for that, and his family, and Pat, large and loving. If you came from small-town America, the life-support systems you had left behind were still there waiting when you came back. He had settled comfortably into his job at Armco and his home overlooking a ravine outside Wampum, Pennsylvania, near where he had grown up, and he was going to school nights for his long-deferred degree in engineering management. Vietnam had seasoned him as a man and strengthened him in his faith; it was the nature and the conduct of the war that he regretted, not his service in it. It occurred to him that his boy, Justin, would someday ask him why he had gone to Vietnam and that he would answer the only way he could: "The country said to go and I went." He never quit believing in that obligation, not even after he and most of his buddies in the bunkers had turned against the war. What baffled him, and them, was why the country never welcomed them home.

JIM SOIKE: BREAKING AWAY

It was his own parish church in his own neighborhood in *Laverne & Shirley* country, the heavily Polish-American South Side of Milwaukee, but Jim Soike, just home from Vietnam, felt suddenly like a leper. He had gone off to war a devout Roman Catholic and had, if anything, been confirmed in his faith by the fact that he had come back at all. He had flown homeward across the Pacific on a C-141 transport with the bodies of six of the dead stacked in GI coffins in front of him and had returned to his roots on the South Side as soon as the Army turned him loose. And now he was sitting with his family in his parish church on a summer Sunday in 1970 with this feeling—*this persecution complex*—

stealing over him. *They're staring at me*, he thought. *They're thinking I committed all kinds of atrocities in Vietnam.*

It was happening in his mind, but it hurt because the church had always been a center of his life; he had grown up with the same sense of belonging there that he had felt at home, in his neighborhood and among his buddies at Boys Technical High. He was settling comfortably into life in their orbit when he was drafted in June 1968. He had flunked out of the University of Wisconsin's Milwaukee branch in his freshman year because it didn't seem as interesting as his job tending trees as a city arborist. He had no sense of mission going to Vietnam beyond what he called the "mild brainwashing" the Army gave its conscripts, but he felt he had kept the faith in the war. He figured in fact that God had spared his life on the night of the Fourth of July in 1969 when the base they called Holiday Inn had come under enemy attack. He was out in a bunker on guard duty when *something* told him to get down. A split second later, a rocket-propelled grenade exploded four feet from his head, shredding the sandbags, splintering his gear and popping one of his eardrums. When the incoming quit, a guy in a tank came over to collect what he figured would be Soike's mangled body. Soike was alive, and he said a silent prayer of thanksgiving for that.

So when he went to church on the South Side and felt its silent accusation all around him, Soike couldn't take it. "It turned me into a sort of radical," he said years later. "I let loose everything I'd known. It was a time when I just felt lost." He walked away from his past on the South Side. He moved to a funkier part of town on the East Side. He let his rust-brown hair grow long and sprouted a heavy beard. He lived with his girl friend Nancy for four years, and when they finally got married, on Valentine's Day, it was at City Hall and not in church. The marriage lasted two years before they realized they weren't connecting anymore through the shell that Soike was living in. "I don't believe in pinning everything on Vietnam," he said, "but I can't say it didn't have a bearing on how I was living, how I was feeling. Vietnam does make you hard. It does make you independent. It does make you think you have to pull things out all by yourself. It doesn't help, trying to communicate with somebody else."

But Soike by then had already started home. He and Nancy had bought a house back on the South Side, and after their divorce in 1978, Soike kept it. He took up with his old crowd from Boys High again. In December 1979 he met his second wife, Julie, while he was doing his shirts at the laundromat next door to his place and discovered how lonely he had been. They were married the next year, and their son, Jamie, was born in 1981. The shell was cracking.

Soike could still go incommunicado about what bothered him. "Honestly," Julie said, burping Jamie on their living room couch, "sometimes you really have to pull things out of him." He still wouldn't leave the safety and the quiet of his house on the Fourth of July, because that was the day the RPG had almost killed him in the war. But life felt good to him again. He was still working as an arborist, ministering to the ills of the city's 35,000 trees, and making stained-glass windows and lampshades on the side; he had a twelve-foot catboat on Lake Michigan for after work and weekends. One day he found himself back in the church where he imagined he had felt the whole parish staring at him in silent reproach. He kept going, and did not feel lost there anymore.

MIKE FETTEROLF: KING OF THE MOUNTAIN

Eleven years after his war in Vietnam, Mike Fetterolf was living in a gimme-shelter cabin on a mountaintop twenty-five miles from Whitefish, Montana, the nearest concentration of people numerous enough to call themselves a town. There was no phone, and the sign in the window warning BEWARE OF OWNER was more joke than threat, since not even the mailman journeyed that far up the rutted logging road to Fetterolf's door. Fetterolf was not really antisocial; on the contrary, he and his brother often drove down the mountain

in his gold pickup after dark to drink with the regulars at the
Silver Palace in Whitefish till closing time at 2:00 A.M., and
even then they sometimes bought a bottle of vodka over the
bar to see them home. But by daylight Fetterolf liked to sit
mellowed out and alone on the front porch with his nearly
waist-length hair tied back in a ponytail—he had not cut it
since Vietnam—and admire the view of Star Meadow sprawling green and glistening at his feet. It was all his, property
of Michael Fetterolf, American entrepreneur. He bought it
with the same layaway-planning genius that once led him to
send a quantity of fine Vietnamese marijuana home from the
war to provide for his recreational future.

He had been "an innocent little boy," by his own ap-
praisal, when he left Kalamazoo, Michigan, for the Army
thirteen years before—a quiet, heartland American kid who
liked home, family, sports, plays, dogs, carpentry and button-down shirts with MF monogrammed on the pockets. He
was, for all that, a little headstrong and rebellious against
discipline, his mother, Pokie Fetterolf, remembered—even,
she thought, groping for the word, a bit troubled. "He was
my first son," she said with mixed amusement and despair.
"Sometimes I think when you have a firstborn son, you
should be allowed to practice for a few years and then send
it back. That's the kind of kid Michael was." But his passage
to young manhood had seemed otherwise unremarkably four-
square. He and his girl, Carol Lynn, had been married for
two months and were at work restoring an old farmhouse
when he was drafted in 1968. Carol Lynn wanted to head
for Canada, but Mike was too straight, too *traditional*, she
thought. He told her that both their fathers would be real
disappointed if he did something like that, and pleasing *his*
father seemed to some of the people near him to be the
central unrealized purpose in his life.

Fetterolf was quite as unremarkable when he arrived at
the war with a fresh shipment of new-meat troopers in January 1969—a serious straight-arrow, Taras Popel remembered, with a chestnut-brown cowlick, a quiet demeanor and
an absorbing interest in real estate. The war transformed him
almost literally beyond recognition. He humped through it
with his folding chair, his stash of smoke and his increasingly
mutinous attitude, leaving a trail of Article 15 misconduct
citations so long that he lost count of them. The only reason

none of them rose to the seriousness of a court-martial, he imagined, was that there were two bird colonels in Pokie Fetterolf's family. He challenged authority and was proud of it. "It wasn't World War II and John Wayne and all that shit," he said. "There's no way a captain could have made us charge a machine gun."

It was on balance a conscripts' army, and, Fetterolf said, the conscripts questioned every order they got. Once, by his own account, he drew a bead with his M-16 on a captain who seemed to him incorrigibly wrongheaded. Fetterolf had a streak of the fabulist about him, nourished by a varied menu of stimulants; the landscape of his Vietnam was blighted by heads on pikes and napalm-broiled babies that, however real to him, nobody else in Charlie Company appeared to have seen. Some of his friends back home in Kalamazoo were under the impression that he had actually killed the captain. He said for the historical record that he had not, and no Charlie Company CO died during Fetterolf's tour in any case, by hostile *or* friendly fire. "Just at the end, just as I was pulling the trigger, I jerked the gun away and missed," he said. "I think that deep down I really didn't want to kill him. I'm glad now I didn't."

The war made Fetterolf a cynic, convinced, like a lot of the nineteen-year-olds in the bunkers, that they were fighting mainly to enrich the munitions makers and the heroin traffickers back home. "That war was designed to go on *forever*, man," he said. "You can't sell arms or napalm unless there's a war going on, right?" But it awakened a certain talent for business and investment in him as well. His first venture into wheeling and dealing came the time when the battalion had pitched camp and he arranged with the villagers to launder Charlie Company's shirts for a dime apiece and pants for 20 cents a pair. His next was a flyer in marijuana futures. Two months before he left Vietnam, he said, he began buying up the local el primo at $20 a pound and shipping some of it home in plain wrappers. It was waiting for him when he came back to Kalamazoo.

He arrived there so transfigured that he didn't even look the same. *Oh, God*, Carol Lynn thought, seeing him, *who's this?* The answer never quite came into register through the cannabis haze around him. They had two sons, one born while Fetterolf was in 'Nam, the second conceived when

Carol Lynn met him in Hawaii for his R&R, and he went to work at the Fisher Body plant in town six days after his return to support them. But Carol Lynn, a few years older than he, was unhappy with his new lifestyle; she protested too much about it, and he walked out after two years to seek his future and his fortune elsewhere. "I quit Fisher Body," he said. "I quit my wife. She didn't like my hair. She didn't like my dope. She didn't like the way I was living my life. So what? I split."

His stake was four houses with a total of twenty units in Kalamazoo's student quarter; Fetterolf had bought them, for $2,000 down, through the shrewd reinvestment of his assets—more precisely, he insisted, with the overtime he had earned working sixty-hour weeks at Fisher Body. He acquired a new lady, a Catholic schoolgirl named Michele who was then a freshman in college and was straining at the traces of her life. Her first encounter with Fetterolf, in the company of some of his friends, had almost been disastrous. He had disappeared briefly on some errand of his own. Some of the others had a white powder that Michele thought was cocaine, and in her impatient innocence she tried snorting some. It turned out to have been heroin; she overdosed on it, and when she came around she was in one of Fetterolf's houses in the student ghetto with people trundling her in and out of the shower to keep her alive. But they hung together. She acted for long passages as a surrogate mother to Fetterolf's sons, and when he wanted to trade up from his four properties in Kalamazoo to a working cattle farm in Paw Paw, Michigan, she put up part of the money.

They spent four years there managing a herd of seventy Charolais, with some of Fetterolf's old running buddies from Kalamazoo as their farmhands, and taking long, exploratory walks on the wild side of life. "I tried everything," Fetterolf said in a CBS News follow-up documentary on Charlie Company. "... abused everything. Everything. Every experience you could find." There were drugs around the farm, pot, coke and Methedrine; people were shooting up in front of Michele and, though it seemed to make Fetterolf incongruously angry, she started shooting up too. There was money—enough money sometimes, she remembered, to throw around. Fetterolf was constantly disappearing, doing deals, in real estate and other items of commerce. For a time they kept a condo in Toronto and alternately commuted there to oversee some of his business undertakings.

Fetterolf had, he said, come out of a world in which you lived one day at a time in an agony of suspense about whether you were going to be dead or not, and once out of it, he had decided consciously to push life to the limit. Michele recalled his having told her once that it didn't matter what he did—he could always say he had been in Vietnam and it had screwed up his head. But the shadow of the war played beneath the surface of his cynicism. Sometimes he would sit for hours on end in the La-Z-Boy chair Michele had given him one Father's Day, no music, no TV and no drugs, just staring. "His eyes were ozone," she remembered. Once, she got out his fine crystal and started breaking it, glass after glass, and she still could not penetrate his silence. He was afflicted by nightmares and flashbacks. He carried a long-barreled Colt .45 and once, Michele said, fired a shot at nothing; the bullet had gone through the wall of their farmhouse and into a neighbor's place across the road.

While their relationship lived, they wrote poems for one another. One of hers, written when their love was still young, closed on a note of foreboding at the distance opened between them by the war:

No one wanted to know why I stared
into my reflection
He's got his memories
of talking old soldiers and me
Sadness again

One of his, in their last days together, seemed to attempt an answer:

The stars demand a change
Through love
Of man's corrupted morality
A change long overdue in me . . .
I have lighted six candles
One for peace
One for understanding
One for compassion
One for friendship

Two for love
My candles burn brighter everyday
I wish to light them for you

But by then it was too late; the candles were guttering low, and when they went out—when Michele felt she could not live with Fetterolf's nightmares anymore—she left him. She heard afterward that he had bought up thousands of dollars' worth of steel fencing and had had it thrown up around his place in the space of a day or two to keep the Viet Cong out. It was a couple of years later when he finally cashed his chips in Michigan and bought his cabin, his land and his free-as-a-bird independence in the northwest Montana mountains. He was still living life to the limit one day at a time, still resolutely refusing to think about yesterday in his pursuit of a new day's pleasures. "Why," his father groaned the last time they saw each other back in Kalamazoo, "do I have a thirty-year-old delinquent for a son?"

A real material success was the only answer Fetterolf seemed able to think of, and Jim Fetterolf died before Michael could achieve it. "I could never prove to him what I could do," he told his mother when he came home for the funeral. From his porch four thousand feet up a mountainside, the possibilities seemed plain enough to him: a condo colony rising one day on Star Meadow and tempting rich Canadian holidaymakers south out of Alberta with their coal, gas and oil money. The dream, if he could make it come true, would be his response to his father and his cenotaph for the war. If the innocent little boy who went to Vietnam hadn't died there, Fetterolf imagined, he would still be on the assembly line at Fisher Body in Kalamazoo and not the king of his very own mountain.

CHARLES RUPERT: A $10 MILLION MISUNDERSTANDING

When Charles Rupert came back from Vietnam, bound for
home in the black ghetto of Detroit, he kissed the ground
and cried. "It was like having ten million dollars in my
pocket," he said, remembering the moment. "I couldn't hold
back the tears." But only the salt aftertaste was left for
Rupert twelve years later. Both his shoulders had been ripped
up when an exploding mine knocked him off a tank; he could
not hold his first job at a Dodge truck plant in suburban
Warren because of them, but the Veterans' Administration
wouldn't pay for the surgery he needed. He was afflicted by
bad headaches, and pus exuded from one nipple if he squeezed
it; he was sure he had been exposed to Agent Orange, but
the VA was slow giving him an appointment. He applied for
a GI loan on a $23,000 house. The VA said no again, even
though Rupert was earning $30,000 by then as a driver for
United Parcel. He and his wife had to park their ten-year-
old daughter with family and move in with Rupert's mother.

He still recalled the VC guerrilla he had surprised one
day in his mama-san's hooch in Lai Khe, telling Rupert that
he was fighting a white man's war and ought to go home.
Rupert had rejected the advice; one of his few positive feelings for his service in Vietnam was that it had put him next
to white men in situations of common danger and had dis-
encumbered him of some of his own mirror-image ghetto
prejudices against them. His grievance instead lay with the
government he had served and with the VA as its most visible
agent in his life. "I risked my life for my country," he said,
"and now nobody gives a shit. If I have a son, I won't let
him go. I'll send him to Canada first."

The day he got the letter refusing him his home loan, he

felt as if the bottom of his stomach were dropping out. He was thankful then in retrospect that he had left his guns behind when he came out of the Army. If he had had one that day, he thought, he might have snatched it up, headed for the VA, hunted down whoever wrote the letter and done what the Army and the war had taught him how to do.

J. C. WILSON: "WE WERE FOOLS"

Until the day his Sherrie made him choose between her and the bottle, J.C. Wilson was drinking himself into trouble and knew it. His poison was beer, and, he said, remembering that time, "It was no trouble drinking three cases a day, one can right after the other." There was one lost winter when the refrigerator in his tract house in Waverly, Tennessee, wouldn't even hold it all; he stashed one case inside and buried two more out in the snow because, he said, "I wanted it ready. Snow a couple inches deep, and I'd be settin' out on the porch there drinking beer." Until Sherrie made him choose, his drinking was crowding everything else out of his life: his work, his marriage, his family. Sherrie understood that before he did. She saw it on paydays, when there *were* paydays; she would look in the icebox for the groceries and find nothing but J.C.'s beer, and she would have to trade some back to the store for milk for their baby.

Wilson didn't understand until later that he had been trying to drown his daydreams and nightmares of Vietnam in a sudsy sea of alcohol. He had gone over expecting to learn how to run a bulldozer and had wound up in Charlie Company instead, a dog soldier in a deadly little war that neither he nor most of his buddies ever understood. "We talked about why we were there," he said, "and nobody could give us any answer. We wanted to know what was the war about, whose side were we supposed to be on, and nobody knew nothing." He was wounded twice, once by enemy shrapnel and once by friendly fire when a grunt sitting up on a bunker accidentally squeezed off a burst of four or five M-16 rounds in his direction. Wilson limped out of the war on crutches after that with a made-in-U.S.A. bullet hole through one foot and the memory of the medic and the kid radioman dying in the body count at Fire Base Julie still burning in his mind. He thought that his scars of the body and soul would count for something. But when he hobbled down the ramp onto the tarmac at Oakland and knelt to kiss the ground, there was nobody there to greet him and his fellow survivors—no reception committee, no brass band, not even a banner saying WELCOME HOME.

Wilson was mystified. "I went over there to do a job and I done it and I survived," he said. "I wasn't ashamed of what I done." But strangers kept behaving as though he ought to have been ashamed, if in fact they noticed him at all. He limped into line for his plane home from San Francisco Airport, still dragging along on his crutches, and people kept skipping and jostling ahead of him as if he were invisible. He understood then, or began to, where he stood in the hearts of his countrymen.

He spent his first years in Tennessee in what he came to understand had been a state of "nervous rage," a gaunt and haunted man careening downhill with a litter of lost jobs, unpaid bills and two failed marriages before Sherrie in his wake. His first wife was a girl he had dated for a couple of years before Vietnam; he married her a day or two after he got back, but she couldn't handle his drinking and he couldn't live with her reproachful silences, so they called it off and were divorced. He tried again, but his second wife was too wild for him, too hell-bent on a good time. His boss of the moment had recognized her once in Memphis and again the other side of Nashville and had asked Wilson, "How you buyin' gas? I ain't payin' you that kind of money." Wilson asked what he was talking about; he hadn't even known his wife had been away. The marriage endured a short while longer, then died the day Wilson came home, found a party in progress and broke it up, forcefully. "Tore up their heads, some of 'em, those that I could catch," he said, "and I walked off and never went back."

He was single again, by annulment, and still drinking hard the day he met Sherrie in a painful case of mistaken identity.

"I was workin' on her daddy's car," he remembered, "because he was crippled. He had sugar diabetes, and they had done took one leg off and was wantin' to take the other one off, and he didn't have no money anyway to take his car and have it fixed." Wilson, handy with a wrench, was bent over the engine when Sherrie slipped up behind him with a thorn about four inches long. "She thought I was someone else," he said. "She stuck me with it in the seat of the pants, and it drove me right up through the hood of the car. I turned around to smack whoever was doin' it. She was with some boy there, and I done grabbed him around the collar and was just fixin' to hit him when I happened to look down at her hand. She had the thorn, and I told this fellow, 'Boy, you awful lucky. If you'd had that thorn, I'd have beat you to death.'"

Sherrie, then in college, was amused but not enough to accept right away when Wilson began asking her for a date. He finally broke through her hesitancy with a bit of a con game, asking her to help him baby-sit with his sister's kids; his sister lived right next door to Sherrie's parents, and Sherrie, feeling safe in their orbit, finally relented. They began seeing each other after that. In 1972 they were married, and Sherrie Wilson, large, wise and patient, dropped out of college thirty-six credit hours short of her diploma to start their family, go to work and undertake J.C.'s reclamation.

It wasn't easy. His drinking and his two disastrous attempts at marriage had left him broke. "All the other ones wanted was a dollar," he said. "They just kept me drained. Every time you turned around, you was just deeper and deeper in debt, and a can of beer's all I was worried about at the time." His bad dreams tormented him with pictures of death and dying; his nights were sleepless, his days dulled by drink and blinded by sudden squalls of anger. "I was trying to keep up with society, trying to put the war behind me," he said, "and I just couldn't cope. I'd blow my check."

"When he *made* a check," Sherrie said. "He couldn't work."

"*Wouldn't* work," J.C. said, correcting her. "I just couldn't hold a job. I couldn't find a decent job, and when I did get work, somebody would rub me the wrong way and I'd blow up and get laid off. It just got to be where you didn't care."

It had been Sherrie who finally saved him by threatening

to leave him—by sitting him down and putting it to him point-blank that either the beer had to go or she and their two children would. He chose them and sobered up starting that day. He found steady work not long afterward as a heavy-equipment operator at Vaughn Contractors, Inc., in town and did not waste much time brooding on the irony that that was the trade he had thought he was joining the Army to learn. Sherrie was still helping out, driving a school bus for kids in the mornings and afternoons and for senior citizens in between. "This one kind of helps me a little," Wilson said. "She pulls with me. Works with me. She works and I work, and we pay our bills."

He still sipped a beer in company, but only then. His revisionist idea of a good time was sitting home nights watching TV with Sherrie and the kids. Sometimes he wished he had a place farther out in the country—a place like the farm he grew up on, just big enough for a garden and a couple of hogs so he could feed himself and his family if times got really tight. Otherwise, he seemed content with his one acre and change in a subdivision outside town, with a creek at the foot of the street where he could fish for bass in his shorts and sneakers in the lazy summer sun. "I'm pretty satisfied with my life now," he said. "I'm pretty well independent. I've got a good job, got two beautiful kids, got a pretty good understanding old lady. I don't really want nothing from anybody."

He was not entirely free of Vietnam. He still had nightmares about it twelve years later, still slept with his hands folded lightly over his throat in case somebody came at him with a blade in the dark. "Even today you don't wake him up too fast," Sherrie said, "and when you touch him you just best stay away."

He still raged at how he had been refused an auto loan when he came home, while veterans of World War II seemed able to borrow any amount any time they wanted. *The World War II guys are heroes*, he thought bitterly. *Drink to World War II*. He still despaired of understanding why he had been in Vietnam at all. He had grown up steeped in country southern patriotism and had never lost faith in America. But the war never made sense to him, and in the absence of any more persuasive answer, he found himself thinking it must have been because of the population explosion at home. *They*

had to have a war to get rid of some of us, he figured.
Vietnam was a good excuse.

What hurt worst was that the country he loved seemed
not to care what the men it sent to the war had been through
there or had endured when they came home—the lost years,
the blighted lives, the wounds of the flesh and spirit. "People
just don't have no sympathy or respect whatsoever for that
guy that went over there and gave his life to keep somebody
free that we didn't know nothing about," he said. "And now
they're right back Communist. The day we pulled out is the
day they moved back, so the whole fight was for nothing.
The guys that died, died for nothing. The guys that got their
legs blown away and their arms shot off got it all for nothing."

He remembered how the boys of Charlie Company used
to brag in the bunkers about how fierce they were in combat—so fierce, they liked to say, that the Viet Cong had
offered to pay a bounty for their ears or their Black Lion
patches. There was no pleasure for J.C. Wilson in the memory. "We were fools, is what we were," he said.

STEVEN MCVEIGH: VIETNAM AND THE ART OF GARAGE DOOR INSTALLATION

If Steven McVeigh hadn't been to Vietnam, he guessed years
afterward, he never would have put up a garage door at his
white shingle bungalow on the North Side of Chicago. It
wasn't a course of instruction he would have recommended
to the kids in his science classes at Dunbar Vocational High
School. It had required that he fight in a war he had never
approved of and hadn't been smart enough to avoid; it had
forced him through a night of hell at Fire Base Julie, then
obliged him to go out for the body count the next morning
and put a bullet into a wounded enemy trooper in what he
persuaded himself was self-defense. He came to despise the

war in fact as he had opposed it in principle, as a hideous waste of American blood and treasure. He became a teacher at Chicago's biggest, blackest trade school precisely because he had despised the war so much. He didn't want another generation marching off to another war, as his had, without knowing enough to reason why.

And yet the mere fact that McVeigh had been to Vietnam and had endured it had been, he thought, a kind of *reinforcement* of himself—a source of confidence wanting in him when he went off, scrawny and unathletic, to the Army. He was fresh out of the University of Illinois's Chicago Circle campus then with a degree in biology, a rare article in a grunt company. They dubbed him The Prof, naturally, and made him hump the radio, and to his own astonishment, he could. He did six months in the field and six months off the line as a clerk, writing up his own promotion to sergeant as one of his last official acts. He came home thereafter with a girl and a calling waiting for him and with a sense of personal well-being that sorted oddly with his turned-off view of the war. He settled with his wife, Sandy, on the North Side, commuting daily to his job in the ghetto, and in the summer of 1981 he found himself putting up a garage door on his own. "I would never be putting up a garage door if I hadn't been in Vietnam," he figured. The skinny, horn-rimmed kid they called The Prof would have been too afraid of falling down.

BOB SELIG: STAYING ALIVE

Bob Selig was back at Northern State University in Aberdeen, South Dakota, feeling bruised and lonely, and this girl he met at a party wouldn't let him alone about the war. "Did you kill people?" she kept wanting to know. "Did you shoot women and children?"

He didn't want to talk about it, but she persisted, and he

blew up. "You don't understand anything about the instinct for survival," he said. "You don't understand that when you're shot at, all you can do—what you *have* to do—is defend yourself."

She still wasn't getting it, so Selig, in dippy inspiration, decided to lay on a little demonstration for her—an elaborated practical joke, really—in the basement rec room at a friend's house out in the country. He borrowed his pal's .22-caliber pistol, loaded it with blanks—he didn't tell the girl that—and stepped out into the hall. "I'm going to come in the door and shoot you," he said, "and when you see me aim at you, you're going to grab for the nearest cheese knife to defend yourself." He burst in. She just stood there. They laughed, but the lesson was a fizzle. *How*, Selig still wondered a dozen years later, *do you explain trying to survive?*

You couldn't, not then; the campus Selig had come back to was fever-hot with passion for a favorite son named George McGovern, and nobody seemed to want to hear what it was really like out in the bush being shot at and having to shoot back. Selig had dropped out of Northern State before 'Nam and had gone to work selling clothes for Shriver's Department Store in his hometown, Sioux Falls, impelled partly by the death of his father and more by his own sense that he was wandering aimlessly through college anyway. He had got through Charlie Company's worst moments in the war at Julie, Cantigny and Junction City without having lost a single member of his squad. The idealism he had carried into the field died there, giving way to a single-minded commitment to staying alive. The short answer to the girl at the party was thus that he probably *had* killed people, to keep from being killed. But trying to explain that in the inflamed campus atmosphere of the early 1970s was like trying to speak to people through plate glass.

Selig felt estranged from a generation—his own. In 'Nam, he had read in the papers from home about kids his age burning flags and draft cards, and it made fighting hard for him and the men in his squad. It told them that the country wasn't behind them. When he first got back to Sioux Falls, his best friends did rally round him for a time, "but," he said, "it was sort of like a wake when somebody in the family dies. All the friends and relations gather round to help out with the arrangements, but then, after a couple of weeks, they sort of drift away and resume their own lives again. They don't keep in touch because they're embarrassed over your loss when they have whole lives."

His own life no longer felt whole to him. Two years had been ripped out of it; he had been off fighting a war he didn't even understand while everybody he knew was doing what he should have been doing with those years—*drinking beer*, he thought, *and getting laid*. He had come home a stranger, a DP from somewhere outside time, and he finally gave up even trying to talk about where he had been. "My job over there was to kill people," he would say, and people would shut up.

The cost was living at the center of a kind of abashed silence, the war upon him like the mark of Cain. He felt a stab of sorrow when South Vietnam fell—sorrow for the buddies who came back maimed or dead and sorrow for what he felt he had lost out of his own life, all for nothing. "Only in the last couple of years has it stopped mattering," he said, twelve years after his return. He was thirty-five then and settled, with a bachelor pad in Sioux Falls and a good job as a salesman for a chemical and construction-equipment company. He never married; the five-year run of his longest romance was spoiled in part by arguments about Vietnam, verbal firefights that nobody ever won. She was antiwar, and so were most of their friends. Their nights out recapitulated the war, the combatants fighting again and again over the same worn bits of ground. The quarrels would always come down to somebody wondering why anybody would have wanted to go to Vietnam anyway, and Selig would finally have to answer: *Nobody does*.

CHESTER WARD: "THERE WAS SO MUCH DEATH"

Chester Ward got out of Vietnam early on a hardship reassignment when his mother died, leaving his father alone in the Long Island resort town of Southampton with a small taxicab business and eleven other kids to feed. But it wasn't early enough, Ward's wife, Bertha, thought when she saw him; it was as if a part of him had been killed in the war. He had gone off a happy-go-lucky black teenager with a crooked smile, a lady-killing manner, a passable high-school transcript and a developing gift for basketball. Girls had buzzed around him like bees around honey; he had fathered three children with his sweetheart at Southampton High and a fourth with Bertha before he went away to the Army. But he came home silent, sullen and angry, *as if*, Bertha thought helplessly, *he was under some sort of pressure*. The crooked smile and the sunshine aura were gone, replaced by quick spasms of temper and long, wordless melancholies afloat on rivers of Scotch.

Sometimes, in her alarm, his wife wondered if he were taking some sort of drug. He wasn't. The monkey on Chet Ward's back, as it turned out, was death. He had seen a lot of it in Charlie Company's Vietnam, and when he got his early out to help his father, the Army, by lot or Kafka-esque design, had assigned him to its corps of professional mourners—those mobile honor guards that traveled the country to stand with the colors at the gravesides of the American dead. He felt on those details like an unwelcome presence, an intruder, though whether it was because he was a black man, a soldier or a messenger of death was never clear. The bereaved families never invited him into their homes. At one

252

burial, the mother of a fallen soldier had turned on Ward beside the open grave and, choked with grief, had told him, "You should be lying in there, not my son! Why are you here alive when he is dead?"

Ward came home shaken that day and seemed to slide deeper than ever into his blank, liquid silences. He was drinking hard, at home and in bars. He was helping out with the cab, but his father worried that his boozing would offend the high-gloss Hampton summer people who made up a major portion of their trade in season. His wife could not penetrate his moods, the long blank passages and the sudden tantrums over nothing. "I just don't want to talk about it," he would snap when she asked him about the war. There were only the intermittent signals about what it seemed to be doing to him inside. "We were over there fighting and dying," he told her once, "but no one knew what they were fighting and dying for." And again: "There was so much death and none of it meant anything."

He hadn't been back very long when he set out from his home one rainy early morning in August 1969 and headed west along the Sunrise Highway toward his post at Fort Hamilton in Brooklyn. It was 6:00 A.M. Ward had been drinking as usual the night before, enough perhaps to leave him heavy-lidded. No one could tell precisely what happened or why; the police accident report recounted only that Ward's car ran out of control, jumped the grassy median strip and collided with an oncoming auto in the eastbound lane. The other driver sustained only minor injuries. By the time they got Ward to a hospital in Bay Shore, he was dead.

The honor guard came to *his* funeral, this time. They assured his widow that Ward had soldiered with great distinction in the war and that they would see to it that his medals were sent to her. Before they left, they gave her and her son the flag from Ward's coffin, folded into a crisp triangle. The medals, if they existed at all, never came, and Ward's name was not inscribed on the official roll of the casualties of Vietnam. The sort of bleeding wounds he suffered there were hidden even from his widow's view until the day he died of them.

HARRY FOXWELL: THE PAST
IS ANOTHER COUNTRY

I was a different person then than I am now, to have been able to do such things, Harry Foxwell thought, sorting through his memories of Vietnam. He had gone off to the Army as a sophomore at a Long Island community college, vaguely pleased with the notion of serving his country and blissfully blank as to what the war was all about. His infantry and instant-NCO schooling, he saw, were directed precisely at turning him into somebody different—somebody who, for the duration of a year, could think of a North Vietnamese soldier as a target, not a human being, and could shoot him dead without reflection or remorse. He had killed a man face to face in his first serious firefight, at Cantigny, firing point-blank into a shape looming up in front of his bunker. When he saw the body by first light the next morning, he was struck by how young and small he looked, not a man at all but a kid as hapless as himself. But it had been a him-or-me situation, and Foxwell didn't torment himself about whether killing him had been right or wrong; it had been necessary. He didn't think much about whether the war itself was right or wrong until he got home, and when he began to feel that it had been wrong, he thought, *That really wasn't me over there. That was somebody else. I'm not the same person now as I was then.*

As Sergeant Foxwell, leading a squad in the boonies, he had limited himself to the standard GI gripe that the tactics of the war seemed pretty dumb, going out in the jungle and waiting to be attacked. He did not rebel, even so; he accepted what he was doing as his duty, trusted his officers, mostly, and concentrated on trying to get himself and his squad home alive. But he found himself even then in sympathy with an old college roommate who, as a pacifist, had been resisting the draft.

"Dear Dummy," Foxwell wrote when his roomie seemed to be losing heart for the fight. "If you could spend one day over here when we're really getting a lot of shit, you wouldn't be able to joke about coming over here. Do whatever you can to stay out of Uncle Sam's reach...and don't even consider letting things ride until you end up here. This is NO JOKE. The sound of a mortar attack or bullets and shrapnel flying toward you is just not worth everything you have back there."

It was only after Foxwell had come home to Long Island and, three days later, to his studies in math at Franklin and Marshall College in Lancaster, Pennsylvania, that he began thinking seriously about what he had seen and done in Vietnam. He found he could justify what he had done as the requirements of duty and survival. He had more trouble with what he had seen, most memorably and most painfully the vanload of Vietnamese civilians hitting a mine on Thunder Road and exploding in a spray of metal, bone and flesh. The memory raised questions about the war that he could not answer and, till then, had not known enough to ask. He began reading about the war—Bernard Fall's devastating *Hell in a Very Small Place* hit him particularly hard—and saw that America was only recapitulating what the French had tried and failed to do in Vietnam a decade and a half before he got there. A light lit. "It was not like I changed," he said long afterward; it was more as if he were seeing the war clearly for the first time, and he was angry.

He found himself drawn to the respectable wing of the student peace movement. He journeyed to Washington in 1970, in the smoky aftermath of America's incursion into Cambodia, to lobby his congressman against the war. He had cast his first presidential vote ever for Richard Nixon in 1968, by absentee ballot from Vietnam, but in 1972 he went door-to-door canvassing for George McGovern's ill-starred peace candidacy. He read a dispatch from Quang Tri in *The New York Times*, quoting a South Vietnamese corporal as having said, "We die easily here, like candles in the wind." The line touched Foxwell; he wrote a poem around it and sent it "in the spirit of peace" to the Lancaster *In-*

dependent Press, which printed it as a letter to the editor. A part of it said:

*The statesmen stand, and prattle on, ten thousand miles
        from here.*
They cannot feel the bullets, see the death, or taste the fear.
They contemplate, negotiate, and tally up the score,
*While my brothers die like candles in the wind of senseless
        war.*

Foxwell's more personal struggle against the war was to put it behind him and pick up the broken threads of his life. He was and he remained a contained man, linear in thought and straight-ahead in spirit, his mind as wiry as his body. He dived under a car the first time he heard a starter's pistol echo across a parking lot from cross-country practice, and he endured six lonely and low-spirited months adjusting to being a changed man in a changed America. But he was not plagued by nightmares or flashbacks and did not feel wounded by the war in anything more significant than his timetable.

He got his bachelor's at Franklin and Marshall in 1973, working part of the time to supplement his GI benefits, and went on to Villanova University for a master's in statistics. It took five road-weary years, commuting seventy miles twice a week from his daytime life teaching school near Lancaster to his evening classes at Villanova. Foxwell hung uncomplainingly in, upgrading his marks from B's and C's in college to A's as a graduate student, and when he came out at thirty, the American Chemical Society hired him as a statistician at its Washington headquarters at what seemed to him flatteringly high pay.

It *was* high, for an ex-schoolteacher, until Foxwell began shopping the Washington housing market at a time of inflationary prices and exorbitant interest rates. He had married his college sweetheart, Eileen, by then, and had fathered two boys, Andrew and Michael. They needed a house with space in a good school district and couldn't afford anything they liked. They wound up renting instead in Burke, Virginia, in the Fairfax County exurbs, and struggling to make ends meet on what had seemed to them a handsome wage.

But Foxwell plowed doggedly forward adapting to his postwar life as he had to the war. He saw no useful purpose in lamenting the time Vietnam had stolen from his career. Instead, he accommodated to it. He learned computers and set up a consulting business on the side. His wife took accounting to bring in a second income. Yes, there had been a price for the war, but times would be better. "You can't go back and change what you went through," Foxwell said, "and it's not good to blame any current problem you might have on past experiences. So I try not to dwell on it."

He was accordingly impatient with the media for what he saw as their fixation with what was bizarre in the war and in the lives of the men who had fought it. He read in a Villanova alumni newsletter that a professor teaching a seminar on the social impact of Vietnam was using the film *Apocalypse Now* as an audio-visual aid to understanding what the war was really like. Foxwell exploded. The war he fought was peopled not with homicidal movie madmen doting on the smell of napalm in the morning but by men like himself, ordinary guys who had coped with Vietnam and were coping with life back home.

For himself, Foxwell was not tormented by replays of what he had seen or guilt at what he had done. He had killed when he was obliged to and had not sought refuge, as some of his buddies did, in the comforting proposition that nobody knew who had shot whom. The Army's tacticians encouraged that fiction, he thought. "How do you take a person and train him in a year to be a killer? You train him to shoot at shadows. You train him to shoot in groups so that they are not individually killing somebody. So a person could convince himself that he never shot anybody or that he didn't know. But there were a lot of Vietnamese killed and a lot of people participated in killing them, so it must be true that *somebody* killed *somebody*."

Foxwell had simply walked away from the fact of his having killed; he had been another man in another country then, a country in which it was sometimes necessary to kill as the cost of staying alive. "I can think back on that now," he said, "and regret that that's the situation I was in and that that's what I had to do. But at the time I didn't think about what it was—I was just defending myself." His regret in hindsight was rather that there had been a war at all. His son Andrew, at seven, had begun asking him what he had done in the war and, with a boy's avidity, whether he had shot anybody. Foxwell tried gently to answer that war was bad and that peace was what people ought to be concerned with. He had already made up his own mind that, if there were another war like Vietnam, he would advise his two boys not to go.

DAVID BEAN: "WHAT'S WRONG WITH ME?"

David Bean had been out of Vietnam for twelve years when he had his first nightmare about it—when he sat straight up in bed, with his lady Diane lying beside him, and screamed, "Kill him! Kill him! Kill him!" Then he was awake, the images dissipating like dope smoke on the air, and he was crying; the tears were spilling down his face, and he was thinking, *Aw, Jesus Christ—what's happening?*

He had been bumping along for a dozen years, dancing through life a half-step ahead of his terrors. He had been through a blighted marriage, a succession of girl friends and a drifter's résumé of underachieving jobs. He had smoked a lot of joints and had fooled with coke and acid. He had had episodes of paranoia and fantasies of superhumanity; he had seen things that other people did not see and had heard music that other people could not hear. He had been in jail and psychiatric wards, once roosting jaybird-naked in a padded cell. He had considered suicide three times and had drawn back from it each time, partly in fear of dying, partly in dismay at what thinking the thought had told him about himself. *What the fuck is wrong with me,* he had wondered for all those dozen years, and when he woke up screaming with his head back in Vietnam, he cried because he was scared.

It scared Bean because he thought he had left the war behind him in Vietnam. He didn't know then that it could sometimes explode inside a man long afterward, like an artillery round with a time-delay fuse, and he had never connected it with his own problems. He had got through exactly five months and sixteen days of it before his foot stopped an NVA bullet looking for Curtis Gilliland's head outside Junction City on Christmas Eve. Twelve years later he still felt some numbness in the foot, and there were pictures that Bean had never completely expunged from his mind. There had been that time at Cantigny when he had flipped over an NVA corpse and the skull had broken open. "I can still see that guy's face sliding away," he said, nursing a beer in the dark outside his mobile home in the Florida Keys. "I can still see those brains running out." But he thought he had persuaded himself that it didn't matter—that he was paid to be a hunter and that the NVA was his prey. He hadn't talked much about Vietnam to anyone since then, because, he thought, *nobody wants to spend one lousy night listening*. Instead, he put his memories in cold storage. When he thought about it at all, he thought of the war as having been worthless for the country and yet formative for himself—an education in the value of life and the ways of men.

He had felt dislocated, even so, when he came home, as if the war had changed him and he could no longer get through to anyone who hadn't experienced it. When the Army sprung him from his post-'Nam tour at Fort Riley, Kansas, he headed straight home to the southern Minnesota lake country and, within two weeks of touchdown, to Mankato State College, fifty miles away. "I thought everything was going to be the same for me, the way it was," he said, but it wasn't; he didn't fit anymore. A girl friend, a phys. ed. major with a nice face and heavy thighs, dragged him along to a peace march one night and he threw a couple of rocks at the local armory windows, but that wasn't him; he had been to the war and the marchers hadn't, and he felt nothing in common with them. He couldn't handle the party scene either. Walking point in the war had left him too sensitized to sounds; he would be talking to a girl and hearing six things at once, and his eyes would be flicking and darting around the room till the girl figured he was tired of her. Or he would be saying something, and nobody would be listening; they would be talking through him, their voices loud over the music, and he would flee out into the night for a joint and a moment's silence.

He made it into his junior year with passing grades, failing interest and fraying nerves, and then dropped out. He knew he could have made it through on brains, if brains had been all that mattered. *People I've seen graduate from college, for chrissakes*, he thought, *I can graduate from college.* But he found himself sliding alone into a kind of limbo, with nobody around he could talk to and no confidence left in himself. He was confused. He was smoking a lot of hash, a hit or two here and a hit or two there, buying peace on the installment plan a quarter-hour or half-hour at a time till the amount he was smoking began to worry him. Sometimes, in a state of dread, he would take off in his beat-up old Dodge and drive off into the countryside, going in circles, not wanting to be anywhere or see anyone. He sank into depression and dreamed of suicide, a reverie that ended when he caught himself lying in bed one day wondering how he would go about doing it. A spasm of fear coursed through him. *What the fuck is wrong with me?*

Bean was frightened enough to check himself into a VA hospital in St. Paul. What he mostly wanted to do was talk to somebody. He tried to tell them about the hash and the panics and how he didn't know what he was doing, but none of it seemed to register. They tranqued him out with Thorazine and parked him on a ward with some gray veterans of earlier wars. He was playing cards with some of the old soldiers when he suddenly passed out. The next thing he knew he was lying in a room with no strength and no feeling, an echo in the gray light was saying, "Blood pressure ninety over sixty," and he was sure he was dying. They told him later that he had had an allergic reaction to the Thorazine, seeming, he thought, to blame him for it. When he came around, they moved him to a younger men's ward and put him in group therapy for an hour a day. That didn't work either. Bean had always been afflicted with stage fright, even speaking up in a high-school class, and he felt nothing in common with the rest of the group anyway—*these people*, he thought, *talking about their petty-ass problems*. He sat mute most of the time, unable to speak and certain that no one would understand him if he did.

He stayed four weeks, then was released in the care of

his lady Sandra. Within three months they were married; within three months more, they began to discover how little they really had in common. They rented a big upper duplex in South Minneapolis, "a humongous place for two hundred dollars a month," Bean remembered, and later bought a house in the suburbs, but neither was large enough to house their mutual discontents. He smoked an occasional joint, purchased from a connection located conveniently down the block; she complained that it made him spacey. She was fighting a weight problem; he bitched that she wasn't fighting it hard enough. She said he never talked. He said he had things he didn't want to talk about and great ideas that nobody could follow anyway. She had a career, in nursing. He had none and didn't want one. He was still searching, he said, knocking along from school to school and job to job in Sandra's relentlessly purposeful train. *I've seen life end just like that*, Bean thought. *I'm alive, and I want to do what I want to do, as long as it's damn near legal.*

Bean had heard people say that if a marriage stuck together for five years, it was probably built to last. His died after five years and one day. He couldn't even remember afterward what their terminal quarrel had been about. One moment he had been lying on their bed, trying to be nice; the next, he was on his feet yelling, shaking, slamming a lamp down on the bedstead and finally giving Sandra a violent shove. He moved out of the bedroom that night and out of the house soon thereafter, to an apartment of his own overlooking the Mississippi River. It had been *one of them seventies marriages*, he thought afterward, a psychologically and financially supportive alliance with no children and no indissoluble bonds; she had never told him that she loved him. The breakup was clean. She got the house. He got his 650 Yamaha and his freedom.

He off-loaded the Yamaha and, having nothing left to lose, he thumbed west to Montana to smoke a little with a friend and then to Alaska to seek his fortune on the last frontier. He didn't find it. Instead, he boarded with a drug dealer, took a job at the Post Office in Anchorage and entered upon a long on-again, off-again dalliance with unreason. He was working one day on the loading dock, exiled there because he had got lippy with a supervisor about the way the Post Office should be run, when it began. He saw that the world was about to end, the only safe place was the top of a mountain, and he had to get his family there fast. *What the fuck is wrong with me?*

He hauled himself to the Alaska Psychiatric Institute, vibrating inside with an incredible energy. *Flying,* he thought, and nothing seemed beyond him. He shot a little pool and felt he could wish the balls into the pockets with the force of his eyes and his thoughts. He tried to explain things to the shrink they assigned him and, failing at that, to the shrink's young assistant, but he wasn't making contact. He wanted understanding and they gave him pills. Some friends visited and asked what he was doing there. Bean was no longer sure. "Hey, man," he answered, "there was nowhere else to go, you know?"

When he came out a few days later, his job was gone, and he was adrift. He drew food stamps for a while, loafed through a job as a janitor in the new federal building in Anchorage for a while longer, then flew off to Sitka spaced out on free-based cocaine to work on the fishing boats. The work was good, and there was a girl named Heather, but his skipper yelled at him one time too many and he quit. He floated back to Anchorage, by sailboat out of Seattle this time, with an ex-Marine buddy who had come out of the war so tightly overwound that he made Bean feel tranquil by comparison. *Kind of screwed up*, Bean thought. *I know, man, I can see it in his eyes. He's a nervous man. He's Vietnam.*

Bean was Vietnam, too, and it was stealing up behind him, a spectral shadow out of his past. There was a sign at the unemployment office in Anchorage when he got back advertising for help for a United States Forest Service research lab. He bluffed his way into a job, hiding his nearly total ignorance of the flora of Alaska. There was a good summer commuting by chopper to a tent camp in the outback, tending plots of trees and vegetation, and a good ego-reinforcing winter helping out at the home office. But the shadows were lengthening, threatening to engulf him, and the second summer tenting out at the foot of Mount McKinley was heavy. *The heaviest period in my life*, he thought. It wasn't dope. He was clean; he was straight as an arrow. He had simply tumbled free-falling out of that reality inhabited by everyone else.

It began when the helicopter ferried him and a couple of co-workers out to the camp. He had been in a water bed in his trailer only that morning with a lady who loved to make love. Then they were clattering out to the boondocks in a 206 Bell, and it could have been Vietnam again. He wasn't sure *where* he was. His nerves were shot. He couldn't sleep. He didn't like the look of the new cook, a big dude with long hair, an earring in one ear, and a .357 Magnum revolver. They were in grizzly country, there were a lot of guns around, but the Magnum was making Bean paranoid, and one morning at first light he caught himself slithering toward the mess tent with a knife in his belt, sneaking up on the cook.

He was acting strangely; he knew that, and he knew people were looking sidelong at him, but he couldn't help himself. One day a chopper put him and a colleague named Paul on the side of a mountain and his eyes quit working; everything was a blur, he was staring into space and Paul was asking what was wrong, and Bean, consumed by paranoia, lied, "Oh, nothing." They trudged down to the helicopter LZ, Bean taking care to keep Paul's hazy form in front of him. On the way he thought he saw the world's biggest grizzly jumping out at them, which never happened, and then that night in camp he thought he was in the movies, like Jack Nicholson, crawling along with the camera always on him in the right spot at the right time until he decided to take a break and go behind the curtain and then come out on camera again asking brightly, "Are you ready?" It was freaking out the soil scientist, a skinny woman with big glasses, but he threw her a little Jack Nicholson look and she went away.

He couldn't sleep at all that night and couldn't go out in the field the next morning. They were standing by the gasoline truck waiting for the chopper when he seemed to see it blowing up and he was running away and people were wondering, *Wow, what's wrong with Dave?* A colleague named Cathy walked him away from the group where they could talk, but he couldn't say anything, so they walked back and the others took off for the field without him. "You guys go to work," he told them. "I got a bigger thing happening." He went back to his tent, seeking shelter, but the cook came in with two other guys and Bean fought and fought, fighting against his paranoia made flesh, until they wrestled him down, got the handcuffs on him and shackled him to a seat in the back of a van.

The boss came out with his daughter, a beautiful blonde, to fetch him back to Anchorage, and Bean felt suddenly at peace. He was staring at the silken blond hair in front of him and hearing music, a kind of mellow jazz only for him, the pianos and cellos playing the same silken figure over and over again, and it was beautiful, it was nice, it was there; he couldn't explain that to anyone, but it was there. He saw the boss up front jabbing at the buttons of the car radio, and he said, "Jim, why don't you turn off the radio and listen?" The music followed him, pacifying his ghosts and his paranoia, and an otherworldly calm fell over him. "I feel fine," he said when he got to the hospital, and they let him go.

That night, thinking he might be God, he went roaming around his trailer court, rapping at doors in the dark. Somebody called the police, but they let him off on his promise not to go outside again. He slept. He woke up. He drank a Heineken's. He listened to some Elvis on the stereo. Some girls came over. He did a dance by the fire and burned his toe. The girls were worried. He went out for a few blasts and got loaded. The last saloon on his rounds was closed. He pounded on the door. The owner poked a gun out the window, pointed right at him. He crossed the street to a hotel to get some breakfast and take a piss. The W had fallen off the ladies' room door; it said OMEN, which looked like a sign to Bean, so he walked in, unzipped and started urinating copiously in one stall just as the woman in the next was leaving.

The woman turned him in. A cop came for him and clapped him in jail, and the next thing he knew, he was shuffling into court manacled to seven or eight other suspected miscreants for processing. A guy in dark glasses was watching him from the back—an Israeli agent, he thought. *I ain't gonna get involved in this*, he was thinking; when they unhooked him from the other detainees, he stood up, circled the jury box, walked out of court, then broke into a dead sprint down two flights of steps, out the front door and into a piano bar across the street. The cops dragged him out, Bean fighting all the way, and put him in a padded cell in a candy-striped jumpsuit and handcuffs. They didn't know what he could do; when they came back, he had got the jumpsuit off with the handcuffs still on and was squatting in the corner naked.

He did ten days in the dangerous ward and five more in jail for indecent exposure, lying drugged out with a white Bible on his chest. Some people came from the VA and told him they were going to take him to Washington. He thought they meant to Washington, D.C., to be a counsel to the President, but they were talking about a hospital in Washington State, and Bean split for home in Mountain Lake, Minnesota. It was the last safe haven in his life, a town that had seemed almost suffocatingly quiet to him when he was growing up. He got an apartment there, and a job at his uncle's construction company. He was doing okay until the day when, in a boozy haze, he set out for church to meet the Ayatollah Khomeini and negotiate a peaceful solution to the crisis over the American hostages in Iran. The police intercepted him and delivered him, in a violent rage, to a state mental hospital in Worthington. He flew at a doctor there in a fury, and when they locked him in his room, unaware of his superhuman strength, he picked up his bed and dashed it to pieces against the wall. They fed him a spaghetti dinner through a slot in the door. He squeezed it back out through the crack between the door and the doorsill.

Bean finally mellowed out enough to be graduated to a VA hospital and then to the street. He did odd jobs around Mountain Lake for a while and put in a summer with the Forest Service in Minnesota. When the job ended with the season, he headed south for the Keys to work on the lobster boats. The Keys had traditionally been a refuge for men and women in flight from mainland society, and Bean felt at rest there, as though he had found home. He had a good lady who told him regularly that she loved him, and a circle of his fellow refugees for company, and lobster on the table any time they wanted it. His boss, a Baptist minister, almost broke Bean's heart the day they found a jettisoned five-pound bag of cocaine bobbing in the water alongside their boat; it was enough to retire on, but the boss slit it open and spilled it back into the sea. It was a measure of Bean's quietude that he didn't care for long. "The ocean is like a dream to me," he said. "I can be out on it or just looking at it, and it brings me a peace I've never had before."

His life remained a walk along a high wire, a series of

suspenseful steps across a void. "I might do one thing in my life," he said, "and I'm going to do it right. I mean I'm going to make it. It's going to take me a while, but I'm going to make it the way I want." He was still a haunted man, twelve years out of the war; the distance in time was not great between his padded cell in Anchorage and his haven in Long Key. "But I'm getting things together," he said, toying with a beer on the trailer-court patio. "I really am."

He had read the story of Charlie Company and discovered that some of his old buddies had experienced torments similar in kind, if not in degree or lurid detail, to his own. He had spent twelve years wondering what was wrong with him, and had only just begun to realize that he was not entirely alone.

ROBERT MASTROGIOVANNI: FIVE DAYS OUT OF THE WAR

The photo lay on the kitchen table in the snug little house in Fair Lawn, New Jersey: the skinny, dark-eyed GI in civvies and the barely teenage saloon girl, his arm around her shoulder, both of them smiling out at the world from a site high above Hong Kong. The memories it called up were practically the only unambiguously happy thing Robert Mastrogiovanni brought back from Vietnam. The Army sent you off to Hong Kong by commercial jet, bussed you into town, warned you which joints were clap traps, changed your money into packeted local dollars and turned you loose in that garden of earthly delights called R&R. Mastrogiovanni had headed straight for one of the bars where the girls were and found one who pleased him, a pretty Chinese of fourteen or fifteen with outsize tinted glasses and long black hair tumbling down over her shoulders. He negotiated a price with the local mama-san to hire her away for the week, then did his own deal with the girl and was surprised at how little she asked.

He spent five happy days with her, seeing the sights in the daytime with a couple of buddies and their saloon girls, spending the nights at an R&R hotel that was accustomed to GIs on liberty and did not ask questions. They chattered like adolescents on a first date, asking a lot of getting-to-know-you questions like where you were from and how many brothers and sisters you had. He bought her a silver bracelet for $20 or $30; she ordered for them at the Chinese restaurant where they celebrated his twenty-first birthday, Mastrogiovanni nibbling uncertainly at delicacies he imagined he might not have touched at all if he had been able to identify them by name. They snapped pictures of the paddle boats on Repulse Bay and took in the view from a high-rise revolving restaurant commanding much of the city. He was a kid on holiday from a sheltered boyhood and an ugly war, but when his five days were up he took the girl back to the saloon and the mama-san and said goodbye. *You can't get too close with them*, he thought. *You know what they are*.

Those five days were an interlude for Mastrogiovanni in a war whose overriding purpose for him, as for most of the men, had become staying alive. He had begun it in what he later recognized as a state of "stark, raving terror," lying in a bunker at Fire Base Julie on his second night in-country and listening to a brother grunt wailing in the dark for his mom. He steeled himself to the blood and the dying, killed two or three enemy troopers himself to his certain knowledge and wondered inwardly if even his officers knew what the war was for. He saw little Vietnamese children begging for C rations and rooting in garbage dumps for food, and felt guilty about it. "Like you're leaving that," he said. "After a year you'll be gone. You'll be back to your showers and air-conditioning and a new car and a refrigerator where you can go get something to eat any time you're hungry, and everything else, and they're still going to be there."

He counted away his days nevertheless like everyone else, and when his time was up he headed home to the safe little world in Fair Lawn he had left two years before. He felt scared going back, wondering how people would take him and how he himself would act; he walked around the family house first thing to assure himself it was the same warm haven he had lived in since he was three years old. His parents laid on a family feast of welcome, a caloric coming-together of uncles and aunts and home-cooked lasagna and chicken cacciatore. He felt like a stranger. "You're not who you were when you left," he said later. "You realize that you never will be again. Your life has changed. Forever. It's like losing your innocence, or losing your virginity. You go over a certain step and you can never go back. You can't undo what you've done."

He sought shelter in the company of his fellow displaced persons, those veterans who had experienced what he had experienced, and for a time had trouble relating to anybody else. He had gone back to the job he had left at the local Post Office, working a night-owl watch from four to eight in the mornings and going to Bergen Community College in Paramus during the day for an associate degree in business administration. His evenings in those days were reserved for what he came to think of as his don't-give-a-damn period. He let his hair grow to his shoulders. He ran with a crowd of guys from the corner, mostly veterans, drinking Mateus rosé and smoking pot when they could score some. He did not want to talk about the war. His letters home had been artful dodges prattling on about the state of his health, which was invariably fine, or the condition of the weather, which was usually rotten. He was accordingly practiced at evasive action when people questioned him about 'Nam, dying, he imagined, to ask him how many people he had killed, and he got good at sidestepping their inquiries.

"How was it?" someone would ask.

"Ah, it was all right, y'know?"

"Well, was it as bad as it was supposed to be?"

"No, it wasn't that bad," he would say, and the catechism would end.

The world he returned to, when he was finally ready, was as precisely and as securely like the world he had left as he could make it. At thirty-three, he was still living with his widowed mother in the house in which he had grown up, with plastic covers on the furniture and a figure of the Madonna reigning over a spotless kitchen. He had quit college after two years of honors-quality work because it bored him. He had resisted marriage because, he thought, the war had made him too self-contained to have somebody else depending on him. He had stayed with the Post Office, rising to a supervisory job managing twenty mail handlers in Je..ey City. Some of them were Vietnam veterans and were considered incorrigibly unruly until Mastrogiovanni took over; they were hard guys, but the nearly tribal bonding among men who had fought in the war was working for him, and he tamed them. He was a bright, articulate and cheery man, and if there was little adventure and less risk in his life since Vietnam, he did not seem to miss it.

But sometimes he would get out the snapshot of himself and the saloon girl and feel a little pang of nostalgia for those five days out of the war. He wondered what had become of her, seeing her smile again. "Someday, maybe, I would like to go back to Hong Kong," he said. "I don't think I've ever had a better time."

BOBBY EUGENE JONES: A DEATH IN THE FAMILY

James Jones, the police chief of the all-black town of Princeville, North Carolina, was crossing the little bridge from Tarboro to Princeville when the Plymouth cruised by with two men in Army dress greens inside. His wife, Eva, saw them next, driving up and down the street outside her house as if they were looking for something. *Not us*, she was thinking, or, more nearly, praying. There had been a telegram ten days before advising the Joneses in brutally spare language that their boy Bobby Eugene had stepped on a booby trap on January 18, 1970, two days before his twenty-first birthday, and had lost both his legs. Further cables had followed almost daily from the hospital in Okinawa, each reporting that Bobby's condition was still serious and that the Joneses would be kept informed. *As long as nobody from the Army don't come, he's still living*, Mrs. Jones's doctor had told

her. She clung to that, but now the Plymouth had pulled up
in front of their place and the two men in dress greens were
standing in the door. They didn't have to say it. She knew
her Bobby had died.

He had gone off to the war an easygoing boy, the kind,
his kid brother James said, who always had a smile for the
world and always got along with everybody. The Joneses
had raised him on a regimen of thrift, hard work and good
behavior; he delivered the Tarboro *Evening Telegram* door-
to-door starting at twelve and began the savings account he
tried to have transferred to his mother's name in the last
days of his life. Once, a white newsboy hit him with a Coke
bottle in a quarrel, and Bobby flattened him. But mostly, his
family remembered, he was the sort who eased on through,
never showing it if there was something you said or did that
he didn't like. His particular favorite, in a brood of eleven
children, was his sister Delores. "I used to call him my Number One brother, and he used to call me his Number One
sister," she said. Eleven years afterward, her eyes still filled
with tears at the memory of him, as if it were still the Friday
she had come home on the school bus and heard he had
died.

She never forgot what she had been wearing that day: the
sweater, the orange plaid skirt and the alligator loafers. The
atmosphere in the house was all wrong; it was full of people,
brothers and sisters and Bobby's girl friend, and it felt empty.
Delores found her mother in the kitchen, appeasing her grief
in the old southern way by cooking up a big family dinner.
Mrs. Jones stood silent over her pots and pans.

"Mama, he's not dead, is he?" Delores asked.

"Yeah," Mrs. Jones answered heavily.

For a time, the family was consumed with bitterness. "I'm
counting the days before I'll be home," Bobby's last letter
to Delores said; she got it the day after the men from the
Army had delivered the news of his death, and it came almost
as a cruel joke. Jones's medals followed, a Purple Heart and
six or seven other tokens of his valor, but the frame displaying them cracked and loosened over the eleven years in
which Mrs. Jones could not find it in herself to care about
them. "It didn't mean nothing," she said. "It's different now,
but for a long time I felt like I hated the world, hated everybody, anything to do with the war or the government. I

couldn't stand it." People in their kindness would try to console her in those days by saying that Bobby had died for his country. "Ain't *got* no country!" Eva Jones would rage in reply.

CURTIS GILLILAND, JR.:
"WE JUST KILLED 'EM"

The woman was squatting in the corner of the Post Office lobby in Somerset, Kentucky, in the Vietnamese way, alone and desolate in a country of 220 million strangers. Her husband, a serviceman, was being shipped to Okinawa and had told her he couldn't take her along; the regulations forbade it. She didn't speak English but he was going to leave her in a trailer with his mother, who didn't have a word of Vietnamese, and the trailer was haunted besides. There were ghosts there; she could see them. She had come to the Post Office in desperation, seeing the flag outside. It had been a symbol of help in her country, and not knowing where else to turn, she had sought succor under it. She was squatting there, as immobile and as patient as stone, and people were snickering and poking fun at her as if she were an animal in a zoo. *That's America in Vietnam*, Curtis Gilliland, Jr., was thinking, angry at their amusement. *We didn't understand 'em. We made no attempt to understand. We just killed 'em.*

Gilliland, Willie to his family and friends, had been trying alone to help. He had been working in the back of the Post Office that day in the middle 1970s, just before the fall of Saigon, when the postmaster came out looking flustered and asked if anyone could speak Vietnamese. "I can," Gilliland answered. He was the only man there who had even been to Vietnam and, having fallen in love with its people, had learned enough of their language to get through a conversation tolerably well—well enough, anyway, for an old Kentucky boy who had flunked out of community college on his first try before the war. The postmaster had led the way to his office, where she was waiting, close to tears. Gilliland spoke to her, the rust flaking away from his Vietnamese as he got into it, and her story came spilling out: She was alone; she was scared; she wanted to go home to Vietnam.

They called her husband finally to come get her, but the scene at the Post Office angered him and he stalked off, leaving her behind. She took up her vigil in the lobby then, squatting in the corner in witness to her solitude and her helplessness, with people gaping and laughing at her, and Gilliland was angry. *There's two cultures fighting here*, he was thinking, the vulnerability of the Vietnamese at war with the selfishness of his own countrymen. Their grins and their japes were telling the woman she wasn't like them; she didn't even know enough to sit in a chair instead of squatting on the floor, and was therefore beneath their concern. Gilliland got some time off and led her across to the courthouse to see a judge. Nothing finally came of it. The woman went back to the trailer and its ghosts. Six months or a year later, she was wandering deranged alongside a highway out of town when a car knocked her down and killed her.

Gilliland felt sick when he heard that. It was, he thought, *kind of like the same way we did the Vietnamese—went over and fought and then decided we weren't doin' no good and it wouldn't make no money so we cut and ran.* He had been there, and he felt they should have stayed for twenty years more if that was what it took; he felt that if it cost a thousand American lives to save a thousand and one Vietnamese, it was worth it. He was just an old Kentucky boy from plain Kentucky stock, his father a carpenter, his mother a day-shift worker at the Palm Beach suit factory to help make ends meet. They had raised him up on a farm outside Somerset to fear God and follow the flag, and he believed in the war. He was a junior in high school, muddling through with B's and C's, when they matched him against the smartest girl in the class in a debate on the American involvement in Vietnam. She contended that the United States ought to pull out. Gilliland argued for staying in and winning and, for all her straight-A report cards, he destroyed her—*tore her all to pieces*, he remembered long afterward, in front of the whole history class.

Three years later he was there himself, having to put his schoolboy patriotism to the proof of combat. *This'll be the best year of your life*, a battalion chaplain told his orientation class when they were new in-country. Gilliland, beginning to be nervous about what he was getting into, thought the man was crazy; he discovered only later that the prophecy had been right. He never quit being scared for his whole ten and a half months in the line. He was hit by bullets twice, once in the hand outside Junction City on Christmas Eve and once in the nose on Thunder Road, and came within eyeshot of death a couple of other times besides. He did not hate the North Vietnamese and praised God that he did not know if he had killed any of them; he did not like shooting at them, any more, he imagined, than they enjoyed being there shooting at him. But he never questioned that the cause he served was just or that it was winnable, if only they had been permitted to win. He was certain that God had smiled on the enterprise and had, for His own unrevealed purpose, spared him.

He had fought the good fight, but what really made his year in Vietnam the best in his life was his introduction to the Vietnamese and to a world beyond the insular bounds of Somerset, or Kentucky, or even the United States. He had been brought up to be accepting of people who did not look like him. His education in tolerance began when his mother taught him never to call a black person a nigger, not even when all the other kids were doing it, and it did not occur to him to consider the Vietnamese any less human than he. Practically his first glimpse of them was through the wire mesh on the bus bearing the new-meat recruits from Bien Hoa to Di An; he saw little children lining the roadside, starving, with their hands out for food, and he felt embarrassed by the terrible distance between their poverty and the plenty waiting for him back home. Most of his buddies kept that distance; even the sex in Vietnam was impersonal in the main, not an act of love but a service to be bought and sold. Gilliland wanted to bridge it. "I loved them," he said. "I really appreciated them. I wanted to get close to them."

He was no less happy to come home, though it meant leaving his Vietnamese friends behind. Gilliland kissed the tarmac at San Francisco, and when his stateside tour was up, he got in his car and raced from Fort Carson, Colorado, to Somerset so fast that doing a hundred meant slowing down. In the red-white-and-blue country he came from, people were tiring of the war but did not blame the warriors for it. No one called Gilliland a baby-killer; his greeting instead was a page-one picture of himself in the *Commonwealth Journal* under a banner reading WELCOME HOME WILLIE.

There were no bad dreams, no sleepless nights, no sweaty wrestling matches with an unquiet conscience. He found work with the state highway department and, later, the Post Office. He went back to Somerset Community College, which had flunked him out before Vietnam, and got his associate degree with a straight-A average. He had broken up with his old college sweetheart before he left, and when he tried to write her from Vietnam, his letter came back stamped ADDRESSEE UNKNOWN. With her mother's permission he followed her to Frankfort, Kentucky, where she was working for the state government, and resumed the courtship. Within a month or so, he proposed, and they were married.

His love affair with the Vietnamese never ended. He remembered having seen a little boy in a ville one day, the homeless love child of a Vietnamese mother and a GI father. The image froze in his mind, along with the twinge of pity he had felt. When he got home he thought he might adopt the boy, but his letter of inquiry came back unanswered, and Gilliland wound up adopting a brother instead. They met while he was still in college, Gilliland stepping out of a classroom into a corridor and bumping into four young Vietnamese men looking lost. They were boat people, refugees from the new Communist regime who had put to sea and been rescued by the United States Navy. They had been taken to Wake Island and then to the refugee relocation camp at Fort Chaffee, Arkansas, until the First Baptist Church in Somerset agreed to sponsor them. One of them, a former ARVN lieutenant, spoke fluent English, but he was only marking time in Somerset until he could rejoin his woman in Iowa. The others needed help with the language, and Gilliland volunteered.

The lieutenant drifted away from Somerset, and so did one of the others; a third died of leukemia. Tri Truong stayed, and Willie Gilliland, who had barely set foot outside Kentucky before the Army, came to count him the best friend he had in the world. Tri was only sixteen or seventeen when the tides of war pitched him up in Somerset, but he had served in the ARVN and had been shot twice in combat. His father had died when he was a little boy, and he had had to leave his mother and the rest of his family behind when he took to the boats a step ahead of what the vanquished South Vietnamese presumed would be a Communist bloodbath. Gilliland saw his loneliness and identified with it; Tri, he thought, was feeling what he had felt as an American in Vietnam, left out and alone.

They fell in together, the old Kentucky boy and his surrogate baby brother from Danang. Tri took an American wife, found work on the night shift at the Palm Beach plant and settled in the garage apartment at Gilliland's parents' place outside of town. They ate dinner out together every Friday night, the Gillilands and the Truongs, and saw each other frequently in between. One day Gilliland's father, who had retired, was sitting out at his place whittling flowers out of sticks of wood with Tri watching at his elbow. They were simple creations, but they looked almost real and had become a paying venture; Mrs. Gilliland was selling them at the factory for 75 cents a flower and people were buying whole bouquets of them. Tri had a quick eye and artistic hands, and when he picked up the knack, he started selling his flowers on the night shift for 50 cents. *Like a son undercuttin' a father*, Willie Gilliland thought, amused and pleased. *It's like he's part of the family.*

He wanted to share his own pleasures with Tri. Gilliland loved the woods, even though he had had to give up hunting. He had been a passionate hunter before Vietnam, but there was no pleasure left in it for him. He went out once with a buddy who brushed a tree limb in a glade, and Gilliland, flashing reflexively back to the jungle, almost shot him. He tried again with his brother-in-law and discovered that he could no longer bear to take a life—any life—for sport. He still liked to walk in the woods, feeling at peace in the solemn cathedral quiet. But it was hostile terrain for Tri, haunted by the fears of his boyhood. They went riding in the woods together when Tri had been in America for six months or a year, the first time he had ever been on horseback, and Gilliland could see him coil tight with atavistic tension. Tri had lived sixteen or seventeen years in a place where you walked in the woods only at the risk of your life, and Gilliland, who had spent a single frightened year there, was thinking: *He's like I was.*

A dozen years out of the war, Gilliland was himself feeling homesick for Vietnam and angry at his own country for its role in the train of events that meant he could not go back. He still believed in the war and still carried around its souvenirs—his dog tags, his Big Red One patch, his P-38 C-ration can opener—as tokens of his pride at having been in it. He and his wife were getting along comfortably enough on their two incomes, his from the Post Office and hers from the state. They were living with their little girl, then seven years old, on a six-acre place outside town and were raising Dobermans on the side. But Gilliland had begun to feel dead-ended as a mail carrier. He had pursued his studies toward a bachelor's in economics with an omnivorous hunger for knowledge, until the 120-mile round trip to the nearest four-year college began to be oppressive. His studies didn't seem to matter to the Postal Service anyway, nor did his tour in Vietnam. It had helped him get the job when veterans of the war were in demand—"I was their token black," he guessed wryly—but he kept getting bypassed thereafter by members of an old-boy network of noncombatants from the Reserves and the National Guard.

He was looking, in the summer of 1982, for something new—something still in government service, since he had eleven years' equity with the Post Office, but more deeply involved in working with people. It was only partly his sense of stagnation that made him itchy to move. He had come home from the war with the conviction that, because he had survived, there must be *something* that God wanted him to do with his life besides haul mail. He was tormented as well by the guilty feeling that America had betrayed the Vietnamese—had lied to them about its intentions and then, wearying of the war, had abandoned them to the Communists. "The country's got to the point where they don't care," he said. "When we get bombed, *then* we'll fight—that's the way I think this country feels right now. We just got too selfish."

He thought of the starving children begging along the highway from Bien Hoa to Di An; he thought of the Vietnamese woman squatting totally alone and frightened in the Somerset Post Office lobby, with his own neighbors staring and laughing as if she were a monkey in a cage. He hoped accordingly that his new life, if and when he achieved it, would take him anywhere on the face of the earth except America—*somewhere*, he thought, *where people appreciate what they've got and want to make it better.* He wished that history had come out differently and that the somewhere else he dreamed of serving could be a free Vietnam. It was as if he wanted to make some personal act of contrition for what he saw as a national act of betrayal. And what, a caller wondered, could one man do? "Be friends," Gilliland answered without hesitation.

DAVID SPAIN: HARD TIME

Encountering David Spain, eleven years out of 'Nam, was like listening to the tick of a time bomb and wondering when—not if—it would explode. He looked like a melting body builder, the slabs of muscle losing out to the billows of suet for possession of his five-foot-six-inch body. His tattooed arms were thick as tree trunks, barely tapering to his stubby hands. His face was spotted with grayish blisters and pitted scars, the results, a chiropractor told him, of having been exposed to Agent Orange during the war. He had violent headaches once or twice a week, "like somebody's beating me with a sledgehammer," he said. When they were upon him, he would fly into raging, roaring furies.

He wasn't always that way, he insisted. He remembered himself as having been an ordinarily peaceable kid when he joined the Army in 1968, an undersized tenth-grade dropout from Rockford, Illinois. It was true, he conceded, that he had been in a jam at the time for having rolled a few homosexuals and that he had *had* to enlist to stay out of jail, a trade-off arranged for him by a preacher friend of the family. But that, he maintained, was different. That was before the Army, before the rages and the pounding headaches that brought them on. "I just didn't like faggots, that's all," Spain said. "Still don't."

He traced his problems instead to Vietnam and to what had been, in the Army's eyes, his inconvenient insistence on his right not to fight. He had been preceded into 'Nam by his older brother, Harry, a combat engineer with the 25th Infantry. The law stipulated that two brothers could not be required to serve in the same war zone unless they signed waivers, and when he arrived in May 1968, Spain almost immediately began agitating to come off the line. His case, he said, reached the Big Red One's commanding general, Keith Ware, who agreed. The problem was that General Ware died when his helicopter was shot down near the Cambodian border in September, and Spain had lost his guarantor. He was hanging around the Black Lions' base at Lai Khe shortly thereafter when a lieutenant ordered him to pick up his gear and get set to go out in the bush on patrol.

Spain said no—General Ware had ruled that he didn't have to go.

"General Ware is dead," the lieutenant said. "Get your shit and go out there."

Spain refused again. To refuse a direct order in a war zone is a court-martial offense. The lieutenant reported him, and, Spain recounted, "they kangarooed me"—found him guilty and sentenced him to six months' hard time in the stockade known sardonically as LBJ, for Long Binh Jail.

Hard time at LBJ was precisely and notoriously that— the military's moral equivalent of a Georgia chain gang— and the stories Spain brought out were as lurid as his fury at the Army for throwing him in. "Before that, I kind of *liked* the Army," he said. "After that, I hated it. Hated it with a passion." There was a sergeant there, he said, who strapped him to an iron cot and beat him with an Army sock filled with soap. There were guards he would kill, he said, if he ran into them now, and something feral in his eyes twelve years out suggested that he meant it.

Spain had burned his bridges to Charlie Company; when he came out of LBJ boiling with hatred, the Army discreetly reassigned him to Bravo Company and extended his time in Vietnam for eighteen more months. He still owed the Army five months when they finally shipped him back to Fort Hood, Texas, to finish out his tour. He stayed five days, then split for Rockford. "You're all disoriented when you get back," he said. "They teach you how to kill a person and then they bring you back and expect you to be normal. I couldn't take it. I left." He hunkered low at home for nearly a year before the Army tracked him down and clapped him back behind bars.

It was a cycle he would repeat again and again; he went AWOL twenty-eight times in what remained of his Army tour and served an aggregate two more years in various stockades before they were through with him. His three-year enlistment had by then taken him six years to serve, two and a half of them in prison and all of them, in his view, as a prisoner.

When he was freed at last, he headed back to Rockford and to the job he had left six years before, working for his father's construction company. He married, had children, grew long hair and a beard, and fleshed out from the 130 pounds he had carried as a grunt to something on the far side of 200 pounds compacted into a massive fleshly ball. "Life is okay," he said; if he had his confrontation with the lieutenant at Lai Khe to do over again, he wouldn't change a thing.

But Vietnam and the Army had left their mark on him, or so he believed. There were the blisters that started appearing on his face a decade out of the war, watery bubbles that burst and left burn scars as if somebody had been snuffing out cigarettes on his skin. He accepted his chiropractor's word that Agent Orange caused them but would not go to the VA with them, "because," he said, "they haven't done anybody else any good." There were the sledgehammer headaches beating at his brainpan, one so violent that he could not move and had to be hauled home by his brother in the back of a truck; he blamed the Army and Agent Orange for them, too. There were the towering rages, uncontrollable paroxysms of anger. "There's no way to *prove* they're related to the Army," he said, "but I suspect they are. I wasn't like that before I went in. Just didn't like faggots." He remembered that long-gone time when he had sort of liked the Army. Thirteen years later, he blamed it for having made him the man he was today.

_____

ED SCHWEIGER:
ONE DAY AT A TIME

In the plotless novel-in-progress he had always imagined his life to be, the post-Vietnam chapters introduced Ed Schweiger in the character of a hippie. He had got part of the way there in the pre-Vietnam pages, coming of age in Janesville, Wisconsin, and bobbing aimlessly through the state university at Madison at his own unexacting pace. When he sat in the morning sunlight after the siege at Junction City, staring at a scattering of pebbles and seeing in them the beauty of life lived for its own sake, it was as much an affirmation of his rambling past as a peek into his unanchored future. But Vietnam seemed to advance his development from a kind of Huck Finn in a '67 MGB-GT into a Jack Kerouac antihero, living literally and figuratively on the road. He grew long hair and a large bushy beard. He set up housekeeping with his girl before she became his wife. He took some courses. He hung out. He went into what he recognized later as a state of "sensory overload," doing what he wanted to do, which usually involved motion and sometimes meant doing nothing beyond being alive.

His marriage became a nomadic wandering, an unhurried search for the right place to settle down. He and his wife spent four years at the quest, nesting for six months at a time in the Southwest, in Maine, in Washington State for the seafood, in California and Florida for the sunshine. They found what they thought they had been looking for closer to home, a log cabin and thirteen acres in Channing, Michigan, on the Upper Peninsula. Schweiger went back to school, at Northern Michigan University, and earned his degree in 1976 in social studies and secondary education. But he didn't feel like teaching then or later, since he thought it inappropriate to do "value clarification" for other people before he had got his own values in working order, and he couldn't find anything else in the contracting Michigan economy. So the Schweigers moved back to the Madison area, and he started knocking around from job to short-lived job as a salesman, a corrections officer at the state detention center for delinquent girls and finally—or, rather, most recently—as a campus security guard at his alma mater.

He had had that job for four years by the fall of 1981 and still thought of it, like most things in his life, as temporary. His marriage had come unglued after seven years, his wife having tired of his wanderlust. "I felt she wanted to be too traditional," Schweiger said. "I thought she was copping out. I thought she wasn't interested in reaching anymore. She wanted to join the bowling team and settle down. That wasn't my idea of fun."

He did not think harshly of her for having dropped out and did not blame the war for his own unmoored existence and unrealized possibilities. What Vietnam did to him, by his own reckoning, was to reveal to him as if in a vision one morning at Junction City that life was beautiful and that living it was all that mattered. He still thought of the life and times of Ed Schweiger as a novel and dreamed of writing it sometime. He would do it "a page a day," he said, with no more than a chapter for the war and no idea whatever as to how the story would come out.

MIKE MACDONALD:
BREAKING THE SILENCE

Perhaps the sweetest words Mike MacDonald ever heard came the day when, a decade after the war, his marriage counselor sat him down and told him, "I think you're a real normal person." He realized then how much he had needed to have somebody tell him that. His six-year marriage was already on the rocks, the victim of a silence that had congealed into lovelessness. He was having nightmares about the war again and was drinking too much beer, trying to narcotize himself into a dreamless sleep. He was driving himself hard—too hard, his wife kept complaining—at his job managing a parking-garage sweeping company in Minneapolis. His faith in God and the Roman Catholic Church had died on the battlefield. He could not talk about the war or read about it. He felt guilt at his participation in it and anger at his country for its ingratitude for what he and his buddies had been through. His life was frayed, raveled, *jumbled up*, he thought, and when the marriage counselor told him he was normal, it was like hearing a doctor say that the biopsy had come up negative. He began then to learn to live with Vietnam.

In their weekly talks, he and the marriage counselor had peeled back the layers of his problems to their core and had found the war there. It was not the sole cause of the disruptions in his life, he came to believe, but it lay on his spirit nevertheless, an unhealed wound that did not hurt so long as he did not touch it. He had an ordinary American boyhood, untroubled in any outward aspect. His father, who had been an Army Air Corps hero in World War II, raised him in the spirit of service to his country; his mother saw to his religious development, tugging him along to mass every morning for long periods of his growing up. He graduated from high school in Minneapolis and took a job parking cars in the base ient garage of a downtown department store, holding off the pleading of his parents while he decided what to do next.

The Army decided that for him when it snatched him up in the draft, trained him as a grunt and dispatched him to Vietnam. He hadn't really wanted to go. "None of us did," he said; he had a girl, a car, a set of drums and a comfortably undemanding style of post-adolescent life. He had tried to join the National Guard to satisfy his military obligation. When its letter of acceptance and congratulations reached him, he was in a bunker in some forgotten Charlie Company outpost in Vietnam.

He had arrived in-country in October 1968, just after the kamikaze assault on Fire Base Julie, and had soldiered val-

iantly against ants, scorpions, jungle rot and the North Vietnamese Army. He won the Bronze Star, among other medals,
and David Arthur, Captain Rogers's successor as Charlie
Company's CO, wanted to put him in for a battlefield commission. "You've got all the talents; you should share it,"
Arthur told him, but MacDonald said no; a commission meant
more time in the Army and in Vietnam, and he had had
enough of death and dying. His own baptism of fire had been
the defense of the patch of elephant grass called Cantigny,
where the rookie listening-posters were caught outside the
wire and killed. "I was in transit and processing with them,
so I knew them real well," he remembered long afterward.
"I knew their expectations, their desires, before we ever
went out there, and then *boom!*—they're gone."

There were too many moments like that for MacDonald,
too much blood spilled for too little purpose. Toward the
end of his tour, he negotiated a fat-rat job off the line as a
jeep driver and was thinking of extending his time in 'Nam
in exchange for an early discharge. He was at the point of
signing the papers when a rocket blew up yet another of his
buddies. The biggest piece of him they found was his mid-
section. *That's it*, MacDonald thought. *I'm getting the hell
out of here.*

He got out whole in body and torn in spirit, changed by
180 degrees from the pint-size boy who went over. "I felt it
was the thing to do then," he said. "My country called on
me to do it and I'd go do it. I thought, 'We're Americans—
let's go over there and mop up and get it over with and get
on with our lives.'" But the rules of play and the constraints
of politics did not allow them to mop up; instead, MacDonald
thought, they were killing and dying piecemeal, for nothing.
He wouldn't even put in for the Purple Heart he had earned
for having been hit by enemy shrapnel; the wound seemed
to him as banal and the medal as worthless as the war.
America's flat tire, he thought bitterly, heading home, *and
I'm the mechanic who couldn't fix it.*

His belief in God was as surely a casualty of the war as
his trust in the word of his government. The boy who had
gone to mass every morning in Minneapolis could not sustain
his faith surrounded by the random and, for him, meaningless
carnage of Vietnam; not even his own survival was evidence
for him that God lived and cared. "It's nice to say someone

is looking out after me," he said, "but the reason I made it was nothing more than blind fucking luck. Why does the mortar hit the guy next to you and not you, if you're in the killing radius? I don't think there's anything that God did, if there *was* a God. It was just luck." His mother's insistently pious letters began accordingly to be a trial for him to respond to. Once, he took some to a chaplain and asked, "How do I answer this?"

"You're not the only one," the padre answered, reading his doubts. "All of our faith gets tested out here."

Mine is no longer being tested, MacDonald thought. *It's gone.*

He came home in a fog, as he remembered it later, feeling changed and uncertain of his footing. He told his family the day but not the hour of his flight into Minneapolis, because he didn't want a to-do over his arrival, and when his plane set down he headed for his girl's place first. He didn't know until he showed up the next morning that his parents had laid on a homecoming party for him and that everyone had waited up till 3:00 A.M. for him to appear. They were supportive, or tried to be, and arranged a series of smaller get-togethers for him. But one night at a dinner party his father said he would never let another child of his serve in Vietnam, and MacDonald took it wrong. He understood only later what his father had been saying—that no one should have to experience a war like that. In his raw state then, just back from 'Nam, he thought he was hearing another unspoken message: *What Mike did was wrong.*

MacDonald endured his lionization for a time, caught between his hunger to be appreciated—"to be treated special"—and his rising feeling of claustrophobia in crowds. Once, he picked up his girl friend and drove to Wisconsin to see his buddy Fritz Suchomel's parents, partly to tell them how sorry he felt that Fritz had died, partly just to be away from home with its round of earnest well-wishing for a couple of days. It seemed to him that people were constantly apologizing to him and that he was constantly having to ask why. "We're real sorry, Mike, that you had to go," they would say, and he would flare: "Why in hell don't you support the guys over there? Why wait till they come back? Support them—don't apologize to me."

He felt equally estranged from his own generation when

he enrolled at the University of Minnesota on the GI Bill and his wages from two jobs. He knocked on doors for George McGovern's bring-the-boys-home candidacy in 1972 and found himself in sympathy with the ends of the student antiwar movement; it was the means he objected to, and the high-pitched moralizing about a morally ambiguous war. "Everyone wanted to decide who was right and who was wrong," he said. "They're *both* wrong, but everybody had to have a big answer. 'Who cares about the war ten thousand miles from here? Let's create our own little war right here.'"

For the three years he spent in college, they kept clawing at him, wanting the big answers, demanding confirmation of their own precast moral judgments on the war. "You're a baby-killer," a guy who had been one of MacDonald's best friends told him at a party. "You were one of those crazy guys over there." MacDonald hit him. They apologized to each other some time afterward, but they weren't friends anymore.

There were times when the questions seemed almost as oppressive as the insults, times when he tired of being asked how many Vietnamese he had killed or what evidence he could supply of the elemental evil of the war; times when his interrogators seemed to him to be ripping great hunks out of his soul, strip-mining him for information without so much as a thank-ou or an acknowledgment of what he had been through. "Goddammit," he would finally say, "I don't *have* any answers!"

What about the civilians, someone would ask—weren't they against the war?

"I don't know. One day people are running up to you and hugging you and the next day a little kid is throwing a grenade at you. What are you supposed to decide from that? What are you supposed to feel? I don't know."

Well, what about his own view, then—was the war right or wrong?

"Shit, I don't know," MacDonald would say and make for the door.

He came away from these encounters feeling empty and deserted, and he turned inward on his own emotional resources, flinging himself into his work at the sweeping company seven days a week and burying his memories of the war out of sight in some far recess of his mind. "I tried to forget for so many years," he said, "that all of a sudden I did." Something impelled him to send in a form for a government bonus being offered in the early 1970s to those who had served in a war. A check came back in the mail in the amount of $600, and while MacDonald needed the money, it turned to ashes in his hands. *It's a slap in the face*, he thought. *They're buying me off.* The check, in his view, was a rough measure of the value his country placed on his service in the war. He no longer wanted to think about it, read about it, or talk about it, even among veteran friends; for them as for him, it was a taboo subject. When he and his fiancee, Beth, were married in 1974, her mother noted in the announcement for the papers that he was a veteran of Vietnam. *What the hell did she put that in there for?* he exploded, reading the copy. He liked Beth's mother too well to hurt her feelings and said nothing to her; instead, he called the *Minneapolis Tribune* to get the reference to Vietnam deleted, but he was too late.

From that point forward, the war cast its withering shadow over his marriage. MacDonald refused to blame its failure on Vietnam; a lot of marriages were breaking up in the 1970s, and he guessed that his would have too. But 'Nam aggravated most of the stress lines in the relationship. The nightmares he had had about it when he first came home had dissipated while he was in college, and he had told himself, *Okay, this is finally clearing itself up.* It wasn't; the dreams came back with a ferocity that scared both of them, propelling him out of bed like a cannonball in the middle of the night. "Jeez, you were soaking wet last night and shaking," Beth would say in the morning; sometimes he would remember and sometimes he wouldn't. His boss suggested that he seek help, but he held back, even when the nightmares invaded his waking hours in flashbacks that seemed "just Technicolor" in their vividness. He read a couple of books and made a couple of appointments to see someone, but it wasn't working and he quit. "I just decided," he said, "that no one could help me with this—it was something I had to get through for myself."

He saw later that that was a mistake for him and an injustice to Beth. His medication for getting through it for himself was beer; he discovered that if he drank four or five a night, more if he were particularly tense, he could make the nightmares stay away. His drinking came between him and Beth. So did his workaholic attention to the sweeping business, though it didn't seem to help when he left it for a year and went into term life insurance instead to be home more. And so, worst of all, did his silences. He was hiding things; sometimes, he would weep in Beth's arms, but he could not talk to her, about the war, or his feelings, or hers, or finally anything else that counted to them. When communication died, love died too. Their marriage was sinking, and he was clinging to its flotsam, more dependent than he had known on her and her approval. He had thought he was happy. He discovered later that he wasn't; he was just scared.

By the time they laid their problem before a marriage counselor, there was not enough left of the marriage for her to save. Beth MacDonald dropped out; the two of them sat down without drawing battle lines, divided their worldly goods in the no-fault way of the 1970s and parted. But MacDonald stayed with the counselor, seeing her once a week long after the question of saving his marriage had become moot, exploring every corner of his life from his childhood on. They homed in on his drinking as a symptom; he put himself through an outpatient treatment program to kick it and then came back to explore its causes. *I have to have some answers*, he thought. *What makes Mike tick?*

The counselor was beginning to think she knew. "Mike," she said when he had been seeing her for a while, "something I've got to tell you—do you know how many times in the last five visits you've brought up Vietnam?"

"I don't think I've ever," he answered.

"Nine times in the last five visits," she said. "Just in passing, and as soon as I question you about it, the subject changes. Mike, I don't think you've come to grips with that, and I think right there is an awful lot of whatever problems you think you might have."

It was then that she told him that he was a normal person, that he was not alone with his problems or more sorely afflicted than anyone else. The nightmares might never go away, she said, but he could learn to use them to his own benefit—to read them as a kind of emotional barometer revealing what was going on in the rest of his life. When he was having a siege, as he was then, it was time to look at the subsurface stresses that might have brought them on:

the fraying of his marriage, perhaps, or the high-octane level of his drinking. Or maybe the heart of the matter lay in precisely those feelings about the war that he had kept stoppered up for so long. Maybe something that had happened thirteen years ago in Vietnam was trying to get out, and maybe he should be talking to somebody about that.

Things began to make sense to MacDonald; he began to see the pieces of his life fitting into place. A veteran friend with similar problems urged him to go to the VA for a work-up to see if he was experiencing what psychiatry had lately recognized as "post-traumatic stress syndrome," a kind of late date with battle fatigue that was hitting some men ten or fifteen years out of 'Nam. MacDonald still couldn't quite bring himself to pick up the phone for an appointment. But after his sittings with the marriage counselor, it was as if the ice cap on his emotions had started to break up at last. His kid sister Monica had moved into his Tudor-style house near Lake Calhoon after Beth moved out; he started telling her his stories of the war, the stories he had never told Beth or anyone else, pouring them out for four hours at a stretch across the kitchen table on Sunday afternoons, and found he could even laugh at some of them. He read up on Vietnam for the first time, clipping and saving articles that interested him. He tried to get an encounter group going among veterans of the war, without success. Those men who did show up were not yet ready, as he was, to break the silence in which they had been encapsulated by society and by themselves.

To his own surprise, MacDonald even applied for membership in the Veterans of Foreign Wars. Like many and perhaps a majority of the men who fought in Vietnam, he had held the old-line veterans' organizations in a degree of mistrust akin to what he felt toward the government, the media and the American establishment. It had to do, he thought, with the way they had been received home from the war: *The sons of bitches didn't need me then, and now all of a sudden they do. Well, fuck them.* MacDonald was past that now. His own life was settling into a comfortable groove. He had a steadying keel, a snug house, a knockout new girl friend named Mary, and a rising place in the Minneapolis Irish community. His nightmares had subsided with the dissolution of his marriage and the advent of his luxuriant new freedom. He still thought that the war had been a tragic waste and that he had been no more than a "military puppet" in it; he still felt that the country owed him and a million others like him a parade for what they had been through. But he no longer felt, as he once had, like a walking time bomb charged full of grievance and frustration. He had begun integrating his year in 'Nam into the thirty-three-year fabric of his life. "Too bad you guys never really fought in a war," an old-timer at his VFW post twitted him one day, and all MacDonald did in reply was laugh.

RICHARD GARCIA:
A HERO COMES HOME

Sharlene Garcia was in a girl friend's kitchen making the macaroni salad for a beach picnic one Saturday night in May 1969 when the premonition stole over her: *Her Rick was going to die.* "I felt very, very alone," she remembered. She sat up talking about it until, at two o'clock Sunday morning, her girl friend told her gently, "Shut up and go to sleep." Sharlene did, thrusting the thought of death out of her mind.

And then it was Tuesday; she had just put a client under the drier at the hairdresser's where she worked when the call came from Richard's mother to come home right away. She was pulling up outside the Garcias' house on Lindo Lane in Morgan Hill, California, when she saw the parked Army van and understood immediately what it meant. She went inside. A kitchen chair lay in splinters where Richard's father had flung it across the room.

The premonition had come true. That Saturday, just as she had felt it, Richard Garcia, not quite twenty-two, had died in the path of an American tank in Vietnam.

He and Sharlene Tracey had been sweethearts at Live Oak High. She was a year younger than he and two years behind him in school. It caused both their families some upset when they were engaged while she was still a senior and he was already in his second year at Gavilan College. He was drafted despite a bad football knee. She thought his Spanish surname might have had something to do with that, but he accepted the Army and the war as his duty, and when she raised the possibility of their fleeing to Canada or Mexico, he laughed her off. They were married when he came home on leave in June 1968, between infantry training and instant-noncom school. She went with him to Travers Air Force Base, outside Oakland, to see him off for Vietnam and clung to him, not wanting to say goodbye. She begged him not to be a hero. He smiled. They wrote one another, planning to meet for his R&R in Hawaii on their first anniversary. She bought a big fire-engine-red piggy bank and began saving up for the trip.

She had always thought he would look good in a moustache, and when she saw him next, in his coffin, he had one. *He finally grew me a moustache*, she thought, and then she was crying. She remembered her premonition of his death and wept again.

Garcia's father, a garage operator, has since died. His mother remarried. His widow moved out of the house on Lindo Lane and, she recalled, "hid out for a while" with her grief. She attempted a second marriage later, to an old school chum of Garcia's. After two children, it failed, and she was wearing Richard's ring again.

In the Army's reconstruction of his death, Garcia dying to save a buddy, he had come home a hero after all—a dead hero, as Sharlene had feared, with a Silver and a Bronze Star for his death in a dying cause. There was no hint of irony in the citation accompanying the Bronze. Garcia's life and death, it said, *materially contributed to the efforts of the United States Mission to the Republic of Vietnam to assist that country in ridding itself of the Communist threat to its freedom.*

PART 3

THE BOYS
OF CHARLIE
COMPANY

Q. How do you explain that so many of the guys are now talking? Not only talking, but it's—it's coming out of them like a waterfall.

A. Somebody asked us.

—DAVID BROWN, at a reunion of Charlie Company, 1981

First there were the recognitions, made difficult by lapsed time and repressed memory. Denny Pierce was out at the windblown little airstrip on Marathon in the Florida Keys waiting for Bob Bowers to arrive for the first gathering of Charlie Company since Vietnam, and Bob Bowers, a walking op-art tapestry in black pinstripes, was descending from the twin-engine Cessna commuter flight looking for Denny Pierce. They had been so close in 'Nam they had called each other Little Brother, but Bowers's face was half-hidden inside a blond beard and Pierce's had been rebuilt since his industrial accident, and they were having trouble finding one another. For a time, they stood side by side at the gate in the hurricane fence, searching from person to person. Once, they looked straight at one another, their eyes meeting, appraising and wandering on. Then it hit them both at once, with the brilliance of an illumination flare lighting the jungle night. Bowers whooped. Pierce yelped. Their two right arms swung wide and met in a roundhouse handshake, and they were Little Brothers once more.

It was that way again and again, the planes settling out of the hot subtropical sky and delivering the boys of Charlie Company from Ranger, Texas, and Wampum, Pennsylvania, and Ottumwa, Iowa, for one more formation. It was not a war that brought them together this time but their shared memories of Vietnam and their mixed success at coping with The World. Thirty of them had been invited south to Marathon with their women in the waning autumn of 1981 for a twelve-years-on reunion, organized by CBS News as a documentary postscript to a lengthy *Newsweek* special report on the company.

If it was conceived as a media event, it became something else for the men, an emotional and often a wrenching journey back to a time and a place that most of them had tried and been encouraged by their country to forget. The intervening years had thinned their hair, thickened their middles, weighted them with mortgages and family responsibilities, and brought them in their early and middle thirties to the threshold of middle age. But for three days in Marathon, they were boys again—the boys of a Vietnam winter turned out in the sun and permitted at last to feel a little proud of who they had been and what they had done.

Old friends and interrupted friendships came together in little explosions of sentiment at the airstrip and among the stuccoed hooches—as they were instantly and inevitably dubbed—at their motel. Kit Bowen and Don Stagnaro found each other and were Doc and Stag again, the distance of a dozen mostly uncommunicative years melting away in ten sustained minutes of bear-hugging. "Oh, man, and I'm supposed to be so strong," Bowen said, suddenly too rubbery-legged to stand, "but I just got two kicks in the heart."

Frank Goins saw Omega Harris through the hurricane wire, turned out sharply in a three-piece brown plaid suit with a hearing aid in his left ear. "My ace, my ace!" Goins boomed, still trying to fit a name to the familiar mahogany face. "How you doin'? Boy, you don't change a bit."

"How you doin'?" Harris answered. "How's everything, man?"

"You remember Red?" Goins bubbled, recalling a mutual friend. "He fell in love with that Cambodian girl?"

"Better than falling in love with that war," Harris said.

"We got a lot to talk about," Goins said, and the two of them fell into each other's arms.

The last plane disgorged the last cargo of old boys on a lowering Friday evening, and Taras Popel was sitting anxiously on the front step of the motel, wondering if his old buddy Stretch Lawrence from the mortar platoon had made it. Tight as they had been in 'Nam, they hadn't seen each other in eleven years, not since Lawrence had stopped in Chicago on his way across country to show off his new bride, Rebecca, to Popel. Would he show up? Popel didn't know until a car pulled up and the Lawrences, Stretch and Reb, stepped out. The two men embraced, their damp eyes shining in the soft Florida night. They stepped apart. Popel extended a pack of English Ovals, the brand they used to smoke in

'Nam. Lawrence took one and they lit up. Then Popel fished up the worn, leather-jacketed hip flask he had carried in the war—"Anybody in mortars knows this flask," he said—and poured them each a Jack Daniel's. They raised the drinks in a silent toast to one another. Their hands were trembling. They downed the Jack D at a single draught apiece. "It tasted better in Vietnam," Popel said, smiling impishly into his emptied cup. He and Lawrence hugged again.

The talk was determinedly lighthearted at first, the men keeping their innermost feelings face down and swapping the kind of stories you could see any week on *M*A*S*H* on television. That was Kit Bowen's game, a drink, a yarn and a laugh to keep from crying. Cowboy Rosson wafted into his ken, instantly identifiable by his western shirt and the Stetson that never came off, and Bowen was saying, "Oh, God, Rosson, I remember him—he thought it would be fun to see a grenade go off. Blew his two bottom teeth out. I had to patch him up and he was jus' sayin', 'Gee, isn't that neat.'"

David Brown hove into view, and more memories rushed back. There was the time Brown got a Dear John letter from home, walked over to Bowen's bunker with a grenade and tossed it in with the pin pulled. Inside, Bowen had never forgotten his fear or forgiven Brown for it, but it had been a joke, and in company, he made a joke of it. "I thought, 'This is it, the Big Blink,'" he said. "I ran out. But he was just pimpin' us—he had taken the powder out."

But as the liquor splashed into the night, the stories got more serious, the tides of emotion deepened and the men drew together in that bonding Stagnaro had thought stronger than they felt for their wives. "The guys are back in Vietnam," Doc Johnson's lady, Donna Daily, said, feeling half left out and half pleased.

Johnson had been anxious all the way to Marathon about the bath of feeling and memory he would be getting into and had considered calling it off. They had got into a little fender-bender of an accident on their way out of Lafayette, Louisiana, to the airport, and Johnson had pulled over and said, "Fuck it, I don't want to go. It's going to be a shitty weekend."

But Donna had urged him to go through with it, and they finally made it on the last flight in. She had sensed, like many of the women, that the men needed to be together—to talk through with one another what they had felt about the war and experienced in The World. They had been encapsulated alone in silence, the men inside and the women outside, for too long.

Laughter and tears, sentiment and anger ran in swift cross-currents among them. Omega Harris was wet-eyed and smiling all at once just seeing them again—"the best goddam fighting men," he said. "These boys *bad*!" Kit Bowen was boozily nominating Kevin Abbott for the Congressional Medal of Honor for having saved a bunkerful of men at Cantigny. Abbott tried to say no, then—deeply moved—fell silent. People kept talking about how Doc Johnson beat the gook to death with his splintered M-16 at Fire Base Julie; Johnson each time would blush furiously and try to change the subject.

Jim the Fox Erwin's homemade chronicle of the suicide assault on Julie made the rounds and found its way to Frank Goins at breakfast the first morning. Goins was strong—"a real horse," Kevin Abbott was telling people. Once, a buddy of his had been killed and Goins, in a fury, had volunteered to walk point, hoping to flush out some gooks for payback time. But when he read Erwin's story, he couldn't help himself; the tears were spilling down his face. "It brought back a lot of memories," he told his wife, Mattie, weeping again. She had never seen him cry before, or heard him speak about the war.

For some, merely being there was a kind of reimmersion in the war and the contending feelings of love, fear and rage it had loosed inside them a dozen years before. *Like pouring gas on a fire*, Kit Bowen thought. He had expected that, and had come with some misgivings, as Doc Johnson had. He roistered through the weekend like a frat-house clown, always on, kidding when there was an audience and hurting so badly inside that he needed two days' R&R in Key West and seven in Nassau afterward to detoxify his emotions. He drank a lot, knocking them back with Doc and Stag and Abbott and others, sometimes signing for $75 champagne on CBS's tab and guzzling it out of the bottle. "I was a total mess," he said. "I'm real emotional anyway, and bringing up all these things—it was real hard, it was a heavy thing. We just pulled all the corks out."

At moments, they might have been back at Lai Khe again,

unwinding with a desperate intensity today to drown out the memory of yesterday and the possibility that there might not be a tomorrow. Doc Johnson pounded at the door of what he thought was Bowen's hooch in the middle of the night, wanting to show him a new fold for a pressure bandage; inside, two terrified senior citizens on holiday were trying to tell him he had the wrong room. Bowen was moving in his own ground fog. At one point—time was a blur—he and Johnson were sitting around Bowen's room with their girl friends, drinking champagne and listening to Jimmy Buffett on a portable stereo singing something laid-back and Key Western:

"With these changes in latitudes, changes in attitudes . . ."

"Why don't you open up?" Johnson asked Bowen suddenly.

"Nothing remains quite the same," Buffett was singing.

Bowen was silent. The music was so they wouldn't have to talk.

"Why don't you open up?" Johnson demanded again.

"With all of my running and all of my cunning, if I wasn't crazy I would go insane. . . ."

"Same reason you don't," Bowen answered, and then they were at one another, each belaboring the other for his coveredness, two old comrades banging away, *As if*, Bowen's girl Myra thought, *they were hitting each other with rubber hoses.* They were at the point of swinging for real when Bowen finally got up and went out into the darkness. It was past midnight. The other guys were off at some strip bar somewhere, raising hell. Bowen walked out on the dock and started to cry. He stayed there for a while, then drifted toward the bar. It was closing. He bought a Bud and, drained and miserable, went back to his room.

There were eddies of tension when, at the sunset happy hour the second night, their old CO Richard Rogers arrived while the men were out on the terrace drinking. He had had to steel himself to come at all. He was then still a lieutenant colonel at Fort Leavenworth, an officer, by every evidence, on the rise. The Army had not discouraged him from being interviewed by *Newsweek* for its report on Charlie Company, but his superiors were openly unenthusiastic about his appearing on prime-time television surrounded by ex-grunts brimming over with grievance against the military and no

longer answerable to its discipline. It had been made clear
to Rogers that if he went to Marathon, he would be going
on his own. That no longer mattered greatly to him; while
he had not yet put in his papers, he had already decided on
retiring to private life. It was the prospect of seeing the men
again that troubled him, and not knowing how he and they
would respond to one another. He knew that every one of
them had disagreed with one or another of his command
decisions and that some held him to blame for the loss of
their buddies' lives. With booze around, he figured, somebody inevitably would get fired up and sound off. He worried
even more about how he would handle his own emotions;
he sensed that, seeing the men, he would feel himself responsible for them again and for what had become of them
since they were in his command.

He was right on both counts. The tension was palpable
when he materialized on the terrace in a polo shirt, khaki
pants and running shoes and moved among the men, shaking
hands and groping for names and faces he hadn't seen or
heard for a dozen years.

"Well, at least he was smart enough not to wear his uniform," Doc Johnson's lady, Donna, murmured. Johnson had
had his quarrels with Rogers and had not forgotten them.

Neither had Bob Selig or Kit Bowen. They had never
forgiven Rogers for the deaths of the rookie listening-posters
he had sent outside the wire at Cantigny or of the top sergeant
who bought it the day the captain marched them into an
enemy base camp near Junction City. Selig watched from
the edge of the crowd as Rogers arrived, then walked off
the terrace. Bowen hadn't even wanted to come out of his
room for the occasion. "Oh, fuck him," he growled when he
heard Rogers was coming and saw the men gathering to meet
him. When Bowen finally did make his way to the terrace,
he would not shake Rogers's hand.

Rogers was wrestling with his own feelings as he moved
from man to man, their faces swimming dimly into register.
Some were friendly, some not; some wanted to be and were
still constrained by the old distance between them, the captain and his company of grunts. "Captain Rogers himself!"
Frank Goins boomed, trying for a bonhomie that was not
quite there. Rogers masked his unease behind a wide smile.
His eyes were shining in the television lights.

"Sir, Mike Fetterolf," someone was telling him, an apparition in a Dior T-shirt with a purple begonia stuck in his waist-length brown hair.

Rogers stared at the apparition, trying to comprehend it.

"Sir," Fetterolf said, seeing his perplexity, "I'm no longer in the Army."

Another face was in front of him, and Rogers was trying to remember it without the beard and moustache. "They called me Doc Johnson," the face prompted. "How can you forget, right?"

"You've changed a little," Rogers said. They laughed.

"Jerry Dickmann," another man was saying. The blond hair was thinner, the face more seamed than Rogers remembered, and a scrub-brush moustache curled down around the edges of the mouth.

"Hi, Jerry, great to see you," Rogers managed. "Put on a little weight."

"Yeah," Dickmann said a little ruefully.

A man in cowboy gear and a big Stetson stuck out his hand next and said, helpfully, "Roy Rosson."

"Roy, good to see you. How you doing?"

"All right," Rosson said, smiling his Marlboro-man smile. "I'm alive."

Rogers finished his rounds, and he and the men alternately sought to break through the awkwardness still lying heavily between them. He tried to tell them how excited he was to see them again, pretending to have recognized more of them than he actually had, and how much he still cared about their lives. They tried in turn to tell him that the war was over, they were okay, he was okay.

"You're the one that installed the idea that we should take care of each other," Bob Bowers said in the grip of a rush of sentiment; it did not come easily to his rebel spirit to compliment officers, but he had respected Rogers and wanted him to know it. "That distinguished Charlie Company from all the other companies," Bowers went on. "We took care of our own, and you're the one that taught us that."

Rogers looked pleased, like a parent whose children had come out well. "The years, the age don't matter; we were boys," he said. "You went away boys and you came home men."

"You taught us to love," Frank Goins said.

"Y'all had pride," Rogers said. "You cared."

Taras Popel, irreverent, asked him why he had stayed in the military anyway.

The moment wasn't right to tell them that he was leaving it. "Y'all had a lot to do with it," he said, his voice low and his eyes glistening with the sentiment of it. "Y'know, we *all* kind of went over, most of us, as boys, and we grew up a lot. For that one time in each one of you's life, you put somebody else ahead of you. Somebody else's life was more important than your own safety, and at that moment you became men."

Strains remained at play beneath the surface. Selig had a talk with Rogers later that night about their differences; Rogers accepted responsibility for the command decisions he had taken at Cantigny and Junction City, but Selig still wasn't appeased. *I can't buy that,* he was thinking. *Three times I asked him at Cantigny to let those listening-posters come back in, and he said no. Those guys died because he wouldn't let them back in.*

When Rogers rose at dinner that evening to raise a glass to the company and to its women—"I think I know you because I know your men and suffered with them"—Selig sat staring mutely at the tablecloth, his hands in his lap, refusing to join the general applause. It wasn't until he had brooded deep into the night that he decided it was time to bury the dead.

In the morning, CBS engineered an on-camera confrontation between him and Rogers, Selig describing what he felt had been bad calls, Rogers once again taking responsibility for them even when Bill Moyers as interlocutor invited him to pass the buck to battalion. "Why does it matter to the troops, to the people in the company," he said, "whether the order came from higher or whether it came from me?"

The encounter, though tense, had lost much of its quality of accusation. Selig had discovered, once the first storm of emotion had passed, that the war was over for him. "Just as a person," he said, "I can respect him for what he had to do. And myself, I've just decided that twelve years ago stays twelve years ago."

Kit Bowen came a longer way around to a less durable armistice with Rogers. Bowen carried his emotions far closer to the skin than Selig and was fueling them amply with alcohol. He avoided Rogers most of the time in Marathon, not wanting to have to speak to him, but it was as if their paths were destined to intersect. Doc Johnson was after Bowen to talk things out. Johnson himself had thought Rogers a bit too emotional as an officer and agreed that he might have made a few wrong decisions, but he figured anybody would have in similar circumstances and there was no profit in second-guessing after twelve years anyway. Rogers's wife spoke to Bowen, too, trying to bridge the distance. "Doc," she told him, standing out front of the motel blinking into the sun, "you don't know how hard it is for him to be here. He knows some of you would like to blow his head off." She was pretty. Bowen liked her and, with Johnson in tow, set out in search of Rogers.

They found him sitting alone at the bar and took seats on either side of him. Bowen had had a lot to drink, and Johnson had coached him hard to be civil. Bowen tried. "I just wanted to say hi, thanks for coming," he told Rogers. "I'm still not the head of your rah-rah fan club, but it took guts for you to be here."

Rogers looked at him. *He hates my guts*, he thought.

Bowen insisted that he did not, but he was teetering close to the line. You think you're hot stuff and everything you did was right, he told Rogers, but I know you were wrong.

"Doc, I fucking blew it," Bowen thought he remembered hearing Rogers say through the mists enveloping him. Doc Johnson doubted it, or doubted at least that Rogers meant it; Bowen was bagged, and Johnson guessed that Rogers was just saying *something* to back him off.

Rogers's own more modulated recollection was that he had said yes, he probably had been wrong sometimes, and sometimes men might have suffered for his mistakes. "I regret that," he went on, "but I'm not going to run from that for the rest of my life, Kit." He had tried in each case to do what he had thought tactically right, and what was tactically right, in his experience, was what was most likely to keep your men alive. In similar situations, he couldn't say he wouldn't make the same calls again.

The conversation wandered on for a time, Bowen leading a veering course among his memories of war and his own turbulent emotions about it and about himself. It was a stand-off, as undecisive as Charlie Company's war. They parted with Bowen still bitter toward Rogers, and Rogers feeling somehow responsible for Bowen. "Hey," he started to tell Bowen's date, Myra, afterward, "if he's been like this..." He seemed to want to apologize.

Myra would not have known how to answer; she and Bowen were no more than a casual pairing, a temporary traveling companionship, and the women at Marathon were consigned mostly to the edges of the event in any case, on the outside looking in. The men had one another in common and the war to talk about, an incomprehensible babel about RIFs and NDPs and hot LZs. The women felt alone at first, at once distant from their husbands and boyfriends in their fraternity and closer to them in their holiday from the silence that had enshrouded so many of them.

That silence had come between Lynn and Jerry Dickmann for a time and had only begun to lift when, some weeks before the reunion, America in the person of a newsweekly reporter had knocked at Dickmann's door and asked him what it had been like in Vietnam. "You see, I had wanted him to be proud of being in the war, and he never could be," Lynn Dickmann said. He had had such trouble speaking to her about it or anything else that troubled him that they had separated for a time. But after the reporter left, Dickmann had drifted up to the attic, rummaged through some cardboard cartons he had not even looked at for years and come down with his old canteen for their son, Eric—*something of his father's from the war.*

At Marathon, the women found each other shyly at first, and discovered like their men that they were not alone—that the breaches in communication that had afflicted the Dickmanns had in some measure touched many and perhaps most of them, too. A few of them were assembled for the television shooting, and as they discovered that in common, it was as if Moyers and the cameras were not there. Mattie Goins was talking about how her Frank had opened up only just that morning for the first time in their marriage, the memories tumbling out until, she said, "He broke down and went to cry. He just cried."

"Had he ever done that before?" Moyers asked.

"Not that I know of, no, because he never talked about it with me, you know."

"Mine neither," Lynn Dickmann said.

"Mine, very little," Nancy Boxx echoed.

"He felt I didn't care," Mrs. Dickmann said. "That I didn't care to know what happened. But I *made* him talk about it."

"They thought *nobody* cared," Mrs. Boxx said.

"It was a bad spot for them," Mrs. Dickmann said, "so they didn't want us to know about it. Why should they share something bad with us? I just kind of said, 'You have to tell me.' I mean, he was a very inward person, and you can't love somebody that's inward. They have to share."

"And he wasn't sharing?" Moyers asked.

"No, he didn't want to share. He just wanted to be left alone. He didn't want to share what happened to him in Vietnam."

Mattie Goins recognized herself and Frank in the Dickmanns' story. She had begged him to tell her about his nightmares, but he would not, and she had fallen into her own answering silence, thinking helplessly, *Talk to me. Tell me what's on your mind so I can help. So I can understand.*

Denny Pierce's wife, Betty, felt her marriage less burdened by the war and was resentful of the media image of Vietnam veterans as psychic cripples who could not cope. She thought in fact that the experience of war had strengthened them—had made them more disciplined and independent and, if anything, more rather than less able to handle the problems of everyday life. But she too understood that there were things in the war that bore heavily on a man's spirit and were too painful to speak about. Nancy Boxx brought it up; Joe, she said, had told her how he had prayed in the bunkers for his survival—"Even like sell his soul," she said, "so he could get home."

"I think that's part of what each one of them is just a little bit ashamed of," Betty Pierce said, "because I think in their hearts that's what they all did. 'You just get me out of this any way, I'll be a better person.' Or 'I'll do anything to get out of this alive.' And if it meant that sometimes they weren't the big hero, then I think they took that road. It was a dirty, dirty war."

The men by then were off together discovering and celebrating what was commonplace about themselves instead of brooding alone on what was different. Yes, some of them had had problems since the war holding jobs, or handling liquor, or keeping marriages together; some of them were still waking up in the night back in 'Nam, sweaty and scared, but they were not freaks or cripples—they were coping.

"You see these movies like *The Deer Hunter* and all that," Jerry Dickmann was saying. "Ain't nothing close to what it was like, really like, over there. They don't tell you about what really happened over there. They don't tell you about people being without showers for thirty or forty days, about people that never ate hot meals for a whole month, or any dry socks, or boots that didn't have no soles on it." He was angry now, almost shouting. "They don't show anything that was really truthfully happening over there. It's all fictional. Guys hallucinating things, guys smoking pot, guys taking drugs, guys raping women, guys molesting kids— that's all you hear about in this country. Like today is the first time all of us ordinary people get to come here and say, 'Hey, we're here and we're ordinary people!'"

They were ordinary people out of the very heart of America, and yet there was hardly a life in Charlie Company that had not been touched in some significant way by the war. J.C. Wilson had nearly drunk a good marriage into ruins. David Rioux was lame, halt and blind. Doc Johnson had lost his dream of a career in medicine while he was practicing medicine on dying grunts in Vietnam. Kit Bowen was still floating along, still looking for a place to drop anchor. Omega Harris was doing well in the Army, smiling out at The World and raging against it inside. Fritz Suchomel had not come home at all; neither had Clyde Garth, Rick Garcia, or Bobby Eugene Jones. Roy Rosson had yet to spend as long as a year on a single job. Jerry Dickmann was still having a six-week siege of anxiety every autumn on the anniversary of Charlie Company's bloodiest days in the war. David Bean had run in jangled flight to shelter aboard a lobster boat in the Florida Keys, Mike Fetterolf on a mountaintop in Montana. Bert Kennish had lost three prime-time years out of a promising career in business and was still catching up. Lloyd Collins and Chester Ward had survived the war and died in The World, each awash in drink and depression. Greg Skeels wanted to be alone, and was. Skip Sommer had lived three years on the lam as a deserter and a dozen trying to escape the keening of dying women and children in his dreams. Alberto Martinez had flung himself off a highway overpass in Miami. Jim the Fox Erwin, the chronicler of Fire Base

Julie, had been asked by a psychiatrist friend of his family to name the most important person in the world. "Me," Erwin had replied without pause, and the psychiatrist was impressed with the resilience of his ego. But Erwin was suffering chest pains at thirty-four, the result, his own doctor told him, of an affliction almost endemic among the survivors of Charlie Company: keeping too much emotion bottled up inside.

Yet they had endured, most of them, with a kind of stubborn American hardihood. They did it alone, most often, believing that they *were* alone. Their own country, in its conflicted feelings about the war, had encouraged that belief—had welcomed them with silence, burdened them with its own guilt on the one hand for having lost the war and on the other for having fought it at all, and left them to heal their various wounds by themselves. It was a credit to them and not to the nation that most of them, however imperfectly, had done so.

They had done so largely out of their own resources. They had come home singly to The World and it was, Charles Hedspeth thought, returning to Puxico, Missouri, *as if I'd been down to the malt shop for a year and a half*. People their own age called them baby-killers. Families and friends treated them often as if they were convalescents home from the hospital, not soldiers home from a war, and avoided the subject of why they had been away as people once drew back from mentioning consumption or cancer.

"What these guys did was something important," Omega Harris said. "They're heroes, but twelve-thirteen years ago, nobody could recognize it." They were accordingly denied that healing agent of past wars called pride. They were America's lost innocence made flesh and come back to the heart of the nation; they were received there with embarrassment, when they were seen at all. They answered silence with silence and found their own ways home.

The boys of Charlie Company were permitted, in Marathon, a measure of pride for their service in the war and for what they had made of their lives in the years since. Toast after toast was proposed, as if it were a victory in the field they were celebrating and not the disparate victories of their own survival. Bob Bowers, the industrial engineer from Wampum, Pennsylvania, raised one "to the guys who didn't come back." Bert Kennish, the real estate salesman from Castle Rock, Colorado, drank to the future prosperity of those who did.

Don Stagnaro, the narcotics cop from Los Angeles, saluted the maimed and crippled: "We're all back and our suffering is over, and the guys that died over there, God knows *their* suffering is over. But there's a lot of guys in hospitals, and we can't get together and forget about them. We love them, and we want them to know we're thinking about them, and Godspeed. And the next life, whatever it is, I hope it's a lot better than the one they're in right now."

And finally Omega Harris, the career Army man from Fort Monroe, Virginia, toasted their right to be proud. "I served with the men," he said. "I know what the men can do. I'm very proud of them. And I'm also very proud to stand here and tell everybody I'm still serving that same Army you guys left. Every time I wear my uniform, I'm representing each and every one of you, and I want you to know that until I give it up, you can feel proud, because you've got somebody standing up for our honor."

There was rebuke as well as pride in their assembly in Marathon, the witness of the pawns against the chess masters who had employed them in a consciously stalemated game. Bill Moyers saw it and, in his own impassioned talk to the survivors of Charlie Company, was moved to remember his service to Lyndon Johnson in the days when the policies that had sent them to the war were set in place. "I was in the White House when many of those decisions were being made," he said, "and had we been able to hear what some of you men have had to say here, and what your wives have said, I think some of those decisions would not have been made." The decisions were made without reference to what the men felt, on the presumption of governments that life is unfair; they left Ottumwa and Muskogee and Brooklyn and Kalamazoo largely without question and did what their country asked of them, waging a war that taxed their bodies, abraded their souls and came to have no purpose for most of them beyond their own survival. "Let everybody remember," Taras Popel shouted across the dining room at Marathon one night, glass aloft, "that we are veterans, not victims." But to be sent to an unpopular war and to be received home in abashed silence is to be a victim of sorts—

the victim of indifference. They had been denied that debt of honor a nation owes its soldiers and were burdened instead with its shame, whether for having waged the war or for having been defeated at it. Their travail was what Vietnam did to them. Our silence is what it has done to us.

THE MEN OF CHARLIE COMPANY

The following men of Charlie Company, or their survivors, contributed their memories of war and peace to this account:

Kevin Abbott	Staten Island, New York	Bank investigator
David Bean	Long Key, Florida	Lobster fisherman
Thomas Kitrick Bowen	Portland, Oregon	Body-building equipment salesman
Bob Bowers	Wampum, Pennsylvania	Industrial engineer
Michael J. Boxx	Ottumwa, Iowa	Welder
David Brown	Lakewood, New Jersey	State job-placement worker
Dan Colfack	Craig, Colorado	Power company assistant shift supervisor
Lloyd Collins	Peoria, Illinois	Died of heart attack, 1978
Peter DeCarlo	Cambridge, Massachusetts	Postal worker
Gerald A. Dickmann	Saukville, Wisconsin	City water worker
Jim Erwin	Tinley Park, Illinois	Unemployed
Greg Etzel	Highland Falls, New York	Deputy sheriff
Mike Fetterolf	Star Meadow, Montana	Retired
Harry Foxwell	Burke, Virginia	Statistician
Richard C. Garcia	Morgan Hill, California	Killed in action, 1969
Clyde Garth, Jr.	Aberdeen, Mississippi	Killed in action, 1968
Curtis Gilliland, Jr.	Somerset, Kentucky	Postal worker
Frank Goins	Boston, Georgia	Body and fender repairman
George Goldstein	Quincy, Massachusetts	Schoolteacher

James L. Green	Sumter, South Carolina	Textile worker
Omega A. Harris	Korea	Sergeant First Class, U.S. Army
Charles Hedspeth	Puxico, Missouri	Schoolteacher
George Hesser	Yukon, Oklahoma	Postal worker
Joseph Jenkins	Queens, New York	Postal worker
Billy Johnson	Lafayette, Louisiana	Unemployed
Carson Johnson	Abilene, Kansas	Baptist minister
Bobby Eugene Jones	Princeville, North Carolina	Killed in action, 1970
Robert Kennish	Castle Rock, Colorado	Real-estate salesman
Wayne Lawrence	Los Angeles, California	Aircraft inspector
Edmund Lee VI	Sydney, Australia	Railroad brakeman
Mike MacDonald	Minneapolis, Minnesota	Manager, parking-garage sweeping company
Ernesto Alberto Martinez	Miami, Florida	Committed suicide, 1982
Robert Mastrogiovanni	Fair Lawn, New Jersey	Postal supervisor
Johnny B. McClure	Fort Riley, Kansas	Sergeant, U.S. Army
Steven McVeigh	Chicago, Illinois	Schoolteacher
Richard W. Olson	Girdwood, Alaska	Drilling company supervisor
Tore Pearson	Sacramento, California	Civil engineer
Joseph F. Pentz	Bellevue, Washington	Railway clerk, sheetmetal worker
Dennis Pierce	Lima, Ohio	Steelworker
Taras Popel	Chicago, Illinois	Machine-shop operator
Leroy Pringle	Sumter, South Carolina	Textile worker
Conrad L. Quezaire	Darmstadt, West Germany	Staff Sergeant, U.S. Army
David Rioux	Oakview, California	Ph.D. candidate
Michel Rioux	Lewiston, Maine	Carpenter
Antonio Rivera Parilla	San Juan, Puerto Rico	Accountant
Richard L. Rogers	Fayetteville, Arkansas	Taco company executive
Roy Rosson II	Ranger, Texas	Oil worker, horse trainer

Charles Rupert	*Detroit, Michigan*	Delivery-truck driver
Thomas Schomus	*Aurora, Oregon*	Carpenter
Ed Schweiger	*Madison, Wisconsin*	Campus security guard
Fred Scott	*Fairbanks, Alaska*	Pipeline security man
Bob Selig	*Sioux Falls, South Dakota*	Salesman
Floyd G. Skeels	*Grand Rapids, Michigan*	Heating and cooling contractor
Jim Soike	*Milwaukee, Wisconsin*	City arborist
John Sommer	*Connecticut*	Bike-shop operator
David Spain	*Rockford, Illinois*	Construction worker
Donald Stagnaro	*Brea, California*	Narcotics detective
George Stover	*Hoquiam, Washington*	Millwright
Frederick V. Suchomel	*Sun Prairie, Wisconsin*	Killed in action, 1969
Tom Swenticky	*South River, New Jersey*	Transportation specialist
Angelo Vittorini	*Chicago, Illinois*	Medical-manufacturing executive
Chester Ward	*Southampton, New York*	Killed in auto accident, 1969
Ronald Warehime	*New Windsor, Maryland*	Fireman
Jake Williams	*Evanston, Wyoming*	Mud engineer
J.C. Wilson	*Waverly, Tennessee*	Heavy-equipment operator

ABBREVIATIONS AND ACRONYMS

A-O area of operations
APC armored personnel carrier
ARVN Army of the Republic of Vietnam (or a member thereof)
AWOL absent without leave
CO commanding officer
DEROS date eligible for return from overseas
DP displaced person
FNG fuckin' new guy
LBJ Long Binh jail
loach light observation chopper
LP listening post
LZ landing zone
MASH mobile army surgical hospital
MP military police(man)
NCO noncommissioned officer
NDP night defense position
NVA North Vietnamese Army (or a member thereof)
OCS officer candidate school

OSS Office of Strategic Services
POW prisoner of war
PX post exchange
RIF reconnaissance in force
RON remain-overnight operation
ROTC Reserve Officers' Training Corps
RPG rocket-propelled grenade
R&R rest and recreation (also called I&I, for intoxication and intercourse)
SOP standard operating procedure
strack smart, sharp, well-prepared (from STRategic Air Command)
USO United Service Organizations
VA Veterans Administration
VC Viet Cong
VFW Veterans of Foreign Wars
XO executive officer

A BIBLIOGRAPHICAL NOTE

This book is a work of original reporting. But in the process of preparing ourselves for it, we took a crash course in the literature of the war in Vietnam and found a number of books especially useful. Frances FitzGerald's *Fire in the Lake*, William Shawcross's *Sideshow*, Michael Charlton and Anthony Moncrieff's *Many Reasons Why* and the memoirs of Lyndon Johnson, Richard Nixon, Henry Kissinger and William Westmoreland helped us understand the historic moment at which Charlie Company was fighting. William L. Allen, et al., *The Vietnam War*, and Shelby L. Stanton's *Vietnam Order of Battle* made valuable desk references. Douglas Kinnard's *The War Managers* is a fascinating and neglected study of the generals who commanded the American effort, written by one of their own number. Charles Moskos's *The American Enlisted Man* was similarly illuminating on life in the ranks and its discontents. The most rewarding books we encountered on the experience of combat in Vietnam included two collections of oral histories, Mark Baker's *Nam* and Al Santoli's *Everything We Had*; two novels, Tim O'Brien's *Going After Cacciato* and James Webb's *Fields of Fire*, and a miscellany of histories, memoirs, reports and chronicles including, most memorably, Michael Herr's brilliant *Dispatches*, C. D. B. Bryan's *Friendly Fire*, Philip Caputo's *Rumor of War* and Ronald J. Glasser's *365 Days*. John Keegan's extraordinary *The Face of Battle* showed us the brotherhood that the grunts who fought at Agincourt in 1415, at Waterloo in 1815 and on the Somme in 1916 shared with the men of Charlie Company.

INDEX

Abbott, Kevin, 49–51, 83
  after Vietnam, 203–206
  at reunion of Charlie Company, 294–301
Agent Orange, 98, 234, 243, 277, 279
Agnew, Spiro, 130
Alcohol. *See* Drinking
Alienation of veterans, 145, 148–151, 170, 250, 266–267
Anger. *See* Rage
Antiwar movement (peace movement), ix, 101–102, 155, 197, 204–205, 212, 214–215, 250, 285
Anxiety attacks, 152, 183, 191
Apocalypse Now (film), 257
Army, United States, in the Reagan administration, 156
Arrival in Vietnam, 3–5, 10, 12–15, 17, 20
Arthur, David, 283
Avoidance of fighting, 112–113, *See also* Resistance
Ayers, Billy, 122–123

Base Area 23,
Bean, David, 22, 46, 48, 51–52, 66, 76–77, 102, 115, 134, 294, 304
  after Vietnam, 258–266
  arrival in Vietnam, 13–14
  Christmas 1968 operation and, 73–74, 75–76, 77

  Larry Sample's death and, 36–39
Bean, Sandra, 261
Big Red One (First Infantry Division)
  mission in Vietnam, 5–6
  reputation of, 5, 7
  traditions of, 5
Body counts, 6, 69, 70–72, 77
Bowen, Thomas Kitrick (Kit or Doc), 17–20, 41–44, 63–66, 82–84, 92, 101, 107, 109, 304
  after Vietnam, 169, 173–177
  arrival in Vietnam, 17–20
  at Cantigny, 47, 50, 52
  departure from Vietnam, 136–137
  R&R of, 114–116
  at reunion of Charlie Company, 294–298, 300–302
Bowers, Bob (Bowser), 10, 43, 81, 111–112, 305
  after Vietnam, 231–235
  at reunion of Charlie Company, 293, 298
Bowers, Pat, 232, 233, 234
Bowling, James Bryan, 6, 7
Boxx, Michael J. (Joe), 47, 303
  after Vietnam, 178–181
Boxx, Nancy, 178–181, 303
Brown, Cherie, 223
Brown, David, xii, 85–90, 110, 135, 291
  after Vietnam, 219–224

317

at reunion of Charlie Company, 295

Callousness, 108–109, 162, 224
Cantigny, Fire Base, 44–52, 60, 283, 298, 300
Charlie Company
early days in Vietnam, 6–7
reunion of (1981), 292–307
Chico, 28
Christmas 1968, 72–77
Colfack, (Danger) Dan, 46, 48, 83, 102, 135, 139
after Vietnam, 159–161
Collins, Lloyd, 53–55, 304
after Vietnam, 157–159
death of, 159
Collins, Nancy, 157–159
Cottrell, Larry, 77, 78
Cranford, Barney, 126
Cruelty, 108, 109

Daily, Donna, 295, 296, 298
Danger (excitement), need for, 144, sense of, 171, 233
Davidson, Nancy, 192–199
Death
exposure to, 22, 28–29, 32–39, 48, 53–55, 59, 65, 66, 101–102, 104, 119, 123–125. *See also* Body counts
premonition of, 26, 61, 86, 126, 289, 290
DeCarlo, Peter, 104, 108, 124
Deer Hunter, The (film), 304
Departure from Vietnam, 134–139
Desertion, 184–188, 189–190, 278–279
Dickmann, Jerry, 27–28, 97, 141, 304
after Vietnam, 151–152
at reunion of Charlie Company, 299, 302
Dickmann, Lynn, 302–303
Discharges, early, 112–113
Disobedience. *See* Resistance
Drinking, 113–114, 161–162

veterans and, 157, 179–181, 221, 243–246, 251, 282, 287–288
Drugs, 114

Emotional problems. *See* Psychological or psychiatric problems
Erwin, Jim (the Fox), 29, 32, 33, 59, 334
at reunion of Charlie Company, 296, 335, 336, 339
Etzel, Greg, 96
Explosives. *See* Rage

Fears, 32, 60–61, 105–106, 123, 189–190, 224
veterans', 258–260
Fetterolf, Carol Lynn, 238, 239
Fetterolf, Jim, 237–242
Fetterolf, Mike, 107, 110, 304
after Vietnam, 237–242
at reunion of Charlie Company, 299
Fetterolf, Pokie, 238
First Infantry Division. *See* Big Red One
Flashbacks, 162, 163, 172, 183, 242, 286
Foxwell, Harry, 33, 44, 48–49, 63, 64, 67–68, 74, 82, 83, 101, 114
after Vietnam, 254–258
French Fort, The, 118, 121–122
Friendly fire, 79–84, 121–122
Friendship (bonding), 169–171, 292–295

Garcia, Richard C. (Rick), 124–255, 134, 289–290, 304
Garcia, Sharlene, 124, 289–290
Garth, Clyde, Jr., 26–27, 35, 225–227, 304
Garth, Daisy, 225
GI Bill, 233
Gilliland, Curtis, Jr., 70, 73, 74, 75, 76, 80, 96, 101
after Vietnam, 271–277

Goins, Frank, 32, 39, 104
  after Vietnam, 216–218
  at reunion of Charlie Company,
    294–296, 298, 299, 302
Goins, Mattie, 217–218, 296, 302–
  303
Goldstein, George, 100, 123
Green, James, 126

Harris, Byrum, 10, 11, 12, 13, 35,
  36
Harris, Jean, 25, 146–150
Harris, Omega, 10–13, 42, 71,
  79–80, 82, 83, 93, 99, 111,
  135–136, 304–306
  after Vietnam, 145–151
  arrival in Vietnam, 10, 11, 12,
    13
  enlistment of, 10–12
  at Fire Base Julie, 26–28, 31–
    33, 34–35
  on R&R, 25, 115
  at reunion of Charlie Company,
    294
Heard, Leome, 26, 225–227
Hedspeth, Charles (Head), 57, 305
Hesser, George, xii, 10
Hicks, Jeff, 47–48, 51
Honor guards, roving, 174–175,
  252

Isolation, 98. *See also* Alienation of
  veterans

Johnson, Billy (Doc), 97, 296
  after Vietnam, 190–192
  at Cantigny, 47, 48, 51
  at Fire Base Julie, 30–31, 35
  at reunion of Charlie Company,
    295–299, 301
Johnson, Deacon, 44, 47
Johnson, Lyndon (Johnson
  administration), ix–x, 23, 306
Jones, Bobby Eugene, 125–126,
  134, 269–271, 304
Jones, Delores, 270
Jones, Eva, 270, 271

Jones, Sgt. (the Top), 62, 65, 67
Julie, Fire Support Base, 24–35,
  38, 39, 53, 89
Junction City, 55–66

Kennish, Faye, 120, 122, 123,
  227–229
Kennish, Robert (Bert), 70–71, 72,
  88, 97, 104, 118–123, 134,
  304
  after Vietnam, 227–230
Killing, feelings about and attitudes
  toward, 48–49, 89–90, 104,
  107–108, 109, 120–121, 148,
  162, 180, 224, 249–250, 251,
  254–255, 256–257

Lai Khe, 6, 7, 39–42
  race relations at, 91–93
Land, war against the, 97–98
Lawrence, Wayne (Stretch), 294–
  295
Lee, Edmund J., IV, 23, 24, 39,
  200–202
  after Vietnam, 202
Leech, The, 71–72
Lieutenants, attitudes toward, 110–
  111
Long Binh Jail, 278–279
Luke's Castle, 79, 84, 86

McClure, Johnny, 101
MacDonald, Beth, 286, 287–288
MacDonald, Mike, 54, 55, 69, 70,
  97, 105, 135, 168
  after Vietnam, 281–289
McVeigh, Steven, 248–249
Marijuana, 114
Martinez, Ernesto Alberto (Al), 8–
  9, 304
  after Vietnam, 192–200
  suicide of, 200
Mastrogiovanni, Robert (Bob), 30,
  34, 102, 103, 108
  after Vietnam, 266–269
Michele (Mike Fetterolf's girl
  friend), 240, 241, 242

Moyers, Bill, 306
My Lai, xiii, 98–99

Napalm, 121–122
Nightmares, 162–163, 171–172,
     179, 184, 204, 218, 223–224,
     241, 246, 247, 258, 282, 286–
     287
Nixon, Richard, x, xi, 95, 102

Officers, attitudes toward, 109–113
Olson, Richard W. (Sea-Tac), 27–
     28, 48, 54, 113–114

Parilla, Antonio Rivera, 91, 96
     after Vietnam, 165–169
Peace movement (antiwar
     movement), ix, 101–102, 155,
     197, 204–205, 212, 214–215,
     250, 285
Pearson, Tore, 57, 106
Pentz, Joseph F. (Joe), 39–41, 66,
     108, 124
Pierce, Betty, 211–13, 303
Pierce, Dennis (Denny or Little
     Brother), 83
     after Vietnam, 181–182
     at reunion of Charlie Company,
     293
Popel, Taras, 9, 55–59, 106, 107,
     306
     after Vietnam, 214–216
     at reunion of Charlie Company,
     294–295, 300
Post-traumatic stress syndrome,
     287–288
Pride, 305–306
Pringle, Leroy, 98–99, 126
Psychological or psychiatric
     problems, 8–9, 77–78, 115,
     183–187, 192–200, 259–266

Quezaire, Conrad, 107

Race relations, 90–94, 166, 216–
     217, 243
Rage (anger), 173

of veterans, 144, 149, 158, 177,
     178, 183–187, 189, 204–205,
     224, 245–247, 277–279
R&R (rest and recreation), 114–
     116, 266–267
Reagan administration, 156, 234
Rebellions, 109–110
Reenlistment, 112–113
Reid, David, 172
Reid, Racie, 30–31
Religous faith, 127–128, 130, 134,
     157, 204, 210–213
Resistance (disobedience), 60, 109–
     113
Reunion of Charlie Company, 291–
     307
Rioux, David, 127–134, 304
     after Vietnam, 206–213
Rioux, Michel, 127–134
     after Vietnam, 206–209, 211–
     213
Rita, Fire Base, 44
Rogers, Richard Lee, 20–25, 56–
     57, 60–67, 110, 134
     after Vietnam, 153–157
     at Cantigny, 45, 46
     Christmas 1968 operation and,
     73, 74, 76
     at Fire Base Julie, 24, 29, 31–
     32, 35
     at reunion of Charlie Company,
     297–302
Rogers, Mrs. Richard, 301
Rosson, Connie, 162–164
Rosson, Roy (Cowboy), 57–59,
     65, 82–83, 99, 113, 134, 304
     after Vietnam, 161–165
     at reunion of Charlie Company,
     295–299
Rupert, Charles, 90–91, 100–101
     after Vietnam, 243–244
Rusk, Dean, ix

Samples, Larry, 27, 28, 36–39, 91
Schweiger, Ed, 57, 59
     after Vietnam, 280–281

Scott, Tiny, 44, 48, 76, 168
Self-confidence, 248–249
Self-control, 149–150
Self-esteem, 229, 230
Selig, Bob (the Roadrunner), 63–67, 81
  after Vietnam, 249–251
  at reunion of Charlie Company, 298, 300–301
Shame, 303, 307
Silence of veterans, 152, 157, 164, 172–173, 217, 221, 236–237, 257, 259, 260, 268, 282, 285–289, 302, 303, 305
Skeels, Floyd G. (Greg), 29, 304
  after Vietnam, 143–145
  arrival in Vietnam, 3–5
  departure from Vietnam, 138
Smitty, 138–139
Soike, Jim, 70
  after Vietnam, 235–237
Soike, Julie, 237
Sommer, John G. (Skip), 65, 68–70, 72–78, 304
  after Vietnam, 183–190
Spain, David, 31, 36–37
  after Vietnam, 277–279
Stagnaro, Donald (Don or Stag), 44, 45, 50–52, 71, 82–83, 97, 100, 104, 106, 116, 136–138, 306
  after Vietnam, 169–173, 177
  arrival in Vietnam, 17–18
  departure from Vietnam, 137–138
  at reunion of Charlie Company, 294
Stover, George, 105, 108–109, 112–113
Suchomel, Frederick V. (Fritz), 93–94, 167–169, 304
Suchomel, Rudy, 167–168
Survival, 59, 61, 63–64, 77, 88–89, 96–97, 104–109, 249–251
Swenticky, Tom, i, xii, 39, 47, 58, 86, 107

Symbols of humanity, clinging to, 107

Talbott, Orwin C., 5
Tet offensive (January 1968), viii, ix
Tour of duty
  one-year, 8, 135
  thirteen-month, 112
Truong, Tri, 274
Ty, 45, 46

Veterans, Vietnam war
  alienation and withdrawal of, 146, 148–150, 170, 250–251, 266–268
  attitudes toward, 145–151, 178–179, 218–221, 234–236, 284–285, 304–306
  lack of recognition of, 143, 145–150, 180, 203–206, 216, 220, 221, 231–232, 234, 245, 247, 248, 280, 285–286, 288, 305, 306
  lost time and broken dreams of, 161–164, 174–175, 176, 190–192, 203, 205–206, 227–228, 252
  psychological and psychiatric problems of, 183–187, 192–200
  rage, explosiveness and violence of, 144, 149, 158, 177, 178, 183–187, 189, 204–205, 224, 245–247, 277–279
  silence about the war, 152, 157, 164, 172–173, 217, 221, 236–237, 257, 259, 260, 268, 282, 285–289, 302, 303, 305
Veterans Administration (VA), 151–152, 194, 208, 215, 234, 243, 244, 279, 288
Veterans Administration (VA) hospitals, 195–200, 260
Veterans of Foreign Wars (VFW), 288
Viet Cong, commitment of, 100

Vietnamese people, relationship to and attitudes toward, 98–100, 151, 271–277

Vietnamization, 95, 99–100

Vietnam war
abandonment of aims of, 208–209, 212, 230, 272, 276–277
attrition strategy in, x, 70–71, 102–104
belief in, 95–97, 127–128, 130–131, 134, 155–156, 168, 208, 212–213, 230, 272–273, 276–277,
as incomprehensible, 96, 99, 103–104, 118, 122, 136, 177, 244–245, 248
public opinion against, *See also* Peace movement
purposelessness and senselessness of, 85–88, 90, 95, 101–102, 103–104, 118, 120–121, 151, 164–165, 178–181, 201,

204–205, 221–222, 248, 306–307
as unwinnable within limited parameters, 6–8, 87–89, 102, 146, 121–122, 153, 155, 173, 205, 218, 230, 283, 307

Vittorini, Angelo (Vitt), 82–84, 102

Ward, Bertha, 252–253
Ward, Chester, 304
after Vietnam, 252–253
Warehime, Ronald, 39–40
Westmoreland, Gen. William, x, 7, 34, 96
Williams, Raymond, 22
Wilson, Doris, 157–159
Wilson, J.C., 15–17, 29, 32, 34, 35, 44, 92, 99, 123, 134, 304
after Vietnam, 244–248
Wilson, Sherrie, 244–247

ABOUT THE AUTHORS

Peter Goldman is a senior editor for *Newsweek*, and Tony Fuller is a national correspondent. They both live in New York City. Richard Manning is *Newsweek*'s bureau chief in Detroit, Stryker McGuire in Houston, and Vern E. Smith in Atlanta. Wally McNamee is a photographer assigned to the magazine's Washington bureau.

The confusion...
the horror...
the truth

VIETNAM

one of the most controversial periods of U.S. history